The Politics of Religious Studies

The Politics of Religious Studies

The Continuing Conflict with Theology in the Academy

Donald Wiebe

MACMILLAN

First published 1999 by
MACMILLAN PRESS LTD
Houndmills, Basingstoke, Hampshire RG21 6XS
and London
Companies and representatives
throughout the world

ISBN 0–333–74154–4

A catalogue record for this book is available from the British Library.

10   9   8   7   6   5   4   3   2   1
08   07   06   05   04   03   02   01   00   99

Internal design and typesetting by Letra Libre

Printed in the United States of America by
Haddon Craftsmen
Bloomsburg, PA

For
Luther H. Martin
and
E. Thomas Lawson

Contents

Part III
Case Studies in the Failure of Nerve

Part IV
Epilogue

Preface

Although the essays collected here were first published as journal articles or appeared as contributions to festschrifts and conference proceedings, they are intimately connected and share a common purpose. Each essay, in one sense or another, defends the academic study of religion as a discipline that is genuinely scientific. By "discipline" I mean a recognized subject publicly available to all students in the field—in this instance, a particular kind of behavior isolated from the whole of human activity—and by "scientific" I mean the attempt only to understand and explain that activity rather than to be involved in it.

The notion of such a study of religion—one free from religious and theological determination—emerged in the last quarter of the nineteenth century, and came to be established in departments of Religious Studies in a number of universities in Europe and North America although it has never fully transcended the tendency to participate in the reality described and explained; that is, it has not adapted itself fully to its new academic-scientific environment. Moreover, much recent and contemporary discussion of the role of such a discipline in the modern university curriculum and of its value to society is determined to rescue it from secularization. The essays in this volume, therefore, are directed to critical analysis of one aspect or another of that rescue effort, from the revisionist histories of the establishment of the discipline of religious studies in the curriculum of the modern Western university to the attempts to reintegrate the academic study of religion with, if not subordinate it to, a religio-theological agenda. Taken together, therefore, these essays constitute what I think is a much-needed book that advocates recovery of the scientific agenda in the academic study of religion, on which basis it achieved cognitive legitimation. I say "much-needed" because without some concerted response to these developments, the study of religion is likely to be reappropriated by religious forces, becoming the avenue through which a religious agenda will be re-established in the university curriculum.

The title I have provided for this collection points to the complex argument presented in the essays: that academic students of religion must eschew politico-ideological interference of any kind, even though the field of religious studies as a whole possesses an inevitably political quality. In essence, this argument deplores the importation of cultural, political, racial, ethnic, or other noncognitive criteria (especially religious criteria, as the subtitle of the volume clearly indicates) in the adjudication of research in Religious Studies or in the assessment of competence for teaching in the field. The latter approach to the study of religion constitutes a betrayal of the discipline as an academic undertaking, because it undermines all hope of achieving a scientifically acceptable understanding of the religious phenomenon, opening the field to the articulation of whatever is valuable to the individual scholar involved or to the community he or she represents, even if the overall result is a set of contradictory propositions and unsubstantiated claims about religions and the nature of religion.

A recurrent theme in these essays is the theological involvement in this discipline. ("Theology" in these essays refers not simply to a particular intellectual activity or discipline, but more generally it denotes any kind of confessional or religious orientation.) This religio involvement stems from the historic nature of the relationship of the study of religion to the religious and theological concerns of the society in which the enterprise first appeared, as well as from similar concerns in modern Western societies in which the study of religion has been granted academic legitimation. And such involvement, I argue, is an unwarranted interference in that scientific undertaking and therefore fuels the conflict between religion and science that has characterized the development and growth of the natural and social sciences in the West—hence the subtitle, "The Continuing Conflict with Theology in the Academy." This conflict is essentially political and ideological rather than scientific, for it involves the attempt to subordinate the commitments of one institution to those of another. Whether or not this conflict alone constitutes a "politics of religious studies" I admit might well be challenged, for there is an obvious sense in which the founding of the sciences, including the "science of religion," constitutes a political act that produces a "politics of science" in general and, more specifically, a "politics of Religious Studies."

Although I find this kind of argument persuasive on one level, it is not relevant to my primary concern about the unacceptable interference of politico-ideological concerns in the academic study of religions in the modern university context. I mention it here, however, because scholars in this discipline often fail to distinguish a more general notion of what is political from what might be called the politics of local concern—a narrower sense of the term that includes not only the notion of party politics but also that of ideological commitment. And in finding a rationale for a "politics of Religious Studies" in the general sense of that phrase, it is often assumed that virtually any kind of political engagement within the field is similarly justified. But that assumption is simply not credible.

It is true that founders are, generally speaking, political actors, because they create the framework within which a particular form of collective life is carried out. On the other hand, the discourse *about* the framework is different from the discourse within the framework. That is, I can agree with those scholars who find an analogy between the founders of political discourse and the founders of academic disciplines, for in both cases the founders dictate acceptable presuppositions, assumptions, and criteria for their respective discourses. In both cases institutions are created that require a certain kind of behavior, and it can be argued that this very act of enforcement is itself political. This obviously applies as much to the founding of the science of religion (that is, the scientific study of religion) as it does to the founding of the other social sciences. But this kind of political activity is still a far cry from the politico-ideological interference in academic matters to which I refer above. The discourse that establishes a science is not a scientific discourse, but that does not imply that it must be political in the narrow sense of the word; it is a discourse about methods for the attainment of a particular kind of conversation rather than a substantive discourse on behalf of a particular set of values. Such a discourse does not, either explicitly or implicitly, sanction the promulgation of a culturally specific worldview or ideology. And the suggestion that founding a science is itself a politico-ideological activity, it is obvious, involves a confusion of the two notions of political and is as little persuasive as the claim that formal logic is political because it too is based on ideological commitments. The argument is not an impossible one, as Peter Munz has pointed out, but it is not compelling:

> . . . the German Marxist philosopher Ernst Bloch even described formal logic as an ideology when he told his students (I was an eye-witness) that the syllogism was an instrument devised by conservatives in that it limited inference to bringing out in the conclusion what was implicit in the premises. Logic, he taught, was an ideology to prevent the discovery of the new in general and of revolutions in particular. Deductive reasoning, he explained, was not eternally valid; but only propagandized to be valid in a society dominated by conservatives who enjoyed its benefits at the expense of the lower orders and wanted to prevent change—for any change would be to their disadvantage. (1988: 333)

What needs bearing in mind here, however, is that the politics of the founding of the sciences implies the political act of consciously attempting to exclude all values from scientific deliberation except the value called "objective knowledge." The sciences, that is, espouse a search for objective knowledge of the world and involve a conscious attempt to avoid (or at least minimize) idiosyncrasy and bias in that search. Their founding is an act of politics in both wide and narrow senses of that term. It is important, moreover, that the modern Western university has developed as an institution dedicated to reflect apolitical rather than political research. This holds even for the study of politics itself within the context of the modern university, which provides us with an excellent analogy for Religious Studies. In *The Nature and Limits of Political Science* Maurice Cowling points to the problem in a noteworthy manner:

> Professors of Political Science who want to engage in political practice (by standing for Parliament, writing in newspapers, advising governments or joining the City Council) are free to do so. But they are, so far as they do this, abandoning their academic function for a practical political one. To do so may, if they are lucky, help them to illuminate the academic subject-matter. But the only rational action to which scholars are committed, the only moral action to which they are commanded and the only "social responsibility" to which their professional position compels them, is to use their energies in order to explain in its full diversity as much as they can of the nature of the world in which they live. (1963: 209–210)

To fail or refuse to demarcate the study of political behavior from political behavior itself, therefore, is to preclude all possibility of a "political science." Moreover, it makes all so-called political science simply another form of political behavior and makes of the university a party in the system of party politics of which it presumes to provide us some objective knowledge. In such a case, it seems to me, those within the university would be left with one option: to defend their form of politics from imperialistic takeover by the politics of their various critics. There is no doubt that explaining aspects of the world is a form of action and is therefore comparable in some broad sense of the word to forms of political action, but it has, as Cowling puts it, its "own conventions, rules, and institutions" (210). Thus Cowling writes: " . . . it is desirable to rid university faculties of the pretension to be schools of political practice, not because of the confusions this induces in the conduct of politics, but because of the damage it does to universities themselves" (120). I maintain a similar confusion exists between religion and the study of religion. And it is equally damaging to the university because it involves the subordination of the academy to the church. Talk of a "hostile takeover" of the university in this way may be considered hyperbolic by many, but it is nonetheless appropriate, as can be inferred from recent remarks by William Dean in his *The Religious Critic in American Culture*. Dean advises "public intellectuals" who currently work in the university—which includes the religious critic, whose primary concern is for the well-being of religion— "to adopt some third sector organization as their psychological home" (160) because the university context will make it "virtually impossible . . . , with its ideology of professionalism," to continue with the work of "convention-criticism and convention-making" (xxi). Despite this advice, however, he exposes the quandary: "[i]f voluntary organizations of the third sector do not offer the best venue and vehicle for the religious critic, and they may not, then what does? Should more hope be placed in the prospect of a deprofessionalized university? Should greater energy be lodged, after all, in reforming the university, in the effort to make it a viable psychological home and vehicle for the religious critic?" (172) Just how serious the damage can be, if one opens the university to this kind of activity, is evident to some extent in James R. Dow and Hannjost Lixfeld's *The Nazification of an Academic Discipline: Folklore in the Third Reich*, in which they show how the connection between German *Volkskunde* and National Socialism so politicized the discipline that it in effect abandoned the path of scholarship and science.

My argument in the essays presented here is: if the academic study of religion wishes to be taken seriously as a contributor to knowledge about our world, it will have to concede the boundaries set by the ideal of scientific knowledge that characterizes the university. It will have to recognize the limits of explanation and theory and be content to explain the subject-matter—and nothing more—rather than show itself a form of political or religious behavior (or an injunction to such action). A study of religion directed toward spiritual liberation of the individual or of the human race as a whole, toward the moral welfare of the human race, or toward any ulterior end than that of knowledge itself, should not find a home in the university; for if allowed in, its sectarian concerns will only contaminate the quest for a scientific knowledge of religions and eventually undermine the very institution from which it originally sought legitimation. To counter that the university's adoption of the ideal of seeking scientific knowledge of the world is itself a political and ideological stance similar to that found in the commitments voiced by the world's religious traditions is not a request for academic legitimation but a political takeover. It is an attempt to replace the methodological founding of the academic study of religion with an ideological founding, and it is supported by arguments resting on the confused notion of what constitutes a political act. The meaning of academic legitimation to those in Religious Studies under these conditions is difficult to perceive, for it would in fact be indistinguishable from ideological or political legitimation; and with this lack of precision we see disappear as well the peculiar contributions of the modern Western university to our general understanding of the world around us and, specifically, to our understanding of religions and religion. Thus I am in full agreement with Cowling when, in drawing an analogy between political science and the study of religion, he insists that "those who propagate religions have renounced the academic task of explaining everything and enjoining nothing" (1963: 161), and I have consequently set out to make the case for a clear demarcation, within the university context, between religion and the scientific study of religion. This is the essential burden of the essays assembled in this volume. There is no argument here that scholars in the field of religious studies ought not to engage in private religious practice, but only that they ought to recognize, as Cowling puts it with respect to the study of politics, that in doing so in a professional context they are abandoning their academic function for a religious one, and that there are institutions other than the university in which the latter function is appropriately carried out. The arguments of these essays attempt variously to show, recalling Cowling, that the only reasonable action to which scholars of religion, "as scholars, are committed, the only moral action to which they are commanded and the only 'social responsibility' to which their professional position compels them, is to use their energies in order to explain" (210) religion.

To assist the reader to see the various elements of the argument against the reintegration of religion and theology with the study of religion in the modern university, I have divided the book into four parts. Part I focuses attention on the emergence of the study of religion as a science. Chapter 1, "Explaining Religion: The Intellectual Ethos," is a response to Samuel Preus's *Explaining Religion: Criticism and Theory from Bodin to Freud* and provides a brief review of the history of the development of Western thought that made possible an ethos in which such a science could be formed. The other two essays in this section, "Religion and the Scientific Impulse in the Nineteenth Century: Friedrich Max Müller and the Birth of the Science of Religion" and "Toward the Founding of a Science of Religion: The Contribution of C. P. Tiele," provide evidence of the commitments to scientific objectivity on the part of the founders of the scientific study of religion. With such arguments as these to separate clearly the study of religion from religious and theological concerns, I maintain, the new discipline achieved academic legitimation as a scientific undertaking.

The essays in part II document a failure on the part of the successors to the founders of the new science to adhere to the principles upon which it had been founded. In chapter 4, "A 'New Era of Promise' for Religious Studies?," I look critically at proposals by Ninian Smart for a study of religion that can be scientific without being insensitive to religion, and I point to the development of a tactic which will ultimately draw the study back into a religio-theological frame. Chapter 5, "Theology and the Academic Study of Religion in Protestant America," provides a brief historical overview of the development of the study of religion in a country from which, given the formal constitutional separation of Church and State, one might have expected less theological interference than has in fact occurred. Chapter 6, "Promise and Disappointment: Recent Development in the Academic Study of Religion in the United States," more specifically focuses attention on that study since the Second World War. In chapter 7, "Religious Studies as a Saving Grace? From Goodenough to South Africa," I show how religion and politics directly affect the field of Religious Studies—not in the sense of the politics of founding the field, but rather in terms of religious and political agendas that transcend the pursuit of knowledge. In chapter 8, "The Failure of Nerve in the Academic Study of Religion," I offer a survey of recent methodological proposals in the field of Religious Studies that provides a clear indication that a large proportion of current students' work in the field rejects the scientific basis upon which it was established. These essays make it clear that not only is there a failure to adhere to the founders' agenda, but there is both little evidence of a clearly objective approach and a marked tendency toward reintegrating the discipline with theology. In the final chapter of part II, "The 'Academic Naturalization' of Religious Studies," I respond to criticism of the "Failure of Nerve" essay and provide argument for the reaffirmation of an academic-scientific agenda for the study of religion.

Part III furnishes a series of illustrations to corroborate the claims made in part II: that the academic study of religion has failed to carry out its original scientific agenda. Chapter 10 is of particular importance because of the widely held view that the phenomenology of religion is a science even though sympathetic to religion. In "Phenomenology of Religion as Religio-Cultural Quest: Gerardus van der Leeuw and the Subversion of the Scientific Study of Religion," I show that the most widely accepted version of the phenomenology of religion is not a genuinely scientific undertaking in that it deliberately subordinates science to a religious agenda. In chapter 11, "On the Value of the World's Parliament of Religions for the Study of Religion," it becomes clear how problematic for academic-scientific study is the confessional concern for religions and interfaith dialogue, given the mixed motives propelling these exercises. In chapter 12, "The Study of Religion: On the New Encyclopedia of Religion," I attempt to show that even in such a broad scholarly undertaking as the creation of an encyclopedia, we have a clear indication of an agenda that cannot help but undermine the scientific credibility of the entire exercise. This must not be understood as a claim that nothing of scientific value is to be found in the Encyclopedia, but rather that the framework within which the task was executed essentially promoted the attempt to "understand" religion rather than to explain it. The last three essays in part III concern specific institutions. In chapter 13, "Alive, But Just Barely: Graduate Studies in Religion at the University of Toronto," I examine closely how within the development of a major Canadian institution the study of religion has been dominated by religious and theological agendas; and in chapter 14, "Against Science in the Academic Study of Religion: On the Emergence and Development of the American Academy of Religion," and chapter 15, "A Religious Agenda Continued: A Review of the Presidential Addresses of the AAR," I show that the world's largest professional organization for students of religion is also heavily dominated by religio-theological rather than scientific concerns. The epilogue, "Appropriating Religion: Understanding Religion as an Object of Science," summarizes the expectations of those who hope to make the field of Religious Studies a respected academic, scientific enterprise.

To repeat, in these essays I attempt to recover for the university a study of religion governed by principles of scientific investigation and I decry the current governance of such study by religious goals. I am aware that in this attempt I might well be accused of following a political agenda. But if so, the agenda does not activate concerns foreign to the university's aims and intentions. It is a "political" act in that it is an attempt to re-establish or re-found the discipline as it first emerged in the latter part of the nineteenth century, and in terms of which it first received legitimation as a university discipline. It is also political in the narrower sense—but not in a way that distorts the scientific agenda of the study of religion. I hope, that is, that the arguments here will persuade various university authorities to scrutinize more carefully their legitimation of departments of Religious Studies as well as encourage national funding agencies to examine more closely the professional societies and associations they support, in order to be sure that they are not unwittingly legitimating one or another religious ideology. Once again, this is a political act that does not introduce an aim or intention into the politics of founding a discipline inconsistent with the search for scientific knowledge of the world (which is the aim of founding the discipline in the first place); therefore it does not implicate me in the very offense against which I have taken up cudgels here. My hope is that, when the arguments contained in these essays become more widely available for discussion in the academic community at large, sufficient pressure will be exerted both from within the field and from the other sciences concerned with the study of cultures and societies so as to require of Religious Studies that it show grounds for legitimation as a part of the curriculum of the modern university.

What distinguishes this collection of essays from their status as individual pieces is, first of all, the added effect to be gained by a concerted, repeated stress on the need for a disinterested approach to the discipline; and second—and more important—that they serve as a response to the unspoken argument that, despite the articles having received some attention in the academic community through the decade (from 1986 to 1997), there has been, as yet, little responsible reaction from the university to the scholarly—let alone financial—implications of the problem enunciated. In fact, in the United States as well as in Canada, there has been an aggravation of confessionalism outlined in these studies, despite an avowed shortage, and consequently more selective deployment of post-secondary academic funding in general.

There need to be tools at hand to facilitate the commandeering of argument and case study, illustrating the motivation behind Religious Studies on this continent. It is my aim that these chapters, amply annotated and supplied with an unseen, detailed index of names and themes, will promote pointed discussion from which a more honest statement will have to emerge about the discipline.

Although no substantive changes have been made to the essays republished here, they have been thoroughly revised with respect to style. On examination of the arguments put forward in these essays—and of the evidence adduced in their support—I found them to be as persuasive now as when they were first published. The presentation of those arguments, however, left something to be desired with respect to clarity and precision— due, I like to think, to the haste in which they were written because of the pressures of teaching and administrative duties. I wish to thank the editors and publishers of the various journals and books in which these essays first appeared for permission to reprint them here (see Acknowledgments), and to recognize my deep indebtedness to Martha Cunningham for her assistance in their revision (though holding her faultless for whatever infelicities and ambiguities that remain). I am, of course, also indebted to many colleagues who have provided me with advice and criticism over the years in which these essays were produced; their assistance is gratefully acknowledged in the notes. Several colleagues, however, have been conversation partners over many years and have deeply affected my views on Religious Studies, and I wish to thank them here for that extended critical contribution to my thinking through the methodological problems of the field: Gary Lease, Armin Geertz, Jeppe Sinding Jensen, Ivan Strenski, Michael Pye, Ninian Smart, Robert Segal, Abrahim Khan, Russell McCutcheon, Bruce Alton, Neil McMullin, and Peter Richardson. Naturally none of them is to be held responsible for the views presented, but more than one or two of them, I think, would acknowledge some complicity. Luther H. Martin and E. Thomas Lawson require special mention here. They have been more than critical conversation partners; they have been joint advocates, if not comrades-in-arms, in a project to secure a scientific basis for the study of religion in the academy. Working with them to found the North American Association for the Study of Religion (1985) and to have it subsequently affiliated with the International Association for the History of Religions (1990) added an important, constructive element to our critical concerns about the religious entanglements of Religious Studies in our universities on this continent. I have therefore dedicated this book to them. Finally, I wish to thank Michael Flamini of St. Martin's Press for many helpful conversations over the years on a variety of matters related to the scientific study of religion; I am grateful to him for his advice and assistance on bringing this project to completion.

Acknowledgments

The essays presented here originally appeared in earlier publications I am most grateful to the editors and publishers listed below for permission to include them in this collection.

"Explaining Religion: The Intellectual Ethos." *Religion* 19 (1989): 305–309.

"Religion and the Scientific Impulse in the Nineteenth Century: Friedrich Max Müller and the Birth of the Science of Religion." *International Journal for Comparative Religions* 1 (1995): 75–96.

"Toward the Founding of a Science of Religion: The Contribution of C.P. Tiele," in Arvind Sharma, ed., *The Sum of Our Choices: Essays in Honor of Eric J. Sharpe* (Atlanta: Scholar's Press, 1996): 26–49.

"A New Era of Promise for Religious Studies?" in Peter Masefield and Donald Wiebe, eds., *Aspects of Religion: Essays in Honour of Ninian Smart* (New York: Peter Lang Press, 1994): 93–112.

"Theology and the Academic Study of Religion in Protestant America," in Dick van der Meij, ed., *India and Beyond: Aspects of Literature, Meaning, Ritual and Thought. Essays in Honour of Frits Staal* (Leiden: Kegan Paul International, 1997): 651–675.

"Promise and Disappointment: Recent Developments in the Academic Study of Religion in the U.S.A," to be published in a volume of papers, edited by J. Plotvoet, emerging from the conference on "Modern Society and the Study of Religion."

"Religious Studies as a Saving Grace? From Goodenough to South Africa," in Luther Martin, ed., *Religious Transformation and Socio-Political Change* (Berlin: Mouton de Gruyter, 1993): 411–438.

"The 'Academic Naturalization' of Religious Studies: Intent or Pretence?" *Studies in Religion* 15 (1986): 197–203.

"Phenomenology of Religion as Religio-Cultural Quest: Gerardus van der Leeuw and the Subversion of the Scientific Study of Religion," in Hans G. Kippenberg and Brigitte Luchesi, eds., *Religionswissenschaft und Kulturkritik. Beitrage zur Konferenz "The History of Religions and Critique of Culture in the Days of Gerardus van der Leeuw"* (Marburg: Diagonalverlag, 1990): 62–86.

"On the Value of the World's Parliament of Religions for the Study of Religion." *Method and Theory in the Study of Religion* 7 (1995): 197–202.

"The Study of Religion: On the New Encyclopedia of Religion." *Annals of Scholarship* 5 (1988): 260–268.

"Alive, But Just Barely: Graduate Studies in Religion at the University of Toronto." *Method and Theory in the Study of Religion* 7 (1995): 357–387.

"Against Science in the Academic Study of Religion: On the Emergence and Development of the American Academy of Religion," in George Bond and Thomas Ryba, eds., *The Comity and Grace of Method: Religious Studies for Edmund Perry* forthcoming (Evanston: Northwestern University Press).

"A Religious Agenda Continued: A Review of the Presidential Addresses of the AAR." *Method and Theory in the Study of Religion* 9 (1997): 353–375.

"Appropriating Religion: Understanding Religion as an Object of Science," to be published in a volume of papers emerging from the Donner Institute conference on "Methodology of the Study of Religion" held at Turku, Finland (1997).

Part I

From Theology to Religious Studies:
On the Emergence of a New Science

Chapter One

Explaining Religion:
The Intellectual Ethos

The scholarly study of religion is now and has always been an essentially religio-theological undertaking for the majority of those involved in the enterprise. It is and has always been predominantly informed, that is, by theological assumptions and religious commitments. But that approach to the study of religion has not been without rivals. There exists, for example, a mode of inquiry concerned with finding explanations of all religious phenomena from within a naturalistic framework alone. Such an approach treats religion as an element of culture like any other and does so by rejecting the assumption that in order to understand it is necessary to believe, in some sense or other, what the devotee believes. And it is the history of the development of this naturalistic framework that Samuel Preus pursues in his *Explaining Religion: Criticism and Theory from Bodin to Freud*.

Preus correctly points out that the new paradigm for studying religion emerged out of criticism of religion, and that its later development rested on the Enlightenment critique of religion. But, he maintains, an historical investigation of early modern European theories of the origin of religion clearly reveals the development of a radically different research tradition. Making heuristic use of Thomas Kuhn's notion of paradigm as both "disciplinary matrix" and "exemplar," Preus identifies a series of minor revolutions in thought about religion over a period of three centuries, the cumulative effect of which, he claims, constitutes the naturalistic paradigm. The history of these minor revolutions he then divides into two periods, the earlier involving a gradually expanding criticism of religion and an increasing degree of detachment from religious presuppositions and commitments, and the later, involving an increasing awareness of the social nature of religion underscoring the curious state of affairs in which we experience both the social persistence and the intellectual obsolescence of religion. The watershed between these two periods is represented by David Hume, his work placing the study of religion for the first time within the context of a scientific study of humanity. In Preus's view, therefore, Hume completes the "paradigm shift" introduced by Bodin, for in Hume we see the conscious substitution of a scientific for a theological framework for the study of religion. "With him," writes Preus, "a line of criticism definitely ends and construction of alternative theory begins . . ." (84).

In the case of Jean Bodin, claims Preus, we have the first extended debate on the problem of the plurality of religions in the world. Bodin was a religious person and worked within a normative framework, but in seeing religion as problematic he was making an intellectual break from Christianity. Although he did not reject Revelation, he put reason above Revelation, thus undermining the generally accepted biblical model for the organization of reality as a whole.

Herbert of Cherbury goes even further than Bodin in the rejection of Revelation: He adopts a global perspective transcending confessional norms. Preus admits that Herbert has a theological agenda but claims the latter's concern to draw general conclusions about religion based on data from all the religions of the world constituted a disregard of the biblical framework.

Bernard Fontenelle's work leaves Deistic theology behind and expands on Herbert's attempt to account for the rise and fall of religious belief without appeal to supernatural causes of any kind. Indeed, according to Preus we see in Fontenelle's search for psycho-historical causes of religious belief the beginnings of a developmental paradigm for studying religion. We have here, that is, "an evolutionary framework . . . [as] a clear alternative to traditional theology, both of revelation and of the innatist, deistic type" (54). Giambattista Vico develops Fontenelle's approach. While not rejecting a Catholic worldview, he nevertheless presents a thoroughly naturalistic account of all human institutions including religion. By exempting Christianity from his analyses, Vico was able to thwart its authority and to give free rein to critical-historical reason.

Hume, as I have already pointed out, completes the development of this stream of critical thought. By rejecting religious explanations of religion, Hume places the study of religion within the realm of human studies; he makes humanity the object of study by extending the experimental method to human motivation and behavior. And his hypotheses in this regard, claims Preus, had a direct documentable impact on later students of religion in Britain, France, and Germany. No longer was the concern in this field focused on the problem of the legitimation of religion, but rather on its explanation. Thus, writes Preus, "Hume's thoroughgoing naturalism, his clear vision of religion as part of a science of humankind, and his development of alternatives to all the contemporary theological explanations of religion together warrant the paradigmatic role he is accorded here. He in effect closes an era of criticism and opens the paths of future research" (100).

Although Hume, in annulling the necessity of accounting for religion in religious terms, brings to conclusion the paradigm shift in the study of religion begun by Bodin, he does not provide a wholly adequate framework for that study. As Preus points out, for example, there is an obvious absence of attention to the social component of religion in Hume's reconstruction of its origin. Hume failed to consider both the possible connection between human sociability and the origin of religion, and the fact that this connection contributed to the establishment and maintenance of a social order. In disposing of the last remaining religious explanations and legitimations of religion, however, he made possible a concern with social dynamics of this kind.

Auguste Comte, Preus then proceeds to argue, moves well beyond Hume's concern with critique; for he recognizes that religion is an ideological complex performing functions indispensable to society. Unlike Hume, therefore, Comte is able to handle the above-mentioned phenomenon of religion's persistence in the face of intellectual obsolescence. Comte, that is, appears able to explain religion without "explaining it away." In terms of his theory of the evolution of human thought, Comte can relegate theology to oblivion while still recognizing its function as a unifying element in society. If religion as explanation cannot hold its own in the modern world and does not provide knowledge about the world as it once did, it can still function beneficially on a social level. Preus points out that there are two theories of religion implicit in Comte's work: one connected to his view of the evolution of the human mind involving a progressive mastery of humanity over its destiny; and the other connected to anxieties created by social crises. These theories, Preus maintains, anticipate the distinction between early British anthropological theorists of religion and French sociologists.

E. B. Tylor's evolutionary anthropology clearly follows the Hume-Comte line in eschewing all possibility of supernatural explanations of religion and in approaching the historical study of humanity as part and parcel of the history of nature in general. Like Comte, Tylor sought an explanation of human behavior, including religious behavior, in empirically based scientific generalizations.

Whereas the line of approach to understanding religion traced from Hume through Tylor is intellectualistic and developmental—it sees the rise of religion in connection with the individual's struggle to explain experience—another line of development, as Preus points out, is evident in the Vico-Comte tradition. In the latter, religion is explained by reference not to individuals but rather to social necessity. Although religion's cognitive import has been surpassed by scientific knowledge, its other functions may still be usefully carried out. Religion is thus "true," not in the literal sense of making correct (acceptable) claims about the world—physical or metaphysical—but rather in the sense that it continues to be socially necessary. Durkheim and Freud, for example, though accepting the Enlightenment critique of religion, do not find it to account sufficiently for the persistence of religion. If religion were merely "a fabric of errors," they maintain, there would be no reason for its persistence. Both recognize that religion, although illogical, is at the same time independent of logic. And both, therefore, like Comte, offer theories to account for the emergence of religion and for its persistence in the face of rational criticism. Their theories refer to forces "deeper than those recognized consciously by the ancient actors themselves, and deeper than the mere curiosity attributed to them by the British anthropologists" (197).

For Preus, then, Durkheim and Freud bring to completion the naturalistic paradigm for the academic study of religion originating ultimately with Hume. That paradigm is complete "because their allegation that psychosocial causes are at the root of religious experience was subject to testing through scientific methods of observation and correction—a process that continues still. Despite the fact that no final scientific 'proof' of their theses can be imagined (a problem shared by the most comprehensive paradigms in the natural sciences as well), the theories were supported by argument and evidence of sufficient power and coherence to support a new generation of specialized studies" (162).

Preus, as this summary of his argument indicates, clearly identifies the emergence and development of a new and coherent intellectual tradition for the study of religion that breaks away from the previous religio-theological paradigm. It is not Preus's intention to provide an account of the institutionalization of the academic study of religion in the curriculum of the modern Western university; rather, and more importantly, he analyzes the intellectual ethos in which an argument for such development could be formulated. His is hardly a whiggish history of the development of Religious Studies, however, for Preus is well aware that even though the study of religion was included in the modern university curriculum it never really entered fully into the academic study of culture in that context. Indeed, even today, Preus quite correctly notes, the study of religion within the university context is still carried on quite comfortably in a quasi-theological or metaphysical mode with most of it still presuming that the origins or causes of religion lie beyond scientific investigation. And his account here of the emergence of a naturalistic framework for the study of religion functions—and is intended to function—as a critique of that theological framework. As Preus puts it, his history challenges the popular notion that the only proper approach to religions is 'from inside' and the implicit corollary that the only proper comprehensive explanation of religions is that they are 'manifestations of the sacred' or responses to 'transcendence'; it argues that a clear distinction between a naturalistic approach with its own explanatory apparatus and religious approaches is necessary to achieve a coherent conception of what the study of religion is about; and, negatively, that such a distinction is needed in order to clarify the difference between the study of religion in the framework of the humanities and human sciences and often hidden apologetic intentions that inform much contemporary writing and teaching about religion. (xxi)

The "insider" approach in Religious Studies is not acceptable to the academy, for it isolates that study from the assumptions and presuppositions of the social sciences concerned with human affairs.

Preus notes in the introduction to his book that the abundance of literature in recent years on how the study of religion ought to be conceived amounts to conclusive evidence of an identity crisis in the field. And he concludes quite correctly that the religious framework for that study is far less likely to provide the unifying paradigm the field seeks than is the naturalistic framework. Consequently, Preus terminates his study with a proposal to adopt the latter:

The naturalistic approach is at once more modest and more ambitious than the religious one: more modest because it is content to investigate the causes, motivations, meanings, and impact of religious phenomena without pronouncing on their cosmic significance for human destiny; ambitious, in that the study of religion strives to explain religion and to integrate its understanding into the other elements of culture to which it is related. (211)

Chapter Two

Religion and the Scientific
Impulse in the Nineteenth Century:
Friedrich Max Müller and the
Birth of the Science of Religion

I t will come as no surprise to most students of religion that there are serious differences of opinion within the field with respect to the nature of
the enterprise. Nor should it surprise anyone that such conflict has characterized the field virtually from the beginning of its acceptance into the curriculum of the modern Western university. The situation is so serious, Eric
Sharpe has recently suggested in his "Religious Studies, the Humanities, and
the History of Ideas," that we might well talk of a "crisis of identity" in religious studies: a crisis created by the pressure to draw a clear line of demarcation between religion and the study of religion (1988: 256). Nevertheless,
Sharpe ventures that the situation may not really be as serious as it seems.
For it is possible that much of the current malaise over the demarcation issue
is simply due to the field's having gone through a period of unplanned, erratic expansion during which little or nothing was done to justify the enterprise, either to ourselves or to the larger academic community. If scholars
were to set the record straight concerning the context out of which Religious
Studies emerged as a new element in the university curriculum, he suggests,
the malaise could be largely dispelled. He writes:

> Above all we have reflected far too little on our own history. For although in
> a sense each one of us has to create his or her own identity, the question of
> heredity is not therefore without importance. The present uneasy relationship
> between the various members of the Religious Studies family could be greatly
> illuminated if we were to look up—and insist that our graduate students look
> up—various family trees. The history of ideas, with or without the sociology
> of knowledge, will not solve all our problems, but might prove to be a useful

diagnostic tool, and might even help to provide the outlines of the disciplinary matrix we are looking for. (1988: 256)

In commenting on his own review of the field in his *Comparative Religions: A History,* Sharpe remarks that in many ways his chronicle turned "into a record of the tug-of-war between Religion and the Humanities for the right to dictate the terms on which religion might be studied" (1988: 245). That tug-of-war is between, on the one hand, those who believe in the necessity of "acquiescence" to the Transcendent as a condition for embarking on the scientific study of religions and, on the other hand, those who believe in "the necessity of *not* submitting to transcendental authority as a condition of getting off the ground in the first place" (1988: 249). Sharpe, therefore, is left with no doubt about the existence of a fundamental contrast of principle among students of religion that can distinguish religious studies from religion. As he puts it: "[O]ver against the way of submission which is the way of Religion, Religious Studies seems to stand for the way of control, at least to the extent to which the investigator exercises discretion, observes, measures, makes choices, and organizes into patterns" (1988: 248). And the story of the development of Religious Studies within the academy, he insists, "is very much a record of attempts to set the study of religion free from [the] submission to transcendental authority" (1988: 248–249). Despite these claims, however, Sharpe goes on in the essay to say that he has drawn this distinction between religion and Religious Studies only "as a matter of principle" and that he is "far from being convinced that it always works out in practice" (1988: 249). In part, he means to draw attention to the fact, as he puts it, that "the [historical] record of Religious Studies is by no means as one-sidedly rationalistic as one might suppose" (1988: 250). Those who would assume that Religious Studies was ever de-theologized, he insists, would simply be wrong (1988: 251). And in support of this claim Sharpe draws the reader's attention to the work of a number of practitioners in the field, early and late, who have affirmed that the causes of "true religion" and "true science" are one and the same. He does not wholly deny, however, that the study of religion was secularized, historicized, and possibly even "de-transcendentalized," as he puts it, but claims, and quite rightly so, that the study did not undergo a wholesale revision in the process. Sharpe asserts that early students of religion were attempting to free the study of religions from the "ultimately authoritarian methods of religious confessionalism" in order to side with science "over against what was felt to be the dead hand of religious orthodoxy" (1988: 251). And with this claim he is ultimately arguing that the impetus for the emergence of the scientific study of religion was a religious one: the study of religion was indistinguishable from religion because what that science did "*was precisely what liberal religion was doing during the same period*" (1988: 251; Sharpe's emphasis). He writes: "[I]f we identify two of [liberalism's] distinguishing features as an insistent moralism and a quest for human universals, coupled with a belief in the infinite educability of the human race, then perhaps we can begin to see how the line of Religion and the line of Religious Studies are (when viewed from this particular angle) not two lines, but one" (1988: 251).[1]

I think Sharpe's assessment here essentially wrong and the argument given in support of it fundamentally misdirected. What particular practitioners in the field of the study of religion did or did not think or do has no logical bearing upon what should constitute the appropriate relationship of that field, either to other fields or disciplines within the academy, or to other institutions in society. Nor is it the case, as some might argue, that because the beginnings of the science of religion "are to be found among Christian theologians or those who were strongly influenced by Christian faith and theology," that those beginnings need furnish the pattern for further scholarship; the scientific study of religion does not "owe a decisive and critical debt to Christianity and its theologians."[2] Furthermore, even if motivations of the religio-theologian and scientific student of religion converged with both ultimately seeking the justification of religion, it is not necessarily the case that each would follow the same procedure in doing so.

Nevertheless, I do think that Sharpe's comments about the ambiguous delineation of the nature of this field of study in the last quarter or so of the nineteenth century are essentially correct; and I also think that a proper understanding of the intention of the so-called founders of the science can make a significant contribution to our own attempts to outline "the disciplinary matrix," as Sharpe puts it, of the field of research in which we are engaged. Furthermore, a critical review of the contribution of F. Max Müller in this regard, I shall argue here, will undermine the conception of the discipline that Sharpe presents in his article and elsewhere for adoption by today's students of religion (1987a: 257–269 and 1986: 294–319).

Friedrich Max Müller, it is generally agreed, is the founder of the modern scientific study of religion in the form in which it has achieved cognitive legitimation in the modern Western university.[3] A proper understanding of his achievements, therefore, should make a considerable contribution to understanding our "heredity" with respect to the identity question under debate. Although I do not think Müller always expressed himself clearly on methodological issues, a careful reading reveals his proposed science of religion to rest wholly upon a scientific rather than a religio-theological foundation, despite his being religiously committed.[4] I shall begin this analysis of his views by paying particular attention to his *Introduction to the Science of*

Religion since, with Sharpe (1986: xi and 35), I see this volume as "the foundation document of comparative religion [the science of religion] in the English-speaking world." Although Sharpe, in his *Comparative Religion: A History,* refers to the *Introduction to the Science of Religion*—a series of four lectures delivered to the Royal Society in 1870—as the foundation document of Religious Studies, he does not provide a detailed analysis of that document. And in a brief discussion of its role in the formation of Religious Studies he claims that these lectures do not provide an "absolutely new departure" in the study of religious phenomena because scholars before Müller had already looked upon religion as an object to be studied (1986: xi).[5] However, even though Müller did not, according to Sharpe (1986: 45), single-handedly found the science of religion, his lectures are foundational to the new science, he maintains, because in them Müller brings order and method to a body of data that until that time had remained relatively disorganized. "Before Max Müller," writes Sharpe, " . . . the field of religious studies, though wide and full, was disorganized. After him, the field could be seen as a whole, subjected to a method, and, in short, treated scientifically" (1986: 46). And this holds true despite Müller's own later claim, in his *Lectures on the Origin and Growth of Religion: As Illustrated by the Religions of India,* that the science of religion is not "a science of today or of yesterday" since its beginnings are as old as the religions to which it gives its attention (1878: 6).[6] Additionally, Sharpe maintains, Müller had popularized the phrase "the science of religion" and in the process "had given the comparative study of religion an impulse, a shape, a terminology and a set of ideals" (1986: 45).

Sharpe has little to say about the content of Müller's lectures on the Science of Religion and the nature of the argument presented. He notes that Müller divided the study of religion into two parts, that he designated with names compounded with the word "theology"—"Comparative Theology," being that part of the Science of Religion dealing with the historical forms of religion (and which constitutes the primary focus of Müller's attention), and "Theoretical Theology," the philosophical element of the Science that explains the conditions under which any form of religion is possible (1986: 43). Sharpe goes on to suggest as well that Müller may have used such designators as "a sign of parentage or at least respectability" (1986: 43), implying thereby that Müller may have failed to distinguish clearly religion from the study of religion. Sharpe stresses that Müller grew up in an atmosphere of German Romantic idealism, as if that fact would account for Müller's being more than a mere scientist (historian-philologist) in his taking up the comparative study of religions (1986: 43). Müller's enthusiastic support for the World's Parliament of Religions in 1893, Sharpe further argues, shows that he was involved in more than a search for knowledge about religions;

he was also actively engaged in a religio-philosophic activity in his comparative study of religions (1986: 44). Consequently, for Müller (as for other founding figures) the Science of Religion (that is, Comparative Religion) "was at root a *practical* activity," and not simply science (1986: 252). This seems a strange conclusion to reach once one has recognized that a major contribution of Müller to the field of religious studies is his use of the phrase "Science of Religion." Moreover, Sharpe arrives at this conclusion without describing Müller's use of that phrase. If Müller and other students of religion in this early period of the emergence of the field incorporated their religious agendas into their study of religions so as to make the discipline essentially "a practical activity," it is difficult to see in what sense they are, then, the founders of a scientific discipline. That is, it would appear that the derivation of this field of research would be primarily religious rather than scientific. I do not think this to be the case, however, for even though one must admit, with Sharpe, that Müller reveals a religious agenda throughout much of his published work, he does not, I think, confound his religious concern with the scientific basis of his study of religions.[7] And despite Sharpe's argument to the contrary, he does seem aware of this. Although having suggested that Müller's advocacy of the 1893 Parliament of Religions constitutes evidence that Müller understood the study of religions to be an essentially practical activity, Sharpe also claims that participation in the Parliament presented a danger to one's scholarly reputation at that time since it was recognized that "whatever the need for interreligious understanding, the scientific study of religion, committed to the quest of truth for truth's own sake, ought not to be saddled with such an onerous and subjective incidental" (1986: 139). And in recognizing that Müller's reputation might withstand the apparent confusion of scientific and religious agendas in supporting such an undertaking, but that the reputation of lesser scholars might not, Sharpe indicates that scholars at the time had, at least to some extent, demarcated the scientific from the religious exercise.

That Müller's science of religion was not a practical activity of the sort defined by Sharpe would have been evident I think, if Sharpe had analyzed Müller's use, in the *Introduction* and elsewhere, of the phrase "Science of Religion." In the *Introduction*, Müller, noting that scholars who study medicine leave the application of that study to others, advises the student of the Science of Religion to invoke a similar "division of labour" in the study of religion. "In practical life," he writes,

> it would be wrong to assume a neutral position between . . . conflicting views [of religion]. Where we see that the reverence due to religion is violated, we are bound to protest; where we see that superstition saps the roots of faith, and hypocrisy poisons the springs of morality, we must take sides. *But as students*

of the Science of Religion we move in a higher and more serene atmosphere (1893: 7; my emphasis).

And in the preface to his earlier *Essays on the Science of Religion,* Müller also draws attention to the difference of intention between the scientific student of religion and the devotee (as he does in his second course of Gifford Lectures, *Physical Religion*). In the *Essays* he admits that the comparative study of religion may have great value for "missionaries and other defenders of the faith," but he insists that the aim of the Science of Religion is not to provide such support: "In order to maintain their scientific character," he writes, "they must aim at truth, trusting that even unpalatable truths, like unpalatable medicine, will reinvigorate the system into which they enter" (1881a: xxvi). In *Physical Religion,* Müller pointedly claims that it is precisely because the Science of Religion is not a practical undertaking that the introduction of this new field into the universities is met "with anything but a friendly welcome on the part of educational reformers." He writes:

> So far as these attacks are directed against all scientific studies which cannot at once show what they lead to, or produce useful and marketable results, no defence seems to me necessary. We surely know by this time how often in the history of the world the labors of the patient student, jeered at by his contemporaries as mere waste of time and money and brains, have in the end given to the world some of its most valued possessions. (1898b: 330)

Being a scientific student of religion, then, involves one in a set of activities clearly distinguished from the activities of the devotee. This does not, of course, mean that the devotee cannot engage in the scientific study of religion, but only that he or she cannot do so "as a religious person"—that is, from a religious perspective of any sort. As Müller asserts in the *Introduction,* "Science wants no partisans" (1893: 28).[8] And even though this injunction is made in a discussion of the relative merits of religions, it also can be applied generally to assumptions about the truth of religion per se. The essence of the Science of Religion for Müller is the commitment of the student to open and honest inquiry unflinchingly and uncompromisingly dedicated to seeking the truth. And such a commitment, quite obviously, stands in potential conflict with the commitments (particular or general) of the student qua religious devotee. Thus Müller writes:

> The very title of the Science of Religion will jar . . . on the ears of many persons, and a comparison of all the religions of the world, in which none can claim a privileged position will no doubt seem to many dangerous and reprehensible because ignoring that peculiar reverence which everybody, down to the mere fetish worshipper, feels for his *own* religion and for his *own* God. Let

me say then at once that I myself have shared these misgivings, but that I have tried to overcome them, because I would not and could not allow myself to surrender either what I hold to be the truth or what I hold still dearer than the truth, the right of testing truth. Nor do I regret it. (1893: 8)

It is true that Müller does not ultimately believe that the Science of Religion de facto will undermine all religious conviction, even though it may be responsible for the modification of some religious convictions once held dear. He emphatically asserts in the *Introduction:* "[I]f we must not read in the history of the whole human race the daily lessons of a divine teacher and guide, if there is no purpose, no increasing purpose in the succession of the religions of the world, then we might as well shut up the godless book of history altogether, and look upon men as no better than the grass which is today in the field and tomorrow is cast into the oven"(1893: 151). This does not, I think, imply that the Science of Religion could not come to such conclusions, but only that if it did, Müller would find the enterprise depressing. Müller's comments here are not methodological so much as they are a confession of his ultimate belief that the truth of religion and scientific knowledge will, in the final analysis, be convergent. As he puts it in the *Introduction:* "I do not say that the Science of Religion is all gain. No, it entails losses, and losses of many things which we hold dear. But this I will say, that, as far as my humble judgment goes, it does not entail the loss of anything that is essential to true religion, and that if we strike the balance honestly, the gain is immeasurably greater than the loss" (1893: 8). Furthermore, in the *Essays* he condemns those who fear to put their faith to critical scrutiny, and who crave "tender and merciful treatment of their beliefs" (1881a: xx-xxi). The issue is most clearly stated, however, in his third course of Gifford Lectures, *Anthropological Religion.* Here he acknowledges that religion is different from other subjects, as it appeals not only to our heads but also to our hearts (1898c: 1); he is willing on that account to listen to objections against its being granted a place among academic studies in the university (1898c: 16). He argues, however, that the possible danger of the study of religion no more warrants its restriction than the existence of poisonous plants precludes the study of botany (1898c: 7). Thus he claims: "To expect that religion could even be placed beyond the reach of scientific treatment, or honest criticism, shows an utter misapprehension of the signs of the times, and would, after all, be no more than to set up private judgment against private judgment" (1898c: 8). He goes on to reiterate that nothing can be more important than to seek the truth (1898c: 13) and to recognize that even if we do not commit ourselves to looking squarely at the facts, they will nevertheless conquer us in the end (1898c: 24, 48). Finally, he reaffirms the value of such a search despite the possible undermining of our fondest and most important beliefs. In this regard, even though he would like to claim a great deal more for the historical study of religion and the religions of the world, he writes:

> [W]e might still claim for the history of religions the same right to a place among our academic studies which is conceded to other historical studies. If at our schools and universities we teach the history of literature, of art, of the various branches of physical science, surely the history of religions ought to form a recognized department in the teaching of every university. Knowledge has a value of its own even if it should not be of practical or marketable utility. Even if religion were nothing but hallucinations as we have been lately told, an accurate knowledge of the causes and different phases of this universal disease might prove useful for its final cure. (1898c: 91–92)[9]

In his *Introduction,* Müller does not supply us with a detailed agenda for the Science of Religion. His intention, as he reveals early in the book, is rather to outline some "preliminary points that have to be settled before we can enter upon a truly scientific study of the religions of the world" (1893: 3), and he provides a summary of these points in the concluding chapter: "I chiefly wanted to show in what sense a truly scientific study of religion was possible, what materials there are to enable us to gain a trustworthy knowledge of the principal religions of the world and according to what principle these religions may be classified" (1893: 145). In addition to his general remarks about impartiality, he argues that a concern for truth and nothing but the truth and a commitment to the rules of critical scholarship are basic to an academic, scientific study of religion. Müller goes on to claim that such a science is essentially an historical and comparative undertaking. In other words, this science, in contrast to theology and philosophy, must deal with religion in its outward appearance—as something tangible and definite rather than as a silent power at work in the hearts of people (1893: 89). Briefly put, this new science, like all the sciences, must deal with the facts as they are found (1893: 74). The historical task, therefore, involves the collection, classification, and analysis of information about particular religious traditions (1893: 17). Müller makes very clear what he has in mind here in volume 1 of the Gifford Lectures, *Natural Religion:* "If the Science of Religion is to be treated as one of the natural sciences, it is clear that we must begin with a careful collection of facts, illustrating the origin, the growth, and the decay of religion" (1898a: 27); in this respect he saw his work on the Sacred Books of the East as providing the foundation "of a new, comparative, and strictly historical study of religion" (1898a: xv). Müller's belief is that such strictly historical work will eventually lead to a recognition of "natural lines of demarcation which divide the world into several great continents" and may permit the discovery of something common to all, granting authentic scientific status to facts known (1893: 8).[10] Müller is convinced that in the process such a study will radically change views (essentially theological and philosophical) held about the origin, character, growth, and decay of the religions of the world, including those about Christianity (1893: 12).

Müller's restriction of Science of Religion to merely the outward, tangible, and definite elements of religion may seem to contradict his division of it into "Comparative Theology," and "Theoretic Theology," the latter can only be addressed once the work of the former is completed (or at least well on its way to completion) (1893: 16–17). But matters are not quite that straightforward. Müller notes, for example, that his account of the Science of Religion here will be restricted purely to Comparative Theology, and he suggests that whatever the tasks of Theoretic Theology, it will be wholly dependent upon the results of the historical and comparative study of religions. He suggests, moreover, that in all likelihood the results of such a Theoretic Theology will contradict what is written about religion from this comparative perspective (1893: 17). Furthermore, in the closing lecture of the *Introduction* he writes rather hesitatingly about the role of Theoretic Theology:

> You will have observed that I have carefully abstained from entering on the domain of what I call Theoretic as distinguished from Comparative Theology. Theoretic Theology, or, as it is sometimes called, the philosophy of religion, has, as far as I can judge, its right place at the end, not at the beginning of *Comparative Theology*. I have made no secret of my own conviction that a study of Comparative Theology will produce with regard to Theoretic Theology the same revolution which a study of Comparative Philology has produced in what used to be called the Philosophy of Language. (1893: 146)

The revolution to which Müller refers here seems, in fact, to involve a rejection of philosophic speculation altogether. In this respect Müller's work shows that he rejects the idealist approach to the understanding of religion exemplified in the work of thinkers like Hegel and Schelling, for example. He finds that kind of work untrustworthy because it is intuitive rather than scientific, and he suggests that it may therefore be at cross-purposes to the work of the comparative theologian. Indeed, in a retrospective essay on the Science of Religion written shortly before his death, the matter is presented much less ambiguously; for Müller in that essay claims that, in trying to account for "religion in general," the philosophers supplanted the historians (1898e: 911). And Müller refers to this development as dangerous because it opened the field "to all kinds of theories long before a sufficient number of facts had been accumulated and critically sifted" (1898e: 911). From an historical point of view, he insists, moreover, "the historical existence of such a thing as religion in general had yet to be proved" (1898e: 911), suggesting thereby that Theoretic Theology of this variety (philosophy of religion as it is generally understood) is not an element of the Science of Religion; as such, philosophical thought simply confuses the enterprise (1898e: 911).[11] In his earlier *Natural Religion* Müller had already pointed to a similar contrast between Comparative Theology and Natural Theology. Though both "projects" worked simply from a human basis without recourse to revelation, Natural Theology (which notion Müller seems to use interchangeably with general theology and Theoretic Theology) differed from Comparative Theology "in that it paid but scant attention to the historical religions of the world, framing its ideal of what natural religion ought to be from the inner consciousness only" (1898a: 53).[12] In further delineating the two disciplines Müller does not deny relevance of one to the other, but he does, I think, suggest that they cannot be conflated. In summing up he claims that Natural or Theoretic Theology has to make room for the study of Comparative Theology or what may be called the Science of Religions, as distinguished from the Science of Religion. While Natural Theology treats religion in the abstract or in terms of what religion might or should be, Comparative Theology studies religions as they have been, and tries to discover what is peculiar to each and common to all, with a silent conviction that what all religions share, whether "revealed" or not, may possibly constitute the essential elements of "true religion" (1898a: 53).

It must also be pointed out here that the apparent basis for Müller's distinction between Comparative and Theoretic Theology would imply that the latter cannot (structurally) constitute a part of the Science of Religion. His division of the Science of Religion here, that is, rests on a distinction Müller draws between two meanings of "religion." In applying to religion Goethe's paradox that he who knows only one language knows none, Müller notes that Goethe was referring to two kinds of knowledge one can have of language, namely, knowledge as "know-how" (*können*) and "knowledge about" (*kennen*) (1893: 12).[13] Thus, though he may be a skillful and poetic master of the language, he might not have much to say on the nature of that language or on language in general. Similarly, Müller suggests that there exist two kinds of knowledge about religion: on the one hand, an insider's knowledge of a given religious tradition, propelling life from day to day; and on the other, an external knowledge of the physical characteristics and social structures of a particular religion (1893: 13). The second kind would correspond to Comparative Theology, the division of the Science concerned with what is empirically available. The first kind of knowledge, then, would be the equivalent of Theoretic Theology. To elucidate the distinction, Müller writes:

The student of Comparative Theology . . . can claim no privilege, no exceptional position of any kind, for his own religion, whatever that religion may be. For his purposes all religions are natural or historical. Even the claim of a supernatural character is treated by him as a natural and perfectly intelligible claim, which may be important as a subjective element, but can never be allowed to affect the objective character of any religion. (1898a: 52)

It is not altogether clear, then, whether Müller thinks Theoretic Theology refers simply to a kind of practical religious know-how that has no relevance to the acquisition of knowledge about religious phenomena, or whether he sees it as referring to a theoretical understanding of the conditions that make religion possible. Theoretical Theology understood as religious know-how, of course, must be excluded from the Science of Religion because it is steeped in subjectivity. Even a Theoretical Theology that frames its ideal on the basis of an inner, quasi-Hegelian consciousness is not arguably an element of the Science of Religion. It is only when the Theoretical Theology of the philosophers is derived from knowledge gained by Comparative Theology that it can be called a bona fide aspect of the scientific study of religion. And it is precisely such a fundamental difference in understanding Theoretical Theology which lends support to Müller's idea of a study of religion as solidly scientific. Müller often compares the Science of Religion to the other sciences such as medicine, botany, and astronomy; and in *Theosophy or Psychological Religion,* the fourth and final series of Gifford Lectures, Müller, after pointing to Hegel's abuse of historical inquiry, draws a parallel between his comparative study of religion and yet another physical science. Unlike Hegel, Müller claims to stick to the facts, his sole aim being "to try to decipher and understand them as we try to decipher and understand the geological annals of the earth, and to discover in them reason, cause and effect, and, if possible, that close genealogical coherence which alone can change empirical fact into scientific knowledge" (1898d: vi). Furthermore, shortly after arguing for the possibility of a scientific study of language in the preface to his *Essays on the Science of Religion,* Müller claims that the study of religion (which, incidentally, he thinks may be the last science we are likely to elaborate) can be scientifically grounded in a similar vein (1881a: xix). As he sums up in his analysis of language, it is in this regard that we have "a truly historical basis for a scientific treatment of the principal religions of the world" (1893: 144).[14]

In the preceding section I have tried to bolster the argument that Max Müller's work was scientifically based. Yet there is no doubt that he was a religious person who did not see serious danger to religion in the role exercised by science. In fact, in his Gifford Lectures he as much as advocated the development of a "Natural Theology" by which the truths of religion could be sustained scientifically. Thus the lectures on *Physical Religion* conclude with the following statement:

> If Comparative Theology has taught us anything, it has taught us that there is a common fund of truth in all religions, derived from a revelation that was neither confined to one nation, nor miraculous in the usual sense of that word, and that even minute coincidences between the doctrines, nay between the external accessories of various religions, need not be accounted for at once by disguised borrowings but can be explained by other and more natural causes. (1898b: 346)

That assertion is reinforced in his preface to the final set of lectures in *Theosophy or Psychological Religion,* when he claims for the historian of religion the capacity to see in history the realization of a rational purpose that can be looked upon as "divine drama" (1898d: v-vi). "It was the chief object of these four courses of lectures," he writes in the closing chapter, "to prove that the yearning for union or unity with God, which we saw as the highest goal in other religions, finds its fullest recognition in Christianity, if but properly understood, that is, if but treated historically, and that it is inseparable from our belief in man's full brotherhood with Christ" (1898d: 538). He thus concludes that "after a toilsome journey, the historian of religion arrives in the end at the same summit which the philosopher of religion has chosen from the first as his own" (1898d: 542).

The duality of Müller's pursuits, as evinced by the above quotations, is pointed out by G. W. Trompf: "Müller could remain a devout Lutheran and yet study religions, as objective historical phenomena at will . . ." (1978: 13). Yet I cannot really agree with Trompf that in Müller's work we have "the emergence of a theory of religion from a faith in a divine providential plan which could be illustrated by the comparative study of religions" (1978: 14). Nor is it acceptable to conclude (with him) that Müller's understanding of the study of religion reveals the supposed "Hegelian fever" contracted by Müller as a student in Leipzig (1978: 12). My analysis of Müller's understanding of the scientific nature of the academic study of religion demands a negative response to Trompf's claims. As I intimate above, Müller rejects the philosophic approach to the study of religion; and he reiterates to a striking degree his commitment to science and scientific method, fully knowing that such an approach could exact a painful change of belief-structures, even to the point of "explaining religion away." Consequently, even though Trompf may be largely correct in his account of Müller's assessment of the science of scholars such as Comte, Herbert Spencer, and Darwin, his suggestion seems wholly implausible that for Müller "[t]here is something in the very nature of history which will constantly elude the tools of the natural scientists, no matter how hard they try to discover its sociological laws" (1978: 62), or that for Müller " . . . the broad historical vision of Hegel retained a prominent place in his understanding of the world" (1978: 12). That Müller's late reflections and conclusions converge with the speculations of the philosophers or with the revelations of particular religious traditions seems incontrovertible, but this does not constitute grounds for Trompf's claim that these beliefs dominated and shaped the entire corpus of his work. Indeed, contrary to Trompf's interpretation, Müller admits the possibility that he could be wrong in having come to such conclusions, at the same time giving no indication that, should research force him to acknowledge that scientific and religious truth do not converge, he would withdraw from his commitment to the scientific study of religions. In other words, despite the religio-theological substance of much of Müller's work, in the final analysis it is a scientific rather than a religious or theological intentionality that informs Müller's research program. Science, for Müller, fundamentally represents the search for truth and is, in his view, essentially subject to falsification, which implies that substantive truth claims do not dictate the basis of the (scientific) research program but rather result from it. Müller's commitment to that ideal (even if theoretical) is clearly evident in his conclusion to the final set of Gifford Lectures, where he writes:

> I do not believe in human infallibility, least of all Papal infallibility. I do not believe in professorial infallibility, least of all in that of your Gifford Lecturer. We are fallible, and we are fallible either in our facts, or in the deductions which we draw from them. If therefore any of my learned critics will tell me which of my facts is wrong, or which of my conclusions faulty, let me assure them, that though I am now a very old professor, I shall always count those among my best friends who will not mind the trouble of supplying me with new facts, or of pointing out where facts have been wrongly stated by me, or who will correct any arguments that may seem to them to offend against the sacred laws of logic. (1898d: 543)[15]

Trompf's further comments on Müller's understanding of the Science of Religion, unfortunately, are not altogether clear. He seems at some points (1978: 62, 64) to be claiming not that Müller denied the value of science but that he denied history or sociology were sciences, and such an admission would mean that nothing historical could receive scientific treatment. Yet at other points he notes Müller's praise for the achievements of the natural sciences, admitting that Müller "was willing to concede that the scientific method could be applied to the study of humanity" (1978: 64), which study surely must be understood in historical and sociological terms. Additionally, Trompf's claim that Müller did not mean by science "positive" knowledge but rather "comparative method" (1978: 64) is equally erroneous. Finally, it is unclear what is to be made of Trompf's seemingly contradictory counsel: (1) that we not overemphasize the role of philosophy in the development of Müller's ideas (1978: 13), and (2) that we recognize that "[f]or all his religious sensibility, Müller was a man of science" (1978: 93). Such inconsistency may derive from Trompf's failure to differentiate between precept and practice in Müller's work. Although Müller's intention in supporting the academic study of religion may have diverged from how he actually undertook the study of religions, this does not provide a basis for inferring that Müller failed in fully elaborating his understanding of the structure or methodology of the new discipline.

In light of Müller's understanding of the nature of the academic study of religion, a description of which I have provided above, Johannes Voigt's assessment of the influence of science on Müller's thought seems more reasonable than Trompf's. Though noting that Müller did not simply overthrow his religion, Voigt writes:

> The tremendous progress that science and scientific thought were making in those days, could not but have its effect upon intellectual life in general. Scientific laws came to be regarded as sacred and took the place of what had hitherto been called divine laws. The scientific method of induction became the tolerated tool for research. Max Müller accepted the challenge of the 'scientific' character of the *Zeitgeist*. (1967: 13)

Beyond this claim, however, Voigt's analysis of Müller on the relation of religious belief to scientific research is ambiguous. Although Müller had adopted the *Zeitgeist* of the second half of the nineteenth century, Voigt maintains that Müller placed upon it his own characteristic stamp, referring to the two-sided nature (academic and religious) of his work (1967: 21). Voigt sees the academic study of religion for Müller as both a scientific and a religious undertaking: "[Müller's] study of nature as well as of history became, in fact, endeavours of a religious character: 'In both [that is, history and nature] we try to read the reflex of the laws and thoughts of a Divine Wisdom'" (1967: 20). But this reading of Müller's stance is flawed because it fails to recognize that for Müller the belief in the existence of God is not presupposed, either in itself or as a necessary element of the framework of analysis of religions but, rather, results from a study of the history of religions undertaken scientifically. Voigt, I think, is actually aware of this despite the way he phrases the matter here, for he recognizes later that Müller's "own religiousness came to be increasingly shaped by his academic studies" (1967: 31), and nowhere does he claim that religious convictions determined Müller's study of religion. Thus, even though Müller's new approach to the study of religion is, as Voigt insists, a kind of theological breakthrough (1967: 22), it is so because of the value Müller considers science to have in the search for any and all truth, including religious truth. Therefore, it is science and the possibility of the scientific study of religions that Müller believes can have a religious significance. Only this kind of interpretation of Müller's notion of the Science of Religion can, I think, account for Müller's positive affirmation of Lord Gifford's understanding of the value of science. "I share with him," writes Müller,

> the conviction that the same treatment which has caused the natural sciences to gain their greatest triumphs, namely, a critical collection of facts, will be the most appropriate treatment of the Science of Religion; nor should I differ from him in looking on man, in his purely phenomenal character, as part of nature, nay, as her highest achievement, so that if religion can be shown to be a natural outcome of our faculties, we may readily accept the Science of Religion as one of the natural sciences in the most comprehensive meaning of that term. (1898a: 13–14)

To return to Sharpe's analysis of Müller and the emergence of the science of religion, one must admit that he is entirely right to have noted that not all those concerned with establishing an academic-scientific study of religion abandoned their individual religious concerns. This fact should not be ignored, he insists, for such religious concerns cannot simply be legislated out of existence. He is quite right to claim, that is, that "even the hardest of hardline empiricists may acknowledge that although what he or she is demanding is professional competence 'within the limits of reason alone,' nothing can prevent the scholar from having immortal longings" (1988: 251; see also 1987a). However, this does not mean that the Science of Religion cannot—or ought not—be wholly secularized; persistent religious longings need not be factored into the study of religion. Reflecting on these nineteenth-century developments, M.C. D'Arcy notes: "Religion, because of its sacred and exalted character, had to become profane before it could be submitted to the scientific treatment which is the ideal of modern thought" (1939: 121). Nevertheless, Müller and others saw this kind of exercise—odd as it may seem—as capable of achieving "religious truth." Religious truth, like all our knowledge of states of affairs in the world, was, after a fashion, considered "scientific" truth.

Given this complex view, then, it is not difficult to see why subsequent discussion of the nature of the new discipline has been attended by a great deal of ambiguity. As Robert Lawson Slater points out, Müller was committed to the study of religious phenomena as a science, and it was that emphasis upon its scientific nature which was new to the religious scene in the nineteenth century. However, what was also new, he claims, "was the conviction that [the] essential unity [of all religions] could now be *proved* by enlightening science" (1963: 26). Even so, Slater rightly argues, to see the possibility of the demonstration of such a unity of religions as a by-product of the scientific study of religion is radically different from claiming the task of the study of religions to be the *creation* of such a unity. In any discussion of a nineteenth-century figure, it is important to remember that the Science of Religion did not emerge in a vacuum; one should examine it against the more general backdrop of the notion of science in Victorian society. David Knight identifies the need for the contextual approach when he states that, in contrast to their French scientific counterparts, there is a sense in which Britain constituted something of a "local culture" within the world of science in the nineteenth century: "science was entwined with other activities [which] . . . were not simply counterweights or antagonists" (1986: 211). In describing this peculiar state of affairs, Knight writes: "A feature of British science which marked it as separate, or provincial even, was its emphasis on natural theology. Science in France had emerged as a distinct activity or profession, justifying itself; in Britain it had not, and claims of utility meant both usefulness in industry and also support for belief in a Creator and Designer, and, thus, in a God-given morality" (1986: 30–31). Knight, however, is not suggesting that somehow the method of study of the physical and social world in Britain was different from that in France; yet in substance the two cultures differed radically, for in Britain there was a widely held view that the scientific method would provide both knowledge of the physical world and of the "religious world." And Knight's useful assessment of the British context (as it differed from the French) goes some way toward understanding the duality of Müller's perception of the relationship between science and religion. For Müller, the conviction that science can ultimately provide us with religious truth is not the same as the assumption that religious truth underlies the scientific project. This is not to say, however, that Müller and other early scientific students of religion did not allow their religious beliefs and commitments to color their research from time to time;[16] but the connection between science and religion did not last long.

Notes

1. In this respect one should also consult Sharpe on the views of Nathan Söderblom in his "[Nathan] he Study of Religion" (1969: 259–274) and his book of the same title (1990). He claims in his essay that for Söderblom, as for other theologians such as Albrecht [Ritschl] and Auguste [Sabatier], the ideal of truth underlies the practice of science, insisting that "the religious ideal and scientific ideal were one" (263). However, Sharpe also notes that

in Söderblom's view, if science is properly undertaken it will always serve the cause of religion. Whether that statement amounts to a prediction or a normative assertion is difficult to tell.

2. Robert T. Osborn, for example, presents such an argument (1992: 75–76; notes 4 and 5). Sharpe makes a similar kind of claim in his book on Söderblom (1990) with respect to the contribution of phenomenology to the scientific study of religion. He writes there that "Söderblom's 'academic contribution to *Religionsgeschichte*' cannot be evaluated other than in relation to his theology. Leave theology out of the reckoning (as one might well be tempted to do in our present-day climate of opinion), and it becomes practically impossible to grasp why Söderblom ever took up the comparative study of religion, or what he did with it" (1990: xx-xxi). Unlike Osborn, however, Sharpe is aware that this "connection" between Theology and Religious Studies in the work of Söderblom does not resolve the logical question of the identity—that is, the structure—of the scientific study of religion. He writes: "I would not for a moment wish to suggest that a study of the Söderblom generation—for Söderblom was by no means the only liberal Christian scholar of his day to grapple with 'the problem of religion'—will resolve whatever 'crisis of identity' there may be today" (xxii). Nevertheless, Sharpe maintains that we must recognize that theology and scientific study overlap in Söderblom's work and that it is a distortion to separate one from the other. He seems also to imply that to recognize this is to recognize the logical inseparability of the two exercises (213). It is as if, as Sharpe puts it (211), in uncovering this root of the phenomenology of religion, one comes to see that the study of religion—at least its phenomenological portion—is not "a 'value-free' exercise in the suspension of belief, but a 'value-rich' exercise in devotion, discipline, and learning" (211). Thus he writes: "'There, then, is one of Söderblom's contributions to the study of religion: that he and the generation of which he was a part subjected the study of religion to the best thinking of which they were capable on a basis of the best and most accurate information available to them. That he, Fredrik Fehr, Samuel Fries, Sabatier, James Hope Moulton, Evard Lehmann, and the rest persisted in believing that the world of religion had a meaning and focus beyond the exercise of human reason does nothing at all to spoil the quality of their work; those who dismiss the possibility of revelation *a priori* or discount it as a 'scientific' irrelevancy may have the greater problem" (210). From this brief account of Sharpe's treatment of Söderblom one can see considerable confusion as concerns the relation of theology to scientific thought in the study of religion. The same confusion can be seen in the work of Gerardus van der Leeuw whose work was inspired by Söderblom's approach. With respect to van der Leeuw's work, I have clearly shown the influence of his theology on Religious Studies in my "Phenomenology of Religion as Religio-Cultural Quest: Gerardus van der Leeuw and the Subversion of the Scientific Study of Religion" (1991b: 65–86, and chapter 10 in this volume).

3. J. M. Kitagawa and John S. Strong (1989: 179–213) maintain that there is some controversy over whether Müller was the founder of the science of religion (185). To some extent this is true. Eric Sharpe (1986: 31,note 7) notes, for example, that the term "Science of Religion" was not invented by Müller. Furthermore, C. P. Tiele, a contemporary of Müller, also consciously refrains from affirming Müller as the founder of the new discipline (1894: 280–286). "Can anyone be said to be the founder of the young science?" he asks. He then proceeds: "Many have conferred this title upon the famous Oxford professor, F. Max Müller; others, among them his great American opponent, the no less famous professor of Yale College, W. Dwight Whitney, have denied it to him. We may leave this decision to posterity. I, for one, may rather be said to side with Whitney than with Müller" (283). Tiele does not deny that Müller had done much for the benefit of the Science of Religion but goes on to say that "a new branch of study can hardly be said to be founded. Like others, this was called into being by a generally felt want, in different countries at the same time and as a matter of course. The number of those applying themselves to it has been gradually increasing, and for years it has been gaining chairs at universities, first in Holland, afterward also in France and elsewhere, now also in America" (283).

An early historian of the discipline, Louis H. Jordan (1905: 522–523), similarly denies foundership to Müller, calling him a prophet and pioneer of the new discipline. Hans Klimkeit in his entry on Müller in the new *Encyclopedia of Religion* (1987: 153–154), more generously claims that "Müller can be regarded as one of the founding fathers of the 'Science of Religion'" (154). All three monographs written on Müller, however, more boldly proclaim him the founder of the science. Ronald W. Neufeldt (1980) insists that there is still wide support for Müller's being called the founder of the science of religion (92). Johannes H. Voigt (1967) writes: " . . . the great pioneer and founder of the subject of comparative religions was unquestionably Max Müller. . . . He became the originator of the academic subject 'comparative religions'" (2,14). G. W. Trompf (1978) asserts that Müller "may be deemed the founder of the modern comparative study of religion. He can be said to have fathered a young social science or (as some might prefer) a recognized discipline which is continuing to gain a foothold in the modern, compartmentalized world of learning . . . (2); [he is] the systematic thinker who established the discipline Comparative Religion in the world of learning" (3). Sharpe (1986) also sees Müller as the founder of the new discipline. Having noted that Müller did not coin the term "Science of Religion" he nevertheless points out that it is only because of Müller that the term gained general acceptance (31, note 7).

Although the phrase "Science of Religion" is often used interchangeably with "History of Religions" or "Comparative Religions," it should be noted that there are significant differences among them. Müller's views about the study of religion were under constant pressure, to the point that, as Voigt insists, "the study of comparative religions that he helped to develop were [sic] rapidly losing their importance in the European intellectual world" (84). But Voigt does not mean to imply here that the scientific approach to the study of religions, so persistently advocated by Müller, was rejected; rather, he merely indicates that the discoveries Müller "had hoped to make through the comparative studies of languages and religions, and mythology failed to appear . . . [and that] new sciences, which were developed already during his lifetime, archaeology and anthropology, were more direct and effective means of exploring the past" (83–84).

4. The distinction intended here is one to which I referred in my essay "The Failure of Nerve in the Academic Study of Religion" (1984: 401–422; 406 note 26; chapter 8 in this volume): there I argue that the intentionality behind the formation of a science of religions must not be confused with the hopes pinned on the results of such an exercise.

5. There is a sense, however, in which Müller did see this as a radically new development. In the preface to the first volume of his *Chips from a German Workshop*, entitled *Essays on the Science of Religion* (first published in 1867), he maintains that even though relatively little new material relevant to the study of the Jews has been discovered, a "new spirit of inquiry" has rejuvenated the study of the Jewish people. Many of the scholars active in this field, he admits, have started out from diametrically opposed premises, and yet they "have all helped to bring out the historical interest of the Old Testament, in a manner not dreamt of by former theologians" (1881a: xii). And the same, he notes, can be said of the study of other Semitic traditions.

6. Müller notes here "that religions and the origin of religious ideas had formed the subject of deep and anxious thought at the very beginning of what we call the history of philosophy" (1878: 6).

7. His attitude might even be considered to be anti-apologetic, as is indicated in the following passage taken from his essay "On False Analogies in Comparative Theology" (first published in the *Contemporary Review* in 1870): "A comparative study of ancient religions and mythologies, as will be seen from these instances, is not a subject to be taken up lightly. It requires not only an accurate acquaintance with the minutest details of comparative philology, but a knowledge of the history of religions which can hardly be gained without a study of original documents. *As long, however, as researches of this kind are carried out for their own sake, and from a mere desire of discovery of truth, without any ulterior objects,* they deserve no blame though, for a time, they may lead to erroneous results. *But when coincidences between different religions and mythologies are searched out simply in support of preconceived theories, whether by the friends or enemies of religion, the sense of truth, the very life of all science is sacrificed, and serious mischief will follow without fail*" (1881b: 122; my emphasis). Müller makes a similar comment regarding the attitude necessary for the study of language in his *Lectures on the Science of Language*: "In the science of language, languages are not treated as a means; language itself becomes the sole object of scientific inquiry" (1891 [1861]/I: 23).

8. Müller was not always this definitive in expressing his views on partisanship. In his *Anthropological Religion* (1898c) he writes: "But while on one side I shall incur the displeasure of those who carry impartiality to the brink of injustice, I expect even stronger objections from the other side" (390). He does not delineate here how impartiality is carried to the brink of injustice and it seems to me that by far his greatest concern is against those who advocate partiality, as the remainder of this essay will show.

9. Müller is not always so conciliatory with regard to challenges to religious belief. In his *Lectures on the Origin and Growth of Religion* (1878), he writes: "How does this arise? What is the historical process which produces the conviction that there is, or that there can be, anything beyond what is manifest to our senses, something invisible, or, as it is soon called, infinite, superhuman, divine? It may, no doubt, be an entire mistake, a mere hallucination to speak of things invisible, infinite, or divine. But in that case, we want to know all the more, how it is that people, apparently sane on all other points, have from the beginning of the world to the present day, been insane on this one point. We want an answer to this, or we shall have to surrender religion altogether unfit for scientific treatment" (169).

10. In the first volume of his *Science of Language* (1891), Müller writes: "An empirical acquaintance with facts rises to a scientific knowledge of facts as soon as the mind discovers beneath the multiplicity of single productions the unity of an organic system. This discovery is made by means of comparison and clarification"(15).

11. In Volume 4 of his Gifford Lectures, *Theosophy or Psychological Religion,* (1898d [1892]), Müller further attacks Hegel, accusing him of being almost entirely untrustworthy; by contrast, Müller claims that he has restricted himself "to try to decipher and understand religions as we try to decipher and understand the geological annals of the earth, and to discover in them reason, cause and effect, and, if possible, that close geological coherence which alone can change empirical fact into scientific knowledge" (vi). He further delineates their differences in the preface to his *Essays in the Science of Religion* (1881a): "There is to my mind no subject more absorbing than the tracing of the origin and first growth of human thought—not theoretically, or in accordance with the Hegelian laws of thought, or the Comtean epochs; but historically, and like an Indian trapper, spying for every footprint, every layer, every broken blade that might tell and testify of the former presence of man in his early wanderings and searchings after light and truth" (ix). That Müller was affected by romantic and idealist reflections on natural religion and the nature of religion there can be no doubt. My point is countered by Peter Byrne (1989) and Gary Trompf (1978), who see Hegel as having a clear influence on Müller's thought. Yet far more important, it seems to me, is the influence of the humanistic and rationalist thought of the seventeenth and eighteenth centuries on the rise and development of science, and the domination of science on the Victorian imagination; and the remainder of the analysis of

this essay will provide reasonable grounds to undermine Byrne's and Trompf's claims.

12. Müller provides an example of the contrast between a philosophical and a scientific approach to the study of religion in *Physical Religion:* ". . . scholarship surely has its rights, and however much we may admire the achievements of the inner consciousness, surely men who have devoted their lives to the study of Egyptian philology, and to whom hieroglyphic, hieratic, and demotic texts are as familiar as Greek and Latin have a right to be listened to, particularly if they are entirely free from predilections in favour of any philosophical system" (1898b: 207).

13. John Baillie seems to miss this point when he claims Müller's "motto" for the science of religion was *Wer eine Religion kennt, kennt keine* (1936: 120). However, as will become clear below (note 16), Baillie seems nevertheless to have accurately assessed the intention behind Müller's approach to the study of religions.

14. There is yet further proof of Müller's role and interest in the scientific controversies of the day, for he participated in the debate on Darwin's theory of evolution. Müller did not simply reject the notion but, rather, argued that it was safer to study the developments of the human mind or rationality rather than natural or biological development. Some discussion of Müller's involvement occurs in Neufeldt (1980), who points out: "As far as Max Müller was concerned, evolution was to be seen as a basic principle for proper historical research, for to be evolutionary meant to be historical and scientific" (158).

15. Not everyone, however, shared Müller's opinion on this matter. Lewis Farnell (1934), for example, noted in his autobiography, "what [Müller] lacked of the scientific equipment was the ability to reconsider his theories" (115). Nevertheless, Müller did attribute importance to such "equipment" in a proper scientific study of religion.

16. John Baillie points out in a review of the new science after its first half-century of existence (1936: 124):

> It is indeed true that the students of this science are nearly always far better than their word and do, in spite of all their protestations, bring their own religious intelligence and the light of their own religious experience to bear upon the otherwise chaotic mass of fact which it is their business to set in order; and when they tell us that this or that change in men's beliefs marks an advance and not a retrogression, they do, in spite of all bluff, mean only that it marks a step nearer to what they themselves believe, or at least that in it they recognise the operation of a principle which they themselves feel to be sound and good. (1936: 124)

This does not automatically mean, however, that, as Baillie would have it, there would arise a deep need for a synthesis of scientific and theological approaches to the study of religion in order to combat an internal incongruity of thought. Indeed, it is because no persuasive argument can be developed (other than an anachronistic one which ignores historical expositions such as Knight's) that Baillie condemns the new science as defective; its very aspiration to be a natural science condemns it in Baillie's eyes (1936: 122). Baillie recognizes that the founders of the Science of Religion insisted on a methodology that precludes argumentation derived from religious "truth." (1936: 123). Yet for Baillie, the opposite must be the case if one ever wishes truly to understand religion. "It is the duty of theological science," he writes, "to provide the historical study of religion with a proper point of view, proper presuppositions, and a succession of proper questions" (1935: 131). By this he means to say that it is the duty of every student of religion to be led to an understanding of religions by religious experience and theological belief.

The question that finally needs to be raised is whether, as Sharpe seems to suggest, a genuine, third approach to the study of religion is possible. In Sharpe's brief analysis of Baillie's view, he suggests that Baillie saw the possibility of theology and historical study of religions working hand-in-hand. I think, however, that for Baillie theology and scientific historiography can only work hand-in-hand if the latter is subordinated to the former. If other religio-theological approaches evade that kind of "subordinationism," as Sharpe has claimed, he has not yet been able to show that to be the case. Moreover, from the point at which the academic study of religions entered the twentieth century, symbolized by the first Congress for the History of Religions held in Paris in 1900, the discipline became increasingly distanced from religio-theological approaches and gradually gained the autonomy it sought. (This is even more clearly visible in Sharpe's discussion of the 1897 Stockholm congress. He finds that congress worth mentioning "as an example of the confusion which can attend a gathering of delegates committed to different ideals" [1969: 268]. He notes "some came expecting an echo of Chicago's Parliament of Religions; . . . others [wanted] a genuinely scientific gathering, [and] most took the opportunity to develop aspects of Christian apologetic" [268]. Significantly, at that Congress, a paper by Max Müller was attacked by the Bishop von Schéele of Visby, an attack which Sharpe sees as "eloquent testimony of the tension between the old and new attitudes to the study of religion in Sweden in the years around the turn of the century" [268]. This confusion did not exist at the Paris congress.) Indeed, it appears that the new science is based on premises that, in the long run, will actually help to undermine the very religious traditions its founders thought it would bolster. But then that is not a result, one could argue, that is peculiar to this science; it is, rather, characteristic of science in general.

Chapter Three

~~~~~~

Toward the Founding of a Science of Religion: The Contribution of C. P. Tiele

In 1988, in a paper read to the Santa Barbara Colloquy on the future of graduate education in religious studies, Eric Sharpe bemoaned the fact that scholars in the field reflected far too little on the history of the development of their discipline. Some understanding of our "heredity," he suggested, would greatly assist us in resolving "the present uneasy relationship between the various members of the Religious Studies family . . . and might even help to provide the outlines of the disciplinary matrix we are looking for" (256). The decade since Sharpe delivered that paper has seen a considerable amount of attention paid to the history of the development of the field. In 1987, Ivan Strenski spearheaded the formation of a program section in the American Academy of Religion on the history of the study of religions, which has produced a number of studies of the pioneers in the field—scholars such as Edward Burnett Tylor, James George Frazer, William Robertson Smith, and Friedrich Max Müller. The North American Association for the Study of Religion has also focused considerable attention over the years not only on the questions of the nature and structure of the field but also on the history of its development. In addition to the various published articles that have emerged from these discussions there have been several book-length studies of developments in and of the field that have made a significant contribution (as Sharpe would have it) to understanding the heredity of the discipline—books like Robert Ackerman's *J. G. Frazer: His Life and His Work* (1987) and *The Myth and Ritual School: J. G. Frazer and the Cambridge Ritualists* (1991), and the collection of essays on the work of Gerardus van der Leeuw edited by Hans Kippenberg and Brigitte Luchesi entitled *Religionswissenschaft und Kulturkritik* (1991). In addition, a number of books have appeared advocating that the history of the Science of Religion be traced back considerably before the nineteenth century and thus are significant in any assessment of the heredity of the field: Samuel Preus's *Explaining Religion: Criticism and Theory from Bodin to Freud* (1987), Peter Byrne's *Natural Religion and the Nature of Religion: The Legacy of Deism* (1989), Peter Harris's *'Religion' and the Religions in the English Enlightenment* (1990), and Robert A. Shepard's *God's People in the Ivory Tower* (1991).[1]

I hope here to add to this growing body of literature. Like Sharpe, I believe there is a good deal to be learned about the nature of the field of Religious Studies from the vicissitudes of its historical development. But the lessons will not be easily learned, for one cannot assume that agreement about the significance of the contributions of the pioneers of the field will be the result of a mere reading of their texts. Not only are there several contextual factors which should contribute to the reading; there is also the possibility of ambiguity and confusion in presentation, of which the reader should be wary. Most of the scholars who helped establish the study of religion as an academic enterprise, as virtually everyone in the field knows, were themselves religious persons concerned for the promotion of their faith, and their religious interests often found expression in their scientific work. But that is not to say that they simply conflated the two enterprises of religion and the study of religion. As I will try to show, particularly with respect to the work of C. P. Tiele, even though such scholars hoped that the results of their scientific study of religion would be consistent with their Christian faith, they were nevertheless concerned to establish the study of religion as an autonomous academic discipline worthy of inclusion alongside the other sciences in the curriculum of the university. It is therefore unacceptable, I shall argue, to claim that, because they expressed the hope that their Christian beliefs might find corroboration in their scientific work, they necessarily made of their so-called new discipline an essentially theological undertaking. And those who would find some justification in the work of such scholars for re-theologizing the contemporary study of religions in the university context simply compound that error of judgment. If Tiele, for example, makes room for theology at all, it is as an externally related complement to the science of religion; he did not, as Ivan Strenski has recently put it, use the Science of Religion to open the door to theology the way Eliade did (Strenski, forthcoming a: 3).

In a recent discussion of the phenomenology of religion proposed by Gerardus van der Leeuw I contrasted his work to that of Tiele as a theological rather than a scientific approach to the study of religion (Wiebe, 1991). Although acknowledging Tiele's own religious concerns, I nevertheless argued that he was intent on establishing a scientific approach to the study of religion wholly independent of reliance on religion or theology. Strenski has suggested, however, that in coming to such a judgment I have not fully "appreciated how deep and subtle was the theology embedded in the original efforts of Tiele" (forthcoming a: 6–7). He continues: "In particular, Wiebe does not understand that for Tiele and others of his ilk, the terms religion and science mean different things than Wiebe's late twentieth-century mind imagines." Strenski holds this view, moreover, even though acknowledging that Tiele's intentions regarding the academic study of religion were in fact scientific (1994: 6). But he claims that I misunderstood Tiele because I fail "to take seriously the historical particularity of terms like religion . . . [that] made it intellectually possible to talk about religion as an object of scientific intellectual inquiry, while granting it special privileges" (1995: 6, 8). What Strenski means by this, apparently, is that Tiele understood by "religion" not only those specific cultural traditions designated "religion*s*," but also something called "religion-as-such," carrying with it—indeed, promoting—"a certain religious worldview similar in most respects to classical deism" (1995: 10). Thus, for Tiele, according to Strenski, "scientific activity led to spiritual vision," for "[b]y contemplating the natural world, people could come to see and know God as he expressed himself in and through his creation" (1995: 10). Strenski therefore claims that for Tiele theology subsumed science and that Tiele's "science" was, as a consequence, merely an apologetic undertaking negating any scientific purposes that may at some point have existed (1995: 13). "He may have thrown a crumb to those who wished to study religion historically . . . ," writes Strenski, "by encouraging the tracing of the evolution of religious changes, cataloguing morphological variations, and so on, but in the final analysis his work did nothing more than shield religion-as-such from scientific examination" (1995: 14, 16–17). Strenski does not, unfortunately, make out a case to support his assertions. He does not, for example, justify the claim that Tiele espoused knowledge of God gained from a spiritual contemplation of the world as an aspect of his proposed scientific undertaking. In fact, as I shall show below, Tiele clearly demarcated such claims to knowledge by the religious devotee from the legitimately acceptable knowledge of the *Religionswissenschaftler.*

That Tiele was a dedicated theologian I do not dispute. Nor do I have any wish to dismiss the claim that his religious convictions may have played some havoc with his work as a historian of religion. But to say that his religious convictions determined the structure of the science he attempted to establish is, I think, not sustainable. I have myself argued the latter claim with respect to Gerardus van der Leeuw (Wiebe, 1991a and chapter 10 in this volume), and I think it equally applicable to a thinker such as Eliade, to whom Strenski refers, but I think it wholly without foundation in regard to Tiele's work; Strenski's attempt to draw a parallel between Tiele and Eliade, therefore, is in my opinion simply not persuasive. Furthermore, I shall accuse Strenski of exaggeration in his claim that Tiele merely threw a crumb to those who wished to study religion historically. Moreover, to base that claim, as Strenski does, on the "fact" that Tiele was in the thrall of the notion of "religion-as-such" is just as unpersuasive. A more discriminating assessment of Tiele's theology, I suggest, is to be found in Lammert Leertouwer's recent essay, "Gerardus van der Leeuw as a Critic of Culture," in which he compares the influence of theology on van der Leeuw with its influence on Tiele. Leertouwer is more discriminating in his treatment of Tiele, I would argue, because he takes seriously the difference of intention in the work of these scholars as historians of religion and as theologians. According to Leertouwer, van der Leeuw was a servant of God first and a professor second; in this van der Leeuw differed from Tiele, whose position as a scientist in no way conflicted with his duty to God. As Leertouwer puts it:

> When we compare van der Leeuw's theological position to that of Cornelius Petrus Tiele, who died a few years before young van der Leeuw began his studies under Tiele's successor William Brede Kristensen, the difference between the two is as striking as it is puzzling. Both of them were dedicated men of the Church and theologians; but whereas Tiele took an extreme modernist position, even to the extent of identifying scientific theology with *Religionswissenschaft,* van der Leeuw developed his ideas about theology in a diametrically opposite direction. (1991: 59–60)

Far from undermining science in order to protect religion, Tiele, if he had an apologetic aim, was concerned to show that, conversely, science was the only way to protect religion. In a sense, therefore, Tiele was intoxicated with science—he wished to see not only the study of religion established as a science, but theology as well. As Leertouwer notes, Tiele's "whole life as a scholar was devoted to the metamorphosis of classical theology into a scientifically respectable science of religion . . ." (1991: 60), and he points out in an earlier essay (1989: 156) that Tiele dedicated his whole life to building a scientific theology in order to rescue it from obscurantism and speculation. He is correct, therefore, in his claim that obtaining scientific knowledge of the world's religious traditions was not Tiele's final goal as a theologian. Leertouwer does not, however, clearly elaborate the sense in which Tiele considered theology to be scientific, even though this is crucial if one is to understand how Tiele's view of the role of the history of religion informed his theology. Tiele, I will suggest, was in many respects Kantian in his understanding of "religious knowledge," for he saw it as lying beyond science but not, on that account, as beyond reason. Thus, even though obtaining scientific knowledge of the world's religious traditions was not his final goal as a theologian, it *was* his final goal as a *Religionswissenschaftler.* Indeed, it is only because of Tiele's clear differentiation between religious and scientific knowledge in this fashion that Leertouwer can maintain, as he does in the later essay on van der Leeuw, that in becoming less haphazard and intuitive, the academic study of religion, in the four decades since the death of van der Leeuw, "has almost fulfilled Tiele's wildest hopes by becoming something like a real science" (1991: 61).[2] Leertouwer, therefore, quite rightly suggests that van der Leeuw, in contrast to Tiele, is no longer relevant for the contemporary student of religion, who takes religion to be a facet of human culture as subject to study as any other cultural element. As he notes in his essay on Tiele's "Strategy of Conquest," "the group of scholars responsible for the field of research [at the University of Leiden] to which Tiele devoted his life still honors the emphasis of the founding father of their department on historical fact-finding" (1989: 167), even though Tiele's laws of religious development were very quickly rejected. This cannot be said, however, for scholars such as van der Leeuw, Leertouwer maintains, for in attempting to make the historical study of religions answer questions of existential import, the discipline overstepped "the bounds of her domain and enter[ed] the realm of theology in the proper sense" (1991: 62).

What is of particular interest in Leertouwer's analysis of Tiele's program for the scientific study of religion is the clear distinction Tiele draws between the positive historical work of fact-finding and the quest for an explanation of the development of religion in the context of a theory of evolution. Had Strenski noted the distinction, and had he taken seriously Tiele's commitment not only to fact-gathering but also to the discovery of laws to explain the emergence and development of religion, he would have understood better why Tiele was, in Strenski's words, in the thrall of "the discourse on religion-as-such" (Strenski, forthcoming a: 8). Although Tiele's ultimate aspirations here may have been (and in all likelihood were) religious and theological, he realized that the laws of development he was seeking could not be established either theologically or speculatively. As Leertouwer puts it, "they could only be reconstructed by following the historical process step by step, from the earliest written sources and artifacts upwards towards the complicated structures of the world's great religions" (Leertouwer, 1989: 156). If Tiele was in the thrall of anything, it was of science, for in his thinking only science could furnish an adequate study of "religion-as-such," not philosophy or religion or theology.

That Tiele was neither in the thrall of "religion-as-such," nor of some speculative interpretive schema such as Hegel's notions of *Wesen und Erscheinung* and *Entwicklung,* is evident from the time of his earliest work in the field of the History of Religions. In the preface to his *Outlines of the History of Religion* (1892), for example, Tiele expresses a concern that the new discipline of the Science of Religion might easily lose itself in abstract speculations based on a few facts at best (1892: viii). It is true that he thinks of his book as a "history of religion" rather than a "history of religions" because his objective is "to show that one great psychological phenomenon which we call religion has developed and manifested itself in such various stages among the different races and peoples of the world." Tiele does not see this stance as itself a clear example of metaphysical speculation, since it is apparent from his interjection that despite taking this approach to understanding religion—one governed by nomothetic accounts of religion—he did not "think it safe to found . . . [this] history on an a priori philosophical basis" (Tiele, 1892: x). He has an interest, to be sure, in the development of religion, but it does not seem to be of the theologico-metaphysical variety suggested by Strenski and others; he demonstrates this in the *Outlines:*

> The history of religion is not content with describing special religions (hierography), or with relating their vicissitudes and metamorphoses (the history of religions); its aim is to show how religion, considered generally as the relation between man *and the superhuman powers in which he believes,* has developed in the course of ages among different nations and races, and, through these in humanity at large. (Tiele, 1892: 2; my emphasis)

Tiele's concern, that is, is a nomothetic one: he seeks a theory to explain the why and the how of religion. In this Tiele's concerns are indistinguishable from those espoused by scientific students of religion such as E. B. Tylor, J. G. Frazer, and others who adopted an evolutionary framework within which to make sense of religion and the human race. This certainly puts Tiele into a different camp from those satisfied with the more purely descriptive work of historical research, but it does not place him unequivocally among philosophers of history like Hegel. Nor does it make of him a theologian à la van der Leeuw or Eliade. It is interesting in this regard to note that P. D. Chantepie de la Saussaye recognized two groups of nomothetically orientated scholars in the field of the study of religion: those influenced by Hegel, and those who followed the lead provided by Hume's *Natural History of Religion* (1757). The latter are considered far more scientific, for they sought to formulate the laws of the development of religion based on natural causes; they deliberately rejected the "essence-manifestation" distinction as subversive of the search for explanations of religion, adopting instead an evolutionary approach to their data. As Chantepie de la Saussaye put it: "Strict evolutionary principles do not admit a real substance and ontological reason of phenomena, nor their teleological destination. The theory of evolution recognizes in history causes and laws, but no aims or ideas; it is occupied only with what is, and not with what ought to be" (1891: 12). In fact, a study of religion influenced by the natural sciences was being "carried out more consistently and more completely" in his day than ever before (1891: 11); of his contemporaries involved in such an approach he lists not only Tiele, but also Albert Réville and E. B. Tylor (1891: 11).[3]

In the quotation from Tiele's *Outlines* above, I added emphasis to the phrase indicating that, for Tiele, religion deals with the relation of persons to beliefs about superhuman powers. I did so because I think it shows clearly Tiele's concern to subordinate his theological to his scientific agenda. The historian of religions, for Tiele, does not deal with superhuman agents and their relations to persons, but only with beliefs about these matters; the theologian may deal with such relations between superhuman powers and human persons, but not the scientist. Tiele is particularly intent on delineating this distinction in his Gifford Lectures twenty years later (1897), because there he wants to show that the Science of Religion should be ranked as an independent science. And for that to be the case, its subject matter, like that of any science, must be objectively—that is, intersubjectively—available to the practitioners in the field; to the scientist, as Tiele puts it, "all religions are simply objects of investigation" (1897, I: 9). Belief in the gods is available for critical investigation, but the gods themselves, obviously, are not. Consequently Tiele defines religion not in terms of the superhuman but rather in terms of social institutions, customs, and beliefs, including the beliefs persons have about their god. He writes: "The object of our science is not the superhuman itself, but religion based on belief in the superhuman; and the task of investigating religion as a historical, psychological, social, and wholly human phenomenon undoubtedly belongs to the domain of science" (1897, I: 5).

The scientific rather than philosophic concern with the general notion of religion—Strenski's "religion-as-such"—is also more clearly delineated in Tiele's Gifford Lectures. Here he explicitly rejects the speculative approach to the study of religion in general (1897, I: 18) and Hegel's approach in particular (1897, I: 249–251), because, according to Tiele, it is an approach that assumes human beings are tools devoid of will in the hands of the "World-Spirit." In opposition to such a teleological approach concerned with "aims and ideas," as Chantepie had put it, Tiele offers as an acceptable object of study only what is empirically available for investigation. He does divide the study of religion into morphological and ontological components, the latter involving permanent and unalterable elements of religion, the former the ever-altering forms in which those elements appear (1897, I: 27, 222, passim). This does not provide sufficient reason, however, to conclude that Tiele adopts a fully Hegelian approach, for he believes it is only by means of examination of the different forms of religion that we come to discern the essential character of religion resident in them all (1897, I: 54). It is through an empirical study of the history of the changing forms of religions, that is, that the laws of historical development can be discerned.

What is perceptible, and what general statements can follow from what is perceived, constitute the essence of the scientific study of religion, which is to be clearly distinguished from any attempt to explain the imperceptible (1897, II: 37–38). The latter Tiele sees as an exercise of faith, and "[b]etween knowledge and faith," he writes in the volume on ontology, "there . . . exists a difference in kind" (1897, II: 36). It is not that he thinks empirical knowledge and faith completely unrelated, but he is adamant that science does "not go beyond the demonstration of the finite causes and the fixed laws which govern physical and mental life," whereas faith ascends "to one or more supernatural causes, in which everything that is finite has its origin" (1897, II: 38). In this respect Tiele is actually Kantian rather than Hegelian, for faith can complement science, if only by providing what science cannot. It is not the duty of the science of religion to supply an apology for religious belief:

> It would fall beyond the province of our science to prove that this belief in the infinite within us is well-founded, and to vindicate the right of religion to exist. Our science is psychological, and its task is *merely* to search for the origin of religion in man's spiritual life. We leave the rest to Apologetics and Dogmatics, and on the theoretical side, to Metaphysics, or that general philosophy which seeks to fathom the deepest foundation of all things. (1897, II: 234–235)

Yet despite Tiele's insistence that it is not the " . . . business of the science of religion to maintain or defend, still less dispute, or destroy . . . [but rather] merely to explain" (1897, II: 119), he nonetheless accedes the indirect spiritual benefit of the scientific enterprise, for it is through the latter that the limitations of scientific knowledge must bow to a greater or transcendental theorizing (1897, II: 262,263). Briefly put, the science of religion is not religion per se and cannot provide what religion provides; science is "solely concerned with gaining knowledge" (1897, II: 245) and has nothing metaphysical about it. As such it is not to be confused with theology. Tiele, moreover, castigates those scholars whom he considers to have violated the canons of science in their study of religion. "If religious persons, or those who are called upon to act as representatives of religious life," he writes, "oppose a science or a philosophy which denies to religion any right of existence, they are perfectly justified in doing so; for such a science or philosophy exceeds its authority, and usurps a right of judgment that does not belong to it" (1897, II: 258). Anti-theologians, that is, fall into the same category as theologians : they both fail to note the clear demarcation between scientific and theological undertakings. Tiele thus concludes: "Though not called upon to prove the truth of religion, our science is not entitled to pronounce it an illusion" (1897, II: 235). Consequently, on the question of the "truth of religion," the scientific student of religion, by definition, must remain neutral.

Whether or not Tiele himself remained wholly neutral in this regard is another matter altogether. There are, as Strenski and others have pointed out, a number of places in Tiele's work in which one finds evidence of religious belief and theological interpretation. There are other occasions, moreover, on which Tiele permits his beliefs to determine the limits of scientific knowledge—his anti-reductionism is an obvious case in point. There is some interference of religion in Tiele's scientific work that, to some degree at least, justifies the claim that he turned his Science of Religion into a Theology of Religion. But to argue, as Strenski does, that Tiele's Science of Religion is simply a kind of "fideism dressed up in the language of the academy"[4] is not justifiable. The theological interference to be found in Tiele's work is better understood as a matter of inadvertence, I think, rather than of design. Tiele makes a fundamental distinction between, on the one hand, science and knowledge, and, on the other, knowledge and faith; but what Tiele interprets those distinctions to mean does not allow his scientific conclusions to be "influenced" by his religio-theological stance. They concern instead questions about the limits of the scientific enterprise undertaken. And in this respect I would agree with Strenski that because of his own religious stance Tiele did not fully grasp the implications of the notion "Science of Religion." But that again was carelessness rather than subversiveness on Tiele's part, for he did not consciously subordinate the scientific study of religion to apologetics. He had demonstrated no intention, that is, to argue that the procedures of science in the "Science of Religion" were permitted to diverge from the customary course followed in the study of other cultural phenomena because of the peculiar nature of the subject matter being treated. And in this Tiele was considerably unlike van der Leeuw or Eliade; for the latter two saw that in order to be able to understand fully the unique nature of religion the "Science of Religion" had to differ in structure and procedure from the other cultural sciences. In other words, scholars like van der Leeuw and Eliade presumed that understanding religion required endorsement, and therefore that the "Science of Religion" must necessarily be apologetic. Tiele, on the other hand, although very much a religiously committed person, believed that science as generally understood in the academic community would never conflict with the fundamental religious beliefs he held dear. Indeed (and somewhat ironically) he saw in science the possibility of a concomitant legitimation of his religious beliefs. This is the essence, I think, of Tiele's argument for a clear demarcation of the Science of Religion from religion and theology. He was convinced of the "truth" of both these enterprises, and believed that in the long run the two undertakings would be mutually confirming.[5]

While allowing that Tiele's intentions, in addition to being theological, were scientific, Strenski nevertheless states that I have not appreciated "how deep and subtle was the theology embedded in the original efforts of Tiele" (forthcoming a: 6–7), and that I fail to understand the real meaning of the terms "religion" and "science" in Tiele's work. My argument, however, is that it is Strenski who misunderstands these terms because he fails to take seriously Tiele's own conscious and explicitly stated rejection of the Hegelianism otherwise dominant in the work of many of his contemporaries and successors; in this Strenski does not grasp the significance of Tiele's attempt to demarcate his work as a scientist from his work as a theologian. What Strenski also misses, it seems to me, is an awareness of how important a matter science had become in late nineteenth-century European and Anglo-American thought, and that Tiele was one of those who fully endorsed the development. I have attempted to show here that with such an endorsement Tiele made a direct and lasting contribution to the field of Religious Studies, despite the fact that he was not wholly consistent in the elaboration of his scientific program.

As has already been indicated in my reference to Chantepie de la Saussaye above, the scientific approach to the study of religion is not peculiar to Tiele. A better idea of this stance may be gained by glancing briefly at some of the other figures mentioned by Chantepie who adopted essentially similar approaches. I look first at Albert Réville because Strenski refers to him, although with quite a different effect than Chantepie. For Strenski, Réville is essentially a Protestant theologian apparently concerned with science only as a subordinate element of a larger spiritual vision. Thus Réville, according to Strenski, is also guilty of a metaphysical usage of the notion of "religion-as-such" undermining the possibility of obtaining scientifically credible knowledge of religion. Such a view, however, does not match Réville's own claims for himself as a student of religion.[6] In his *Prolegomena of the History of Religions*, Réville, contrary to what one would expect by reading Strenski, categorically rejects any suggestion of Hegelian influence in his understanding of the science of religion. Indeed a Hegelian interpretation of the data would only introduce distortion in the understanding of what religion is (Réville, 1884: 21–22). Hegel's metaphysical system, Réville insists, makes it virtually impossible to take history seriously (1884: 22). To illustrate his claim he writes:

> How, for example, can we, without forcing its terms, apply [Hegel's philosophy] to Buddhism? Is it in accordance with reality to apply to the religious development of humanity as a whole these categories of infancy, of youth, of maturity, which would infer a continuous and simultaneous development? Is there a difference of form only between religion and philosophy, and does the

Hegelian philosophy take sufficient account of that practical realism, so different from theoretic abstraction, whence it results that a religion may become philosophical, but that no philosophy has ever founded a religion possessing true historical power? And does not the illusion under which the illustrious master fell, when he believed that he had victoriously re-constituted Christian orthodoxy, already prove that there was much that was arbitrary, not only in his method, but also in the principle of identity from which he set out? (1884: 22)

Nor is it only Hegel's a priori theorizing that Réville rejects—all theories that avoid methodical examination of the facts, as he puts it, are to be removed (1884: 58), for science requires no less than "the methodical, experimental and constantly verified knowledge of facts of all kinds that the world offers to our observation" (1884: 224). Réville, therefore, like his teacher Tiele, rejects a teleological approach to the understanding of religious phenomena; his concern as a student of religion is to gain critically testable knowledge about the world's religious traditions. This does not mean, of course, that Réville was not also a theologian; indeed, he was a theologian. He did not consider it necessary to reject theology just because there were some who did not think it demonstrable (1884: 174), for he clearly distinguished theology from science as a radically different undertaking. Theology, although different from science, was not necessarily irrational, according to Réville. There is a sense, in fact, in which he thought theology could house the same degree of disinterestedness about its subject matter that science did, thus allowing theology to relate to religion as science ("methodic knowledge") relates to empirical data (1884: 185). Although such a view may appear to ascribe to theology the designation of knowledge, thus putting it into potential conflict with scientific knowledge, Réville denied any such implication and affirmed a complete independence of religious thought from science; in effect, then, he also affirmed the autonomy of science in cognitive matters. For Réville, science (including the Science of Religion) could not clash with religion. As he expresses it:

> But above all, it is well to recognize that definitively, and when thoroughly understood, religion in itself and independent science never ought to be hostile, because in fact they do not respond to the same needs and cannot be substituted the one for the other. If science springs out of the intellectual need of knowing the real and the true in everything, religion meets aspirations of another kind which are not less natural, less inherent in the human spirit. Science proceeds methodically, using hypothesis provisionally only, always subject to experience. It is essentially analytic; and it is on that account that it cannot end in the universal synthesis which the spirit nevertheless also demands. (1884: 228)

Contrary to the claim Strenski makes, then, Réville and Tiele do not see their scientific activity as connected (causally or otherwise) to greater transcendental awareness; rather, they posit no clash between their science and a worldview obtained through religion. As Réville puts it, science may be the "sovereign mistress in the domain of the finite," but it cannot "go beyond it without contradicting itself" (1884: 228). As with Tiele, Réville, although interested in theology and ready to use it to place limits upon the Science of Religion, was thoroughly committed to establishing a context within which a bona fide scientific study of religion could be undertaken. Thus it is not justifiable to lump Réville into the same camp with religious phenomenologists such as van der Leeuw, Otto, or Eliade, for in his work there is a clear intention of establishing a line of demarcation between science and theology, whereas the religious phenomenologists refused to countenance the autonomy of the scientific undertaking, in this field of research.

That E. B. Tylor's work differs even more radically from the phenomenologists I have listed above needs little defense here. Its "reductionism," when compared to their work, is beyond question. Nevertheless, I can imagine the argument that because of his concerns for the practical import of his discipline, Tylor was not a truly scientific student of religion but rather a crypto-theologian. In concluding his work on the origins of culture he writes: "It now remains, in bringing to a close these investigations on the relation of primitive to modern civilization, to urge the practical import of the considerations raised in their course" (1958, II: 529). Indeed, the science of culture—and, therefore, the science of religion—he insists, "is essentially a reformer's science" (II: 539), for in his opinion it can be of great assistance in advancing society. Furthermore, in claiming such a value for this new intellectual undertaking Tylor does not exclude the theologian and metaphysician. He writes:

> In the scientific study of religion, which now shows signs of becoming for many a year an engrossing subject of the world's thought, the decision must not rest with a council in which the theologian, the metaphysician, the biologist, the physicist, exclusively take part. The historian and the ethnographer must be called upon to show the hereditary standing of each opinion and practice, and their enquiry must go back as far as antiquity or savagery can show a vestige, for there seems no human thought so primitive as to have lost its bearing on our own thought, nor so ancient as to have broken its connection with our own life. (II: 238)

However, the fact that his work is, in some sense, complementary to that of the theologian and metaphysician—and concerned with the spiritual dimension of human existence insofar as his work is concerned with the progress of human civilization—hardly provides sufficient reason to claim that Tylor's anthropology or Science of Religion is essentially crypto-theological. And the same, I think, can be said for the complementarity perceived by scholars such as Tiele and Réville between their religion (theology) and their science, even though they express their religious or spiritual convictions more openly than Tylor. They, like Tylor, were concerned that their interpretations of humanity and society be consistent with the methods and theories of the empirical science they espoused, even though they may have issued statements that science could not support. This does not imply that these scholars expected the science of religion, in the process of its investigations, to "recognize" religious doctrines, nor did they expect it to fulfill an apologetic role in that respect; and despite the assumption that theology would go beyond scientific knowledge about religion, their discipline could not contradict that scientific knowledge. Such a separation of the two realms of thought by Tiele and Réville freed the student of religion to seek explanations of religions and religious development in a purely scientific manner. As with Kant, the notion of the limits of knowledge became a useful tool for Tiele and Réville in defining a new set of boundaries for the proper scientific study of religion, since it prevented others within the field from assigning a determining role to theological concepts and beliefs. In seeing too much of Hegel in these scholars, and not enough of Kant, Strenski has missed the serious commitment to the natural sciences implicit in the Kantian character of their work. It seems, moreover, that Strenski is unaware of the vogue in which science was held in Europe in the second half of the nineteenth century, and of the influence it played in virtually every field of research in the academic community, including that of the History of Religions.

Like Strenski, Eric Sharpe insists that a proper reading of the history of the study of religion must not forget "that many of the founding fathers of comparative religion were liberal Christians," and that they viewed the history of religion as indicative of the advance of the human race "towards a truer knowledge and a deeper love of God" (1986: 148). But unlike Strenski, Sharpe is aware that such views are not presented as the conclusions of scientific research but rather as complementary theological views consistent with the results of scientific labor (even if related only "externally" to those results). As he puts it:

> We have had frequent occasion to be reminded, in the course of this book, that the comparative study of religion was capable of making an appeal to two types of mind, the "scientific" mind and the "religious." The "scientific" mind was concerned to apply a particular method to a body of data—data taken as a rule to refer to only the workings of the human mind, and not to any type

of transcendent reality. The "religious" mind, on the other hand, had as its essential point of departure a stance of faith in the actual existence of a transcendent order of being; and although the emergent data of comparative religion might well come into conflict (or appear to do so) with certain traditional answers to questions of religious authority, these could not contradict the basic stance of faith itself. (1986: 144)

Sharpe suggests, therefore, that many of these "liberal Christians" viewed the Science of Religion as both a pure and an applied science (1986: 252). As proof of this he argues that they were "willing to have their names associated with such public manifestations as the Chicago World's Parliament of Religions in 1893"; it is well known that Tiele was one of those scholars (1986: 252). But this is not to say that Tiele subordinated his neutral, scientific-historical methodology, and the results achieved by means of that methodology, to an a priori determination of religious faith.

Strenski maintains that Tiele espoused a view of science far from anything I would likely acknowledge as scientific (forthcoming a: 11). In some respects he is entirely right to say so. Although Tiele's demarcation of the Science of Religion from theology clearly establishes a framework for the scientific study of religion as a purely cultural phenomenon, it also partly protects the affirmations of faith from critical analysis. Strenski thus makes the acceptable claim that Tiele's anti-reductionism retarded the formation of theory in the study of religion and arbitrarily impeded the further development of the discipline. But unlike the later phenomenologists (van der Leeuw, Otto, Eliade, and others) Tiele did not attempt to blend his scientific and theological positions into one. There is some degree of affinity, therefore, between the work of Tiele and the later, more reductionist scientific students of religion who rejected the pure-versus-applied distinction, because the pure historical research undertaken by scholars in both camps was carried out according to essentially the same methodological rules. However, the phenomenologies of van der Leeuw, Otto, and Eliade transcended that framework and made of the History of Religions a "historical" enterprise radically different from the historical study of other aspects of human culture. The later phenomenologists, therefore, effectively subverted the growth of the scientific study of religion by pulling it back into the theological domain (by means of the blending referred to above) from which it had previously been emancipated (at least in part). Tiele, although not fully freeing his History of Religions from religious motivation, did set a course for the study of religion permitting its further development in a scientific direction. It is important that this be clearly recognized, because there have been several recent attempts to harness scholars like Tiele to a program for "re-integrating" (blending) the scientific and the religious (theological) in the creation of a "new methodology" suited to the study of the peculiar nature of religious phenomena—it being assumed that the peculiar nature of the religious phenomenon is its mixture of the otherworldly and the here and now.[7] This would make of the Science of Religion a "unique" scientific undertaking, which is to say not a bona fide scientific undertaking because it would somehow transcend the methodological framework within which all other sciences operate. Such a peculiar methodology, in fact, would require of students of religion that they respond to religion not as to data for analysis, but rather as to something addressing the "core" of their being. The latter response certainly reflects the proposals offered by the religious phenomenologists to whom I have referred above; but, importantly, it does not describe the work of Tiele (or Réville), nor the work of that other founding figure Friedrich Max Müller.[8] This is so despite the relative parity of the substantive religious beliefs held by the two groups of scholars. The parity can be accounted for, however, in other ways than by the assumption of an identity in their approaches to the academic study of religion.[9]

In the second volume of his *Protestant Thought in the Nineteenth Century,* Claude Welch dedicates two chapters to an analysis of the emergence and early elaboration of the objective approach to the study of "religious subjectivity," and of the History of Religions, as well as to the influence of those developments on theology. He correctly notes that these developments constituted a new impulse within the religious ethos of Europe at that time, but he does not fully explain in what sense the impulse was "new," nor provide clear indication of the consequences of that impulse for subsequent twentieth-century thought. In fact, he seems to suggest that the "new impulse" did not make a very significant impact at all. He writes:

> What can we conclude about the theological response to the late-nineteenth-century study of the history of religions? Surely a new kind of openness to other religious claims was emerging. But even leaving aside the orthodox thinkers who believed it possible still to maintain the exclusive truth of Christianity, we are surprised by the relative ease with which the superiority of the Christian religion was affirmed, both by the liberals and by the historians of religion. Christianity was no longer the only religious truth, but even a sympathetic consideration of the values of other religions seems to have left confidence in the supremacy of Christian faith largely untouched. In this respect, the theological judgment at the end of the century does not seem much different from the position of Schleiermacher at the beginning of it. (1985: 144–145)

Welch's conclusion describes Tiele's theological stance as a Christian (as well as Réville's and Müller's), as it does the stance of other representatives of late nineteenth-century and early twentieth-century students of religion such as van der Leeuw and Otto. But this is not the end of the matter, for it does not take into serious consideration the tangible effects of the divergent approaches to the study of religion represented by these scholars. Despite seeing little development in theological judgment about "other" religions during the nineteenth century, Welch does not argue that the new impulse was insignificant; for in part that impulse was a logical by-product of the scholarly atmosphere fostered by the liberal theologians' exploitation of the theory of evolution. He also notes "the study of the history of religions was still in its infancy" (Welch, 1985: 145), implying that any expectation that such a new science could radically transform, in the space of a generation or two, the worldview of the culture within which it had been born is unrealistic. And yet the academic study of religion—with its views on Christian theologians' positions on "other religions"—has changed substantially since the end of the nineteenth century and with it the attitude of Christian theologians toward other religions. I would argue that Müller, Tiele, and Réville played a significant role in the creation of that reality—a role diametrically opposed to that of the religious phenomenologists or Eliade-style historians of religion.

In this regard it is useful to note that the first International Congress of the History of Religions was held in Paris under the presidency of Albert Réville, and that its honorary presidents, although not present at the meeting, were Max Müller and C. P. Tiele (Sharpe, 1986: 123). This is of some significance because, as Sharpe points out, the Paris Congress differed markedly from the previous international meetings of scholars concerned with religion in Chicago in 1893 and in Stockholm in 1897. He argues:

> [Since Paris] we have been able to see the field being gradually taken over by the advocates of comparative religion as a pure science. The irenic enthusiast was not welcomed, and soon came to realise that his interests would only be served by an entirely independent kind of gathering devoted to the goal of the final unity of all believers. The separation became more and more marked as time went on, and the scholarly climate of opinion began to turn away from unilinear evolution and world-wide comparison, and towards culture history, culture circles and the uniqueness of religious traditions. Thus by the 1920s the two paths [of the study of religion as a pure science and as an applied science] had become almost entirely separated. (Sharpe, 1986: 252)

I would argue that such a separation follows from the framework for the study of religion adopted by the three presidents of the Paris Congress, because in distinguishing religion-as-an-object-of-study from religion-as-an-address-to-the-human-soul, in effect they were also distinguishing *practice* from *study*, thus facilitating the eventual separation of the two approaches.

The work of the later phenomenologists, in contrast, precluded any such separation, for they blended religion-as-object and religion-as-address.[10] Such is not the case with Tiele, for his clear demarcation of the study of religion from theology establishes in effect the autonomy of the new discipline. Here, then, is to be found a deliberate (even if not full) redefinition of the field rather than a half-hearted contribution toward its emancipation from religion and theology. For this reason Lammert Leertouwer is justified, as I have noted above, in saying that, insofar as the academic study of religion today has refused to treat religion "as an intrinsic source of information or as the product of extra-cultural information," it has become "far less intuitionist and haphazard [and far more] advanced . . . in precision and methodological finesse," in which process it "has almost fulfilled Tiele's wildest hopes by becoming something like a real science" (Leertouwer, 1991: 57, 61).

Notes

1. Eric Sharpe's most recent contribution to this kind of enterprise is his *Nathan Söderblom and the Study of Religion* (1990). Ivan Strenski's *Four Theories of Myth in Twentieth Century History* (1987) also makes an important contribution to the issue of the "heredity" of the field with respect to influential twentieth-century theorists of myth who influenced the field of Religious Studies.

2. Leertouwer is less clear about these matters in the earlier of the two essays, claiming that "[t]he conquest of valid knowledge about the world's religions was for Tiele not a goal in itself . . ." (156). Leertouwer does not here, in my opinion, distinguish clearly enough between Tiele the *Religionswissenschaftler* and Tiele the theologian; this entire essay is much less clear than the later essay in its delineation of Tiele's contribution to the development of the Science of Religion. However, it is clear that Leertouwer even here speaks of Tiele "as one of the founding fathers of the science of religion" (154), noting that Tiele was concerned not only with "trying to save his own theological bacon" but also with "trying to formulate a fundamental rule for the science of religion as he saw it . . ." (163).

3. A similar assessment is found in Alexander Le Roy's introductory chapter, "The Science of the History of Religions Applied to the Primitives," in his *Religion of the Primitives* (1922: 22).

4. Strenski uses this phrase in a study of sacrifice provisionally entitled "Struggle over Sacrifice: Civil Religion, Social Science, and Theology" (forthcoming b: chapter 6, part 2). I am grateful for his having made that material available to me before publication.

5. Alexander Le Roy provides a clear statement of the kind of position Tiele in fact adopted. He writes: "[L]et it be noted that, while our predecessors in the history of religions have often been influenced by anti-Christian preoccupations and in consequence have begun by removing the supernatural from

their scheme, such a display of bias is no reason for us to adopt our dogma as a predetermined principle, in opposition to theirs" (1922: 24). And this stance toward the Science of Religion is taken up regardless of whether it is "to the advantage of friends or enemies of Christianity" (1922: 11). The problems raised by the Science of Religion founded on such anti-naturalistic assumptions must be faced squarely, Le Roy maintains, and that means without rejecting the scientific character of its approach to data. "With that simplicity of spirit which is considered one of our Christian virtues," he writes, "we, who invoke the Gospel, will permit ourselves to be enticed upon the ground which our adversaries have chosen and where they have already taken the precaution to dig our tomb" (1922: 25). This stance is taken without fear for the Christian faith since, Le Roy insists (quoting Réville), "religion in itself and independent science should never be hostile to each other, because as a matter of fact they do not answer the same needs and can not be substituted for each other" (1922: 295).

6. Nor would others agree with Strenski here. Le Roy, for example, notes that Albert Réville "was a Protestant professor, driven from the chair of theology at Montauban, Paris, and Geneva, because of the radical nature of his ideas . . ." (1922: 7) and includes him among those who approached the study of religion from a non-religious point of view. After noting that the new Science of Religion has finally become fashionable, he writes: "But most of the names and works just cited require at once a qualifying remark: up to the present this 'science' seems to have been conducted in a deliberately anti-Christian spirit. The theories thus set forth could not fail to provoke replies. On the Protestant side, the liberal school has a simple and original way of closing its opponents' mouths—by admitting their conclusions. The following seem to belong to this school in different degrees: O. Fleiderer, H. Preiss, W. Bousset, in Germany; E. Caird, F. J. Gould, and F. K. Ingram, in England; and in France, A. and J. Réville, A. Sabatier, etc. . . ."(1922: 8).

7. I raise this concern at some length in my article "The Failure of Nerve in the Academic Study of Religion" (1984 and chapter 8 in this volume). There I show in some detail the prevalence of the attempts to invoke one or other of the founders of the field as justification for merging the theological and scientific enterprises.

8. I have argued this at length in the case of Müller in my "Religion and the Scientific Impulse in the Nineteenth Century: Friedrich Max Müller and the Birth of the Science of Religion" (1995a and chapter 2 in this volume).

9. Many (if not most) scholars and scientists in the late nineteenth century supported not only the scientific method but also the ideology of progress that appeared an inseparable aspect of it. It is the progressive aspect that would account for many early scientific students of religion assuming the role of cultural critic as well. Twentieth-century developments in science, however, have undermined that ideology by showing there is no essential connection between moral progress and the development of science. The effect of this on the academic study of religion has been beneficial, although it has meant

the loss of the role of "critic of culture" for the student of religion. Leertouwer expresses this situation in his claim:

> By becoming just another branch of science, the science of religion finds itself no longer in what Fokke Sierksma preferably called "the central fighting area at the European front." If Gerardus van der Leeuw has become a stranger to us—as I believe he has—it is not because we have become so much more clever historians of religion than he was, but because we are unable to share his theological zeal. Who cares about theology nowadays? Nobody, of course, but theologians, and therefore nobody cares about what historians of religion have to say about the culture of which they are part of [sic]. Whenever something like the Rushdie affair happens, the encyclopedic knowledge of historians of religion comes in handy to explain a few satanic verses—but that is all. Questions like what the very occurrence of such an affair and the panic it created mean in terms of the nature and destiny of Western culture are anybody's competence—not particularly to be claimed by historians of religion. For questions like those touch upon something like theology—in the end, they cannot be answered by some kind of aesthetic humanism in the vein of Mircea Eliade's *The Quest* (1991: 61).

10. Commenting upon the contribution to the Science of Religion of Nathan Söderblom and Gerardus van der Leeuw, Waardenburg notes that "they could not afford the revolution of de-theologizing *Religionswissenschaft* completely..." (1991a: 45). "Their first care," he writes, "over against the threatening orthodoxies or tempting liberal theologies, was to see *Religionswissenschaft* as a legitimate discipline with a positive role for theology and this was the case they fought for" (1991a: 45–46). Despite the qualifications made, they in effect, therefore, subordinated *Religionswissenschaft* to theology. In introducing *Religionswissenschaft* into the theological program in an effort to broaden the horizons of their theological students they, according to Waardenburg, "willy-nilly promoted the emancipation of *Religionswissenschaft*" (1991a: 45), but the "emancipation" extended only to administrative concerns and not to methodological independence.

I have doubts about whether these scholars contributed to such an emancipation. (See my argument to the contrary, with respect to van der Leeuw, in my "Phenomenology of Religion as Religio-Cultural Quest: Gerardus van der Leeuw and the Subversion of the Scientific Study of Religion," [1991b] and chapter 10 in this volume.) Waardenburg has objected that I have failed to understand not only van der Leeuw but also the Dutch religious studies "scene" both before and after van der Leeuw's time. He claims, for example, that in van der Leeuw's day "no system of *Religionswissenschaft* existed to be subverted," and that "van der Leeuw was quite frank and open about his manner" in the study of religion and therefore "scarcely capable of illegal action" (1991b: 87). If my position on Tiele in this chapter has any merit, however, then it is obvious that a tradition of some sort was already extant from which van der Leeuw could well have deviated. And the fact that van der Leeuw was frank about his theological intentions does not necessarily lay to rest all questions about what he was up to in his attempt to establish a special phenomenological approach to the study of religions. Strangely, Waardenburg admits in this essay that van der Leeuw was "not a scholar of science of religion as we understand it nowadays," but he fails to recognize that Tiele came much closer to that ideal before van der Leeuw even started his career in the field. In fact, Waardenburg appears to see van der Leeuw's failure to adopt the scientific conception of the study of religion as of direct use to the emergent discipline. He writes: "The de-absolutization of the ideal of the objective science after the First World War was a legitimate affair not only for theologians but for any intelligent researcher, and van der Leeuw participated in it" (1991b: 91). Whether that de-absolutization benefited society may be a question worth asking; but his other point is questionable. That is, I do not see how one can say that by undermining the autonomy of science one improves science; and Waardenburg provides no justification for this claim, regarding either the Science of Religion or any other science. His suggestion, moreover, that those who seek some uniformity of principle and practice in the sciences constitutes a kind of inquisition (1991b: 89) is in effect a mechanism for evading critical thought about the nature of the task in the field of religious studies. I fully agree with him that there is a pluriformity of principle and practice in the field (1991b: 87), but I cannot support his claim that such a pluriformity ought to exist.

Part II

*A Return to Theology:
On the Resistance to Scientific Method*

Chapter Four

A *"New Era of Promise" for Religious Studies?*

In the conclusion to his analysis of the study of religion in his *Science of Religion and the Sociology of Knowledge* Ninian Smart maintains "[w]hat we need to do ultimately in the study of religion is to break down that simplified opposition between learning *about* religion and feeling the living power of religion [; for] the two can go together and indeed must go together if the study of religion is to enter boldly into its new era of promise" (1973b: 160).[1] How transcending that distinction can set Religious Studies on a new course, however, Smart does not indicate clearly. Indeed, it might well appear that his advice here is more likely to entrench the traditional, religio-theological study of religion from which the academic, scientific study of religion first emerged. That is, if the opposition between learning about religion and feeling the power of religion is questioned then the distinction between the disinterested scholar-scientist and the concerned teacher-guru would also be at issue—and that would leave the old-style *Religionswissenschaftler* indistinguishable from the new. Despite wishing to transcend the opposition between "learning about religion" and "feeling its power," Smart nevertheless asserts that for the student of religion, theologians should be looked upon more as rivals (7, 13–14), for, as he argues, if "we are to justify the science of religion, it is centrally upon intellectual grounds, not on the ground of its utility or of its capacity to improve people" (8). Religious Studies is not, as he puts it, "a pious dogmatism, girding its loins with the cloth of . . . scholarship" (14). Though this last statement would appear to clarify his position, in fact it only complicates the issue, for as a claim it stands in opposition to his opinion about the nature of the study of religion quoted above. The pure intellectual grounds Smart invokes here to justify the study of religion would seem to establish only a scientific learning about religion. But, with reference to the first quotation above, Smart also posits that knowledge of religion can be increased by "feeling the living power of religion." Smart has set up a contradiction here, however, for if "feeling the living power of religion" adds something beyond pure knowledge of the phenomena, then that "feeling" takes on a meaning greater than Smart's intended phenomenological one: it becomes religious. The apparently flagrant contradiction between the two descriptions of the study of religion underpins Smart's book and ultimately deflates his argument about the "New Era"; and therefore that argument bears closer examination here.

In discussing the relationship of theology to the study of religion in the second chapter of *The Science of Religion and the Sociology of Knowledge*, Smart acknowledges that there are other concerns for students of religion in addition to that of learning about religion—namely, the concern with religious truth. Despite having explicitly claimed that theology and the study of religion stand in a conflicting relation he appears nevertheless to suggest that this is in appearance only. To illustrate his point he draws attention to a distinction he sees as important between two kinds of nontheological and nonreligious approaches to the study of religion. "It is useful," he writes, "to make a distinction between religious studies and the scientific study of religion. . . . The latter is part of the former, but religious studies legitimately can include aims other than the scientific study of religion. For example, much of the philosophy of religion is concerned with probing questions of truth, directly or indirectly, and is a legitimate part of religious studies" (41–42).[2] Whether or not this argument effectively re-establishes earlier ties between the academic study of religion and piety seems, on this account, to be a valid question, and in this discussion I shall attempt to examine whether Smart's methodological proposals for Religious Studies involve such a relationship. In a sense I shall be raising critical questions about the meaning and significance of his proposal that we distinguish Religious Studies from Theology as well as from the scientific study of religion. The analysis will be restricted essentially to his position as it appears in *The Phenomenon of Religion*, since it is in this book that he consciously addresses the issue of methodology in the study of religion. Religion, as he puts it, "is sufficiently important in human existence to be properly understood and the present book is meant to be a small contribution to thinking about that project" (1973a: 4).

Smart's concern in *The Phenomenon of Religion* is to try to establish what is entailed in coming to a scientific understanding of religion. In contrast to his analysis in *The Science of Religion and the Sociology of Knowledge*, he does not in the former work explicitly distinguish a scientific study of religion from a more general study of religion. This does not mean, however, that such a distinction is missing altogether or plays no significant role in the methodology he elaborates here for the academic study of religion. At first glance Smart's argument in *The Phenomenon of Religion* appears straightforwardly scientific. As in *The Science of Religion and the Sociology of Knowledge* Smart sees a notable contrast between theology as a scholarly discipline and the scientific study of religion. The contrast derives from a difference of intellectual approach by the practitioners of the respective disciplines. Theology, claims Smart, involves what he refers to as "Expression," by which he means a response of commitment, on the part of the scholar, to the "object" under investigation culminating in testimony to that experience. The approach of the scientific student of religion to the object of inquiry, on the other hand, precludes such "involvement" and is therefore more objective. In summary Smart writes: "The critique of the anatomy of theological studies can be summed up as follows: that we always need to make a distinction between historical and structural enquiries, such as sociology, phenomenology, etc., which are the proper province of [the study of] Religion, and the use of such materials for Expressive ends, that is, the doing of Theology. The critique implies that some restrictions and inconsistencies have been placed upon scientific studies by the needs of Expression" (16).

Smart knows that it is exceedingly rare, if not impossible, to maintain a wholly objective position from which to undertake the study of religion. Nevertheless he maintains that the study of religion need not on that account proceed as though any degree of bias were admissible for students in this field. There are different degrees of bias, with different degrees of significance; as Smart puts it, "some omnipresent bias does not legitimate universal great bias" (17). Indeed, if it did, one would have to conclude unhappily that to understand a religion would require endorsement of it. On the contrary: Smart insists that recognition of some omnipresent bias "by no means entails that it is necessary to Express [that is, to endorse religion] in order to do Religion [that is, to study religion]" (28).

The "anatomy of the study of religion" also provided by Smart in the opening chapter of *The Phenomenon of Religion* supports such an interpretation of his analysis of Religious Studies. It is clear from this discussion that, for Smart, the "understanding" of religion that should be the concern of the scholar in this field is scientific rather than hermeneutical. He expands upon the tasks of description and explanation: description always precedes explanation, uncovering the content, so to speak, of the religious phenomenon under scrutiny; whereas explanation clears up any puzzles presented by that content.

Given this understanding of the nature of the scientific study of religion it is not surprising that Smart should see himself as providing a neutral framework for the discipline. What must be noted here, however, is Smart's rejection of what he refers to as "flat neutralism." Neutralism, to be sure, requires a "bracketing" of Expression, (a refusal to adopt the religious attitude of the persons or community being studied), but "bracketing Expression," he insists, is not the same as ignoring Expression altogether; to do that would simply be to take up the old-style empiricist study of religious phenomena restricted to a discussion of the external characteristics of religion only. That type of analysis, he argues, "flattened out" description and made it impossible to capture the "fine grain," which led to a distortion of the phenomenon's true character. Consequently, according to Smart, the student of religion must always take seriously the Expression characterizing the lives of the devotees in the tradition being studied. Of course, for Smart, "taking seriously" does not mean an endorsement of the faith, but rather a willingness of the scholar "to enter into engagement with those who carry on the Expression of the faith . . ." (31). He continues: "[This does not] entail that [the scholar] is thereby chiefly concerned with Expression" (31). The engagement merely helps avoid description of the religious phenomenon that does not do it justice. However, to insure that the Expression of the devotee is properly understood, while not allowing that element of Expression to dominate in an apologetic thrust, Smart suggests that the Expression of the devotee always appear in brackets; bracketed Expression simply being a faithful "re-presentation" of another's commitments without either endorsement or rejection.

It is clear that given Smart's notion of neutralism in the study of religion and its differences from a straightforwardly empirical approach to that study (that is, to a flat neutralism), he is entertaining a notion of a study of religion broader than the scientific (that is, an approach permitting questions that even though not outrightly theological are more than merely scientific). Indeed, Smart sees in the work of Mircea Eliade—and in particular in Eliade's notion of a creative hermeneutic approach to the study of religions— an example of the kind of study that is "more" than science but "less" than theology. He maintains, in agreement with Eliade, "[i]t would be artificial for the Religionist [that is, the student of religion] to present the meanings of faiths and cultures and then simply to contract out of the question of their significance in the larger perspective of human history and a new global humanity" (49–50). Thus, on the problem of objectivity Smart concludes: "Religion [the study of religion] incorporates, by bracketing, Expression into its descriptions, and that there is no strong reason to hold that particular commitment is necessary to the practice of [the study of] Religion" (34).

Close scrutiny of this conclusion reveals a lack of precision regarding the task of the academic student of religion; nor is it clear whether the study of religion in fact implies endorsement, if not of a particular religion then of religion in general. Smart's conclusion to the argument of the book as a whole exposes that ambiguity even more pointedly. Acknowledging that the task of theology is to Express a worldview and to Express commitment to it, he writes: "If Religion [that is, the study of religion] has any share in this activity, it is at one remove. It cannot easily affirm, out of its own substance, that men are sinful or that the Creator is good. What it can do is to show that the understanding of religion and even of ideology, is a necessary and indeed illuminating part of the human enterprise of accounting for the world in which we live" (148). If the academic or scientific study of religion, however, is directed toward gaining knowledge about religions rather than toward testifying to religious values, then it must be said that the latter, if not a specifically theological task, is nevertheless a metaphysical one and should therefore be left to philosophers and metaphysicians.

It is not difficult to understand Smart's reasoning and the source of its ambiguity, for a description of a religious phenomenon must include reference to the object of worship—to what Smart calls the Focus of religion. And since the Focus of a religion transcends human boundaries, it might appear as though the student of religion, like the devotee, assumes religion to be more than simply a human phenomenon. Consequently Smart is right to insist that the student ask the question "Is the Focus . . . part of the phenomenon which the observers witness?" He also rightly maintains that the student cannot answer this in the same realist fashion as the devotee. Consequently, the principle of "bracketing" is once again invoked in relation to questions about the existence of the Focus of religion that allow the student to acknowledge the reality—but not the truth or falsity—of the Focus in the life of the devotee. Smart refers to this approach as "bracketed realism" that does not so much leave the question of the existence of the Focus unanswered as unasked (62).

From Smart's analysis it might appear that the student of religion must treat religion as a merely human phenomenon. Yet no such conclusion is actually drawn. Having rejected Peter Berger's methodological atheism because it requires a priori reductionistic explanations of religion—making his methodological atheism indistinguishable from atheism *tout court*—Smart maintains that only a phenomenological description of religion recognizing the reality of the Focus is acceptable. Unlike the a priori reductionism of Berger's methodology (which assumes a projected character for the Focus of religion), the phenomenological description eschews ontological assumptions. Ultimately Smart asserts: "Now if we have rejected projectionism within phenomenology, we cannot hold that phenomenology simply deals with human events and products, though it certainly does at least this" (68). Were Smart to leave the discussion of this matter here, no critical concern would emerge. However, he further elaborates:

The phenomenological description of the [Christian] Eucharist (for example) brings out the interplay, so to speak, between the Focus and the participants. From the point-of-view of phenomenology, the question of whether the Focus exists does not arise; but if it *does* exist, then the phenomenological description does actually describe a manifestation of the Focus, or in other words it is not just a description of human events, etc. (68)

In this statement he seems to contravene the very essence of the phenomenological approach to the study of religion, because he suggests that the question of the existence of the Focus is left unanswered, whereas, as he himself has already acknowledged, the phenomenologist is one who ought not to pose the question in the first place. Furthermore, his discussion of "the mythic firmament" in chapter 3 is not at all clear. He sees some analogy between mythic or metaphysical explanations on the one hand, and modern historical, scientific explanations on the other; yet he thinks our acceptance of phenomenological description will preclude use of the latter type of explanation in accounting for religion. "[I]f we are to pursue the method of phenomenological bracketing," he writes, "we must not, in understanding the historical aspects of some myths, let these twentieth-century assumptions get in the way of understanding" (83). If "understanding" in this passage means that descriptive account of religion outlined by Smart in earlier chapters of the book, then it is not clear how he will distinguish this approach to the study of religion from the approach of the theologians. He devotes the final chapter to that express problem, as well as to the disparity of attitude between the devotee and the academic student of religion— although he does not solve these problems entirely satisfactorily, it seems, as I will attempt to show.

As Smart points out, religions themselves explain the world—or attempt to explain the world. Such explanations, of course, involve supernatural causes and therefore clash with the naturalistic explanations sought by scientific students of religion. As an illustration Smart contrasts a religious ("internal") explanation of the conversion of Saul of Tarsus (later Saint Paul) with the scientific ("external") explanation of the experience; but he asks in the process whether the latter's reductionistic assumption—that is, that Paul's religious experience could be solely explained in psycho-historical terms—is any less metaphysical than Paul's "explanation" of the experience in terms of an encounter with the transcendent (the supernatural). Ultimately Smart urges the student of religion, even though he or she is in search of natural explanations for religious phenomena, to leave open the possibility of alternative explanations going beyond the scientific; for Smart at least, these would be based on a phenomenological description of the Focus of the devotee's experience and would not conflict with the scientific explanation.

The student of religion would apparently remain agnostic with respect to the role of the supernatural in human affairs while paradoxically recognizing the power of the supernatural. The tension between the two positions is expressed by Smart as follows:

> To this extent the Religionist's (or historian's) account is compatible with the Theological Expression of faith, namely, that it was through the power of God that early Christianity was established. Though compatible, however, it differs from the Theologian's description. The historian is not uttering any kind of faith statement: he is not *qua* historian, speaking as a Christian. Rather he is accepting a phenomenological description of the Focus of Paul's experience, and recognizing that Paul's actions were highly influenced by what he (Paul) took to be the object of his experience. The historian is also recognizing that such an experience has its own validity as power, as a force (to put it crudely) in the determination of the affairs of mankind. (136–137)

The significance of this account is that it uses what Smart refers to as phenomenological explanation—that is, explanation that invokes the supernatural without assumption as to its ontological status. A precise elaboration of this is not provided by Smart; no detailed account of "phenomenological explanation" is given beyond the examples employed that illustrate its character. And for this reason I find Smart's argument too thin to be persuasive.

Many students of religion see a "new era of promise" for the field of Religious Studies in its identification with the sciences and its concomitant legitimation as an independent entity within the modern university; Smart, however, quite clearly does not. He acknowledges that the study of religion needed emancipation, so to speak, from theology, but he denies that such emancipation is only possible by total identification of the academic study of religion with the naturalism implicit in a scientific methodology. The alternative methodology he attempts to elaborate in *The Phenomenon of Religion,* however—one permitting objective learning about religion without decrying the feeling of its living power—is not without flaws that ultimately keep it from being distinguished from theology. There is an indication of this early on in Smart's analysis when he borrows from Eliade's notion of "creative hermeneutics" in his new ("phenomenological"?) approach to the study of religion. For Smart, of course, the notion allows the student to say something about the value and significance of religion for human beings. The flaw, however, lies in there being no ground on which that value can be established and no means by which it can be delimited. Smart does claim to be aware that such an approach might incur a sliding into an (implicit) theology, but I do not think he adequately perceives the seriousness of this situation. Eliade's work, to be sure, involves historical and scientific analysis, but in the end it is fundamentally a theological undertaking; and only with difficulty could the academic student of religion lift the notion of a creative hermeneutic—an essential element of his interpretive framework for Religious Studies—from that framework and apply it with any degree of validity, the academic work being shaped by an altogether different collection of assumptions and presuppositions. An example of the incongruity I identify in Eliade is seen in the following passage from his essay "Crisis and Renewal" in the collection entitled *The Quest*. Eliade writes:

> The fact that a hermeneutics leads to the creation of new cultural values does not imply that it is not "objective." From a certain point of view, one can compare the hermeneutics to a scientific or technological "discovery." Before the discovery, the reality that one came to discover was there, only one did not see it, or did not understand it, or did not know how to use it. In the same way a creative hermeneutics unveils significations that one did not grasp before, or puts them in relief with such vigor that after having assimilated this new interpretation the consciousness is no longer the same. In the end, the creative hermeneutic *changes* man; it is more than instruction, it is also a spiritual technique susceptible of modifying the quality of existence itself. This is true above all for the historico-religious hermeneutics. (1969: 61–62)

As the passage just quoted clearly shows, the object of Eliade's creative hermeneutic is not to provide us with knowledge about religions or even knowledge about the values held by a given religious community, but rather to recover the abandoned transcendental values and meanings once provided to their devotees by those traditions. What it is important to note here is that Eliade simply accepts the validity of the religious meanings once held. Consequently the hermeneutic invoked to re-establish these values is actually a religio-theological one. A further instance of the theological character of Eliade's "creative hermeneutic" is seen in his reference to the message of primitive religious traditions in the preface to this volume of essays. He writes: "The interest in such 'messages' is not exclusively historical. They do not 'speak' to us about a long-dead past, but they disclose fundamental existential situations that are directly relevant to modern man" (ii–iii). The scholar's task, he implies, is not simply to look for the historical significance of such tradition; indeed, this would entail a reductionistic distortion of the truth *of* religion and therefore, it seems, of the truth *about* religion. In "The Quest for the Origins of Religion" in this same collection we read:

> He [the historian of religion] knows that he is condemned to work exclusively with historical documents, but at the same time he feels that these documents tell him something more than the simple fact that they reflect historical situ-

ations. He feels somehow that they reveal to him important truths about man and about man's relation to the sacred. (53)

In Eliade's understanding, such a "creative hermeneutic" allows for a study of religion different from the pursuit of both the scientific student of religion and the theologian:

> In brief the history of religions affirms itself as both a "pedagogy," in the strong sense of that term, for it is susceptible of changing man and a source of creation of "cultural values," whatever may be the expression of these values, historiographic, philosophic or artistic. It is to be expected that the assumption of this function by the historian of religions will be suspected, if not finally contested, by the scientist as well as by the theologians. (66)

In supplying a systematic hermeneutic of the sacred and its historical manifestations, then, Eliade hopes to transcend science and supplant particular theologies with a general religious undertaking, restoring the sacred to a desacralized culture.

If this is the intention behind Smart's hope for a study to go beyond the search for mere knowledge about religions, then it is essentially a religious undertaking. Such a project, however, not only exceeds the scientific intent of the academic study of religion but also runs contrary to it; it does not restrict itself to legitimate claims to knowledge as do other disciplines within the modern university.

The foundation upon which Smart attempts to establish his distinction between the study of religion (Religious Studies) and the scientific study of religion is the principle of phenomenological bracketing. In this Smart is influenced by the work of Gerardus van der Leeuw, making explicit many of the implications of phenomenological bracketing left implicit by the latter (1973a: 53). Smart's argument, however, is not persuasive. There is no doubt that van der Leeuw, like Eliade, wished to use the scientific study of religion for nonscientific ends. For van der Leeuw, the (phenomenological) study of religion was a religious exercise to which the scientific study should contribute. But, as I have shown elsewhere,[3] to require the scientific study of religion to make such a contribution would rob it of its scientific character—and I am not sure that van der Leeuw addresses this problem any more successfully than Smart.

The primary issue at stake in Smart's bracketing methodology involves the philosophical problem of the nature of the religious phenomenon; that is, should the student of religion treat religion as a purely human phenomenon? As I have already pointed out above, Smart raises this question in chapter 2 of *The Phenomenon of Religion* when he asks, "Is the Focus . . . part of the phenomenon which the [scientific] observers witness?" (56). One would expect the response to this question to be in the negative, for the concept of bracketing rules this out; otherwise, in effect the Existence of the Focus would be conceded, rather than merely its Reality for the devotee. Smart, however, rejects that negative response—not simply because of its destructive implications for religion, but because in his mind a simple 'no' to the question would carry over to questions on the existence of the gods, therefore lending legitimation only to reductionistic accounts of religion. Thus Smart writes:

> [I]f phenomenology is to be assimilated into its brother sociology, then it also ought to proceed with a methodological atheism - but already this is to suggest that a certain kind of description has to be given of, for example, the Eucharist, a description, that is, which comments on the "true state of affairs." Such a comment would include reference, presumably, to the projected character of the Focus. At this juncture methodological atheism would be effectively indistinguishable from atheism *tout court.* (59)

And although the point of "bracketing," according to Smart, is to keep such philosophical issues from intruding upon the scientific study of religion, a simple substitution of "yes" for "no" to the question equally constitutes an ontological judgment without the benefit of philosophical argument. If, following Smart's argument, the Focus is to be a part of the phenomenon witnessed by the scientific observers, then it can be neither the "Focus-as-it-is-in-itself" (if it exists, that is) nor the "Focus-as-projection," but rather the "Focus-as-it-is-in-the-mind-of-the-devotee." This Smart refers to as Bracketed Realism (61). Further difficulties exist with such a position, however, for it assumes that the Focus is real for the devotee because the devotee believes the Focus to exist. But the assumption that this holds true for all devotees is obviously problematic, especially with respect to those who have reinterpreted the tradition in liberal, post-Enlightenment terms.[4] It is not at all clear, then, whether the notion of bracketed realism resolves the critical problem about the value of the religious phenomenon.

Bracketed Realism, in Smart's view, avoids both the reductionism of projectionist, social-science theories of religion as well as the realism implied by the devotee's commitment. But lest Bracketed Realism be allowed to evolve into a form of nefarious methodological atheism repugnant to a proper understanding of society, Smart backs up his proposed approach with reference to Peter Berger's work in which the latter unacceptably forces treatment of religious phenomena as entirely human in character. Smart writes: "My argument . . . is directed to the conclusion that it is wrong to analyze religious objects in terms simply of religious belief. A description of a society with its gods will include the gods. But by the principle of the bracket we neither affirm nor deny the existence of the gods" (54). Smart does not entirely reject Berger's analysis, but he counters that a methodological agnosticism can retain what it has to offer while yet adhering to the principle of the bracket. Although methodological agnosticism should by definition differ from methodological atheism, in what way this is so is not made clear. In fact the argument could be made that the two are not different at all. And Smart draws more from this analysis of bracketed realism than is warranted in his insistence that phenomenology does not deal simply with human events and products. His earlier rejection of "projectionism" had been the rejection of an a priori theoretical stance and not a falsification of all projection theories, actual and possible. His claim here seems to rule out, in an a priori manner, all possible projectionist accounts of religion; this is tantamount to asserting the actual Existence of the Focus, and in so doing runs afoul of the requirement of bracketing. The most Smart ought to claim here is that phenomenology may in some sense "be in touch with" more than simply human events and products.

Robert Baird has properly assessed this problem from the point of view of the academic student of religion. Paralleling Smart's analysis of the phenomenon of religion, Baird writes:

> The historian is certainly interested in Sankara's or Guadapada's view of nondual Reality, Tillich's ground of Being, the view of the Buddha in the *Lankavatara Sutra*. But, historically speaking, these are all men's views of Ultimate Reality. While it is undoubtedly true that all views of Ultimate Reality are human in the sense that it is men who hold them, to ask "What is the nature of ultimate Reality?" is a different level question from "What is Sankara's view of Ultimate Reality?" (1972: 19)

Baird quite properly qualifies this apparent reduction by insisting that it is methodological only—not ontological: "When we state that the history of religions is the study of man rather than the study of God we are making a methodological stipulation and not a theological proposal" (20). Given Smart's rejection of Berger's methodological atheism it is unlikely that he will find Baird's conclusion acceptable. Yet Smart's own analysis seems to drive him in the same direction, despite his refusal to articulate the matter in the same way. He does seem to come close at one point, although only ambiguously so, in his discussion of the Eucharist cited above. What becomes apparent here is that unless the existence claim is taken to be true— a claim that, by definition of the use of the bracket, cannot be so taken because it must not even be raised—the phenomenological description of the Eucharist is a description of merely human events, of the relation of persons to a transcendent reality they take to be there (that is, believe to exist).

In fact, much of Smart's argument actually seems to support my critique of his position. The "analogies" he uses to explicate the meaning of his Existence-Reality distinction do not always carry the force he thinks they do. The "pen-friend" and "Father Christmas" scenarios, for example, have more to say about the Reality of "transcendent" Foci in the minds of their devotees than they do about their objective existence, and therefore they support reductionist rather than nonreductionist interpretations of religion. A closer look at the Father Christmas analogy will help clarify this point. A phenomenological description of the "Father Christmas Event" must make clear that the character is "real" in the lives of the children. However, the description also must make clear that this "reality" is only created by the fact that the children believe him to exist. (The reason for the "reality" of Father Christmas in the lives of adults who do not believe that he exists will, of course, find a different kind of explanation.) The description of the children's relationship to Father Christmas, therefore, is no more than a description of a human condition. And if so here, then one may ask why not so in the case of religious "realities." The phenomenological description, to be sure, must involve a description of the "existence-belief" of the devotee, but it does not require acceptance of that belief. The latter would, in fact, define a philosophical or religious undertaking that the bracketing is designed to avoid.

Nor is the fact that the devotee finds reductionistic accounts of religion unacceptable a sufficient reason for the student of religion to adopt a metaphysical position assuming the existence of the Focus. Smart's account of the conversion of Saul of Tarsus to Christianity, to which I have made reference once already, seems to illustrate this, but he does not draw from the account conclusions I think inescapable. That is, he underestimates the potential for a phenomenological description to undermine the metaphysical in the context of "explaining" the world. For such a phenomenological description is superior to one that excludes the reasons devotees provide for the metaphysical claims they espouse. Of course, a nonreductionistic description of the reality claim, which attempts an understanding of why the claim is made, is a fuller description of the religious phenomenon—and therefore a better description. But the validity of the devotee's stance constitutes another matter and one beyond the concerns of the academic student of religion. And, if the student of religion accepts that the theologian's claim somehow goes beyond the account provided by the academic study of religion, the principle of the bracket is violated. This would seem obvious; however, Smart, rather surprisingly, disagrees. In fact, he entertains the notion of a supernatural (theological) explanation to complement the explanation provided by the student of religion. Smart agrees that the student of religion must remain agnostic but seems to maintain that in so doing the scientist need not deny the cognitive value of such complementary theological accounts. Clearly, a rigid agnosticism of this kind would reject adoption of such explanations; therefore, one may ask in what way the methodological agnosticism proposed by Smart can be distinguished from the methodological atheism rejected by him as atheism *tout court*.

Such a conclusion is not reached, however, for Smart insists that his methodological agnosticism would only apply to the scientific student of religion rather than to the more general student of religion (whose concern is not only with obtaining knowledge about religion but also with feeling its power). Without such a restriction, of course, concern with Smart's proposal would vanish, for methodological agnosticism no less than methodological atheism would be forced to seek scientific explanations of religious phenomena as wholly human products. Given Smart's distinction between a scientific and a nonreligious (but simultaneously nonscientific) study of religion it is clear that methodological agnosticism applies only to the former enterprise. Yet Smart cannot bolster the distinction with any argument that is not circular—other than the thin claim that methodological agnosticism allows the student of religion to draw certain kinds of conclusions about the *meaning* of religion not permitted by scientific study. It would appear, therefore, that the more general study of religion is close to the religio-theological study of religion that does not operate within such an agnostic framework. The principle of bracketing, then, is a kind of crypto-theological enterprise, predisposing the student of religion to assume the "truth" of religion (that is, to assume that the Focus of religion exists).

The religious nature of such a phenomenological approach becomes even clearer once one recognizes that the principle of bracketing taints the search for explanations of religious events. For all his talk of explanation in *The Phenomenon of Religion* (and elsewhere), Smart ultimately restricts the study of religion to providing descriptions of the phenomenon. This follows from the fact that explaining any phenomenon, in violation of the methodological rule of bracketing, depends upon whether one assumes the "truth" to be illusory or veridical. Admittedly the descriptions Smart seeks are far more complex than those usually provided by the kind of empiricistic students he criticizes. But it is precisely because of the complexity that Smart's restriction of the study of religion to description takes on an apologetic tone. Bracketing, it will be remembered, requires the student of religion to assume, even if only for the sake of accurate description, that the devotee is always right. Thus, thorough description will include accounts of the devotees' own explanations for their religious affiliation. Although such accounts are provided within brackets, so to speak, so that the question of their truth or falsity is not at issue, they nevertheless lend more coherence to the phenomenon.[5] Yet Smart gives no consideration here to the fact that such supernatural explanations as the student of religion is required to include in describing the phenomenon may stand in outright conflict with naturalistic explanations that constitute the acknowledged findings of the academic student of religion. (His own analogy of the child's belief in Father Christmas presents precisely such a case in which one would be well advised to seek an external explanation about the reality of the phenomenon since any existence claim would immediately be seen to be implausible.) For to ask the scientific student of religion to give up the cognitive framework that diverges from that of the religious devotee is tantamount to asking the researcher to give up the scientific project pure and simple. To take the scientist seriously in this regard would amount to according privilege to the scientist's worldview over that of the religious person—and this Smart finds objectionable. What Smart fails to recognize here, however, is that this privilege only operates within the framework of the academy. In fact, it is difficult to see how it could be otherwise, just as it would be inconceivable for the devotee to give up the worldview that gives meaning to existence. Even if religion holds the truth, and science is incapable of seeing it because of a restrictive methodology, that does not constitute grounds for arguing that the academic study of religion ought to be anything other than scientific. And if "the more general student of religion" seeks "explanatory" accounts of religion outside the cognitive universe of the scientific student of religion, then such a student stands in conflict with the scientific approach and has no greater right within that setting than the devotee or the theologian. At best, one could concede Smart's claims that religion cannot be studied within a scientific setting. That "something more" than the scientific should be sought obviously involves a recognition of at least the plausibility of religion's truth; and such recognition could only be due either to religious experience of some kind or to metaphysical or theological argument, neither of which is appropriate to the activity of academic departments set aside for the scientific study of religious phenomena.

Though this critique of Smart's understanding of phenomenology of religion and his "bracketed realism" cannot claim to have falsified his methodological proposal for Religious Studies as distinct from the scientific study of religion, it does, I hope, call it into question. For it points out that Smart has not been successful in arguing for a distinction between a scientific study of religion and a more general study of religion that is nonscientific but also simultaneously a nonreligious, nontheological study of religion. The claim on behalf of a "New Era of Promise" in the study of religion is illusory and therefore a disservice to science.

Notes

1. My analysis of Smart's argument here will draw essentially upon two works in which he concentrates on matters of method in the study of religion: *The Science of Religion and the Sociology of Knowledge* (Princeton, NJ: Princeton University Press, 1973) and *The Phenomenon of Religion* (London: Macmillan Press, 1973).

2. Smart's claims here with respect to the philosophy of religion are questionable, not as regards its task but rather with respect to the function it should have in the academic study of religion. Most practitioners in the field see the kind of philosophical enterprise Smart describes as being redolent of metaphysics and therefore as lying outside the field of Religious Studies. See, for example, C. J. Bleeker's "The Relation of the History of Religions to Kindred Religious Sciences, Particularly Theology, Sociology of Religion, Psychology of Religion and Phenomenology of Religion" (*Numen* 1 [1954]: 142–152), and his "Comparing the Religio-Historical and the Theological Method" (*Numen* 18 [1971]: 9–29). A critical philosophy of religion and concern with questions of methodology in the study of religion, however, have generally been accepted as meriting a role in the field.

3. See my "Phenomenology of Religion as Religio-Cultural Quest: Gerardus van der Leeuw and the Subversion of the Scientific Study of Religion," in *Religionswissenschaft und Kulturkritik: Beitrage zur Konferenz, The History of Religions and Critique of Culture in the Days of Gerardus van der Leeuw (1890- 1950),* eds. Hans G. Kippenberg and Brigitte Luchesi (Marburg: Diagonal-Verlag, 1991): 65–86 (and chapter 10 in this volume). Relevant comments in this regard can also be found in my essay "The Failure of Nerve in the Academic Study of Religion," *Studies in Religion* 13 (1984): 401–422 (and chapter 8 in this volume).

4. Nor does this apply simply to modern devotees, as Paul Veyne, for example, makes clear in his *Did the Greeks Believe in Their Myths? An Essay on the Constitutive Imagination,* trans. Paula Wissing (Chicago: Chicago University Press, 1983).

5. These "thick" descriptions accepted in the absence of better explanations for the phenomenon recall the work of Clifford Geertz, especially *The Interpretation of Culture, Selected Essays* (New York: Basic Books, 1973), and *Local Knowledge: Further Essays in Interpretive Anthropology* (New York: Basic Books, 1983).

Chapter Five

———❦———

Theology and the Academic Study
of Religion in Protestant America

My concern in this essay is with the role of theology in the academic-scientific study of religion in the United States. More precisely, I will consider whether theology *rightfully* has a role to play in the scientific study of religion in the publicly funded university, for it is only in the light of that question of legitimacy that I think we can make any sense of the developments in the study of religion in the United States or understand the debates regarding its current status within the American scientific community.[1] The question of the legitimacy of theological and religious studies in U.S. universities is, of course, very complex and is not easily addressed, for in this context it constitutes both a political and a scientific (or methodological) question.

It is obvious that in the privately funded universities and colleges in the United States, not to mention the privately funded seminaries and divinity schools, the question of the teaching of religion and theology faces no crisis of legitimacy at all. Whether in privately funded venues the methodological, and therefore scientific, problem is posed at all depends on whether such instruction sees itself as derived from (or an aspect of) *Religionswissenschaft*. The teaching of religion or theology in the publicly funded university, on the other hand, would appear to be in direct violation of the First Amendment of the U.S. Constitution, which clearly advocates a separation of Church and State, prohibiting the latter from promoting any activity involving the inculcation of religion.[2] In this respect the study of religion in Europe is considerably different from its counterpart in the United States, because theology actually forms a part of the curriculum in European universities. The question of whether theology ought to be allowed similar status in the curriculum of publicly funded universities in the United States, however, has been answered indirectly at least—via the Constitution—in the negative. But that has not prevented theologians and other theologically minded scholars in the university from trying to find other means to bring theology back.[3] And without some understanding of that fact, it is not possible to understand fully the character of what is called Religious Studies in the United States. With this in mind, I proceed to an overview of the historical development of the field of Religious Studies in the United States in which the problem of the relation of theology to the study of religion will be made plain.

Within a single essay I cannot hope to provide a full history of the study of religion in the colleges and universities of the United States. What I propose, therefore, is to give a brief review of some recent treatments of that history, with special focus on the emergence of the academic study of religion as a curricular element in the publicly funded university. In proceeding along this line I should first indicate that that history is antedated (and very much influenced) by a scholarly—although pious—approach to religion that constituted a fundamental element in the early colonial university in America. University education in religion essentially meant the training of the Protestant clergy, with advanced study of theology introduced upon the acquiring of a classical undergraduate education (to include the study of the Christian religion) common to all students. (To speak of a Protestant hegemony here is quite appropriate given that the first Roman Catholic school was not established in America until 1789.) By the end of the eighteenth century, however, explicit instruction in Bible and Theology had been removed from the curriculum of the Protestant universities and relegated to seminaries and divinity schools, with moral philosophy replacing it as "integrator" of the undergraduate arts program. This displacement of the study of religion also meant that the discipline was not likely to develop in the same way as other arts subjects, for as D. G. Hart maintains, "the upshot of these developments was to remove serious study of religion from the liberal arts curriculum [altogether]" (1992: 200).[4] One sees in the early history of the study of religion in the United States, then, an assumption that religious experience and commitment are necessary preconditions for the study of religion, and that such an assumption was essentially of a Protestant nature; as Charles Long put it in a recent essay (1992), one sees in the early history of the study of religion in America the foundations of a cultural Protestantism that becomes the basis for future developments in the study of religion, or at least that profoundly influences those developments.[5]

The only book-length treatment of the study of religion in the United States is Robert S. Shepard's recent *God's People in the Ivory Tower: Religion in the Early American University.* Shepard's project in this book is to trace the development of the early programs of religious studies in six American universities: Boston, Cornell, New York, Pennsylvania, Chicago, and the Divinity School at Harvard. He focuses his attention, however, chiefly on developments in the latter two institutions, because in his opinion, William Rainey Harper of the University of Chicago and Charles Eliot of Harvard (presidents of the respective institutions) "provided an academic structure for the scholarly treatment of religion . . . [and] promulgated a new rationale [and] new conception of the place of religious studies in the academic environment" (1991: 42). The "educational landscape" in the postcolonial period was rather bleak for those interested in the study of religions other than Christianity; the cause of this, as Shepard somewhat circularly posits, was the "irregularity and fragility of the American university's interests in the scientific study of religion" (9). Yet Shepard is also aware of the importance of the Protestant hegemony in religious education in American colleges and universities, pointing out that, despite the emergence of a liberal form of theological reflection embracing science and the importance of scientific method in all learning, and despite the availability of scientific models for the study of religion in various European contexts, most study of religion in American institutions of higher learning in the late nineteenth century was still dominated by theological and ministerial concerns. This was the case, he insists, at Boston University even though as early as 1873 it had made the appointment of a professor of Comparative Theology whose work was to be dedicated to the "historic and scientific study of religions" (12). For in fact, Comparative Theology did not become a distinct academic unit, free to develop in terms of principles peculiar to itself, but remained ultimately defined by the School of Theology. There was no revision of the School's program, claims Shepard, "from its primary mission of ministerial education" (15). Comparative Theology was welcomed as handmaiden to theological study—that is, only in so far as such study helped "broaden" the perspectives of potential ministers and missionaries.

The comparative study of religion at New York University, on the other hand, was intended to be scientific in the sense of treating "other religions" fairly, claims Shepard, but it was nevertheless driven by a predominantly apologetic impulse. "There was no design," he writes, "to support a strong academic program in the emerging discipline of *Religionswissenschaft*" (27). Although some of the members of the teaching staff there thought an objective, scientific approach to the study of religion appropriate for their university—which, after all, claimed to be nonsectarian—there was no intention on the part of those doing the teaching "to engage in serious research in the science of religion" (26).

Cornell University, Shepard claims, had only a "brief flirtation with the science of religion" (18) that failed to become established because of its relatively weak status as a component of Cornell's School of Philosophy. That "flirtation," however, was important for its influence on Morris Jastrow of the University of Pennsylvania who recognized it as an important contribution to the emergence of a scientific study of religion in the university context, and he expanded upon it in his own work. Although no formal program for the academic study of religion emerged at Pennsylvania until the twentieth century, Shepard writes that when it did, "there is little doubt that serious scholarship was the objective of the history of religions group [and that] ministerial training had no formal role to play" (36). Since it was originally founded as a secular institution without affiliation to a divinity school of any kind, the study of religion could be established by Jastrow in a way that accepted the historical method as the basis of the study of religion—although shortly after Jastrow's death, George A. Barton reintroduced a religious tone into the program so that, as Shepard puts it, it "became a haven for ministers and rabbis of proximate churches and synagogues to continue their studies" (38).

Although Shepard, as I have already noted, sees Harper at Chicago and Eliot at Harvard as providing for Religious Studies in the context of the academy, their conception is closer in intent to the traditional Protestant religio-theological approaches found at Boston, New York, and Cornell than it is to Jastrow's European-influenced idea of the study of religion at Pennsylvania. Shepard nevertheless maintains that both Harper and Eliot were convinced of the value of scientific learning and that both also saw a role for the study of religion in the curriculum of the university. Consequently, "the outcome in both cases," he insists, "was a welcoming of *Religionswissenschaft*" (59), although it was very unlike the originally founded discipline of the European scholars.[6] "For both men," Shepard continues, "the university was the proper place to study religion and to study it—Christian theology included—scientifically. Moreover, the scientific study of religion was appropriate for minister and scholar alike" (59). And on further reading it becomes clear that, even though Chicago established the "first nonsectarian, graduate research program in religious studies in America" (51), it received the majority of its students from the Divinity School and, as Shepard admits, never really became "a significant training ground for scholars of religion" (68). As for Harvard, Shepard also recognizes that its fundamental vision was carried out in "the training and preparation of ministers" (68). Thus it is quite apparent, I think, that the academic study of religion as conceived by either Harper or Eliot was not developed along the scientific lines of Jastrow's program at the University of Pennsylvania; for at both Chicago and Harvard the role of the university was considered to be not only that of the mediator of a knowledge about religions but also the mediator of religious knowledge (teaching *about* as well as teaching *of* religion). Their programs were indeed based upon an acceptance of the role of scientific method in higher learning, containing, as Shepard claims, "a sympathetic and harmonious role for the study of *Religionswissenschaft*" (124); but the influence of the seminary within the framework of the university had a major—and negative—impact on the development of *Religionswissenschaft* as an independent and autonomous undertaking in that setting. Those who supported *Religionswissenschaft* in the university, that is, were also—and primarily—involved with religious instruction and with the professional training of clergy and missionaries, and they made the emerging discipline of *Religionswissenschaft* at best an ancillary subject in a theological curriculum (107, 111, 113, 119, 120–121). This meant that there was not a simple openness to and acceptance of *Religionswissenschaft*, but rather that the results of such scientific research depended to some extent, for missionary purposes, on the assurance of the supremacy of Christianity among the religions of the world (125). Indeed, Shepard comes to very much the same conclusion when he writes: "Whether apologetic or moralistic in purpose, the important fact was that *Religionswissenschaft* programs arose within a Christian—mostly Protestant—ethos" (126). This must be clearly recognized if one is to understand why the current debates over the role of theology in programs of Religious Studies in the university curriculum have unfolded as they have. Early *Religionswissenschaft* in the American university context was, in effect, a "Christian *Religionswissenschaft*." And although its influence in the nineteenth-century university certainly helped raise the level of scholarship on religion in the university—essentially by helping it transcend ecclesiastical boundaries placed upon thought about religion and religions—it also prevented the development of an authentic, scholarly *Religionswissenschaft*. Shepard himself concedes the truncated development of the academic study of religion, even though it undermines his earlier claim that Harper and Eliot produced a new rationale for the place of the study of religion in the academic environment. "As the theological school within the emerging university became the place to study religion," he writes, "*Religionswissenschaft* became subject to the particular curricular structure, objectives, and ethos of the seminary" (128). *Religionswissenschaft*, he continues, was unable

> to separate [itself] from the theological and professional concerns of the nascent university, particularly the rising seminary within the university. A theological agenda accompanied the entrance of comparative religion in American higher education despite the arguments, some rhetorical and some sincere, that the new discipline was objective, scientific, and appropriate as a liberal arts subject. Students valued the new science of religion for its professional utility; few even considered its potential as a discipline coterminous with other humanities disciplines. (129)

In effect, then, Shepard concludes that the study of religion failed to emerge as an independent academic enterprise with its own identifiable group of scholars; it was not until after World War II that the discipline acquired the identity of *Religionswissenschaft* (129).

In coming to the above conclusion Shepard claims to adopt the view on the development of Religious Studies in the United States first put forward by Joseph M. Kitagawa in his "History of Religions in America" (1959) and "Humanistic and Theological History of Religion with Special Reference to the North American Scene" (1983). The claim, broadly outlined, is that the religious liberalism of the World's Parliament of Religions served as the fundamental impetus leading to the establishment of the study of comparative religions in American universities; furthermore, by this impetus, interest in that enterprise was kept alive until the late 1920s, thereafter declining (along with the liberalism) because of the dominance of neo-orthodox theology in American thought in the 1930s. For the most part, Shepard's reading of Kitagawa is quite acceptable; the latter does talk of a decline of interest in the scholarly study of religion in the 1930s, and of a renewed interest in the field "after the end of World War II" (Kitagawa,1959: 5; 1983: 556). But Kitagawa's claims in these essays are less straightforward than Shepard intimates. In the earlier essay, for example, Kitagawa notes that a number of scholars figured among the participants at the Parliament, including students of religion, but he emphasizes that "they attended the parliament as representatives of their faiths or denominations and not of the discipline of the history of religions" (1959: 4). In drawing attention to this, Kitagawa underlines the fact that the academic study of religion in the United States has more than one dimension—indeed, that it is of two distinct kinds. Furthermore, in "The History of Religions in America," he distinguishes the History of Religions from the "theological History of Religions," insisting that the former—as a scientific endeavor—"developed only at the dawn of the modern period, namely, during the Enlightenment" (16), and he insists that in America such a *Religionswissenschaft* "did not develop . . . until a relatively recent date" (1). The reasons for America's tardiness in adopting the scientific approach, he claims, are to be found in the religious character of the education established in U.S. universities during the colonial period. In his later essay, "Humanistic and Theological History of Religions," Kitagawa argues that "any attempt to assess the development of the History of Religions during the past 100 years, especially in North America, cannot ignore the impact of two of the major international assemblies on the discipline, namely the World's Parliament of Religions, held in Chicago in 1893, and the first Congress of the History of Religions, held in Paris in 1900" (1983: 553). He acknowledges, however, that it is in the United States that the Parliament of Religions becomes "inseparably related to the aim of Comparative Religions or History of Religions" (553), but he can only half-heartedly claim that the tone for later developments in the History of Religions in America was set by the 1900 Paris Congress (554). In his brief review of the IAHR's (International Association for the History of Religions—the official body formed in 1950 to oversee the congresses that followed the Paris meeting of 1900) discussion of the nature of the scientific study of religions he does not show *how* the IAHR influenced developments in the United States. Excluding the influence of a few European-trained scholars such as Morris Jastrow, it is really not possible to agree with Kitagawa that the IAHR—or even the Paris Congress—has greatly affected developments of the field in the U.S. The American Society for the Study of Religion (ASSR)—formed in 1959, and until 1990 an affiliate member of the IAHR—has had a negligible effect on the field; its severely restricted membership has simply not allowed it to play a significant role.[7] In fact, the American Academy of Religion (AAR), the main professional association representing the majority of those who teach religion in institutions of higher education in the United States, not only has never had either a formal or informal connection with the IAHR, but has deliberately kept itself apart from—if not opposed to—their activities.[8]

This should account for Kitagawa's rather ambiguous understanding of the development of the field of religious studies in the United States. Although as early as 1959 he recognizes the emergence of a scientific study of religion in the Enlightenment (1959: 17), he insists that *Religionswissenschaft* is not simply scientific but rather "religio-scientific," being obliged to "view the data 'religio-scientifically'" (21). And in the 1983 essay he refers to the History of Religions (*Religionswissenschaft*) as "an autonomous discipline situated between normative studies . . . and descriptive studies" (1983: 559). Unlike other social sciences, then, for Kitagawa this discipline does not simply seek descriptions or explanations of events and processes; rather, it inquires after the meaning of religious data and is therefore a mode of research linking descriptive with normative concerns (560). This hybrid enterprise he refers to as the "humanistic" History of Religions, which he contrasts with a more explicitly normative theological History of Religions. The former, according to Kitagawa, derives from the work of scholars involved in the international congresses (and later the IAHR) and is what Kitagawa considers to be a bona fide scientific undertaking—but he provides no evidence to support this claim. He is entirely correct, of course, that such a humanistic History of Religions serves as a justification for the field of religious studies after World War II. But the argument that such a view of the field derives from the work of the Paris Congress and subsequent congresses, or of the IAHR, is difficult to maintain, since those scholars quite clearly saw themselves involved in a scientific enterprise similar in structure to any other scientific work fostered by the modern university curriculum. Moreover, if the IAHR were in fact the source and foundation of a humanistic *Religionswissenschaft* (as Kitagawa maintains), the lack of co-operation with—and even outright hostility toward—the IAHR by the American Academy of Religion becomes a virtually insoluble puzzle.

That the academic study of religion in the United States experienced some kind of rejuvenation after the Second World War is, I think, fairly generally accepted. Whether Kitagawa has adequately characterized and accounted for it, however, is another matter. Whereas Kitagawa attributes this renewal of interest in religion to factors such as a sudden interest in things Eastern, a growing fascination in the social sciences with myth and symbol, and an interest on the part of influential theologians in inter-religious dialogue (556), D. G. Hart maintains that Religious Studies became a growing concern in large part because of "the cultural crisis generated by the two World Wars" (1992: 218). "Science and technology," Hart ventures, "seemed to be more of a threat than a salvation to social ills, and educators took steps to ensure that undergraduates received a proper training in values and morality" (218).[9] He notes in this regard that in 1943 the American Council of Learned Societies (ACLS) "recognized" the value of religion to a liberal education as self-evident, despite the dangers of indoctrination accompanying the teaching of religion; the benefit to be accrued from this widespread concern for a general liberal education of America's youth was immeasurable and had an obvious impact upon the growth of Religious Studies in the postwar years. As Hart points out, from the end of World War II until 1960, programs in Religious Studies in American universities doubled, with student enrollments increasing dramatically (211). But what one in fact sees here is the coincidence of the concerns of the ACLS with those of American Protestantism and not with those who wished to establish a Science of Religion; liberal Protestants were not concerned with the objective study of religion but rather with showing the relevance of religious ethics and spirituality for the modern, fragmented world. Hart writes:

> Calls for unity in higher education provided Protestants concerned about the study of religion with added leverage. Generated by the crisis of the second World War, many books and articles by mainline Protestant leaders appeared that picked up on the sense of upheaval within American universities . . . [lamenting] the increasing fragmentation of knowledge and the secularization of learning. (209)

Given this informal alliance between Protestant Christianity and the defenders of the humanities, one is not surprised that programs in Religious

Studies departments simply resembled programs and curricula of Protestant seminaries and divinity schools.[10] Therefore the rejuvenated *Religionswissenschaft* of which Kitagawa speaks—the humanistic History of Religions— amounts to a continuation of the programs Shepard calls "Christian *Religionswissenschaft*," since it took on the character of the Christian (meaning mostly Protestant) ethos from which it emerged (1991: 126). Shepard is right to point out that, after World War II, this "Christian *Religionswissenschaft*" was less directly associated with the professional training of theologians and ministers, and that it attempted—with some degree of success—to become a more scholarly and therefore academically acceptable enterprise; yet he provides no indication that its more humanistically based identity made of it something fundamentally different from what it had been throughout the late Victorian and Edwardian periods of American history. The so-called new, humanistically based *Religionswissenschaft*, that is, far more nearly resembles the theologically orientated History of Religions in the early American university described by Shepard than it does either the contemporary work of European scholars connected with the IAHR (and its international congresses) or the new ideal of *Religionswissenschaft* said to have emerged in the academic community in the 1960s. As Hart puts it: "Proponents of religious studies, which often meant the ethos of liberal Protestantism, made common cause with humanistic scholars and resurrected the philosophical idealism of the old genteel tradition under the label of general education" (1992: 218). Consequently, the period from 1945 to 1960 not only represented no advance in the development of Religious Studies as an academic or scientific undertaking; it amounted to a retrograde step, in that, like the classics in the colonial curriculum, it defined itself only in terms of a reaffirmation of "commitment to civilization," thus "reaffirming" its opposition to the sciences.

The 1960s, Hart maintains, saw a decline in the consensus between the university and the Church, with the dominant Protestant Church claiming automatic—because spiritual—superiority over its secular opponents. Although Hart does not provide an explanation for this development, I would argue that it was due in large part to the growing religious pluralism of Western civilization and its impact on the academic community, which made it no longer possible to assume the superiority of Christian ideals and beliefs. It became obvious, therefore, that if the Study of Religion were to remain part of the university curriculum it would have to find a clearly scientific or objective justification. And according to Hart, "the formation of the American Academy of Religion signalled . . . [that] reaction against the humanistic and liberal Protestant orientation of religious studies during the 1940s and 1950s" (219) and provided the discipline with a new, radically altered structure. Hart is right, I think, to claim that the formation of the American Academy of Religion was a reaction against the "Christian *Religionswissenschaft*" dominating the study of religion in the American university, but he is seriously mistaken in his claim that the AAR successfully put Religious Studies into a more objective and scientifically acceptable position. Without understanding this, one cannot properly grasp the present status of *Religionswissenschaft* in the American academic context. I shall therefore proceed to a brief analysis and critique of Hart's 1992 essay "American Learning and the Problem of Religious Studies."

The essential element in Hart's analysis is the claim that the debates and discussions among students of religion in the early 1960s leading to the formation of the American Academy of Religion constitute a watershed in the history of the study of religion in America. According to Hart this is so because the formation of the AAR involved the students' accepting the scientific commitments generated by the Enlightenment; in other words, they moved from seeking religious, theological, and humanistic explanations to seeking scientific explanations of religious phenomena. As he puts it, they "abandoned the notion that religious guidance or belief was necessary for the study of religion and insisted instead that religious phenomena could be explained in naturalistic categories as well as any other artifact" (197). Unfortunately Hart fails to make his case. There is no doubt that the study of religion had a very uncertain status as an academic discipline prior to the 1960s because it was neither sufficiently "classical" to be wholly accepted as one of the humanities nor sufficiently "scientific" to be included among the sciences; as he points out, it was not until 1979 that the ACLS listed the AAR as one of its learned societies.[11] The formation of the National Association of Biblical Instructors in 1909 and the American Association of Colleges in 1915, he claims, provided some academic legitimacy because they promoted standardization of religious instruction in both universities and ecclesiastical educational institutions; in my opinion, however, they did not make a significant impression upon the broader academic, scientific community. Teachers of religion were still not readily accepted by the academy at large because any academic status accorded Religious Studies arose from its link with the humanities rather than with the sciences. Hart's further claim that many within the field of religious studies felt their historical associations with ecclesiastical institutions constituted a problem, and that the perception of bias and lack of objectivity in their work required some response, is also accurate. Whether their response to the problem was adequate—namely, the self-study of the National Association of Biblical Instructors leading to its being renamed the American Academy of Religion—is in fact a connected issue, but it cannot be pursued here.[12]

According to Hart, the emergence of the AAR marked a radical change in the way religion was studied and taught in the United States. "The new methods of studying religion advocated by the AAR," he writes, "signalled the demise of this Protestant dominance as professors of religion became increasingly uncomfortable with their religious identification. . . . By striving to make their discipline more scientific, religion scholars not only embraced the ideals of the academy but also freed themselves from the Protestant establishment" (198). The National Association of Biblical Instructors, he argues, established the self-study committee to review the status of the field within the academic community and to see what the NABI could do to improve the health of the discipline—"to make the study of religion more academically respectable" (212). To that end, he maintains that the members of the Association sought to establish their field on empirical and scientific grounds, "rejecting not only their Protestant associations and affiliations but also the idea of religious studies as a humanistic discipline." Thus he claims that, from the time of the self-study report, "[t]o be religious was no longer as important for professors of religion as methodological sophistication and academic achievement" (213).

Hart bases his argument essentially upon an analysis of Claude Welch's *Graduate Education in Religion: A Critical Appraisal* (the result of a major two-year research project on graduate studies in religion, as distinguished from professional theological education). As president of the American Academy of Religion, in 1970 Welch presented a preliminary report on the results of his research in an address to the Academy entitled "Identity Crisis in the Study of Religion? A First Report from the ACLS Study." Hart's claim that Welch's report "helped to legitimate the discipline within American higher education" (1992: 214) is entirely correct. He also claims justifiably that Welch's report, which "called for increased methodological sophistication within the profession" (1992: 214), to some extent achieved the desired results. His further statement, however, that the report "marked a clear defeat for the older humanistic and Protestant orientation of religious studies . . ." (214) is an exaggeration. It is true that Welch called for the independence of Religious Studies from ecclesiastical interference; it is also the case that his study helped undermine the Protestant hegemony that until then dominated religious education and the study of religion in America. But I would argue that he did not persuade scholars to shift their loyalty from the Church to the academy; his study simply clarified the nature of the relationship of the scholar to the Church and to the academy. Part of the reason for Hart's faulty assessment may be the reasonableness of Welch's claims that, as of 1970, students of religion clearly saw the distinction between Theology and Religious Studies, formally accepting the fact that Religious Studies alone was the concern of the university teacher of religion. But

Welch's claims do not do justice to reality; for although a formal kind of recognition of the scientific character of the study of religion had been achieved, that notion was only paid lip-service at best. In fact, Welch seems to be aware of this, for he comments that, despite the successes in programs of Religious Studies in a number of public universities, there were still many signs that the issue of identity had not been settled; that is, there were a number of serious, unresolved matters that in Welch's consideration still left the field of religious studies at risk of "falling back into the arms of confessional interests" (1970: 12).

Indeed, D. G. Hart himself seems aware of the issues that concerned Welch, but he does not appear to admit the seriousness of the situation. He points out the irony in Holbrook's chairmanship of the Self-Study Committee that brought about the change of name of the NABI, given the fact that Holbrook had argued strenuously for a view of religious studies as a humanizing and liberalizing discipline in his book, *Religion: A Humanistic Field*, published the same year. Hart acknowledges that the change in name of the professional body from the National Association of Biblical Instructors to the American Academy of Religion did not settle the issue of advocacy and indoctrination—aspects essential to the teaching of theology and religion in seminary and divinity school contexts (Hart, 1992: 213). For scholars in the field, while seeking increased academic respectability, nevertheless retained their aim of making students more humane, religious, and moral (213). And although allowing that scholars shifted their loyalties from the Church to the academy, while eschewing a similar shift of loyalties away from religion, Hart does not stress clearly enough that these scholars were in contradiction with the new ethos because the methods advocated in the study of religion by the AAR meant that being "religious" was no longer important for professors of religion (213–215). Had Hart made a closer analysis of the presidential addresses to the AAR, I think he would have seen that his claim regarding the defeat of the "older humanistic and Protestant orientation in religious studies" was precipitate. For within two years after Welch's first report of the ACLS study to the AAR, the real state of affairs in the field was exposed in Robert Michaelson's presidential address: "The Engaged Observer: Portrait of a Professor of Religion." Michaelson acknowledged that, despite the avowed intention of the Academy to make a clear demarcation between religious instruction and teaching about religion, the opposite tendency was re-emerging in the field, which rejected objective scholarship in favor of "involvement" (1973: 422). In fact, so strong was that "opposite tendency" that he describes it as giving birth to what he appropriately terms "classroom religion" (422). Although Michaelson expresses some surprise with respect to the scholars involved in this development, he himself seems to share their concerns, and therefore to contribute to their project (to replace the objective and scientific study of religions with a more traditional model of Religious Studies). Michaelson is concerned in this essay, that is, with the risk to the soul represented by the secular study of religions, and he claims that the teacher of religion, even in the university context, has an obligation to help students achieve "wholeness." Consequently, he proposes a scarcely credible study of religion combining detachment with involvement; his contention is that the scholar cannot separate scholarly from existential concerns. "That much," he concludes, "the age of involvement has taught us" (423).[13] In light of Michaelson's comments it is not surprising, then, that Eric Sharpe came to quite a different conclusion about the history of the development of the field in America. Contrary to Hart, Sharpe maintains that " . . . by the early 1960s the American schools were moving firmly into the acceptance of this wider role" for Religious Studies (1986: 280).

Although there is more one could say about the history of the growth of the academic study of religion in the United States, it seems to me that enough has been cited here to allow some significant conclusions to be drawn. I think it abundantly clear, for example, that although there has been much activity and apparent shifts of attitude within the field, the discipline has not really developed much beyond what it was at its origins in the nineteenth century. Kitagawa's suggestion, followed by that of Shepard, that a new style of Religious Studies emerged in the years immediately following World War II, and D. G. Hart's contention that the birth of the American Academy of Religion in the 1960s signaled a transformation catapulting the study of religion in American universities from the religious and humanistic realms into the scientific are simply not substantiated; for I have shown that the arguments provided on behalf of such claims are internally inconsistent and the evidence amassed in their favor either weak or illusory. Briefly put, the study of religion in the United States is, for the most part, still approached with religious or quasi-religious presuppositions. Two recent essays solicited by the AAR make this incontrovertible: the first is Leo O'Donovan's overview of the 75th anniversary meeting of the AAR in Chicago (December 1984), and the second is Ray L. Hart's 1991 study on religion and theology in American higher education.

Although according to O'Donovan the program of the AAR meeting was designed to provide "a general indication of the disciplinary challenges which have emerged for the *scientific* study of religion today" (1985: 560— my emphasis), these "challenges" did not include the issue of "advocacy-learning," nor that of theological—or ecclesiastical—involvement in the study of religion. Evidently O'Donovan and his colleagues in the Academy assume that such learning and "involvement" are necessary elements to any proper academic study of religion, for O'Donovan does not hesitate to encourage the Academy to involve itself in the current reshaping of the American religious scene. "If a new appropriation of faith is under way in the United States," he writes, "we shall need guidance in understanding the experience and courage in learning how it may be socially constructive. The American Academy of Religion is, of course, the largest single professional association for students of religion who might contribute to meeting that need" (1985: 558). In his review he places great emphasis on the contribution of theologians—particularly those who call for a contextual or "relativised" theology—because he thinks that the scholar can bring out the emancipatory potential of religion for the betterment of society. Members of the Academy may expect, he says, that theology will "be more—or less— challenging to the society in which it exists and to be more—or less— concerned for the unity of purpose among members who are both citizens and believers" (1985: 564), and accordingly he urges the members to construct versions of such religio-social agendas as may be found in various documents of "the World Council of Churches and by Vatican II's Pastoral Constitution on the Church in the Modern World" (1985: 565). One might imagine such reconstructed versions, redolent of appropriate ethical, religio-social, and theological concerns, as we read in this revealing, if lengthy, passage from O'Donovan:

> Whether the academic study of religion can respond to this social situation will surely be a matter of concern for its largest organization when it meets again next year at the Anaheim Hilton just before Thanksgiving. Will the grand contemporary sculpture of Chicago—Calder and Picasso and Miró— be replaced in a dispiriting way by Disneyland? Next year we will again be searching for images that travel well, images that even bear transcendence. If our study of religion is genuinely concerned for its cultural context, then there should be time enough for a good-humoured visit to the Enchanted Kingdom. But if we pursue religion for our own sakes alone, then the Meeting will pass by emptily. Next fall in California, it seems, there will be another opportunity to see which face of religion will be uppermost, the timelessly trivial or the historically transcendent, the giddiness of self-centered human ceremony or the true joy that accompanies God's pleasure in creation. (1985: 565)

Surprisingly enough the sentiment expressed here is shared by most members of the Academy. And that naturally means that such concerns also dominate the programs of study in those scholars' respective college and university departments in the United States. Given this picture of the study of religion in the Academy, one would be very hard pressed indeed to make out a case for "a radical transformation" in the discipline, resulting from the transformation of the NABI into the AAR.[14]

In light of O'Donovan's account of the work of the Academy and its members, it is difficult to talk of "new and radical developments" in the scientific study of religion in American academic circles. The so-called new developments in the field in the 1940s and the 1960s have proven not at all to be departures from the "Christian *Religionswissenschaft*" model first established in the nineteenth century. Of course there can be no doubt that the theological character of today's *Religionswissenschaft* is considerably less Christian and Protestant. But it is far from religiously or theologically neutral—having replaced religious ethnocentrism with pluralism—and therefore far from scientific. The intention to make the academic study of religion currently existing in the university curriculum more scientific was no doubt held by some of the contributors to the formation of the American Academy of Religion, but that intention was obviously short-lived, perhaps overwhelmed by more pressing concerns. Nor has a scientific impulse actually re-emerged in the Academy (or in very many departments of Religious Studies in American universities and colleges) in the thirty years since its formation, despite the rhetoric sometimes voiced in this regard.[15] Although no full-scale account of the current status of Religious Studies has been undertaken to provide evidence in support of these claims, the results of the recent report of the AAR's Committee on Education and the Study of Religion—billed as an update on the Welch report—go a long way toward substantiating them.

If any radical changes have indeed taken place in the academic study of religion in the three decades of the AAR, one would be justified in expecting to find some indication of it in Ray Hart's report on behalf of the Committee on Education and the Study of Religion entitled "Religious and Theological Studies in American Higher Education" (1991). But in actual fact the Religious Studies scene seems not to have changed at all over that period of time; the report shows that Religious Studies has not advanced since the NABI stage, if we may call it that, which reflects (as did the substance and structure of the NABI) what the academic study of religion was all about at its first emergence—an inchoate enterprise often indistinguishable from theology and laced with apologetic and moral concern. As Hart's report makes clear, the members of the Academy are still divided between "study of religion" (those concerned with knowledge about religion) and "practice of religion" (those concerned with the "truth" of religion) (1991: 734, 778).[16] They therefore differ little from their NABI predecessors. Moreover, it appears that by far the majority of the members of the Academy favor the style of scholarship combining the two activities (or at the very least eschews a clear demarcation between them), for one of Hart's concerns is to try to resolve the tension between them without dishonoring the social virtues the field claims to inculcate: "tolerance, pluralism, respect for opposing positions, etc." (1991: 790). In stressing social virtues at all costs over the demarcation issue,

Hart is in effect supporting the status quo. What appears to be at stake here is a loss of power in the Academy brought about either by alienating a large contingent of members and risking internal schism, or by losing academic legitimation as a result of close association with religious and theological matters. Taking seriously the tension between theology and the study of religion would constitute a radical threat to structures presently in control of the field. It is not wholly surprising, therefore, that Hart holds the conflict of approaches to the study of religion revealed by his report to be a problem in the definition of the field that has "not yet been sufficiently named to permit whatever is at stake to come to the fore" (731).

There are hints in Hart's report to suggest some change in the field since the days of the NABI, but the changes do not amount to much. Although Hart notes the discomfort of many "with the nomenclature that discriminates 'religious' from 'theological studies,'" he does admit that the term "religious studies" is now generally used to refer to "the scholarly neutral and non-advocative study of multiple religious traditions (1985: 716). He is also aware of the fact that the younger scholars recently out of graduate school find theology in the study of religion to be problematic in the university context (1985: 732). All he concludes from these "discoveries," however, is that the study undertaken was unable to get to the bottom of this opposition. Significantly, the "opposition" is indistinguishable from that which plagued the academic study of religion in the American setting from its inception in the late nineteenth century. It seems, therefore, that one is forced to agree with Shepard in his analysis of the early history of the field: namely, that authentic academic or scientific status has not yet been granted the field of Religious Studies in the United States.

Three decades after the report of the NABI Self-Study Committee, the Academy has received a submission from another self-study committee—that of the AAR (De Concini, et al., 1993a and b). Although the number of aims delineated has increased in the latter version of the Academy's mission statement, the two reports are in all essential respects identical. As an example, its stated seventh goal, which requires that the Academy accept a "conversation" of "the various voices in the field of religion," appears to be directed toward ensuring that the academic or scientific study of religion within the Academy never strays from its original religious foundations. Such religious intention, inimical to the scientific aspirations of the 1960s, receives less opposition from scholars of religion today. Barbara De Concini (current executive director of the Academy) illustrates the possibility—or desirability—of the combination of religious views with academic endeavor in the field. According to her, it is no longer possible to assume "a clear distinction separating scholarship from advocacy," and therefore "all disciplined reflection on religion" must be endorsed by the AAR and, by implication, the academy in general (Frisinia, 1993a: 5). Furthermore, she suggests that a number of the recent presidential addresses to the Academy have shown "that religionists have an important contribution to make to the entire conversation in the academy—small 'a'" in this regard because of the particular insights and understandings of the religionists with respect to "knowledge and power, evidence and advocacy" (1993a: 5). In putting matters this way, however, it seems fairly clear that the AAR has succumbed to the temptation—a temptation Welch thought the student of religion had transcended in the NABI to AAR development—to look upon the study of religion as a religious undertaking as much as a scientific one.

Given the dominant view of the nature of the study of religion within the academic religious studies community, it seems that the teaching of religion and theology within the public university in the U.S. has become a reality, and that this is so because the scientific study of religion has been described in such a way as to make it virtually indistinguishable from theology. This constitutes a victory for the American theological community in a double sense, for not only does it evade the strictures of the Constitution regarding the separation of Church and State; it also provides a kind of scientific legitimacy to the undertaking that it did not have when ensconced in the seminary and divinity school setting. The price for this victory is rather high, because the development, when fully understood, is not acceptable to the academy at large. I expect that the broader scientific community within the university will consider the AAR to have sacrificed the very thing they appear to have set out to gain in the process of transforming the National Association of Biblical Instructors into the American Academy of Religion—namely, a genuinely objective and scientific knowledge about religion. For those in the field still concerned to achieve that ideal, there is ground for deep disappointment in the history of the development of Religious Studies in the United States. There is nevertheless some hope to be found in the "hints" of progress in the field evident in Hart's report. These hints say nothing of the current status of the discipline, but they may well be indications of a genuinely new and radically different future for the academic study of religion in America.[17]

Notes

1. This is the essential point of contention in an exchange of views between Francis Schüssler Fiorenza and me in the *Bulletin of the Council of Societies for the Study of Religion* (Fiorenza, 1991, 1993, 1994; Wiebe, 1994d, 1997d).

2. Around the time of the transformation of the National Association of Biblical Instructors into the American Academy of Religion, the decision in the

Abington Township School District vs. *Schempp* case (1963) signaled a profound change in the broader social context of the academic study of religion. According to Kathryn Alexander it "altered the total picture of the study of religion in America by introducing the language which has governed its subsequent development in secular public colleges and universities" (1988: 389). The distinction it introduced into the field was that between the teaching *of* religion and the teaching *about* religion, with the former being excluded from public institutions by the Constitution, and it opened a window for the inclusion of the academic study of religions in the curriculum of the modern public university. The claim that theology is an essential aspect of the academic study of religion, of course, re-kindles the debate about the legitimacy of Religious Studies in the state colleges and universities.

3. See, for example, Schüssler Fiorenza (note 1 above) and Linell E. Cady (1993).

4. It should be remembered, however, that the displacement mentioned here refers to the removal of the Bible and Theology from the arts curriculum as elements of religious instruction and therefore represents an element of the secularization of the university's ethos. That, of course, should have opened the way to a more hospitable general ethos for the scientific study of religion, were it not for the fact that other venues for the teaching of religion sprang up in their place—venues in which religious intention predominated. Given those developments, one can accept Hart's assessment that the removal of the study of religion from the liberal arts community made it nearly impossible, ironically, for that study to develop as did other disciplines in the university curriculum.

5. Long's ultimate intention in his analysis of the development of Religious Studies in America differs from mine in a number of respects. A pointed example of that divergence of opinion can be inferred from his statements on the problematic nature of an "objective" scientific study of religion in his essay on the past and future of the discipline in the United States (1985): he cautions his readers against the assumption that the study of religion in the public university either is, or ought to be, a guarantee of its objectivity (32). He writes: "Constraint by law, and most probably from conviction by the members of its faculties, enables these institutions to present their teachings on religion in a non-proselytizing style; such institutions could then be declared the objective centers for the academic study of religion. This temptation must be resisted and denied because it does not portray an authentic appraisal of the meanings and nuances of the history of the study of religion prior to this innovation, nor does it pose in a correct manner the relationship and matrices of the meaning of American academic life as it is related to a serious concern for the understanding of religion" (32). The remainder of this essay should serve to support my opposing view that an objective approach is not only possible but desirable. Long's caveat regarding the approach leaves it no choice but to be religious. The Enlightenment model of scientific study, he insists, "thwarted the development of a full range of

methods for the study of [the] ultimate meaning of these [religious] expressions" (39). As should become clear in my argument, Long's desire for a deeper probing of the "essential meaning of 'the religious'" (37), as he puts it, makes of the academic exercise a religious one. Despite this difference, however, we are in at least partial agreement on some matters, especially on the meaning of the scientific study of religion for the emergence of the AAR in the early 1960s. As Long puts it in his essay "A Common Ancestor: Theology and Religious Studies" (1992): " . . . the American Academy of Religion, in taking over from its predecessor, the National Association of Biblical Instructors, stayed within the limited arenas already defined by religious and secular Protestantism. When the change was made from NABI, very few of those involved in making the transition knew anything of the scholarly study of religion that had been inaugurated in the early part of this century by Professor Morris Jastrow, Jr. This was the tradition of *Religionswissenschaft.* While this orientation might not have solved the American dilemma of the study of religion, it would have placed its problem and meaning within a wider historical and comparative context" (144). I also agree with Long in his assertion that there were cultural reasons for the AAR's course of action—reasons involving the fundamentally Protestant character of its constituency. Nevertheless, it should also become evident that the objective, scientific model for the study of religion represented by Jastrow is the only appropriate model for the study of religion in the public university; thus Long's claim that such study needs "the critique of theology to save it from the illusions of objectivity and to point out the ethical and teleological nature of all our intellectual endeavors" (149) is to be rejected. Such "authentic Human science" (150) I would argue, is not science at all.

6. An elaboration of this state of affairs is to be seen in my essay "Religion and the Scientific Impulse in the Nineteenth Century: Friedrich Max Müller and the Birth of the Science of Religion" (1995a, and chapter 2 in this volume).

7. It is important to note here, moreover, that the ASSR's understanding of the task of *Religionswissenschaft* was radically at odds with the IAHR's views. Eric Sharpe correctly points out that for the ASSR, even though philological, historical, archaeological, and other techniques in the study of religion ought to be conscientiously cultivated, they were not to be regarded as the ultimate end of the study. The greater human questions about the meaning of life, that is, were also—and more importantly—the concern of the student of religion, and E. R. Goodenough's presidential address at the inaugural meeting of the ASSR in 1959, according to Sharpe, made that quite clear. Furthermore, writes Sharpe, " . . . it was equally clear that these were the tones which scholarship would have to be prepared to hear from the United States for some time to come . . . [for] from all sides the American position seemed to be crystallising into one in which the old historicism was being weighed in the balance and found seriously wanting, because it was incapable of answering even its own deepest questions" (1986: 274–275). By contrast, Sharpe claims that the IAHR rejected such an approach to the field

at its Marburg conference in 1960, especially when it reaffirmed its understanding of the character of the academic study of religion. "[I]t is clear," he writes, "that Marburg was in many ways to be a watershed for the simple reason that there methodological discussion established itself for the first time as an integral part of IAHR procedure" (1986: 277).

8. Further details on this matter can be found in my essay "Against Science in the Academic Study of Religion: On the Emergence and Development of the AAR" (forthcoming a; and chapter 14 in this volume). It should be noted that in the early years of the AAR, connections with the IAHR were considered by some as a mark of the former's having achieved academic status. Michaelson in the mid-sixties wrote: "During this past summer [1965] the Claremont Colleges hosted the first meeting in the Western Hemisphere of the International Association for the History of Religions, a meeting which brought together scholars in religion from all over the world. This event symbolised the fact that the history of religions is well on its way toward becoming an established discipline in America" (1967: 13). This was, obviously, a minority opinion, and an attitude, if actually shared by others in the AAR, that was very short-lived indeed. Eric Sharpe's view of the matter is significantly different. He claims that "in a great deal of what was said and done at Claremont it was clear that the ideal of disinterested, objective scholarship *for its own sake*, while not abandoned, had been relegated to a position of only relative importance" (1986: 284).

9. It is interesting to note that in the United Kingdom religion was considered inadequate for such a task, so that an alternative kind of study—Cultural Studies—was approved to fill this role. On this see Fred Inglis, 1993.

10. This was so much the case, in fact, that with the increase in interest in the study of religion in the postwar years there simply were no teachers available who had been trained to lecture on *Religionswissenschaft*. As Kitagawa points out, the majority of those hired in this period came from seminaries and divinity schools. He writes: "In a real sense, the chaotic picture of the undergraduate teaching of the history of religions can be traced to the lack of adequate graduate training centers for *Religionswissenschaft* in North America. Thus when teachers of world religions are needed at many undergraduate colleges, they usually appoint either philosophers of religion, historians, biblical scholars, or theologians who happen to have personal interests and perhaps had taken two or three courses in the history of religions or comparative religion" (1959: 11).

11. Even today it does not appear that the social sciences, let alone science more generally, recognize the work of the so-called student of religion as worthy of consideration. It should be noted here, for example, that Murray G. Murphy makes no mention whatsoever of scholars in the history of religions or *Religionswissenschaft* in his recent essay "On the Scientific Study of Religion in the United States" (1989). *Religionswissenschaft* as it is practiced in the United States and represented by the AAR, it appears, does not merit consideration as a scientific undertaking. Nor does Murphy mention the work

of the members of The Society for the Scientific Study of Religion, which is more directly concerned with the social scientific study of religious phenomena. The reason for this, however, may be the tendency of some scholars to call one form of sociology more scientific than another. Roland Robertson, for example, writes: "More, perhaps, than anywhere else, the sociology of religion in the USA has occupied an interstitial position between sociology as a very secular discipline and religious studies as both a defence of religion and a critique of Western secularity. To that extent, much of American sociology *of* religion might more aptly be described as sociology *and* religion—a seeking of a conciliation between sociological science and privatized religion . . ." (1993: 10).

12. On this matter see my essay "Against Science in the Study of Religion: On the Emergence and Development of the American Academy of Religion" (forthcoming a; and chapter 14 in this volume).

13. A review of all the presidential addresses to the AAR since the change of name from NABI further supports my critique of Hart. Of the twenty-seven addresses delivered and published since 1964, eleven deal directly with the problem of the relation of "theology" to "Religious Studies," of which nine argue strenuously for a kind of merger of the two enterprises (if not a subordination of the latter to the former). (The other two appear to argue the opposite: Welch's address (referred to in my text) puts the matter ambiguously, while the address by William C. Clebsch ["Apples, Oranges, and Manna: Comparative Religion Revisited"] clearly favors a scientific or academic approach over the religio-theological in the comparative study of religion.) Three addresses—the only ones not based on Western and Christian themes—pay attention to the Theology-Religious Studies debate indirectly, and all, in my opinion, favor some form of integration of the two. Of the remaining addresses, ten are directly concerned—and in a rather traditional manner—with Christian religious and theological issues, while three deal with humanism and hermeneutics, which topics are clearly Western and Christian in inspiration. I have provided a fuller analysis of these addresses in my essay "A Religious Agenda Continued: A Review of the Presidential Addresses of the AAR" (1977a; and chapter 15 in this volume).

14. Even a cursory review of the scholarly contributions of participants in the annual general meetings of the AAR (and in the various regional meetings of the Academy) provides incontrovertible evidence of the primarily religious or theological concerns of its members. A review of other scholarly associations and societies affiliated some way or other with the AAR would likely provide even further evidence in this regard.

15. There are a few programs of study in the U. S., however, that are scientifically respectable. In reviewing their undergraduate program, the Department of Comparative Religion at Western Michigan writes:

During the early years of the department, its faculty wrestled with this principal issue: How should religion be studied in a public university? In the course of developing its undergraduate program, the faculty argued that the study of religion in a public university must occupy a valid and intellectually defensible place within the university curriculum. Thus, the model for the study and teaching of religion could not come from the divinity school or theological seminary. (E. Thomas Lawson, "Ph.D. Proposal in Comparative Religion," working paper, Western Michigan University, Kalamazoo, Mich. 1994: 3).

Similar comments regarding the undergraduate program at Western Michigan had already been made by T. Lawson in his essay "Rationale for a Department of Religion in a Public University" (1967). And the same could be said about the undergraduate program at the University of Vermont; see the interview with W. Frisinia, Chairman of Vermont's department in *Religious Studies News* 9 (September 1994): 6–7.

16. In "The Academic Study of Buddhism in the United States: A Current Analysis," Charles S. Prebish comes to a similar conclusion about the attitude of scholars in Religious Studies. He writes "[a significant number] of colleagues who have come to the study of Buddhism, and hence to academe, [have done so] as a result of their strong personal commitment to Buddhism as a religious tradition [and] for many this has created a tension between scholarship and religious commitment, between Buddhology and personal faith" (278). It is important to note here that Prebish used Ray Hart's "Religious and Theological Studies in American Higher Education" as a model for his own research project.

17. Another "hint" of the future direction of the field, I think, is to be seen in the emergence of the North American Association for the Study of Religion (NAASR) in the 1980s. The association was founded in order to support the historical, structural, and comparative study of religions and to provide a forum of discussion and debate for those scholars whose interests focus on achieving a scientific explanation of religions and religious phenomena. In part the association emerged to represent scholars in the United States in the IAHR, since no connection currently exists between the AAR and the IAHR. Although there had been a link between the American Society for the Study of Religion (ASSR) and the IAHR (until 1995), ASSR's restrictive membership policy left most American scholars interested in this connection without possibility of representation.

Chapter Six

———✧———

Promise and Disappointment:
Recent Developments in the Academic Study
of Religion in the United States

My aim in this essay is to provide a brief account of the development of the study of religion in institutions in the United States since World War II.[1] There is a general consensus of opinion among students of religion and historians of the field to the effect that the revival of academic interest in the study of religion in America dates from the early post World War II period after a lengthy decline in its fortunes beginning in the mid-1920s. In the five decades since, there has been an unexpected and unprecedented growth in the scholarly study of religions in American colleges and universities, and it is my intention here to provide not only an account of this advancement but also, in the process, to sketch out the elements of an explanation.

There have been many changes and developments in institutions of higher education and in American society more generally that have significantly impinged upon this scholarly enterprise. There have been many technological advances to expand and accelerate scholarly research, improve dissemination of the results of that research, or affect pedagogy in the field; but these advances will not receive treatment here. Although such developments are of interest, it is too early to evaluate properly their full impact. In my opinion, moreover, they have not been determinative in the development of the academic study of religion in the United States.

Factors that have been determinative can be described as socio-political and cultural; these include the ambiguous if not insidious legacy of the emergence of the scientific study of religion (often thought of as the Science of Religion)[2] in what Conrad Cherry (1992) has called the "age of the American University," from 1870 to 1920. And it is to these socio-political and cultural factors that I shall be devoting my attention here. I do not aim to provide a comprehensive geo-political account of the larger social world in which this revival of the academic study of religion in the United States has occurred, although such matters may arise indirectly. Rather, I shall focus on several important aspects of that revival that, on the one hand, show great promise for the field of religious studies and, on the other, lead to disappointment due to the developments' ultimate impeding of the establishment of a science of religion—of a study of religion and religions in American colleges and universities—whose orientation is primarily scientific rather than religious. I begin with an account of the early development of the academic (that is, scientific) study of religion in the United States.

The Academic Study of Religion: The Emergence of a Confused Science

The college curriculum in the colonial period in the United States provided in essence a religiously determined education inspired by a philosophy of education of medieval origin that presumed a unity of knowledge could be derived from an understanding of the unity of God. Although this philosophy did not outlive the eighteenth century, its core notion of the unity of all truth did survive and persists in some forms even to this day. Religion in the colonial period virtually dominated student life and thus effectively determined the structure of higher education. The latter was in effect a spiritual discipline in which the ideal of scholarship did not threaten the framework of denominational catechetics. Scholarly study of religion was indeed an essential element in the classical college curriculum, but it was entirely a confessionally based study designed primarily to form "character"; college education, that is, was *paideia*.[3]

New philosophies of education emerged early in the nineteenth century and gained considerable strength with the rise of interest in the natural sciences. These changes in educational philosophy led to the removal of biblical and theological scholarship from the arts curriculum and to the isolation of scholarship dedicated to the training of ministers for the Church in alternative structures within the university. The creation of seminaries for this task, however, was not followed by a secularization of the ante-bellum college, for despite the removal of biblical and theological scholarship from the curriculum, the colleges retained their concerns for the religious—that is, for the spiritual and moral—formation of their students. The ideal of the unity of knowledge that had dominated the colonial college—namely, the notion that all knowledge is essentially a knowledge of God—was still retained, although considerably transformed. That unity would now be achieved, not by the teaching of Bible and Theology, but rather by promoting a new kind of general course in moral philosophy, usually taught by the president of the college (often a Protestant clergyman), constituting the culmination of a student's post-secondary education. As Julie Reuben puts it in her history of the American university, such a course was intended to "draw together all the knowledge learned in the previous three years and place it in a Christian framework" (1996: 23).[4]

With the increasing interest in the sciences throughout the second half of the nineteenth century, further radical developments in American higher education followed—developments appearing to involve secularization that greatly threatened the notion of the unity of Truth upon which college education had been founded.[5] Cherry, as I have noted, refers to this period as "the age of the American University" and he argues—correctly, in my opinion—that without a proper understanding of this time we cannot understand the shape of contemporary American university education; nor, therefore, can we properly assess the possibilities and limits of the study of religion in that setting. Two major movements, claims Cherry, are responsible for this transformation of colleges into universities: specialization and professionalization. With the growth in science, new fields of study emerged that could not simply fit into former college curricula. Rather than expand the curriculum and increase the length of time required to complete a program of study, university reformers elected to concentrate on method over substance. Education, that is, would train students to think scientifically rather than provide them with authoritative bodies of information as it had done in the past. A new scientific "search for truth" became the focus of university education; "[t]here was no longer any particular body of knowledge that distinguished the educated from the uneducated" (Reuben, 1996: 67). New, elective curricula came into existence, requiring students to choose from a variety of fields of study no longer aimed at achieving the comprehensive knowledge of the old system. Concentration on a particular field fostered a depth of education, moreover, that led to professionalization, the result of which was the further undermining of the unity of university education sought by the earlier college curriculum. Research became a fundamental aspect of the university enterprise, and this required the protection of academic freedom.[6]

Although these developments, as Cherry argues in his review of the reform of university education in America, "drove the university away from any unifying center" (1992: 116)—especially one based on eternal verities (1995: 34)—they did not bring about wholesale secularization. It is true that the new curriculum was contrasted with the old in that students were allowed to pursue any and every subject matter, free from religious constraint, but university reformers, despite their espousal of the notion of free inquiry as a necessary prerequisite for science, were still committed to the concept of the unity of truth as essential to good education. Reuben points out that those seeking to reform university education still believed in the ultimate harmony of scientific with religious truth but that they rejected any approach to science favoring *sectarian* systems of religious belief, and they set out to find ways of reconceiving the relationship of religion to science that would allow the two to be blended. In effect they did not renounce the original aims of the early American college to " . . . encompass students' intellectual, moral, and spiritual education" (Reuben, 1996: 73). In an attempt to reconcile the two truths, argues Reuben, "[i]ntellectuals proposed a new alliance, in which scientific methods could be applied to religious questions. . . . By discarding the practices of dogmatic theology and adopting those of science, people could progress both in their understanding of religion and in their knowledge of nature. Wedded to science, intellectuals believed that religion would experience a veritable renaissance" (1996: 60). What happened to the modern American university in this period of transformation, therefore, is not the secularization of education but rather a "desectarianizing" of it. As Reuben puts it, "[t]he creation of new universities in the late nineteenth century reflected the contemporary aversion to church control . . . [and b]y the end of the nineteenth century educational leaders presented nonsectarianism as an essential feature of university government" (1996: 83,87). It is crucial that we understand this if we are to understand properly not only the emergence and growth of a science of religion in America, but also the impact of recent changes in American society upon its development. The reformers of the university, as I hope will become evident, provided a favorable environment for the scientific study of religion and yet impeded that study by failing clearly to demarcate it from religion itself.[7]

The desire on the part of the reformers of the university to assure a place for religion in higher education while avoiding direct ecclesiastical control led to the attempt to create a form of religious education compatible with science. Working on the assumption that science provided the most reliable foundation for knowledge in all fields, they tried to create "a modern scientific form of religious education" (1995: 123). It is this project that eventually led to the introduction of the "scientific" study of religion. "While reformers fought church affiliation," writes Reuben, "they did not intend to banish religion from higher education . . . [for they] believed that the university had an 'obligation to cultivate the religious spirit'" (1995: 124). Consequently, they argued for an application of the scientific method to religion, claiming that it could assist to revitalize religion and integrate it into modern intellectual life. The "Science of Religion" that first emerged in the American university, then, aimed at the expression of a knowledge of religion to provide a basis for "spiritual education" *and* be an acceptable part of the curriculum of the modern university. But such a "Science of Religion" does not exactly coincide with the current application of the term—that is,

with a nonreligious, academic study seeking description, analysis, and theoretical explanation of religion free from the burden of apologia. Nevertheless, the earlier form of the Science of Religion did often lead to the kind of
study of religious phenomena that made valuable contributions to an objective account of religion. In its apologetic form, however, the Science of Religion was ultimately unsuccessful in that early period, for even though it
flourished between 1890 and 1930, it did not, as Reuben shows, "recon-
struct religious doctrine and establish it as part of a scientific knowledge"
(1996: 135). That is, "scientific religion" neither stimulated a "religious
awakening" on university campuses nor attracted students to courses in the
scientific study of religion. University officials thus looked to extracurricular
activities to supply the religious needs of their students, who in the process
lost all interest in the science of religion for its own sake. This situation obviously created room for the development of a nonapologetic, academic
study of religious phenomena, in that it allowed the study to continue, un-
concerned with the metaphysics of religious belief and practice, but it was
devoid of spiritual motivation. In looking to the extracurricular to respond
to students' religious aspirations the university officials "reinforced the func-
tional differentiation of religion and science that emerged from the scientific
study of religion" (1996: 118). By the end of the second decade of the twentieth century, Reuben concludes, they turned away from the Science of Religion because they "began to realize that academic study of religion was not
inherently religious . . ." (1995: 142). This recognition, she claims, undermined the study's initial motivation and delayed the growth of religious
studies programs in U.S. universities until the end of the Second World War.
On the other hand, the notion of a strictly scientific approach to the understanding of religious phenomena had clearly been established.

Although I think the picture Reuben paints of the emergence of the Science of Religion in the early modern American university is essentially correct, I do not think it accounts for all aspects of its development or applies to
all its early practitioners. Eric Sharpe has argued in his *Comparative Religion:
A History* (1986) that that emergence was essentially bound up with the intellectual history of late nineteenth-century and early twentieth-century Europe. He insists "the situation of comparative religion in America at the turn
of the century, modifying factors notwithstanding, did not differ fundamentally from that obtaining in many parts of Europe at the same time. The same
elements—motive, material, and method—were in evidence. Liberalism,
both theological and political, provided the ground in which it was able to
flourish" (138). European contributions to the discipline, he argues, helped
"to create in America a climate in which comparative religion of a kind could,
and did, flourish" (97). And even though the U.S. academic community "was
scarcely in a position to make a similarly large-scale contribution to the

development of the subject" (97), he maintains that it made a distinctively American contribution to the field in developing the psychological study of religious behavior (104). Sharpe, however, also admits that this scientific study of religion suffered "something of an eclipse, despite its promising beginning, under the pressure of conservatism and orthodoxy" (138), and in this belief Sharpe does not differ much from Reuben. Nevertheless, these exceptions to the general progress of the study of religion, which survived despite pressure from a dominant Protestantism,[8] show that conditions enabling a nonapologetic study of religion were in fact present in the early modern American university.

Joseph Kitagawa suggests that the development of the science of religion in America was significantly dependent upon the progress of that science in Europe, referring especially to the first International Congress of the History of Religions held in Paris in 1900, although he acknowledges that much of the impetus for the new discipline came from the World's Parliament of Religions held in Chicago in 1893 (1983: 553). The impact of the Parliament of Religions on comparative religion in the United States is clear,[9] but the influence of Europe as a major factor in the development of the science of religion in America is less convincing. To be sure, there is some traceable influence in the work of scholars such as Morris Jastrow, but these are exceptions to the rule. The Paris Congress, unlike the Parliament of Religions, made a clear distinction between "religion" and "the study of religion"; therefore it did not hold the same interest for the university reformers as did the World's Parliament of Religions.

In his analysis of the emergence and development of the science of religion—of *Religionswissenschaft*—in early American higher education, Robert S. Shepard comes to a conclusion similar to that of Julie Reuben. He recounts this history primarily as it unfolds at the level of graduate education and argues that even though the science of religion was a scholarly enterprise aimed at winning a place for itself among the empirical sciences, it was so subordinated to religio-theological concerns that it was severely hindered in its development "as an autonomous, independent discipline" (1991: 107). "Comparative Religion's emergence in American universities," he concludes, "was inchoate and accompanied by occasional apologetic and moralistic motives." He continues:

> Its success, in terms of student enrollment, was due to the interest it held for ministers and theological students. It failed to garner a group of professional academicians with a Religionswissenschaft identity. It was, in short, hindered in its development by its auxiliary role for the professional training of theologians and ministers. An academic, humanistically based identity eluded its grasp until after World War II. (129)

Since the Second World War, the study of religion in the United States appears to have flourished remarkably. This success story, however, is not unambiguous; unclear is whether the resurgence of Religious Studies in the American university since that time is the resurgence of an independent, autonomous Science of Religion in the European sense or the resurgence of the apologetic religio-scientific undertaking dominant in the early modern American university. Reuben, while granting that the academic study of religion claimed to have become an independent scientific enterprise, accuses it of nevertheless having remained haunted by religious aspirations (1996: 142). And Shepard's suggestion that "an academic, *humanistically based* identity" (emphasis added) for *Religionswissenschaft* in the United States eluded the university's grasp until after World War II intimates the re-emergence of a richer enterprise than that of a discipline concerned with the mere description, analysis, and explanation of religious phenomena. The undertaking was "richer" in that its concern was not simply with the scientific truth about religion. For in addition, it was perceived to have a spiritual value. Furthermore, as D. G. Hart points out (1992: 207–208), in their defense of the study of religion students now drew support from the humanities by stressing, as did the humanists, the spiritual relevance of their studies to the natural sciences.

I shall argue here that the factors leading to the post World War II study of religion in higher education in the United States largely recalls the ambiguity of the earlier period. I will demonstrate that the "religious studies community" in America, while laying claim to scientific status for the enterprise in which it is engaged, and even though adding significantly to our scientific knowledge of religion, seems primarily intent upon establishing itself as a clerisy, a secularized group who express great anxiety about modern developments in society and who are dedicated to protecting the soul and spirit of humanity in what they see as a period of fragmentation and decay.[10]

A New Interest in Religion:
Re-establishing the Academic Study of Religion

Joseph Kitagawa attributes the sudden decline in the study of religion in the 1930s to "the impact of theological neo-orthodoxy, the depression, the impending war, and other factors" (1983: 556). Others have argued that it was the increasing role of the sciences in university education that in all likelihood played the most significant role in the decline. Conrad Cherry, for example, maintains that, in addition to the depressed economy and the concern over violating the First Amendment relating to the question of the separation of Church and State,[11] the increasing importance of science in the university curriculum and the poor quality of work in the study of religion relative to other disciplines led to the curtailment of the academic study of religion. "Above all," he writes,

> an American social order shaped by the natural sciences and technology contained little sympathy for an approach to the study of religion that was at best a pale imitation of scientific ideals in its claims to inductive method and practical importance. Observers of the role of the study of religion in higher education were forced to admit in the 1930s and 1940s that the large universities catering to the interests of diverse classes of American society were emphasizing 'the technical or vocational as distinct from the cultural' aspects of higher learning, and that even the denominational colleges were succumbing to the pressures of technical vocationalism. (1995: 101)

By the mid-1940s, however, Americans entered a period of anxiety in which the benefits of a scientific education were not as unalloyed as they had at one time appeared, and there was, as Cherry puts it, "a national turn to religion" (1995: 104). D. G. Hart similarly claims that religion gained leverage because of the fragmentation of the university science curriculum. He writes: "Generated by the crisis of the Second World War, many books and articles by mainline Protestant leaders appeared that picked up the sense of upheaval within American universities ... [and lamented] the increasing fragmentation of knowledge and the secularization of learning" (1992: 209).[12] University leaders once again looked to the study of religion as a way of providing coherence and meaning to their curriculum and of administering to the needs of the student. In 1943, for example, the American Council of Learned Societies (ACLS), although recognizing in the revival of religion the danger of indoctrination, nevertheless affirmed the value of religion to a liberal education. And, as Hart points out, this was obviously beneficial to the study of religion in the university, for the number of religious studies programs in the United States doubled between 1945 and 1960, with a corresponding increase in student enrollment (1992: 210–211). The scholarly study of religion that wrought this increase, then, was not the objective, scientific approach to religions in disinterested search of empirical discoveries or theoretical explanations. It was, in fact, a religio-theologically inspired study directed to the great themes and concerns of human existence. Indeed, according to Walter Capps, in his recently published *Religious Studies: The Making of a Discipline* (1995), it is possible to trace much of this resurgence of the scholarly study of religion in postwar America to the influence of one theologian:

> One can make a strong case for the contention that the academic study of religion gained sufficient intellectual stature to enter the world of the state or public university within the United States and Canada in the late 1950s and

1960s largely because of the Tillichian conceptualization of the theological enterprise. . . . In institution after institution, from Bloomington to Tallahassee to Missoula to Santa Barbara, many of the scholars and teachers who took the initiative in organizing religious studies were of a perceptible Tillichian mind. Most of them had been trained in Christian theology in seminaries and divinity schools. Consequently, the curricular models that became operational when such programs were inaugurated gave expression to intellectual transition: Tillich's theology gave its adherents forceful and clear access to the more inclusive cultural worlds, and in ways that could be sanctioned religiously and theologically. (289–290)

Kitagawa acknowledges that the scholarly study of religion received significant impetus from theologians in postwar America, and in particular he acknowledges the work of Paul Tillich as "[o]ne of the most serious attempts to set forth the principles of a 'Theological History of Religions' . . . (1983: 557). He also admits that a number of historians of religion in North America have been influenced by Tillich's normative approach to the study of religion. He does not, however, come to the conclusion drawn by Capps that theology was the main cultural force behind the rapid growth of the field of religious studies in the early postwar years; for Kitagawa it is essential to a proper understanding of the field that one admit a clear line of demarcation between theological and humanistic approaches to the study of religion. Thus, in looking at the causes behind the renewed interest in the History of Religions after the war, he lists, alongside "a new interest among influential theologians in a dialogue not only with Judaism but also with Eastern religions," "a sudden interest in things Eastern, including historic Asian religions and modern Eastern cults . . . [and] the growing fascination among some social scientists in non-Western myths, symbols, cults, social structures and cultural patterns . . ." (1983: 556), suggesting that the aim of the humanistic approach to the study of religion is significantly different from that of the theologian. The study of religion, he insists, is an autonomous discipline, and not simply a rubric covering a variety of related studies. It is neither a purely descriptive (scientific) enterprise nor a normative (religious) undertaking like philosophy or theology. Its primary concern, he claims, is with meaning, and it is directed toward achieving an integral understanding of the overall religious history of humanity. He admits, however, that such an inquiry into the meaning of religious phenomena reveals, paradoxically, both descriptive and normative aspects in its execution. Consequently, despite Kitagawa's claim that it is not theological, the humanistic study of religion is nevertheless a kind of religious undertaking: it is a religio-scientific enterprise that, as he put it in an earlier essay, ought to be a part of all institutions of higher education because " . . . in this bewildered world of our time, students ought to be exposed to some of the deepest issues of life, as they have been experienced and understood by the noblest men and women through the ages, in the East as well as in the West. . . . [I]t can widen the intellectual and spiritual horizons of students by bringing to them these deeper dimensions of life and culture in the dreams and faith by which men live" (1959: 30). Such a study, while not a form of sectarian theology, is still considerably more subjective than the scientific interest in description, analysis, and explanation of religious phenomena; thus it is essentially indistinguishable from a theological study of religion.[13]

This humanistic or scholarly study of religion, which Kitagawa takes such pains to distinguish from religion and theology, I suggest is really little more than another aspect of the "national turn to religion." Such a study of religion is no less religious than Tillich's "theological history of religion"; even if not, to be sure, a sectarian form of religion, it is nevertheless a liberal form of Protestantism.[14] And with its establishment in the Divinity School of the University of Chicago, it wielded immense influence in the development of the field of religious studies in colleges and universities throughout the United States. Although the re-establishment of this approach to the study of religions at Chicago must be attributed to the work of Joachim Wach,[15] the turning point in the growth of the Divinity School's national profile coincided with the arrival of Mircea Eliade in 1956. Indeed, given the power and range of Eliade's work, it is not entirely inappropriate to think of Eliade himself as a cultural force shaping the field, and therefore worthy of attention here.

In "A Tribute to Mircea Eliade" on the occasion of the establishment of a chair in his name, Frank Reynolds argued that because of Eliade's productivity, force of personality, and vision for the field of Religious Studies he "will stand as a model of, and a model for, the history of religions for many generations to come" (Reynolds, 1985: 21). Franklin Gamwell, on the same occasion, claimed "should the distant future decree that only one scholar of religion from our time shall be remembered, his constitutive influence upon the course of our enterprise will recommend that it be Mircea Eliade" (Gamwell, 1985: 19). Although these appraisals come from Eliade's colleagues in the Divinity School, I think the claims are justified with respect to the influence Eliade exerted on the field in the United States. And it is quite clear to those colleagues that his influence was one that advanced a study of religion directed at the enhancement of religion per se, and that therefore was wholly consistent with the aims of the Divinity School's overall mission. In his discussion of "Mircea Eliade and the Divinity School" on this occasion, Jerald Brauer, for example, commented upon Eliade's pleasure at being a member of the Faculty because it "permitted him the freedom to move ahead with the serious study of religions without having to argue the problem of the reality of the sacred or of religion itself" (Brauer, 1985: 27).

For Eliade the study of religion embraced more than a simple scientific or scholarly enterprise. Reynolds points out that the Eliaden vision "is not simply an exercise in scholarly erudition designed to address an audience of isolated academics [but rather] is itself an activity of cultural creation that dares to imagine the possibility of what Eliade has himself called 'a new humanism'" (Reynolds, 1985: 21). There is little to refute, then, in Brauer's contention that Eliade's coming to the Divinity School marks a third major phase in the development of the theological agenda of the School.[16] And there can be no doubt that the dominating influence of Eliade and Chicago on the development of the field was a religious and theological one. On this score Eric Sharpe's assessment is justifiable despite the fact that he maintains that "the Chicago hermeneutical programme was not meant as a counterblast to the IAHR's five principles [of the scientific study of religion]" (1986: 280). Sharpe insists that it widened considerably the scope of the historian of religions, and he goes on to say:

> Most important, it acknowledged that the historian of religions might find himself playing an active role in the world's cultural dialogue, rather than merely sitting on the sidelines as a disinterested observer; also it committed the scholar to a search for the inner meaning of religion, and not only to a quest for historical fact and circumstance. The 'objective' historian of religion was in danger, one feels, of being acknowledged as a skilled craftsman whose work might be admirable in itself, but who would have to learn new concerns and new techniques if he were to be of real significance in the new world. That some of the historians in question found difficulty in even understanding this position, much less in adopting it, is further evidence of a growing gulf between them and the new hermeneuts. (280)

Eliade's influence, Sharpe therefore asserts, was detrimental to those concerned with furthering the disinterested, objective study of religions, moving the study of religion in America away from the scientific ideals upheld by the IAHR (1986: 289).[17]

Professional Societies and Associations:
A Conflict of Interest in the Academic Study of Religion

Although the predominating influence on the development of the study of religion in the early postwar years was religious in intent, there was, nevertheless, some continuing concern with a more genuine scientific study of religion. The desire on the part of the theological and humanistic historians of religion for academic legitimation within the college and university, for example, has had a considerable effect upon the work of many scholars in the field; many of them, when not considering the Truth of religion, make valuable contributions to understanding various aspects of particular religious traditions from a scientific viewpoint. Reflective of this trend, a more direct concern for the scientific study of religion emerged in 1949 with the creation of the Committee for the Scientific Study of Religion (CSSR).[18] Early members of the Committee, and early statements of the Committee's goals, reveal some overlap between the aims of this group of scholars and the historians of religion already mentioned; but the evolution of the group reveals a serious disparity of views on "the problem of the relationship between the religious and scientific functions of the organization" (Newman, 1974: 138). Despite lack of overall consensus, however, as William Newman points out, "successive statements of goals place stronger emphasis upon the scientific rather than the apologetic aspect of studying religion" (1974: 139). "Similarly," Newman continues, "the transmission of scientific knowledge gains more and more ascendancy as an explicit goal as compared, for instance, to the earlier goal of increasing dialogue between social scientists and 'religious persons.'" (139). In 1955 the CSSR officially became the Society for the Scientific Study of Religion (SSSR), and the principle of maintaining its scientific status increased in importance, even though it often co-operated with religious functionaries on various research tasks, as Newman puts it (1974: 144). Having developed independently of the National Association of Biblical Instructors (NABI), it nonetheless became associated with NABI's successor organization, the American Academy of Religion (AAR). The same concern over the clash of theology with science plagued this relationship, however, and led finally to the "withdrawal of the Society for the Scientific Study of Religion in the mid-seventies from the alliance forged between the SBL [Society for Biblical Literature] and the AAR" (Alexander, 1988: 393).

It is also important to mention, as Murray G. Murphy points out in his essay "On the Scientific Study of Religion in the US, 1870–1980" (1989), that the scientific study of religion was very much alive elsewhere—in the social science departments of many colleges and universities. Murphy admits that the social sciences originally "took Christian doctrine as a premise and so considered religion not as a subject for study but as a frame of reference within which questions of human behavior were to be viewed" (1989: 136); and he argues that "the Darwinian revolution changed this situation" for psychologists, sociologists, and anthropologists (1989: 137). The work of social scientists on religion has not, however, achieved a high profile in the various social science professional organizations, and this mode of the study of religions has, therefore, not played a very large role in shaping the field of Religious Studies in the United States despite the significant influence of several prominent social science theorists such as Durkheim, Weber, and Freud. Interests of the social sciences obviously overlap significantly with interests of members of the SSSR, but Murphy makes no reference to this overlap. It is also worth noting that Murphy makes no allusion at all to the work of members of the societies and associations that emerged in connection with the work of the religiously and humanistically orientated students of religion, even though, in an important sense, they dominate the field of religious studies. It can be argued, therefore, that for Murphy, the work of historians of religion does not count as scientifically acceptable work.[19]

Despite this continuing interest on the part of some scholars in the historical and social-scientific study of religious phenomena, the influence of professional associations on the development of the study of religions in America has been from the outset primarily a religious one. By far the greatest number of societies and associations devoted to the field are confessional in nature (some of the more significant are the National Association of Baptist Professors of Religion, the Catholic Biblical Association, the Catholic Theological Society of America, and others, more recently formed, including the American Society of Missiology, the Society of Christian Ethics, and the North American Academy of Liturgy).[20] Others societies who claim a nonconfessional basis[21] such as the Society of Biblical Literature (originally the Society of Biblical Literature and Exegesis [SBLE], founded in 1880 with the change of name occurring in 1962) and the American Academy of Religion (originally the Association of Biblical Instructors in American Colleges and Secondary Schools, founded in 1909 with a change of name in 1922 to the National Association of Biblical Instructors and a further change of name to the American Academy of Religion in 1963)[22] began existence primarily as supports, in varying degrees, to teachers of religion in colleges and universities and were as much concerned with the religious lives of faculty and students as they were with the scholarly advancement of the field. Robert Funk, for example, pointed out in 1975 that the Society of Biblical Literature (SBL) was essentially "a fraternity of scientifically trained biblical scholars with the soul of a church" (Saunders, 1982: 69), for its members committed themselves to the scientific study of the biblical texts while accepting the texts as Scriptures. Ernest W. Saunders, in his history of the Society, claims that its first century of existence closed on the same note on which it had opened. "While heresy trials and teachers' oaths might be a thing of the past," he writes, "a resurgence of militant Fundamentalism, with political as well as ecclesiastical consequences, raised anew the question of whether the learned society is an arcane group whose members enjoy themselves in sealed isolation from public life or a sector that must accept responsibility for a larger world" (1982: 70). And the issue, he insists, will continue to plague future work of the Society because it turns on the divisive question of whether taking the Bible as normative for faith is compatible with its scientific study. "Historical criticism may not be bankrupt," he claims, "but the question of theological meanings of tradition and scripture both in the ancient situation and in the situation of the interpreter will continue to sue for recognition" (1982: 102).

The National Association of Biblical Instructors (NABI), although committed to sound scholarship, distinguished itself from its parent organization (the SBLE, see note 22), as primarily a support group for teachers of Bible and religion "in secondary schools, colleges, universities, and theological schools" (Mould, 1950: 14) rather than as a strictly scholarly society. In a paper on "The Function of the NABI," Ismar J. Peritz, a founding member of the organization, provided a description of its orientation in his claim "[o]urs is the delicate task to propagate the noblest ideals in the face of fundamentalism at one extreme and a materialistic and mechanical philosophy at the other" (Mould, 1950: 14). And a review of the titles of the early presidential addresses to the Association ("Biblical Instruction in Its Relation to Church Loyalty" [1927], "God's Continuing Revelation" [1938], "The Unity of the Bible" [1945]) confirms its religious intent and function.[23] The task of providing scientific knowledge about religions that would bring students face to face with the issues of truth, value, and the meaning of human existence remained the mandate of the Association into the 1960s.

The NABI, however, was not altogether satisfied with its image in the wider academic community, and in the early 1960s it created a self-study committee "both to determine the kind of public image [it wanted] to project and to increase the effectiveness of the Association" (Buck, 1962: 2). As a result of the Committee's deliberations, the Association changed its name to the American Academy of Religion (AAR), but it is clear that little else changed; the AAR, that is, essentially continued with the mandate of the NABI and retained all connections to other associations such as the American Association of Theological Schools (AATS).[24] And the AAR will continue with that agenda, as is clear from its recent Self-Study Committee Report (De Concini, et al., 1993a and b). Although the 1993 Report recommended some changes in the number of goals and aims of the Academy, their overall mandate is nevertheless essentially faithful to the original aims of the NABI: to support a scholarly study of religion that maintains and advances the concerns of religion.[25]

Although the majority of the organizations devoted to the support of the scholarly study of religion in the United States have some religious affiliation or intention, this is not true of all such groups. I have already referred, for example, to the formation of the SSSR in 1949 and its support of a strictly social-scientific approach to the study of religious phenomena. A decade later the American Society for the Study of Religion (ASSR) was formed at the second *ad hoc* meeting of a group of scholars representing a diversity of fields concerned with religion. The ASSR has remained small and has not taken on any of the tasks of a professional association. It has nevertheless been very influential in the support of the scientific study of religion in its close association with the International Association for the History of Religions (IAHR), forged within a few years of the ASSR's establishment. Not only did the ASSR sponsor, after a fashion, the eleventh International Congress of the IAHR, it has subsequently (until 1995) represented American historians of religion to the IAHR because until then there was no other organization in the United States interested in supporting that kind of scientific enterprise internationally. Given the AAR's professed interest in scientifically respectable scholarship in religion, one might have expected at least some degree of cooperation with the IAHR, but that simply has not happened. In fact, it seems as though there has always been a considerable degree of hostility in the attitude of the AAR toward the IAHR and its activities.[26]

It is because of this apparent hostility (and because for some the ASSR had in effect become a kind of "honor society")[27] that a new association emerged in an attempt to represent to the IAHR those North American scholars interested in the scientific study of religion. With this aim, the North American Association for the Study of Religion (known as "NAASR") was founded in 1985 and immediately sought affiliation to the IAHR, which it was granted at the 16th International Congress of the IAHR in Rome in 1990. Recognizing the role played by the AAR for the majority of scholars and teachers of religion in the United States, NAASR attempted to work co-operatively with the AAR to represent those of its members interested in the strictly scientific study of religion to the IAHR. Its request for affiliation with the AAR for this purpose, however, was rejected, and further attempts by NAASR to bring the AAR into a positive relationship with the IAHR have all failed, despite the recent claim by the executive director of the AAR, Barbara De Concini, that the AAR is committed "to genuine plurality, diversity, and inclusiveness—both as regards persons and as regards all the various sub-fields within the field of religion" (Frisinia, 1993a: 5).

Given the size of the AAR (and its sister organization, the SBL), which quite correctly describes itself as "the major learned society in the field" (De Concini, et al., 1993a: 4), it is quite obvious that the scientific study of religion in the United States is not likely to advance beyond the stage it reached in the late 1920s unless the AAR radically alters its goals and intentions. The combined membership of the SSSR, ASSR, and NAASR number fewer than 2000, whereas the membership of the AAR is 8000 and that of the SBL, 7000.[28] Given those numbers, there is an obvious danger that the approach to the study of religion taken by the AAR and the SBL will overshadow the scientific approaches promoted by the other organizations. This is not to deny all value to the research of scholars belonging to the AAR, the SBL, and other more confessional societies and associations; much of the work produced by members of those groups constitutes superb scientific undertakings. And given the large number of scholars involved, it is clear that the field of religious studies has greatly benefited from the existence of those organizations; since the 1960s, that is, this field has received considerably more attention than at any other time in its history. New fields and subfields of study have been created, and the increased specialization that has occurred has improved immensely our understanding of the range and character of religion.

Despite these advances, however, it is also clear that the field of religious studies still does not enjoy the academic prestige of other disciplines in the university. In a recent commentary on the renewed mission statement of the AAR, for example, it is acknowledged that departments of religion still find their existence challenged by their university colleagues. It is claimed, however, that this is at least partly because the AAR has not adequately made a case for what it does, nor adequately explained its value to colleagues, students, or the public at large (De Concini, et al., 1993a: 4). What is far more likely, I think, is that the case the field has made for itself is rejected because it is not a case for the Science of Religion within the university curriculum but rather a case for the value of religion itself—"scientific religion"—as a source of meaning and, therefore, as a means of remedying the fragmentation of the curriculum.

Religion and the Law:
A Scholarly or Scientific Study of Religion and Religions?

It has often been argued that developments in the interpretation of the First Amendment by the U.S. Supreme Court are largely responsible for the very rapid development of new programs and departments of religious studies in colleges and universities and for the consequent growth of the major professional organizations devoted to the study of religion. The First Amendment legislates against both interference with the free exercise of worship as well as the promotion and advancement of religion, and is often referred to as promulgating a doctrine of the separation of Church and State. The teaching of religion in public colleges and universities, therefore, is considered unconstitutional and consequently has often been seen as an impediment to the development of religious studies programs in such public institutions. Although no specific court case has yet dealt directly with the establishment and operation of departments of Religious Studies in public institutions of higher education, there are a number of U.S. Supreme Court decisions in which the justices, as David Fellman puts it, "have gone out of their way, in *obiter dicta*, to say . . . that public colleges and universities are free to give courses about religion that are not designed for indoctrination purposes" (Fellman, 1984: 83). One such case in the early 1960s had a particularly dramatic effect on the field of Religious Studies, even though its concern was merely with the practice of opening the school day in primary and secondary schools with a Bible reading and prayer. The decision in this case (*Abington School District* v. *Schempp* [1963]) reinforced the doctrine of the separation of Church and State but, as Robert Michaelson has noted, also resulted in the promotion of the study of religion in institutions of higher education. Michaelson quotes one of the justices writing for the Court as saying: "Nothing we have said here indicates that . . . study of the Bible or of religion, when presented objectively as part of a secular program of education, may not be effected consistently with the First Amendment" (1977: 295). This did not amount to establishing departments of Religious Studies in public institutions constitutionally, but many in the field never-theless seem to think that it did. Many, in fact, seem to think the Schempp case alone is responsible for the very rapid increase in the number of de-partments and programs in Religious Studies in the 1960s and 1970s. In his history of the discipline, Walter Capps notes that the case "reinforced the separation of church and state while adding legitimacy to the academic study of religion" (1995: 337). And Kathryn Alexander suggests that the Schempp case constituted a watershed in the development of the field in the United States, because it "altered the total picture of the study of reli-gion in America by introducing the language which has governed its subse-quent development in secular public colleges and universities" (1988: 389). Reference is usually made to the comments of Justice Goldberg who, going beyond the majority decision of the Court, argued that the government must be neutral with respect to religion, but that this means it cannot sim-ply ignore religion as if it had never existed. Religion, he therefore insisted, ought to be a part of one's education; but such education, in order to be neutral, must be a "teaching about" religion rather than a "teaching of" re-ligion (Michaelson, 1977: 295). And since Schempp, Goldberg's argument on the teaching *about* religion rather than the teaching *of* religion, Alexan-der correctly points out, has been repeatedly invoked in support of the cre-ation of departments and programs of religious studies in U.S. institutions of higher education.

There is a sense in which this influence of the legal implications of the First Amendment on the field of Religious Studies is really quite surpris-ing, given that the Court acknowledged as acceptable only the objective study of religion for academic (scientific) rather than religious purposes— few of the newly created programs, as has been made clear above, have re-stricted themselves to such study. There can be no doubt, moreover, that the major professional associations that support such programs move far beyond the boundaries placed on the study of religion permitted by the Court. An anecdote related by Robert Michaelson in a discussion of the

Court's attitude to the objective study of religions brings out clearly the conflict between the Court's ruling and many who are involved in programs of Religious Studies in America. "About ten years ago [the mid-1960s]," he writes, "at the height of the Berkeley Free Speech Movement, I quoted the Court's language—'objectively as part of a secular program in education'—in an address to a group of Danforth and Kent fellows, all graduate students. Their reaction was stormy. *Objectivity* had become by then a very bad word and a totally unacceptable notion" (1977: 295–296; emphasis in the original). Michaelson's response to that event ten years later still suggests that the student of religion in the United States need not take the matter of the separation of Church and State—of the "teaching of" and "teaching about" religion—too seriously, all the while invoking decisions of the Court in support of the public establishment of programs of Religious Studies. He admits that the notion of objectivity in the Court's decision cannot be dismissed out of hand, but he attempts to diminish its significance by equating the notion of objectivity with "a completely detached, mechanistic, and inhuman stance" (Michaelson, 1977: 296). He then concludes: "If 'open, free, critical, and scholarly' can be taken as legitimate extensions into the academic realm of 'objectively,' 'neutral,' and 'secular' from the judicial . . . then scholars in religious studies should have nothing to fear from court decisions in this area" (298). W. Royce Clark, however, views this whole matter quite differently, and, I think, more astutely. Although he notes that Supreme Court decisions may have required public education not only to assist students to be critical but also to inculcate values in them that will help them to become good citizens, such inculcation of values ought not to be of a religious nature. Aware of the character of most religious studies programs in American colleges and universities, Clark expresses concern for them should the Court ever rule directly on their legality, and he advises a reconsideration of the usual defense of their programs on the basis of the "teaching about"/"teaching of" distinction (1990: 112). He complains, moreover, that the Schempp *dicta* have forced an impossible task upon teachers of religion not imposed on other disciplines; namely, that of sustaining pure objectivity in their research and teaching. In doing this, he argues, the Court has espoused a notion of objectivity as an "ultimate concern" that is in conflict with and detrimental to religion. For Clark, as for most others in the field in the United States today, it appears, the study of religion must not show itself inimical to faith, and a scientific study of religion simply does not abide by such a principle.

What is clear in regard to the issue of the First Amendment is that the Supreme Court has in fact provided support for the creation of a Science of Religion and for the teaching about religion in public institutions of higher education,[29] but that despite this support, the development of such an enterprise has not really got off the ground. Rather, the religiously orientated study of religion that was already in place in many colleges and universities, and sanctioned by organizations such as the AAR and the SBL, appropriated the ruling of the Court for their own approaches by reinterpreting the notions of objectivity, neutrality, and secularity that lay at the heart of the Court's decisions. Its thriving, moreover, in large part accounts for the lack of any significant advance in the scientific study of religion in the departments of religious studies in American colleges and universities.

Religion Reaffirmed:
The Postmodernist Challenge to the Science of Religion

Despite the ascendance of a religiously orientated study of religion in American colleges and universities, there is still considerable dissatisfaction among its practitioners with respect to its status in the university community. It appears, that is, that it has not achieved the academic respectability they had expected; although accepted as part of the university curriculum, the study of religion is still regarded as suspect by many within the scientific community. In 1991, for example, the AAR commissioned Ray Hart to undertake a review of the field because it appeared to them that Religious Studies in higher education was becoming marginal and that this was occurring because many in academia saw it as concerned with inculcating religious knowledge rather than undertaking the scientific study of religion (1991: 723). Barbara De Concini, Executive Director of the AAR, noted in an interview, moreover, "[r]eligion doesn't enjoy the self-evidence of other disciplines in the humanities and social sciences" (Frisinia, 1993a: 5), although she maintains that this is due to ignorance of the nature of the discipline rather than to a thorough knowledge of it. A similar judgment is reiterated in a commentary on the report of the 1993 AAR Self-Study Committee in two issues of *Religious Studies News* (De Concini, 1993a and b). And the authors of "Religious Studies and the Redefining Scholarship Project: A Report of the AAR Committee on 'Defining Scholarly Work'" (Myscofski, 1993) subsequently wrote:

> Religious Studies, however defined or wherever located, remains suspect in the eyes of many within the rest of the academy and continually finds itself marginalized or otherwise obscured due to the fact and/or perception of blurred boundaries between studying religion and being religious, or between education about and education in religion. (7)

This recognition of the academic marginality of their discipline, however, has not encouraged leaders of the AAR to seek a rethinking of the field to give it the scientific orientation it needs if it is to achieve the academic recognition it so craves. Following that path, it seems, would require more than they are willing to give up, for it would require them to reject the notion that they can "blend" religion with the "Science of Religion" in such a fashion that the enterprise would be of significance to our lives and not simply make a contribution to our empirical and theoretical knowledge of religions and religion. Along with the other humanities, their discipline, according to most American students of religion, involves not only research directed at obtaining knowledge but also a concern for the formation of the student as a whole person. This view finds collective expression, for example, in Stephen Crites's "Liberal Learning and the Religion Major," a report written on behalf of the AAR Task Force on the Study in Depth in Religion, undertaken in co-operation with a national review of Majors in the Arts and Sciences initiated by the Association of American Colleges. "The quest about religion," according to Crites,

> plunges the student into the densest and most elusive issues of value, introduces the student into an ancient and enduring conversation, not always peaceful, about ultimately serious matters, engages the imagination of the student in the most daring imaginative ventures of human experience. . . . For many students it is a disciplined encounter with an order of questioning that has affinities with their own struggles for personal identity. It is one way of joining the human race. (1990: 13)

Crites is quick to point out that the aim of the study of religion is not to convince students to join any particular religious tradition—that would be unacceptable sectarianism—but he nevertheless insists that the study of religion must assist students in discovering that religion makes sense and that "the sense it makes enlarges her or his own horizon of human possibility" (1990: 14). And that, obviously, is an apology of sorts for religion. Crites is not unaware of the Supreme Court ruling in the Schempp case requiring a clear distinction between teaching of religion and teaching about religion, but he chooses to read that ruling not as banning in-depth involvement with religion but only the study of religion for sectarian purposes (1990: 4). And Ray Hart points out in his report, to which reference is made above, that a clear decision on the part of the AAR as to whether it represents and promotes a Science of Religion or a "blended" study of religion combining both the study and promotion of religion could be disastrous for the AAR, and, presumably, for the various programs of Religious Studies, because it would alienate a large part of its clientele. Hart insists, that is, that "any heavy weighting to either side [of this debate] risks alienating students drawn to the other (not to mention dishonouring the virtues the field is claimed to inculcate: tolerance, pluralism, respect for opposing positions, etc.)" (1991: 790).[30]

Although taking such a path, the AAR nevertheless attempts to make a case for its brand of Religious Studies not only as a scholarly discipline, but as the only truly scientific study of religions. This is so, it is argued, because, unlike the so-called scientific students of religion, its members have recognized the illusory character of claims to objectivity in scientific research. Barbara De Concini insists, therefore, that we can no longer assume "a clear distinction separating scholarship from advocacy" and claims, furthermore, that "the Academy welcomes all disciplined reflection on religion" (1993a: 5). Her sentiments are echoed in a discussion of the seventh aim of the new AAR mission statement contained in the 1993 Self-Study Committee report captioned "To Welcome into Our Conversation the Various Voices in the Field of Religion" (De Concini, 1993a: 4). Recognizing that the membership of the AAR includes not only university professors but seminary professors as well as members of churches and other fields outside the higher education framework, the AAR, it is claimed, must remain committed to keeping this conversation going, "[w]elcoming scholarship that cannot be separated easily from advocacy (e.g., feminist, theological), while at the same time promulgating the policy and practice that scholarship in the Academy opens itself to criticism and makes itself vulnerable to correction through public discourse and scholarly exchange" (De Concini, 1993a: 2). This, however, is merely *conversation;* it is not science. What determines "knowledge" here is not critical thought involving "conjecture and refutation," but rather *negotiation* among various advocacy groups posing as scholarly discourse within the academy.[31] Clearly, then, the AAR has decided to resolve its internal conflict not by simply rejecting the objective, nonadvocacy approach to the study of religion in favor of its religious approach to that study, but by attempting to show that such an objective approach is not good science. As Martin Marty put it some years ago, those so-called scientific students of religion still "cherish a scientific ideal which other humanities and the social sciences no longer seek" (1983: 83). They are, he insists, avant-garde religionists who fail to recognize that the scientific-enlightenment culture to which they are committed is a culture in serious crisis—in fact, a culture in demise.

In the face of this crisis, then, it might be suggested that postmodernism is to be the savior of the religiously orientated study of religion; indeed, in showing that science as it once was conceived is not possible because objectivity is impossible, one presumes that the alternative, "religio-scientific" study of religion, is as scientific as anything else. In a recent article, Frank Reynolds echoes Marty's sentiments when he claims that we can no longer believe "that the Enlightenment mode of rationality provides a prejudice-free mechanism for discerning and exploring the factual truth about the one purely objective natural and social world in which human beings, whether they know it or not, are destined to live" (1990b: 11). For Reynolds this is clear because we are now critically aware of our socio-historical context, which includes recognition of the constructed character of all social reality. He allows that we might still retain for practical purposes the differentiation between natural sciences, social sciences, and humanities, but he insists that "there would be no unbridgeable gap between the three segments; nor would there be an implicit hierarchy that ranked them in terms of their conformity to a single ideal of purely 'objective' rationality" (1990: 14). A so-called scientific perspective on religion, therefore, would really be structurally indistinguishable from any other perspective on religion. It is little wonder, then, that members of the AAR have been so quick to espouse postmodernism, for the latter is clearly antiscientific. Nor is it any wonder that, with the ascendance of the AAR as the major professional organization representing the study of religion in colleges and universities, the scientific study of religion in the United States has languished to the extent it has.

Conclusion

The scholarly study of religion in the United States has experienced a renewal of interest since the 1940s that until recently[32] has been sustained at high levels. Today there exist in the United States more than 1200 college and university departments of religious studies, numerous societies and associations devoted to the support of research in one area or another of the field,[33] and well over 15,000 scholars and teachers whose primary academic commitments and responsibilities are devoted to this discipline. With the increase in the number of scholars working in the field and of the number of organizations dedicated to assisting their research, the discipline showed great promise at mid-century and beyond. There were gains in terms of the increased breadth of interest in the field, and a significant increase in sustained attention to non-Western religious traditions and comparative studies.[34] The development of specializations enriched the field, encouraging a depth of knowledge in a wide range of issues and themes. And the ever present concern for academic legitimation and scientific status within the broader university community held out the promise of growth in methodological sophistication that would lead to progress in the conception of the field as a bona fide scientific enterprise, genuinely distinguishing the field of religious studies from religion and freeing it from apologetic burden and a redemptive agenda. That promise, however, has not been fulfilled. Scholars in this field, unfortunately, generally perceive themselves not simply as scientists seeking and transmitting knowledge about and explanations of religious phenomena, but rather as humanists charged with the "understanding" and advancement of religion as an element in the overall formation of their students, and through them, of culture and society.[35] Hence the recent, rather persistent concern with the scholar as "public intellectual"[36] among students of religion in the United States, and the insistence that the responsibilities of the student of religion include three publics rather than one: the *ecclesia* and the republic as well as the academy.[37] This is, I believe, to conceive of the students of religion, and other humanists, as a clerisy for the university and for the nation: as persons who have a kind of spiritual power that makes them capable of achieving an integrated view of all disciplines in the university curriculum and of providing for the social welfare of society at large. It appears in this view that the only student of religion "who takes religion seriously" is the one who is religiously engaged. Wilfred Cantwell Smith puts the point succinctly: "The study of religion is no longer an idle curiosity, but has begun to be a recognized aspect of the total intellectual Quest. And not only of some armchair intellectual quest. It is an integral aspect of the quest for a viable world: the practical problem of what we all are to do about it" (1995: 9).

The developments in the study of religion in the United States over the last half-century or so, then, are in the final analysis a disappointment; for the potential and promise of many of those developments were subordinated in service of other goals than academic and scientific.

Notes

1. I wish here to thank Luther Martin for his critical comments on earlier drafts of this essay, and Martha Cunningham for her critical comments and editorial assistance with the final version.

2. What I mean by "science of religion" and "the scientific study of religion" is clearly and concisely delineated by Claude Welch in his book *Protestant Thought in the Nineteenth Century, Vol. 2, 1870–1914* (1985):

   In the literature we have been examining, the term *science of religion* (Müller, Tiele, Tischhauser, Jordan) is for all practical purposes interchangeable with the term *history of religion* (Réville, Chantepie de la Saussaye, d'Alviella, Tiele, Moore) and *study of religion* (Jastrow). What does this term *science* mean in this context, beyond the free and impartial spirit of inquiry? Plainly, it was intended to suggest the emergence of a discipline of study comparable to the sciences of anthropology and philology (among the *Geisteswissenschaften*) and even to the natural sciences. It means the thoroughgoing application of a principle of criticism to all religion(s) considered as phenomena of human experience (hence *Religionswissenschaft* rather than *wissenschaftliche Theologie*). (133)

3. My comments on this period of the history of higher education in the United States rest on the work of W. Clark Gilpin (1996) and Conrad Cherry (1992, 1995). For the remainder of this brief historical account I

draw heavily from Julie Reuben (1995, 1996), D. G. Hart (1992), Conrad Cherry (1995), and Robert S. Shepard (1991).

4. Reference to cited material will appear in the text of the essay.

5. George Marsden (1992, 1994, 1997) argues that the academy has been secularized and that a disestablishment of religion in American colleges and universities took place during this period. As this account will show, however, his thesis is not persuasive; such a claim is valid only to the extent that the control of institutions of higher education once wielded by American Protestantism has certainly declined. A diminution of "sectarian" control, however, cannot be equated with the rout of religion from higher education.

6. I assume agreement here on the importance of academic freedom in the growth and development of the modern research university and will not, given limitations of space, elaborate on that matter here.

7. The ambiguity of this situation is captured by Frank E. Reynolds (1990b). He admits that *Religionswissenschaft* emerged in the early modern period of the university but correctly points out that it "had great difficulty establishing its scientific credibility" and so was "not able to carve out for itself a viable space within the institutional structure of American universities" (8). Drawing on R. Shepard's doctoral thesis, "The Science of Religion in American Universities 1880–1930: A Comparison of Six Universities" (later published as *God's People in the Ivory Tower: Religion in the Early American University* [1991]), Reynolds talks of "the aborted attempt to establish *Religionswissenschaft* in American universities at the end of the 19th and the beginning of the 20th centuries" (8n7).

8. Conrad Cherry's claim that most scholars of religion wished to blend "the aims of scientific study with the practice of piety and training in religious leadership" (1995: 100) is an accurate description of the effect of an apologetic science of religion.

9. The Parliament was influential, that is, in stirring up public interest in other religions, which in turn stimulated an interest in the study of religion per se, certainly of benefit to the universities and divinity schools; but the study fostered thereby was not a comparative study of religions but rather an interreligious dialogue. James A. Kirk's claim that over the course of time the World's Parliament of Religions "led to the International Association for the History of Religions, which continues to this day" (1993: 133–134) is simply wrong. As Eric Sharpe points out, scientific students of religion, even though they may have been involved in the 1893 Parliament, held themselves "aloof from any further such gatherings simply on the grounds that whatever the need for inter-religious understanding, the scientific study of religion, committed to the quest of truth for truth's own sake, ought not to be saddled with such an onerous and subjective incidental" (1986: 139). This was to become, in a sense, a major bone of contention between American and European students of religion in the mid-1960s; see note 17 below.

10. Ben Knights states in his study of the idea of the clerisy in the nineteenth century : "Amid the encroachments of chaos the function of the clerisy was to

maintain a cosmos in which literature and history made sense and in which, consequently, human actions and aspirations would still have meaning" (1978: 13). Access by the clerisy to such a cosmos, for Knights, transcends "dependence on naturalistically conditioned knowledge" (20). The clerisy, therefore, had a noumenal basis that enabled it to represent and bring unity to a badly fragmented world. A clerisy, in other words, takes on the social and moral functions of religion, providing the world with a set of commitments and values that anchor the world, so to speak, during a time of peril. The notion of a group possessed of a wisdom sufficient for such a task, according to Knights, is deeply rooted in Renaissance humanism. He claims, moreover, that such a function requires an institutional framework: "An institutionally based clerisy is necessary," he writes, "because the prevailing social pressures are inimical to enlightenment; in the face of a materialist civilization, high mental culture (which is that civilization's hope) does not stand a chance" (199). Only such an institution, for example, can bring about the subordination of the sciences to the humanities. Consequently, the domain of the clerisy is not the university but the faculty of humanities specifically; for only the humanist scholar can protect against wholesale symbolic collapse and insure the dominance of the higher elements of the mind (see 220).

It appears, as I will elaborate below, that the student of religion in America—sometimes in concert with other humanists—conceives of those who study religion as a clerisy and the enterprise in which they are engaged as a kind of theology.

11. Robert Michaelson writes: "The law of the land, stated at the beginning of the First Amendment, is that 'Congress shall make no law respecting an establishment of religion or prohibiting the free exercise thereof. . . . ' That is the controlling doctrine [regarding the separation of Church and State]. All U.S. Supreme Court decisions in this area revolve around it" (1977: 293).

12. Hart sees this as a mere continuation of earlier policy in which a variety of organizations such as the American Association of Colleges and the National Association of Biblical Instructors worked to have religion itself, rather than the study of religion, considered a viable component of liberal education. Thus Protestant justifications were now bolstered by the defense invoked by humanists on behalf of the humanities: that religion provided an integrating spiritual focus to an otherwise fragmented science curriculum. Hart writes: "Two organizations that built upon Protestant extracurricular activities and began to give more credibility to the study of religion were the American Association of Colleges [AAC], and the National Association of Biblical Instructors [NABI]. These bodies were especially influential in establishing a consensus among educators that provided religious studies with a coherent framework" (1992: 205). More will be said below about the influence of these and other societies in the growth of the study of religion in American institutions over the past five decades.

13. I use the phrase "theological study of religion" in a broad sense to refer not only to studies informed by a sectarian view of the world but also to studies

based on the assumption of the existence of a reality beyond the bounds of the natural world available to scientists.

14. It is helpful to keep in mind here that in its extreme form, such liberal Protestantism came to pervade American culture and can be said to have become a form of civil religion. And a study of religion operating from within the framework of such a broad cultural Protestantism is still a theological rather than a scientific study of religion; see note 13 above.

15. Time does not permit analysis here of the influence of Wach on the development of the study of religion at the University of Chicago. Although of considerable importance his influence on the national development of the field was negligible because of his premature death in 1955.

16. According to Brauer, William Rainey Harper's expectation of the Divinity School at its founding was twofold: that the school would educate people for thoughtful ministry and that it would "advance knowledge in religion through the pursuit of rigorous scholarly research" (1985: 27). The first phase of the School's development, he claims, was dominated by the historical method characteristic of its approach to the study of theology through the 1930s. In the second phase—lasting through the 1950s—systematic and constructive approaches dominated the organizing principle of the institution, and the Divinity School was identified during that period as a center of process theology. The third phase was initiated with the arrival of Eliade in Chicago and was marked by a return to historical analysis, although, as Brauer puts it, "of a new kind" (27). Brauer writes:

> Eliade's fundamental concern not to reduce the reality of religion to any other phenomenon, his insistence that the central concern of the total faculty was to understand, interpret, and analyze the reality of the sacred, his affirmation that religion represents a distinct and particular way of living in the cosmos, his search for the manifestation of the sacred in concrete and particular forms, his insistence on locating and analyzing the universals within the particulars without dissolving or reducing the particulars, his subtle and imaginative elaboration of the meaning and structure of myth and symbol—all of these activities came to pervade the life of every area or field in the Divinity School. . . . If one wishes to argue that this marked a shift from theological to religious studies, that is one way to designate the change; however, it must be done with great subtlety. (27)

17. The Chicago school is as influential today as it was during Eliade's time, as can be seen from the concerns of the "Berkeley-Chicago-Harvard Program" mentioned by Frank Reynolds and Cheryl Burkhalter in their introduction to *Beyond the Classics? Essays in Religious Studies and Liberal Education* (Reynolds, 1990a). As they put it, the program "aimed at enlarging the role and scope of religious studies in the undergraduate liberal arts program," meaning by that the development of an "expansive vision" of Religious Studies that would see its courses serve "as integrators for the humanities and so-

cial sciences." And there can be no doubt about the hegemonic intent of the Chicago approach to the field. "Taken as a whole," write Reynolds and Burkhalter, "the essays in this volume convey the basic commitments and perspectives of the Chicago group. It is our hope that when the essays are read as a unit, these basic commitments and perspectives will prove convincing not only to those involved in religious studies, but to administrators and teachers in other areas as well" (xiii).

18. This CSSR (1949) is not to be confused with the later Council of Societies for the Study of Religion (1969), an umbrella organization formed, with assistance from the American Council of Learned Societies (ACLS), to coordinate the projects of the various societies and associations related to Religious Studies and to help avoid duplication.

19. I find Murphy's judgment about the promise of the social sciences to achieve a theoretical understanding of religion is rather dismal. Perhaps resulting from a poverty of theoretical development over the value of various categorical schemas employed, there was, and is, he argues, a marked lack of agreement on what is being studied, on the approaches adopted by the various social sciences, and finally on their relative achievements. A field so promising at its emergence and throughout its early period of development, he insists, now looks much less promising; although he does allow that with a change of focus on the units of analysis used by scholars the situation could well improve. Murphy's views on the future of the social scientific study of religion, therefore, seem to bring him into more favorable alignment with the humanistic—and even theological—historian of religions; thus he undermines the very notion of a genuinely scientific study of religion. This is unfortunate because he ignores a great deal of theoretical development in the study of religion, much of which has come from advances in the cognitive sciences. In this regard, see E. Thomas Lawson and Robert McCauley (1990), Stewart Guthrie (1993), Pascal Boyer (1993, 1994), Dan Sperber (1996), Rodney Stark and William Sims Bainbridge (1987), and Lawrence Young (1997), among others.

20. These organizations are all members of the Council of Societies for the Study of Religion (CSSR).

21. One might here usefully distinguish "capital-c" from "small-c" confessionalism, using the former designation to refer to societies and associations directly connected to religious organizations, and leaving the latter designation to refer to those groups that assume the existence of some transcendent religious reality but that do not have a direct affiliation with any other religious (sectarian) body.

22. Ernest W. Saunders writes: "What's in a name? The 1962 meeting thought that it was not without significance. By majority consent an abbreviated form of the historical title was adopted; henceforth the organization would be known as the Society of Biblical Literature. A descendant organization [of the SBLE] followed suit a year later: the National Association of Biblical Instructors was christened the American Academy of Religion" (1982: 53). It

will become clear below that the changes of name were essentially a concern with image-management—the apparent religious orientation of the names of these groups, it seems, hindered their achieving broader academic recognition in the university community.

23. It is interesting to note that Charles Foster Kent, who was president of the NABI from 1910 to 1925, was also the founder of the National Council of Schools of Religion in 1922, which was dedicated not only to improving the quality of religious teaching in colleges and universities, but also to enhancing the spiritual lives of teachers and students. Kent did not differentiate between Religious Studies in university and in the divinity school. This organization is still alive and active, although it has gone through several changes of name: National Council on Religion in Higher Education (1924), Society of Religion in Higher Education (1962), and Society for Values in Higher Education (1976). It was in effect an organization through which Protestant divinity schools attempted to influence the course of higher education in America by strengthening the role of religion in the undergraduate curriculum. Religion was to provide the integrating factor in an otherwise fragmented university curriculum.

24. Argument and evidence in support of this claim is to be found in my essay "Against Science in the Academic Study of Religion: On the Emergence and Development of the AAR" (forthcoming; and chapter 14 in this volume).

25. I find exaggerated the claims of scholars such as D. G. Hart (1992), George Marsden (1994), and Conrad Cherry (1995) that the change of name from NABI to AAR signaled a major shift in the nature of the kind of "religious studies" to which it gave support. In particular, I would deny that it signaled in any significant way a move toward a secularized, scientific study of religion. I have set out arguments to that effect in "Against Science in the Academic Study of Religion," cited in note 24, as well as in "A Religious Agenda Continued: A Review of the Presidential Addresses of the AAR" (1997a and chapter 15 in this volume). There is a sense, however, in which Stephen Crites's claim has merit that the change of name signaled a substantive change in the Association, because it brought about a radical alteration in the way Religious Studies was taught on many campuses; but the change was little more than a move from an avowedly sectarian (Protestant) approach to a generically broader religious approach to the field.

26. The 11th International Congress of the IAHR, it is of interest to note, was not sponsored or supported by the AAR. Arrangements for the Congress, it appears, were made by members of the then recently formed ASSR, although the ASSR did not formally sponsor the Congress. What is clear is that there was sufficient difference of opinion between American and European scholars about the nature of the academic study of religion to lead to the resignation of at least one of the Congress's organizers (see Sharpe, 1986: 286). The tension is clearly seen in the opening address to the Congress by C. J. Bleeker, Secretary General of the IAHR. Speaking about the theme of the Congress (or at least one major symposium in the Congress—

"The Impact of Modern Culture on Traditional Religion"—and on the formulation of that theme sent to prospective participants in the final circular before the meeting took place), Bleeker expressed concern with the subsequently formed question for discussion at the Congress: "What can critical scholarship contribute to a better understanding of the problem raised by contemporary relations among religions?" Bleeker insisted that the IAHR was not the appropriate forum for such a question. Other organizations such as the World Fellowship of Faiths or the World Council of Churches, he noted, have such a mandate, but not the IAHR. Consequently he proceeded to "introduce" the American scholars to "the spirit and the work of this organization [the IAHR]" as a scientific enterprise. He went on at length to say:

The I.A.H.R. has always drawn a sharp borderline between its own activities and those of the organization I have just mentioned. The primary object of the I.A.H.R. is purely scientific research in the extensive field of the history of religions. The historians of religion belong to different churches, confessions and religions, or do not adhere to any special form of belief. One of the fascinating features of our organization is exactly that we respect one another as scholars without any reservation and that we fully co-operate in research for scientific truth. Therefore we should refrain from making statements which in their religious aspect possess a normative bearing. Neither can it be expected that the symposium will yield resolutions suggesting an actual solution of the problem at stake. However, historians of religion who really keep in touch with what happens on the stage of the world, cannot remain unmoved in regard to this crucial issue. They will feel obliged to let others, who wrestle with these problems, profit from their knowledge. That is the sense of this symposium. Our contribution to the solution is rather modest. It consists in the right answer to the question: what can critical scholarship contribute to a better understanding of the problems raised by contemporary relations among religions? (Bleeker, 1968: 4–5).

Some American scholars (particularly those of non-Western, non-Christian traditions) saw this attitude of the IAHR as condescending and offensive—one presumes because many at the Congress wished to speak in a directly relevant way on the problems of the relations of religions. But it also offended the Americans, it appears, because the ideal of a disinterested, objective scholarship in religion clashed with their own ideal of "involved" scholarship and they objected to being lectured by the Europeans on how to be more scholarly. Others, however, saw the holding of the Congress in America as a sign of the maturation of the science of religion in the United States. As R. Michaelson put it, "[t]his event symbolized the fact that the history of religions is well on its way toward becoming an established discipline in America" (1967: 13). This was, nevertheless, a minority opinion. As Eric J. Sharpe has noted, "in a great deal of what was said and done at

Claremont it was clear that the ideal of disinterested, objective scholarship *for its own sake*, while not abandoned, had been relegated to a position of only relative importance" (1986: 284). In further describing the aftermath of the Congress Sharpe writes: "I do not propose to dwell on this unfortunate episode, except to note that for a few years thereafter, the history of religions in America and on the continent of Europe tended to drift apart" (1986: 286). I think it would be more accurate to say that the history of religions practiced in Europe and America had never actually been very close to begin with, and that after this "unfortunate episode" the relationship that had existed simply soured and has remained in that state to this day. I have described something of that relationship in my earlier essays on the AAR (Wiebe forthcoming a and 1997a, chapters 14 and 15 in this volume). For further information on the nature of this rift, see Charlotte Allen's "Is Nothing Sacred: Casting Out the Gods from Religious Studies" (1996).

27. Some would dispute the suggestion that the ASSR is an honor society. Conversation with those who were involved in the founding of the Society provides clear indication that it was not established as such. It is equally clear, however, that over the years it has come to operate as if it were an honor society in that it has severely restricted its membership by means of a peculiar set of rules for the election (and "non-election") of members; refusing to take on responsibility to represent all American scholars who have an interest in being associated with the IAHR. The Society voluntarily relinquished its membership in the IAHR in 1995 because it recognized that it did not represent American scholars committed to IAHR principles for the study of religion and acknowledged that it had no intention of changing its character in order to do so.

28. The ASSR limits itself to roughly 100 members; NAASR, although it has approximately 200 on its membership list, has only slightly over 50 dues-paying members; and the SSSR has 1300 United States members and 260 international members. There is some overlap of membership among these organizations.

29. It is important to bear in mind here that a distinction is made in the Court decisions between, on the one hand, primary and secondary institutions, and, on the other, colleges and universities, with respect to what is appropriate to teach students at different stages of maturity (see Fellman, 1984: 82–84).

30. Although Hart's report to the AAR recommended that the AAR/SBL develop a meaningful dialogue between members holding these opposing points of view, nothing of lasting significance developed from the sessions devoted to this debate at several annual meetings of the AAR. Nor were members from other, opposing, societies and associations (the SSSR, the IAHR, or the NAASR, for example) invited to participate in these brief public forums; working sessions at committee and board levels across association boundaries were rejected by the leaders of the AAR. Indeed, instead of working in co-operation with the IAHR at the international level, the AAR

looked rather to creating an international version of itself (on this see R. Hart [1991: 790–791], and Wiebe [1993b]).

31. See William Scott Green (1992, 1994b, 1996), Warren Frisinia (1993a), Richard B. Miller *et al.* (1994), and Richard B. Miller (1996).

32. R. Hart (1991: 724), for example, refers to the apparent recent marginalization of religious studies. See here also the essays in *Pathologies in the American Study of Religion: North American Institutional Case Studies*, edited by Gary Lease, a special issue (7/4[1995]) of *Method and Theory in the Study of Religion.*

33. There is a serious need for a thorough history of these organizations and their relationships to each other if an adequate account of the development of the academic study of religion in the United States is to be rendered.

34. The situation here is not without ambiguity. Van A. Harvey (1970), for example, pointed out that although non-Christian studies entered the curriculum they were not allowed substantially to inform the development of the field; he insisted that such studies were essentially "tack-ons" to a fundamentally seminary-type curriculum. He argued, moreover, that "[t]his was reinforced by regarding study of religion as belonging primarily to the humanities—aimed at helping students come to grips with their own life posture" (25). Eighteen years later William R. Darrow (1988) made a similar claim about the style of religious studies at Harvard University. Even though comparative religion courses were fostered at Harvard in the 1960s, there are still a number of noteworthy features about the study of religion there that show it to be tied "to the continuing unfolding of the Protestant heritage in this place" (233–234). This situation still exists at Harvard today.

35. William Scott Green, for example, espouses the same goal as the NABI and as Peritz raises in the discussion above: namely, to protect the student from fundamentalist religion and a mechanistic (nonreligious) philosophy. Green writes: "By depicting belief in God as inherently lowbrow and intellectually unworthy, we make one of the most serious and persistent of human questions seem immune to critical reflection, and we also give religious communities license to dismiss the value of academic inquiry in their own lives and thought" (1996: 27).

36. On this point see Cady (1993) and Dean (1994).

37. See Martin E. Marty (1985). The scientific agenda does not transcend the religious; in fact it is in some sense determined by the religious agenda. Marty writes: "To yield all to the academics [by which I assume he means scientists] might be to obscure commitment to religion. To yield all to the religionists might be to produce a clerisy or theocracy. The interaction profits all" (9). Yet he admits that the concern of the *ecclesia* is to present a coherent worldview, and it is difficult to see how interaction between such a worldview and the *ecclesia* could do anything but undermine the academic enterprise, especially since, according to Marty, the "[t]eaching about religion instead of teaching religion is its own kind of quasi-credal commitment" (8).

Chapter Seven

~ひな~

Religious Studies as a Saving Grace?
From Goodenough to South Africa[1]

In this paper I will not concern myself directly with the complex relationship between socio-political change and religious transformation in society at large. Instead I shall focus on methodological concerns arising in the study of religion, which of necessity must also analyze the nature of such relationships. In so doing I am indirectly taking up the theme of our conference, for such methodological clarification will involve analysis of a variety of claims about the nature of the socio-political structures within which the academic study of religion takes place, and of the implications of those claims. Indeed, a fundamental question arises as to whether such socio-political structures are, in fact, involved in personal or social "religious transformations" at all—or ought to be.

The official policy of departments for the study of religion in the academic setting is that this enterprise, like others in the university, belongs to the cognitive-scientific domain alone and should not serve to further religious, cultural, political, or other ends. As I have shown elsewhere, it was because of the adoption of such a scientific framework, clearly demarcated from religio-theological concerns, that the study of religion succeeded in achieving the academic legitimation it sought from the university.[2]

Though this policy was not officially a part of the institutionalization of the academic study of religion in the International Association for the History of Religions at its inception, when the Association found many theological and religious matters appearing on the agenda of its periodic congresses, a five-point statement was formulated by R. J. Z. Werblowsky, giving "the basic minimum presuppositions" for the pursuit of historical and comparative studies of religion.[3] According to the statement (signed by a number of members of the IAHR), the academic student of religion engages in a scientific discipline: to study religious phenomena as empirical facts of human existence and history and not as embodiments of transcendent truth—this despite its classification among the Humanities within the university structure. Such study naturally rejects the claim that religion is a *sui generis* phenomenon.[4] And, although admitting that the scholarly study of religion may have originally had a nonacademic motivation, such is no longer the case—indeed, it has a duty to keep itself free from ideological commitment.

Not all scholars involved in establishing—or reestablishing—the academic study of religion necessarily agreed with the clear demarcation between the religious and the student of religion. Erwin Goodenough, for example, in his address to the group of American historians of religion who would soon form the American Society for the Study of Religion (ASSR), although distinguishing the scientific study of religion from traditionalist and theological approaches, does not discount the religious point of view in understanding the nature of the study of religions. "The hope of reviving study of the science of religion," he writes,

> lies . . . not in courting the traditionalists and theologians, but in coming to recognize that science itself is a religious exercise, a new religion, and that science and religion have fallen apart largely because traditionalists have done what they have always done, failed to recognize a new approach to religion as it has formed itself in their midst, challenging thereby old conceptions and comfortably formulated adjustments.(Goodenough, 1959: 85)

He continues: "Historians—of religions, that is—must include in their study, and in their sympathy, the new religion of science, or of scientists, along with the religions and thought ways they have hitherto considered" (85). For Goodenough, religion is a matter of adjustment to "the universal reality," and science, like religion, seeks relationships and meaning in trying to find the principles behind the empirical data. That search for meaning from facts is, he insists, "a new formulation of man's relation to the *tremendum*" and is therefore "a totally new form of religion itself"(90). Goodenough describes the new religion succinctly:

> The new religion takes a new attitude toward the *tremendum:* It no longer hides its head, ostrich-fashion, in myths asserting that the *tremendum* is less perilous than it is; it no longer surrenders to the *tremendum,* and asks to be reabsorbed into it. Instead, refusing either to run away or surrender, it accepts the *tremendum,* and the individual's helplessness and insignificance before it. It drops no curtain, but faces the overwhelming within and without, while it seeks to find relationships and meaning as far as it can by its own method. (90)

This spirit, he argues, also characterizes the academic-scientific study of religion. As he puts it,

> we can hardly call ourselves scientists of religion if we systematically define religion so as to leave out this great approach to the *tremendum* going on all about us, and refuse ourselves to share in it. . . . [W]e combine science and religion in our very marrow, combine them into a dedication to learning about religion by the slow dogged approach of science. I know no other way in which we can hope eventually to understand better the *homo religiosus,* religion itself, and avoid the agony Sanday felt when he killed in order to dissect. For if we still have to kill the old dream that religion is a matter of revelation, through *Religionswissenschaft* we may discover that the scalpel itself has become a sacramental instrument. (91, 94–95)

The new institutional framework for the academic study of religion proposed by Goodenough, it is obvious, is not simply a neutral framework within which a peculiar kind of intellection takes place. Goodenough's proposal is, in fact, a call for radical socio-political changes in academic structures that will not only disenfranchise, so to speak, a particular kind of scholar, but that will also effect a religious transformation. Furthermore, the change of approach he seeks in the academic study of religion is necessitated by the broader influence of science on society, with what he sees as science's generally corrosive effect on traditional modes of religious belief and existence.

Willard Oxtoby (1968), reviewing the development of the history of religions in America with particular focus on Goodenough's essay, quite rightly points out that Goodenough's version of scientific humanism, like the new phenomenology of religion (599) and the dialogic approach to the study of religion (603) taken up by many American scholars, renders the science of religion "a religious exercise," which in turn makes the study of religion indistinguishable from religion itself (607). Oxtoby concedes that Goodenough's thesis about science as a religious exercise is not likely to gather a very large following, since the majority of American scholars in the field are identified—happily or otherwise—with one of the traditional religious bodies in America and thus are more likely to emphasize the notion of religious community over the philosophical interests raised by Goodenough. Despite the religious character of Goodenough's *Religionswissenschaft,* however, Oxtoby maintains the latter's essay on the nature of that study is "one of the important statements in the history of the discipline . . . enshrin[ing] points with which any discussion of scientific attitude in the study of religion must come to terms"(608). And yet the only reason Oxtoby gives to back up such a statement is that in Goodenough "there is a searching openness . . . which goes beyond the sterile isolationism and externalism of Werblowsky's Marburg platform"(605). So that although Goodenough tries to ascribe to *Religionswissenschaft* a scientific character denied it by theologians, he himself appears to undermine it by refusing to adhere to the academic conventions adopted by other university disciplines—a surprising move given Goodenough's active part in the Werblowsky "Manifesto." And if Oxtoby on the one hand lauds Goodenough for insisting on the restoration of a neglected scientific rigor, he is nonetheless guilty of contradiction in accusing "pure academics" of aridity in its approach to the study of religion. He acknowledges that Goodenough's essay on *Religionswissenschaft* is oracular yet does not wholly condemn it for being so; in his view, we should in fact visit oracles from time to time(608). However, students of religion ought not to consult oracles, for to do so would simply draw us back into the furor of inter-religious conflict that is exactly what the academic study of religion is designed to avoid(598, 605n1)—which conflict I shall proceed to outline.

Goodenough, as Oxtoby notes, laments the fact that *Religionswissenschaft* was ignored by his fellow scientists. Given the American academic context, however, it is not difficult to understand why Religious Studies was virtually ignored. In a country whose Constitution insists on a clear separation of Church and State, study of religion such as Goodenough proposes would amount to little more than the teaching of religion with the support of the State—it accords privilege to a particular (if relatively new) religion over established traditions and is bound to create conflict not only between the religious and the secularists but also within the ranks of the religious themselves. Some traditionalists—Randy Huntsberry, for example—have echoed the complaint of the secularists that Departments of Religion are little more than havens for the propagation of a new religion. In "Secular Education and Its Religion" Huntsberry argues that the academic study of religion has spawned an interest in what he calls "generic religion," which stands as a direct challenge to the historical religious traditions constitutionally excluded from the classroom. "Teaching 'about' religion," he writes, "has become the teaching 'of' religion. We are messiahs whether we like it or not"(1974).[5] Robert Michaelson similarly points out that much of the so-called academic study of religion has fostered the creation of a "classroom religion."(1972: 422). And Robert Bellah, in his "Confessions of a Former Establishment Fundamentalist," not only admits as much but actually advocates it. He maintains that the professor of religion ought "to stir up the students' unconscious religious depths . . . [and] to get the students to face the religious dimension of existence directly . . . (1970c: 4)," since no religion scholar ever remains aloof from religious commitment, or its equivalent, anyway. This equivalent for Bellah, consists of a fundamental scientific stance, structurally indistinguishable from religious commitment—it also assumes its concepts to bear a "higher ontological status than the [religious] realm [being] studied"(1970: 3). Bellah, therefore, in his espousal of symbolic realism as doctrine and as methodological framework for his thought, blurs the boundary between religion and the study of religion both in research and in teaching.[6]

In his *Journal* for March 2, 1967, Mircea Eliade (who also signed the Werblowsky "Manifesto") noted: "The history of religions, as I understand it, is a 'saving' discipline"(1977: 296). A little more than a year later (April 21, 1968) he wrote: "Very interesting, this remark of Fingarette: 'In psychoanalysis Freud brought into the most intimate partnership, a science of human change and the art of self-liberation.' . . . I attribute a similar function as well to the history of religions"(309–310). It is obvious from even the very brief review of the literature provided here that Eliade is not the only scholar who has desired scientific legitimation for his work—even though that work is essentially emancipatory in character. But the cost of Eliade's taking up an emancipatory or salvific task (as Kurt Rudolph, among others, has clearly shown) has been the abandoning of *Religionswissenschaft* as a scientific discipline. As Rudolph puts it: "[Eliade] attempts to tie the history of religions to a programme that would not only rob it of a firm basis in philology and history but would also bind it to a one-sided view of humanity and the world, to the narrow view of a romantic crypto-religious vision that cannot be harmonized with the discipline's aspirations to universality and with its critical distance as a science"(1989: 109). Eliade's approach to the study of religion, therefore, makes of it little more than "a kind of personal confession" bound to clash with the confessions of others (115). This obviously would dismantle the work of those students of religion who achieved academic legitimation in the field by creating a methodological framework that allowed them to transcend such inter-religious wrangling. The study of religion, therefore, if it is to survive as an academic and scientific undertaking, is in need of being "saved" from becoming a salvific undertaking. Unlike Jacob Neusner, then, who like Eliade argues for Religious Studies as our next vocation—that is, as a task *beyond* the scientific study of religions—we must see and treat the Science of Religion as our *academic* vocation. And a brief look at Neusner's work will reveal the contradictions in his study of religion that undermine its scientific integrity.

In his "Religious Studies: The Next Vocation," Neusner maintains that, having transcended the framework of the study of religion by the religious (and thereby having created an academic study of religions), it is necessary to move beyond that new enterprise into "Religious Studies" if we are to fulfil the academic mandate. Neusner's argument here is reminiscent of Ricoeur's unpersuasive claim that the intention of the critical thought in which we transcended our original naïveté can only be fulfilled if we move beyond it into a "second naïveté." Neusner admits that the academic study of religion came into being by ridding itself of "empty-headed preachers, pastors, and rabbis," and by "making a place for people who could teach and with a measure of detachment and objectivity take up the tasks of interpretation" (1977b: 117). But thereupon he complains of the "rather technical and desiccated way in which we have made religious studies into a tolerable science"(119). He announces: "What has happened is that religious studies have ceased to raise those central issues which are addressed in the humanities. We have moved too far toward the pretense that there is a science of religions, even adopting the jargon and obfuscation of pseudo-sciences . . ." (119). He advises that we "turn our attention once more to the critical exposition of the central issues of religiosity; to the questions raised and answered both in diverse historical religions and by our students here and now" (119). And he points out our duty to tell the students "that it is in religions that humanity has asked its basic questions about making the world fit for them who are in God's image and made in God's likeness" (120), for only then will we and they "measure and shape our own capacity to transcend our small and limited selves" (119). That in doing this we would effectively be taking up the tasks of our "empty-headed predecessors" presents no problem for Neusner, since they—"the preachers, pastors, and rabbis of the 1950s, and . . . the freaks and crackpots of the early 1970s"—never lost sight of what is most important, "the human dimension of religions"(119).

Other scholars, like Neusner, focus attention on the "human dimension" of religion even to the point of refusing to demarcate the study of religion from religion and other forms of personal engagement. David Chidester, for example, in his "Religious Studies as Political Practice," argues that the central approach to the understanding of religious phenomena is to be found in the phenomenology of religion, and he maintains that there is an inherent political activity of nonviolence in such a phenomenology. Consequently, as a political practice, "religious studies refuses to deny the humanity of even those who deny the full humanity of others"(1987: 17). Insofar as the phenomenology of religion points up the religiously pluralistic nature of South African society—and therefore undermines the state propaganda, in Chidester's view, that the country is a "Christian nation"—one might say that the phenomenology of religion is "implicitly political." That, however, does not mean that such a phenomenology is essentially a political undertaking; nor does it justify the claim that it ought to be. Chidester, however, concludes that the implicitly political character of the phenomenology of religion in South Africa obliges us to see that the political task of the academic study of religion is the criticism "of all private ownership of the sacred"(17). His argument, however, is not convincing; in fact, it is less an argument than a pronouncement. And the impact of his statement is not

very successfully muted when he hastens to elaborate: "[t]his political practice does not begin with the announcement of a political programme,
but . . . has already begun in the disciplined, academic, plural study of religion and religions" (17). His thought does not extend, however, to the prag-
matics of the constructive political program he thinks students of religion
ought to take up. This is left for us to read in the work of his colleague,
Martin Prozesky.

Prozesky's essay evaluating "South Africa's Contribution to Religious
Studies" presents a much more expansive notion of the political responsibilities of the academic study of religion. In speaking about the political climate in South Africa he writes:

> Amidst all this [political oppression], Religious Studies in our context will
> damn itself . . . if it imagines that all it must do is document, analyze, inter-
> pret, and explain the reality of religions in South Africa, for the situation
> cries out for something more. It cries out for *a new ethic of religions, a new,*
> *creatively critical interrogation of religion in relation to both socio-personal lib-*
> *eration and oppression.* . . . [T]he field [of Religious Studies] cannot now be
> credibly studied without prioritizing the problem of religions in the struggle
> for a more humane world order in general, and in the apartheid state in par-
> ticular. (1990: 10–11)

For Prozesky, moreover, this socio-personal concern can only be adequately
addressed if personal religious well-being is an essential aspect of the study
of religion. He writes: "Lest these sentiments make it seem that I view religion as no more than a socio-personal reality, as no more than a mode of
being human, let me add that in South Africa as anywhere else, the central
claim of religion to reveal to us the ultimate and deepest truth and to relate
us beneficially to it, is in its own right a profoundly absorbing and important matter . . ." (11). The contribution he believes South African students
of religion can make to the discipline, therefore, is in promoting its development "as a significant, humanizing force in the context of the struggle for
a post-apartheid society *by problematizing religion as a socio-personal force*"
(18). This will require that students of religion engage in "a genuinely liberative praxis in South Africa" (17). Recognizing the human suffering of the
context in which their research and teaching are conducted, he insists, forces
the realization "that the one thing our work cannot be is apolitical," and
that, as students of religion, we must join in "moral allegiance with other
forces working to humanize South Africa, without compromising our duty
to remain critically independent" (17).

Unfortunately, apart from exploiting the general ethical sensibilities of his
listeners, Prozesky's statement for a politics of Religious Studies does not

constitute a convincing epistemological or methodological argument. His paper to the 16th IAHR Congress (Rome, 1990) on "Proposals for a Criteriology of Religion, with Special Reference to Religion in South Africa" attempted to do this, but not, I think, with much success.[7] It might be said, however, that to provide a generally acceptable structure within which to distinguish (scientifically) between salutary and harmful forms of religion is virtually doomed from the start. Yet Prozesky's (and Chidester's) position does find justification, according to Gregory Baum, in a hermeneutic understanding of the human (social) sciences; for it is here, he insists, that truth reveals its transformative character. And for Baum, ultimately, "religious studies, and the human sciences in general, should not only aim at understanding reality but also at transforming it"(Baum, 1990: 4–5).[8]

According to Baum, an acceptable study of any phenomenon must not concern itself solely with the description and explanation of events but must also include evaluation, which implies commitment to particular moral values. Simply to study something objectively is to leave things as they are. To assume that science by definition has nothing to say regarding injustice and oppression in society is to label it a conservative and ideological enterprise at best, which, indirectly, supports the status quo. As Baum puts it: "The objectivity of science understood in this sense is actually a powerful ideological instrument that helps to reconcile the intellectual community with the existing social order" (1990: 7); in accounting for conditions as though they were necessary, science places those conditions beyond criticism. It is apparent, Baum therefore argues, that the ethical relativism of "objective scientific analysis" must be transcended, and that "truth" in the human sciences requires more than a mere scholarly "demonstration of an hypothesis on the basis of empirical data and more than an act of interpretation in keeping with the self-understanding of the actors" (1990: 6). He elaborates:

> If we study the subjugation of women in religion, or the manner in which some religions treat outsiders, or the blessings pronounced by religions on rulers and princes, we cannot be content with understanding what these actions meant to the believers at the time. They truly believed that these actions corresponded to ordinances of divine origin. Here religious studies must move from the 'empirical research' and 'hermeneutics' to a 'social analysis' of the situation (Habermas). Here the researcher must try to discover the social function of these religious practices and entertain the possibility that the self-understanding of the believers was distorted. (1990: 5)

That university departments of Religious Studies, past and present, have not always been religiously or politically neutral is not news—despite their avowed ideal to keep the academic study in those contexts as neutral as possible. But what does constitute "news" is the explicit—and often belliger-ent—attack upon that avowed ideal; and this transformation is profoundly detrimental to the field. There is a sense in which it has split the Religious Studies academic community into two camps and has created conditions for an antagonistic schism within the field. What is in store for Religious Stud-ies with the continued rejection of the neutrality ideal can be seen in Jacob Neusner's account of "The Civil War in Jewish Studies," the crux of which dispute, he demonstrates, lies in the split between Jewish scholars concerned with humanistic learning and those concerned with preserving Jewish values (1986). The critical stance necessary for the academic community, Neusner forecasts, will be discounted as disrespectful and inappropriate to the subject matter. And disagreement with those who approach the study of religion critically and scientifically will escalate condemnation and unscholarly in-sult. Indeed, this scenario is already being lived-out to a considerable extent in the field of Religious Studies. Gary Lease, for example, points to precisely such conflict as the cause for the " . . . fall of Religious Studies" at Santa Cruz: "Religious Studies, at the height of its popularity and success at Santa Cruz," he writes, "attempted to define itself as concerned with individual students' own religious traditions; with the possibility and value of religion; and with the cultural components from three such traditions . . ." (Lease, 1995b: 315–316). And the consequences, he notes, were not long in coming:

> As might be expected, a deep inability on the part of Religious Studies fac-ulty to reach unanimity concerning the program's academic identity quickly surfaced. There was, in other words, trouble in paradise. The split which de-veloped can most easily be characterized as a division between those who viewed a religious studies program as *also* directed towards the development of each individual student's religious growth and sensitivity, and those who considered such a program to be concerned *only* with making intelligible what people *claim* as religious experience. . . . In a larger faculty such a split may well have meant nothing more than infrequent disagreement at meet-ings; in a board as small as Religious Studies this ideological divergence had a powerful impact on the program itself. Above all, it was manifested in the lack of a planned and coherent curriculum dedicated to commonly shared goals. (316)

Similar tensions disrupt discussions in my own—much larger—university department at Toronto and in the Centre for the Study of Religion, and they have led to some uncivil exchanges including accusations of "witch-hunts" by one faction against the other.[9] The reasons for the underlying tension can only properly be discerned, I think, by examining the papers in connection with the formation of the original Centre for Religious Studies; for this material reveals clearly differentiated objectives between the Graduate unit and the undergraduate Department of Religious Studies, the latter being dominated by a religio-theological perspective.[10]

More broadly, however, these tensions are widely evident in academic societies and associations dedicated to the study of religions. Although limitations of space prevent my going into a detailed analysis, I would like to draw particular attention to the discussions concerning the St. Louis Project on Theology and Religious Studies in the *Journal of the American Academy of Religion*, in which Strenski refers to those who wish to bring about an integration of Theology with Religious Studies as "our very own contras" (1986: 324).[11] And the response by Charles Davis to my article "The Failure of Nerve in the Academic Study of Religion," condemned by Hans Penner as "[even] beneath the standards that are commonly accepted among colleagues" (1986: 165nl).[12] It is not inappropriate in this regard to refer as well to the comments of Michael Pye, secretary-general of the International Association for the History of Religions (IAHR): in his introduction to the conference he identifies the attack upon the work of the IAHR implicit in the attempt by Ninian Smart and others to establish a World Academy of Religion to reintegrate (like the American Academy of Religion on which it would be patterned) the religio-theological study of religion with the academic, scientific study of religion.[13] Germane here also is the kind of editorial liberty exercised against the scholarship of one group by the other, as is seen in the note Kurt Rudolph attached to his paper on Eliade to which I have referred above:

This article originally appeared as "*Eliade und die 'Religionsgeschichte'*" in one of three German *Festschriften* that Hans-Peter Duerr edited on the occasion of Mircea Eliade's 75th birthday: *Die Mitte der Welt: Aufsätze zu Mircea Eliade* (Frankfurt/Main: Suhrkamp, 1984: 49–78). Professor Duerr invited contributors to write a critical essay on Eliade or on a theme that Eliade had discussed, so as to set a precedent for a new kind of *Festschrift*. The plans for an American edition of—or rather, an American selection from—the *Festschrift*, to be published by the University of Chicago Press under the leadership of Wendy D. O'Flaherty, have by now excised almost all contributions to the German edition that were critical of Eliade; as a result, it will simply replicate the model of the traditional *Festschrift*. I venture to doubt that such was the desire of Eliade himself, who is unfortunately no longer among us. Eliade was always kind enough to tolerate justified criticism. (1989: 118)

And as Terrence Tilley clearly indicates in his review of J. Samuel Preus's *Explaining Religion: Criticism and Theory from Bodin to Freud*, the polemics and politics of explaining religion are likely to continue for some time and, I suspect, in a rather heated mode, given what is at stake—namely, who is to control the study of religion in the modern university and what the agenda of that study is to be (Tilley, 1991: 252). There is no doubt that socio-political change and concerns with religious transformation are interrelated in the determination of these matters. Just how they are (or ought to be) related is less clear. As far as Tilley is concerned, it is not only the religious researchers whose missionary role in the university has been detrimental to critical analysis and research. Besides these, he insists, there are *academic* missionaries: "As the former want to bring people to a commitment to a religious faith so the tradition may thrive, the latter want to bring people to a commitment to learn the skeptically based academic study of religion to carry on that tradition. Naturalists are no less guilty of missionary work than are theologians"(253).[14] One might justifiably conclude, therefore, that the academic students of religion in Tilley's view are responsible for introducing religious warfare into the academic context.

In light of these developments in the field of Religious Studies, it seems to me that if we are ever to regain the position on whose basis our field achieved academic or scientific legitimation, we will have to take up Weber's battle regarding the role of science in modern society. As Aron describes it: "He fought on two fronts: against those who threatened to corrupt the purity of rational thought by bringing in political convictions or sentimental outpourings, and those who falsified the meaning of science by attributing to it the capability of unlocking the secret of the nature of man"(1985: 340–341). Those who see science as but another ideological structure have not understood its nature; they fail to see that what is special about science is that it concerns restrictions. Science, that is, attempts to obtain reliable beliefs about the world; it attempts to understand the world as it is and to represent it as accurately as possible. That is its only task. As Weber put it: "Science today is a 'vocation' organized in special disciplines in the service of self-clarification and knowledge of interrelated facts. It is not the gift of grace of seers and prophets dispensing sacred values and revelations, nor does it partake of the contemplation of sages and philosophers about the meaning of the universe"(1946: 152–153).[15] Consequently, "in the lecture rooms of the university," Weber insists, "no other virtue holds but plain intellectual integrity"(155–156). Some may argue that scientists are then less than human because they "evade" their moral responsibility by restricting their influence simply to teaching, research, and writing. If that is the case, then those who wish to retain their moral or religious integrity should feel compelled to forego all involvement in science—an implausible situation at best.[16] But the precise point of science, as Weber clearly sets it out, is to limit itself to this kind of purely academic function.[17] In his essay "'Objectivity' in Social Science and Social Policy," he shows that no empirical science can create—"in the form of generally valid ultimate value judgements"—a lowest common denominator for the resolution of spiritual, social, or political problems (1949: 57). It is only the dogmatically bound religio-ideological groups (particular religious traditions, for example) that can confer upon cultural values the status of unconditionally valid ethical imperatives. Thus he writes:

> The fate of an epoch which has eaten of the tree of knowledge is that it must know that we cannot learn the *meaning* of the world from the results of its analysis, be it ever so perfect; it must rather be in a position to create this meaning itself. It must recognize that general views of life and the universe can never be the products of increasing empirical knowledge, and that the highest ideals, which move us most forcefully, are always formed only in the struggle with other ideals which are just as sacred to others as ours are to us. (1949: 57)

The academic implications of that Weberian analysis are expressed by Maurice Cowling nearly fifty years later, when he tries to make clear the difference between politics and political science: " . . . the only rational action to which scholars, *as scholars* [emphasis added], are committed, the only moral action to which they are commanded and the only 'social responsibility' to which their *professional* position compels them, is to use their energies in order to explain in its full diversity as much as they can of the nature of the world in which they live"(1963: 210).[18] To go beyond that mandate, whether in political science or in the academic study of religion, by engaging in political or religious activity "in the classroom," is to reject what Weber might well have called "the morality of scientific knowing."[19] As he puts it:

> [O]ne cannot demonstrate scientifically what the duty of an academic teacher is. One can only demand of the teacher that he have the intellectual integrity to see that it is one thing to state facts, to determine mathematical or logical relations or the internal structure of cultural values, while it is another thing to answer questions of the *value* of culture and its individual contents and the question of how one should act in the cultural community and in political associations. (Weber, 1946: 146)

Those responsible for introducing the "warfare" into the field of Religious Studies, therefore, are not, contrary to Tilley's claim, the "naturalists," but rather those who have claimed to take up a scientific study of religion while attempting to integrate it with their own religious or political aspirations.[20] This is precisely why Werblowsky, having seen the specter of turmoil in the peculiar circumstances of the Marburg international IAHR congress, wrote: "The facts and analyses of *Religionswissenschaft* may become the raw material for a *theologia naturalis* or for any other philosophical [socio-political] or religious system. But this is . . . outside the terms of reference of *Religionswissenschaft* and therefore no longer the concern of the student of religion"(in Schimmel, 1960: 237).[21]

My account of these developments in the academic study of religion is not, I think, difficult to comprehend. Contemporary students of religion want to be scientists because they see in science a valid mode of thought. However, they also want to be socially responsible citizens, seeing their function as intellectuals to be the development or protection and refining of the ideology (that is, the framework of meaning) of their own society. For many of them, religion is absolutely essential to a meaningful life within a coherent social framework, and a naturalistic study of religion seems to undermine religion. Consequently they experience a dilemma, for their intellectual role as scholars or scientists conflicts with their perceived function of sustaining the myths of their culture.[22] In a very important sense, therefore, the conflict of views I have briefly delineated in this paper regarding the nature of the inter-relations between religions (with their salvific-emancipatory aims) and the academic institutions within which we seek to understand them is but another reflection of the science-religion conflict characteristic of so much of Western civilization. What is required in that debate—not only in the field of the study of religion but there especially so[23]—is an either-or choice, for it is not scientifically acceptable to mix our science with modes of thought that contradict its fundamental intentionality. Walter Burkert's comments in this respect are fitting as a conclusion to my remarks here:

> The language that has proved the most generally understood and cross-cultural is that of secularized scholarship. Its practice today is determined by science in its broadest sense, its system of rules by the laws of logic. It may, of course, seem the most questionable endeavour of all to try to translate religious phenomena into this language; by its self-conception, a religion must deny that such explanations are possible. However, scholarship is free to study even the rejection of knowledge and repudiation of independent thought, for scholarship, in attempting to understand the world, has the broader perspective here and cannot abstain from analyzing the worldwide fact of religion. This is not a hopeless undertaking. However, a discussion of religion must then be anything but religious. (1983: xxi)

Notes

1. This paper was delivered at a special conference of the International Association for the History of Religions, hosted by the North American Association for the Study of Religion at the University of Vermont, August, 1991, on the theme "Religious Transformations and Socio-Political

Change" (with particular attention focused on Eastern Europe and Latin America).

2. See my article "The Failure of Nerve in the Study of Religion" (401–422 and chapter 8 in this volume).

3. See Annemarie Schimmel, "Summary of the Discussion," (1960): 235–239.

4. What is meant by this is that "religion" is deemed to be like any other subject matter—it is not somehow special. It is determined, not by some peculiar essence it somehow possesses, but rather by particular problems and interests raised by data relevant to it. Without intending to open a discussion of the place of the religious in the realm of cultural anthropology, I find it interesting nonetheless to compare Religious Studies to what Ernest Gellner says of anthropology: "The idea of anthropology is rooted not so much in the distinctiveness of man as in its denial. As long as man stood outside nature, his special status exempted him from ordinary inquiry. It was his demotion to an ordinary, if distinguished, member of nature which made it inevitable that something like anthropology should arise" ("The Stakes in Anthropology" [1988]: 17).

5. Note especially John B. Carman's comment: "We clearly wear the secular garb of the modern academician, but we, too, have our vocation and our mission" ("Inter-Faith Dialogue and Academic Study of Religion," [1971]: 86).

6. In my article "The Failure of Nerve . . ." (mentioned in note 2 above), I refer to such a generic religion as "small-c" confessionalism. The critique I provide points clearly to the difference between this and the "capital-c" confessionalism seen by all academic students of religion as unacceptable in the university context. It is difficult, therefore, to understand how some of those same scholars insist on identifying "small-c" confessionalism as essential to the academic study of religion. The article also provides documentary evidence of the pervasiveness of generic religion in the university setting. My essay "Postulations for Safeguarding Preconceptions: The Case of the Scientific Religionist" reinforces the point by providing a brief overview of presidential addresses to the American Academy of Religion. Subsequent addresses reveal similar problems; see Wendy Doniger O'Flaherty, "The Uses and Misuses of Other Peoples' Myths"; Robert L. Wilken, "Who Will Speak for Religious Traditions?"; and the plenary address to the American Academy in 1989 by Huston Smith, "Post-modernism's Impact on the Study of Religion."

7. Prozesky's paper expands upon themes raised in his 1985 address to the 15th IAHR Congress in 1985 (Sydney, Australia), later published as "Explanations of Religion as a Part of and Problem for Religious Studies."

8. Although Baum's paper was to have been presented at the conference on the "Contribution of South Africa to Religious Studies and Theology" at the University of Cape Town in April of 1989, Professor Braum was not granted a visa and, thus, could not present his paper in person.

9. Those charges are to be found in correspondence generated by a debate held at the Centre for Religious Studies in Toronto in the Fall of 1984 on the topic: "The Relationship Between Theological and Religious Studies: What Should the Toronto Model Be?" Some of this information is also contained

in the Archives of Trinity College, Toronto. The debate was taped by Marion Wyse and was deposited in the University of Toronto Archives (accession number B84–0043). A more detailed account of the problems with the study of religion at the University of Toronto can be found in Wiebe 1995b (chapter 13 in this volume).

10. The relevant reports and correspondence in the University of Toronto Archives indicate quite clearly that both theology in general and the Toronto School of Theology in particular were important concerns. The fact that the undergraduate department emerged from the combined resources of the various Departments of Religious Knowledge in the religious colleges on the university campus constitutes a major factor in the discord.

11. In his essay, Strenski argues that the report of the "Saint Louis Project" concerned with the re-integration of Theology with Religious Studies (see *Journal of the American Academy of Religion* 52[1984]: 727–757), and the inclusion of an award for excellence in constructive religious-theological thought, are counter-revolutionary developments undermining Religious Studies scholars' optimism about the academic character of their field. The force of Strenski's anxiety about the possible results of those developments is well expressed in the following paragraph:

"I cannot see how this 'constructive-reflective study of religion' belongs in the AAR's list of award categories. The AAR might just as well create a 'Saint's List' for practical excellence in *being* religious. An award for *thinking* religiously is not all that different. There may well be a 'new religious consciousness' welling up across the land, at least among intellectuals estranged from the 'hippopotamus churches.' But America has known well how to give such feelings voice and nurture—in the *agora*, in the churches. And, if existing churches are hostile, America again gives us a time-tried solution—found a new church. But, leave the *akademia* to be itself. Religious studies does not need to undermine its own academic aspirations. It needs to get on with the job. Without lapsing into a discredited positivism, we in religious studies must resist its re-theologizing—even if these days the new theology speaks often in the seductive pseudo-universal language of continental Hermeneutics, the archaic religion of Eliade, or the post-critical faith of Ricoeur. Our job is still to *study* religion, not to *make* or 'construct' it." (331–332)

Walter Capps, in "A Response to Dr. Strenski," sees Strenski's remark as "uncommonly vitriolic commentary" (125) filled with "ill-mannered volleys of rhetorical venom" (126). Capps maintains Strenski has simply misunderstood the "Saint Louis Project," which was essentially a broadening of Religious Studies in the context of a Catholic university in which a theological approach to religion had thus far been the sole rule. Though there may be some validity to Capps's claim here, his account does not really capture the nature of the Project's full intention. I have provided a brief analysis of it in my "Postulations" article cited in note 6 above. The intention of the "Saint

Louis Project" is, in fact, similar to Davis's in his "The Reconvergence of Theology and Religious Studies (*Studies in Religion* 41975]: 205–221. See also his "Theology and Religious Study" 2[1981]: 11–20). Support from Max Weber for Strenski's assertions can be detected in "A Catholic University in Salzburg," *Max Weber on Universities: The Power of the State and the Dignity of the Academic Calling in Imperial Germany,* ed. and trans. Edward Shils (Chicago: University of Chicago Press [1973]: 46–47). As Weber points out, the appointment of persons to religiously controlled universities presents serious problems: "they are absolutely incompatible with a selection of candidates according to strictly scientific and scholarly criteria . . . Such a university would naturally not be one likely to be viewed by academic institutions as of equal standing and rights, nor would it indeed by accorded equal privileges" (46).

12. Hans Penner, "Criticism and the Development of a Science of Religion?" *Studies in Religion* 15 (1986): 165–175, especially 165,n 1. My essay and the response by C. Davis ("Wherein There Is No Ecstasy") had appeared in *Studies in Religion* 13 (1984): 401–422 and 393–400. Other essays directed to the Wiebe-Davis exchange by Lorne Dawson (145–151), Bruce Alton (153–164), Barry Henaut (177–196), and me (197–203) are also found in Volume 15.

13. For Smart's comments in this regard, see his "Concluding Reflections: Religious Studies in Global Perspective," in *Turning Points in Religious Studies: Essays in Honour of Geoffrey Parrinder,* ed. Ursula King (Edinburgh: T. and T. Clark, 1990), 305. See also Smart's review of *Marburg Revisited: Institutions and Strategies in the Study of Religion,* ed. Michael Pye (Marburg: Diagonal-Verlag, 1989) in *Method and Theory in the Study of Religion* 2 (1990): 298–304.

14. I think Tilley's comments here are without foundation. Clearly Weber was no proselytizer: "Whether, under such a worthwhile 'vocation' for somebody, and whether science itself has an objectively valuable 'vocation' are again value judgements about which nothing can be said in the lecture room. To affirm the value of science is a presupposition for teaching there" (Max Weber, "Science as a Vocation," [1946: 152]). See also Weber's comments in this regard in his "The Academic Freedom of the Universities," (1973): 18–23.

15. Weber continues: " . . . if Tolstoi's question recurs to you: as science does not, who is to answer the question: 'What shall we do and, how shall we arrange our lives?' or, in the words used here tonight: 'Which of the warring gods should we serve" Or should we serve perhaps an entirely different god, and who is he?' then one can say only that a prophet or savior can give the answers. If there is no such man, or if his message is no longer believed in, then you will certainly not compel him to appear on this earth by having thousands of professors, or privileged hirelings of this state, attempt as petty prophets in their lecture-rooms to take over his role. All they will accomplish is to show that they are unaware of the divine state of affairs: the

prophet for whom so many of our younger generation yearns simply does not exist" (153).

16. Weber in fact thought the scientific (objective) study of values was possible and not without benefit to the communities espousing those values. Lack of space here prevents my analyzing the relationship of values to science. With respect to the scientific study of religion, see E. Thomas Lawson and Robert N. McCauley's "Crisis of Conscience, Riddle of Identity: Making Space for a Cognitive Approach to Religious Phenomena" (1993): 201–223. For comments on the meaning of science, see note 17 below.

17. Peter Lassman and Irving Velody, in "Max Weber on Science, Disenchantment and the Search for Meaning" (the concluding essay of *Max Weber's 'Science as a Vocation'* (1989: 159–204), claim that the question of the meaning of science is a central issue for Weber. The main problem in his account of the development of science, they argue, is that of its own legitimation or justification. Although I am in agreement with them on this point, I do not think Weber's handling of that question nearly as ironic as they do, nor as internally inconsistent. Our implicit differences of interpretation, however, cannot be addressed here. (See also E. Shils's introduction to the translation of *Max Weber on Universities.* Here he speaks of Weber's moving confession of faith in "the value of science and scholarship" coupled with "a tragic awareness of their limits" [1973: 3]).

18. Religious Studies in this respect is like Political Science and the other social sciences—a cognitively orientated scientific undertaking—and not like Philosophy, which has generally been understood to provide a kind of supra-scientific, foundational knowledge.

19. I have provided an account of this notion in my article "Is Religious Belief Problematic?" (1977). One might also consult the essays in *The Ethics of Belief Debate* (McCarthy, 1986).

20. I am thinking here of such claims as those of John Carman (cited in note 5 above) in his "Inter-Faith Dialogue and Academic Study of Religion" (1971): "We clearly wear the secular garb of the modern academician, but we, too, have our vocation and our mission" (1971: 86).

21. See also Werblowsky's "Marburg—and After?" (1960).

22. This point is made particularly clear by William H. McNeil in his *Mythistory and Other Essays* (1986), which I discussed in relation to the "history of religions" in my "History or Mythistory in the Study of Religion? The Problems of Demarcation" (1989: 31–46). Raymond Aron, in his *Main Currents in Sociological Thought* (II: 1967), shows how acutely this dilemma affected sociologists such as Durkheim, Pareto, and Weber: "This is the contradiction peculiar to our sociologist; the contradiction between the need for scientific precision in the analysis of society and the conviction that scientific propositions cannot unite men, since the coherence and order of every society is always maintained by ultra-, infra-, or supra-rational beliefs" (3). It appears that they did not fully understand their task as scientists, confusing it with the one intellectuals apparently have always

performed—namely, that of developing an ideology for the society in which they lived. J. Z. Smith points to a similar problem for students of religion in his essay "Map Is Not Territory" (1978). Although for Smith the human sciences (including history and the history of religions) "serve as limiting perspectives" on the understanding of religion—"as boundaries of concreteness over against which to judge more speculative and normative inquiries in religious studies" (289)—he restricts the task of the scientific student to non-speculative and non-normative matters. The philosopher and theologian, he concedes, may have "a standpoint from which he may gain clear vision" (289), but the historian (scientific student of religion) is a person of hints and insights at best, which cannot ground such "vision." The latter, therefore, approaches religion simply as a human phenomenon, "as one mode of constructing worlds of meaning" (290). Consequently, "Religious Studies are most appropriately described in relation to the Humanities and the Human Sciences, in relation to Anthropology rather then Theology" (290). In summary, then, religion is seen as the power to relate to the natural and social world "in such a way as to guarantee the conviction that one's existence 'matters'" (291). Thus, "[w]hat we study when we study religion is the variety of attempts to map, construct, and inhabit such positions of power through the use of myths, rituals, and experiences of transformation" (291).

23. I have argued this point in depth in my book *The Irony of Theology and the Nature of Religious Thought* (1991a). I have also addressed it in: "Religion Transcending Science Transcending Religion . . ."(1985b); "Is Science Really an Implicit Religion?" (1989b); and "Religion, Science and the Transformation of 'Knowledge'" (1993a).

Chapter Eight

The Failure of Nerve in the Academic Study of Religion[1]

M y concern in this essay is with the relationship of theology to the study of religion, and, more particularly, to the "academic study of religion." I shall not, however, focus attention here on how theology has received the results of academic research on religion,[2]—its concerns may be legitimate—nor on historical and institutional questions about the two communities of scholars,[3] or even on the notion that theology as an element of religion overall constitutes a focus of interest and concern to the academic student of religion.[4] My interest here is in the methodological problems implicit in that relationship—even though the matter thus expressed hardly reveals the depth of the issue. Briefly put, the question of theology's methodological relationship to the academic study of religion jeopardizes the existence of such an academic study, for it re-opens the debate about who controls the agenda for such study—is it the scholar-scientist or the scholar-devotee, the academy or the Church, scientific procedure or transcendent subject-matter, and so on.

As I shall show here, it was in the precise act of distinguishing itself from theology that the study of religion gained a political identity within the academic community. I shall also show that there is currently an argument being made for an explicit role for theology in Religious Studies in the "interpenetration" of the two.[5] And I shall argue that, even though under constant pressure from a hidden (if unconscious) theological agenda of many of its practitioners, the re-establishment of such an explicit role for theology constitutes a rejection of scientific, academic goals and, therefore, amounts to a "failure of nerve" by the academic community in Religious Studies.[6]

Some clarification of the term "theology" must precede the argument of this paper—both to counter criticism of my "ambiguous" use of the term in earlier discussions,[7] and to correct misinterpretations of my position which would place me within the "theological camp."[8] Moreover, I would like to pre-empt, if possible, an attack on my perception of historical fact, as might be attempted by those who, like Charles Davis, see the conflict between theology and religious studies as due to a failure of the antagonists to recognize a radical shift of meaning in the use of the concept from medieval to modern times.[9]

In trying to account for the history of "God-talk" ("god-talk") and talk about God (the gods, or any other functionally equivalent Ultimate) I find it helpful to distinguish "confessional theology" from "non-confessional theology." The basis of the distinction is essentially presuppositional. Confessional theologies presume the existence of some kind of Ultimate Transmundane Reality, whereas non-confessional theologies recognize only the cultural reality of "the gods" (that is, of some transcendent reality) and attempt to account for it rationally but without subscribing to the supposition that the Ultimate exists.[10] Such a "theoretical theology"—or theology proper—in attempting to provide a rational account of the reality of the gods, leaves open the possibility for a reductionistic account.[11] For as a truly scientific enterprise, theology must hold God (the Ultimate) as problematic, as I shall argue below.[12]

I point out, furthermore, that not all confessional theologies are of the same order. For example, I distinguish "small-c" *confessional theology* from "capital-c" *confessional theology*—the latter being commonly used to refer to (exclusivist) theologies of particular creeds and confessions in the history of Western religious thought.[13] "Small-c" confessional theology, however, is used to cover even the more general acknowledgement of the ontological reality (existence) of the "Focus" of religion—that is, the independent existence of some Ultimate or other to which religious discourse points.

Such distinctions, I suggest, will help students of religion recognize the radical difference between those persons who acknowledge the claim of a transcendent and sacred reality on their lives and those who do not—even when that claim is not tied to a particular historical and exclusivist understanding of some form of divine revelation. Such a non-exclusivistic "confession" I nonetheless take here to be "confession" despite its lack of specificity.

To clarify further the notion of theology as it is used in this essay, I shall respond briefly to Charles Davis' claim that a properly critical theology, which emerged with medieval Christendom, is wholly compatible with Religious Studies. Even for Davis there is a form of theology from which the academic study of religion should be separated, namely, the theology which is nothing more than an elaboration of a particular religious tradition or faith and which, therefore, merely presupposes and reconfirms that tradition. This corresponds to what I have referred to above as captial-c confessional theology, and is rejected by Davis in favor of a critical or theoretical theology. The distinction between such a confessional (or naïve in Davis's terms) and critical theology is not, however, clearly drawn; his conception of critical or theoretical theology will be seen to differ vastly from mine and to reveal in fact the character of the "small-c" confessional theology described above.

Confusion is generated in Davis's discussion of this matter by several apparent contradictions in his use of theological terminology. This occurs, for example, when he compares and contrasts concepts of "theology as a whole," with "the properly theological," and with the various theologies—historical, systematic, theoretical, foundational, confessional, etc. And at one point Davis insists that capital-c confessional theology is not really theology at all (1975: 221). Furthermore, his claim that systematic theology is concerned essentially with the ordered exposition of the doctrines of a particular tradition which rests on revelation and authority (212) is contradicted by his further claim that the science of religion is simply a more advanced stage of systematic theology rather than something essentially different (219), though he still maintains that he has kept the term "theology" simply to refer to "reflection" upon religion as opposed to the process of expression and communication proper to religion as such (220).

His claim to be using "theology" in a non-partisan, critical fashion is undermined in the underlying assumption of his work that "the religious"— whether it be experience, expression, or activity—is sufficiently different from other social phenomena for it to become the object of a distinct and special science.[14] The assumption excludes reductionistic explanations of religion for the rather circularly-argued reason that "[r]eligious phenomena [. . .] call for a direct [special] investigation to analyze their common elements . . ." (1975: 214). This specious and ultimately tautological argument reappears later in the essay in the claim that "the science of religion is an empirical enquiry distinguished from sociology and psychology by its primary concern with religious data as religious" (219). All of this amounts, of course, to the patent non-sequitur that since theology, as "rational discourse about God," exists, then God too must exist; and this effective "presumption of theism"[15] I would argue, makes of Davis a "small-c" confessional theologian.[16] To conclude: I do not take issue here with theology of the theoretical kind which recognizes the Ultimate as problematic; for such a theology leaves open the possibility of a reductionistic account of it. All uncritical thinking about God or the gods which relies on revelation or on the "presumption of theism"—therefore, refusing to countenance the possible non-existence of the divine—is "confessional theology." Such theology constitutes a species of what I call "religious thought," operating within the framework of general religious assumptions or traditions and is therefore in-compatible with what will be referred to below as the basic minimum pre-suppositions for the academic study of religion.

The study of religion as a scholarly exercise has a very long history;[17] ante-dating by far the institutionalized, academically-legitimated study of religion which emerged in the late nineteenth century.[18] And it is important to see that its acceptance in the academic domain was not occasioned by a natural, spontaneous recognition either of its academic style or methodological sig-nificance. Rather, it came about as a result of a quest for such recognition that required establishing the scientific objectivity of religious studies—a quest which, as has often been pointed out, is the product of the Enlighten-ment. This in turn required giving up the theological interests and confes-sional stance so characteristic of that study in the past.[19] Indeed, in some countries—France being a case in point[20]—the teachers of the new disci-pline replaced the Theological Faculty altogether. In this sense Jacob Neusner is right to suggest that the new academic student of religion at-tempted to overcome an unwanted past, although I think he exaggerates when he claims that the attempt was successful (1977b). Similarly Joachim Wach (1951, 1958) and Joseph Kitagawa (1958) speak of the study of reli-gion as being emancipated from a theological agenda, and Robert W. Friedrichs (1974) talks of the "detheologizing" of the subject. The study of religion, they assert, was becoming more neutral, objective, and scientific. This meant adopting a notion of a universally applicable mode of inquiry, implying that religions could be studied in exactly the same way as any other social phenomenon. The scholar *qua* scholar, therefore, was to eliminate re-ligious commitments from all scholarly analysis. The several concerns of the "new" discipline included: (1) morphology of religion, involving primarily a description of rites, rituals, beliefs, practices, art, architecture, and so on of the various historical religions; (2) stages of religious development; (3) par-allels among the various traditions; and, later, (4) the phenomenology of re-ligious meaning and the structure of religions. The discipline, then, was primarily empirical, heavily centered on philological and historical concerns, and resulted in the production of scholarly monographs and interpretive studies.

The institutionalization of this new discipline was not only to be found in universities; an international association (The International Association for the History of Religions [IAHR]) was eventually formed in the 1950s al-though International Congresses had been held from 1900 on, and under the pressure of various religious sentiments—especially as the Association expanded membership to include religion "scholars" from the Far East[21]—theological and religious matters began to appear on the agenda of its Congresses. This unforeseen regression led to a stricter formulation of the scientific goals and intentions of the new discipline (*Religionswissenschaft*) by R. J. Zwi Werblowsky. His five-point enunciation of the "basic minimum presuppositions" for the pursuit of historical and comparative studies of religion was reproduced in *Numen*, the official publication of the IAHR (Schimmel, 1960).[22] A summary of that statement here will provide a kind of benchmark for the "retreat to theology" I shall attempt to document below: [23]

1. "Comparative religion" or *Religionswissenschaft* is a scientific discipline;
2. *Religionswissenschaft* is a branch of the humanities, and as such it is an anthropological discipline, studying the religious phenomenon as a creation, feature and aspect of human culture. The common ground on which students of religion, *qua* students of religion, meet is the realization that the awareness of the numinous or the experience of transcendence (where these happen to exist in religions) are, whatever else they may be, undoubtedly empirical facts of human existence and history, to be studied like all human facts by appropriate method;
3. *Religionswissenschaft* rejects the claim that religion is a *sui generis* phenomenon that can only be understood if ultimately seen to be a realization of transcendent truth;
4. Although the study of religion may arise from non-academic motivation, it needs no such external justification (and ought not to rely on one);
5. The IAHR must keep itself free from all ideological commitments.[24]

Some critics have seen this program as Comtean *ersatz* religion.[25] But Werblowsky's review of Wach's "theological" approach to the study of religion counters that: "Of course historical analysis can never yield the norms without which life is not worth living . . . but, then, nobody ever supposed historical analysis to do just that. There is, after all, a world of difference between study and living, between studying history and making it" (Werblowsky, 1959: 354).

Religious Studies did in fact gain the academic legitimation it sought. But it failed to live up to the commitments it had given the academic community to pursue its agenda in a religiously non-partisan fashion. E. J. Sharpe (1986 chapter 6) points out, for example, that in the early days of the "discipline,"[26] Religious Studies was still considered by many to be religious instruction even if not on the confessional scale found in theological faculties—an impression bolstered by the close association of some of its leading practitioners (such as F. M. Müller) with movements such as the World's Parliament of Religions held in Chicago in 1893. Kitagawa has noted, in a review of the subject as taught in the United States, that although its early formation followed European scientific lines, it eventually submitted to the pressures of conservatism and orthodoxy (1959, 1983). This seems less surprising when one considers that the majority of those in the field hail from a religious background and likely entered the discipline with theological baggage if not an agenda.[27] The situation is further compounded by the connected complaint—voiced by C. J. Bleeker (1961, 1975) and still heard today—that the IAHR has not been able to attract social scientists interested in the study of religious phenomena. As Oxtoby put it, Religious Studies was simply "not scientific enough" (1968: 591).

I do not mean to suggest here, however, that scholars were being duplicitous—in fact, they made the conscious effort to "bracket" their own beliefs and made this "bracketing" a requirement of the discipline. In so doing there emerged a general methodological agreement that the truth-question not be raised in Religious Studies—that is, that the academic study of religion forego the philosophical-metaphysical justification of the various historical religious traditions which had thus far been such an unsuccessful and divisive exercise. So it is not that those who adopted the bracket—*epoché*—denigrated that metaphysical exercise or denied its value in other contexts but just that, for the sake of achieving a convergence—however short-range—of scholarly opinion on general religious issues from a wide range of competing theological frameworks, they restricted their concerns to less speculative, more positive matters where all could agree on the criteria for assessing claims.

The *epoché* (or bracketing) freed the student and the study of religion from ecclesiastical domination, although there was still a certain amount of theological suspicion attached to those so engaged (Oxtoby, 1968: 591). However, there are methodological corollaries implied in the *epoché* to suggest that such a study of religion, even though free from a certain ecclesiastical—and therefore capital-c confessional—domination, is nonetheless influenced by religious or theological commitment. The most damning corollary, as I have indicated elsewhere, is the "descriptivist doctrine"—whereby the substance of the Science of Religion is reduced to phenomenological description—especially when connected with the widely-held belief that such a study constitutes a new discipline, (namely, the "Science of Religion."[28]) The corollary requires that the study of religion remain free from theory and forego explaining religious phenomena. For to explain is to grant that the phenomenon is somehow illusory or veridical—in other words, to invoke the very category of truth which the *epoché* banished in its attempt to achieve academic neutrality. However, the enterprise, if it is to be scientific, must necessarily move beyond mere ideographic description to a more nomothetic explanation and theory.[29] This can be done without entering the metaphysical or theological fray—and so, without contravening the conventionally adopted stratagem of the *epoché*—by means of analysis of the cognitive components of the religious tradition concerned compared with the cognitive universe of the investigator. If the cognitive "worlds" clash, the student of religion then proceeds to consider alternative accounts of the religious phenomenon by regarding factors or aspects of human existence not in themselves religious. It is this potentially reductionist accounting for religion that the "descriptivist doctrine" is meant to preclude. For descriptionists, "to explain" is "to explain away" and that, it appears, must be avoided at all costs. But to avoid that possibility altogether is to assume that it can never be "explained away." That assumption, however, indicates a religious or theological bias, for it grants an ontological reality to religion which the latter may not really possess.

The first corollary—the descriptivist doctrine—is complemented by the doctrine of "the autonomy of religion." The obviously circular argument is given that since the discipline of Religious Studies exists, it must have a peculiar subject-matter inviting an equally peculiar method of analysis. Religion being a *sui generis* phenomenon, it is to be treated "on its own terms." Ultimately, to see it as anything other than "religious" is not to take religion "seriously."[30]

To reiterate, the *epoché* and its corollaries, taken together, imply that Religious Studies is a science with a methodology peculiar to itself, distinct from theology-religion on the one hand and the physical and social sciences on the other. I have shown elsewhere, however, that this argument is flawed because it is based on mutually exclusive sets of assumptions and because it fails to delineate clearly the methodology assumed peculiar to itself (Wiebe, 1978).

My arguments on this issue have been criticized as distortions of the original intent of the founders of this "new" science as well as of their successors (Widengren, 1983). It has been claimed that the science is not restricted to the descriptive or ideographic level but rather that it extends to "understanding." Widengren chooses as illustrative of such an approach the work of C. J. Bleeker, who goes beyond mere "fact gathering" in his study of religion to phenomenological understanding (Bleeker, 1954, 1971). I do not deny that Bleeker wishes to go beyond the fact-gathering stage—as do most of his colleagues—but I must point to the problems inherent in that exercise. The "understanding" Bleeker seeks quite obviously presumes the validity of the devotee's position, for the bracketing is still very much in effect in this exercise. The devotee's self-understanding in effect provides the point of departure for this task. This principle was accepted early on in "Science of Religion" circles which we see in F. M. Müller's adoption of "Comparative Theology" as an element of that science. The student, he insists, must deal with the facts as discovered, so that "if people regard their religion as revealed, it is to them a revealed religion and has to be treated as such by every impartial historian" (Müller, 1893: 74).[31]

There is no doubt that the understanding sought by phenomenology "goes beyond" descriptive, historical and philological fact-gathering. The question which needs raising, however, is whether that "understanding" is still description (perhaps at a deeper level), or whether in fact it goes beyond that ideographic to a truly nomothetic grasp of religious phenomena. And if the latter, its *epoché* in fact amounts to an *a priori* acceptance of an ontological reality although it refuses to commit publicly—or even privately—to that reality. Therefore, it is assumed that reductionist accounts are unable to provide an understanding of religion; and that means, conversely, that religion necessarily involves persons with what is ultimately "real," and "good." *Understanding,* then, would by definition preclude causal explanation; because the latter, where applicable, is of limited value, for this kind of understanding is broader than explanation.[32] Such an "understanding," to conclude, amounts to a non-specific theology, for it assumes the ontological reality of the religious phenomenon without consciously espousing any particular historical religious tradition's view of that reality.[33] It rests uncritically on the assumption of the metaphysical validity of "religion in general."[34]

What I hope to show in this section of the paper is the hidden theological agenda of Religious Studies.[35] Neusner's relatively recent suggestion (1977b) that the academic study of religion in the United States and Canada has developed a set of norms which exclude religiosity from the classroom, and that there has developed a consequently detached and objective approach to the study seems a fairy tale, which ignores the significance of the literature produced, as the discussion to follow should demonstrate. Furthermore, with respect to "what goes on" in our Departments of Religious Studies and in our other academic institutions, the evidence simply does not support his claim, but documentation of this will have to be left for another paper.[36]

Space does not permit a detailed analysis of all the positions and arguments against what amounts to a "detheologized" academic study of religion; nevertheless I shall attempt to delineate here the major stances taken. I am not sure that the two major arguments (and their subdivisions) I shall deal with are clearly distinguishable from each other—nor are they set out by their authors in a pure and pristine form. However, the typology I shall offer should be of some use in assessing what has grown to be a large body of literature; and the overview provided should at least indicate a trend in Religious Studies which threatens to jettison the gains it has made since the Enlightenment.

The most common type of argument to be found in this literature might best be designated the "complementarity thesis." The claim usually put forward in this case is not that Religious Studies is of no use to our search for understanding religious phenomena but simply that it is inadequate. The "heart of religion," that is, cannot be perceived if the subject is approached "in purely informative, descriptive, scientific terms" (Kegley, 1978: 280). According to Mostert: "One must go beyond the historical and socio-scientific approach that adheres simply to empirical methods of data collection and description or even explanation" (1976: 8–9); or as Ladner puts it, the proper study of religion "entails more than employing the intellectual instruments of criticism and analysis to investigate various forms of faith and belief" (1972: 216)—something which has been neglected recently in the shallowness fostered by an expansion of Religious Studies, while it blindly vaunts "that we are finally getting our intellectual foot in the academic door of secular education . . ." (Ladner, 1972: 216).

In an early essay in this genre, Bernard E. Meland raises questions about the assumption that the student of religion need only be concerned with "objective methods" (1961). According to Meland, the student of religion must be distinct from the regular historian or the run-of-the-mill social scientist. The student of religion "is not *just* a historian or a scientist in the sense that defines the anthropologist or social scientist. He is a student of religions in a specific and specialized sense" (269–270, emphasis added), involving "deeper" dimensions of religion. And Kees Bolle, while admitting that the study of religion—historically at least—is an enterprise in its own right, and that emphasis on such study in the early days assisted the establishment of Religious Studies in university centers and departments, denies that it alone will "make our field acceptable in a modern academic framework" (1967: 98). Indeed, he predicts that, without complement, the pure academic approach would bring the discipline to an end: "Religious phenomena are never just intellectual propositions or just individual affairs. Hence neither can the manner in which religious phenomena are approached have its centre in logical investigation and a resulting synthesis of general laws *alone,* even if the individual following this method is a master in the fields of logic and anthropology" (100).

Such complementarity might best be characterized as "incremental," the academic study of religion being supplemented by theology as, say, physics is "exceeded" by chemistry. Theology, that is, is an entirely different way of "knowing" than the "knowing" of science which increases our information. As Kegley expresses it, the student of religion cannot remain detached in an information-gathering exercise but rather must share in the religious experience of the devotee. And, he maintains, "this [. . .] is not a call for indoctrination but for the wooing of the spirit" (1978: 280).[37] Kegley, however, does not see the complementarity as unilinear but rather as a "mutual benefiting" of Theology and Religious Studies: "Theology without serious religious studies tends to pious arrogance; religious studies without theology tends to parasitical aloofness. In a dialectical encounter, both may thrive" (1978: 282).

A similar "mutual complementarity" thesis is to be found in the work of R. H. Drummond: "If theologians need the history of religions to give full-bodiedness and contemporary relevance to their own work, the historians of religion need theology in order to come to grips with that which they are really supposed to deal—the central elements of the religious life of humankind" (1975: 403). J. P. Mostert insists "it rests with theology to illuminate [religion's] ultimate depth dimension" (1976: 12); as do Meland and Bolle (among others), although Bolle at least calls for a "deprovincializing of Christian theology" in the process (1967: 116).[38]

"Incremental complementarity," however, is not the only response to the issue of the relationship of Theology to Religious Studies; there is an alternative, which I will refer to as "incorporative complementarity." It is a position halfway between the simple "complementarity thesis" and the "identity thesis" (to be discussed below), which does not fully insist on the distinction between Religious Studies and Theology but instead points to the subordination of the former by the latter. The position seems well expressed by A. Jeffner in the conclusion to his paper on "Religion and Understanding":

> [R]eligion can be seen as a kind of understanding and explanation of a part of reality. Such religious understanding is parallel to other kinds of understanding, e.g., the scientific one. But religious understanding aims at an understanding of our total situation, in other words an all-inclusive understanding. The religious all-inclusive understanding need not be opposed to a scientific understanding of a part of reality, but it is opposed to a scientific world view and a scientific all-inclusive understanding. (1981: 225)

Science, then, has a place, but it is secondary; it can only make its contribution within a wider frame of reference. Theologians taking up this stance effectively "hybridize" disciplines, tending to talk of "religio-sociology," or "religio-ecology," or "religio-history," and so on.[39] As J. Kitagawa (himself a proponent in this category) puts it with regard to J. Wach's work, there is an attempt to "combine the insights and methods of *Religionswissenschaft,* philosophy of religion, and theology" (1958: xxxviii). As one sees in Wach's writings and activities, this implies that although as a student of religion one does not wish to give up the ideal of objectivity, one comes to recognize that such objectivity falls short of the broader vision in which neutrality is precluded. "What is required," he writes, "is not indifference, as positivism in its heyday believed [. . .] but rather engagement of feeling, interest, *metexis,* or participation" (Wach, 1958: 12). And to settle for less is to adopt a form of scientism.[40] Kitagawa echoes Wach in this matter, advocating the exploiting of such "new" disciplines as religio-sociology and religio-science to show the possible "syntheses" and "interpenetration" of disciplines sought by Wach.[41]

But Wach and Kitagawa are not the only scholars to hold this position. Indeed, as Kitagawa points out, the line of thought goes back to Wach's Marburg teachers, including F. Heiler and Rudolph Otto (Kitagawa, 1971: 49). What Wach envisages in his redefinition of Religious Studies, according to Kitagawa "is the interpenetration between constructive theology, which is informed and purified by careful studies of history of religions, and history of religions, itself liberated from the 'narrowly defined' scientific approach to the study of religion" (1971: 52). Other scholars in this tradition include Paul Tillich,[42] Mircea Eliade,[43] and Eliade's many followers.[44] What all have in common is what Kitagawa found essential to Wach's attempt at a deep penetration into the nature of religion—namely, "the recognition of the objective character of ultimate reality" (1971: 46). In other words, what is implied (if not sought) is a concept of "meaning" as a "transcendent something" unaffected by the dictates of science.[45] The sciences (including the scientific study of religion) are thus in effect contaminated by the religious vision. Science, it appears, cannot ultimately comprehend religion; the latter remains, in Wach's words, "one of the inexplicable mysteries which have accompanied the ascent of man . . ." (1944: 307).

This mysteriousness, I maintain, is essentially a religious attribute—and proof of a confessional stance. And I would argue that such a pronouncement reveals a similar approach wielded by all those methods for the study of religion which subordinate the detached, scientific "outsider" approach to religion to the confessional "insider" approach.[46]

The last type of argument for a re-theologized Religious Studies mentioned above as the "identity thesis," amounts to a variation of the preceding forms. Its claim is that following analysis of the nature and task of Theology and Religious Studies the two will in fact be pronounced essentially the same enterprise. This position has been set out elaborately by W. Pannenberg (1976) within the framework of a defense of theology as a science (and therefore as an academic discipline). He allows that theology can be described as the "science of Christianity," but if Christianity is seen as only one religion among many others in the context of the history of religions, it should rather be placed under the general heading of the Science of Religion (1976: 256). The kind of unity which "reduces" theology to a sub-discipline, however, he rejects, arguing that theology does justice to Christianity only as a science of "God," where "God" stands for "reality-as-a-whole" while admitting that an "anthropological turn" has taken place in theology to make both the concept and theology itself problematic. He then goes on to ground such a hypothetical theology in the Science of Religion (346), theology's concern being, as he puts it, "the communication of divine reality experienced in [religions . . .]" (365). This amounts to a critical theology of religions "in virtue of its attempt to examine the specifically religious theme of religious traditions and ways of life, the divine reality which appeared in them, and not some other psychological or sociological aspect" (365–366). Theology, therefore, he equates with the Science of Religion when that task is being properly carried out. In an earlier essay Pannenberg describes an identical characterization of Theology and the Science of Religion, but there he admits that the exercise is not simply historical but rather a kind of "religious-historical" research and therefore a religious exercise. Such an admission unwittingly supports the thesis that academic and religious pursuits are mutually exclusive (1971: 116).

Pannenberg's kind of stance is taken up by a number of other scholars as well. A similar but much briefer statement is presented, for example, by B. Hebblethwaite (1980). Carl-Martin Edsman contends that Religious Studies, when placed in Faculties of Theology as it has often been, has not fared badly; and he maintains that those who call for a separation of the two disciplines are propagandists ignorant of the strictly scientific scholarship of both fields (1974: 70). A. D. Galloway maintains that it is in the human quest for truth that we see "the unity and integrity of our discipline" (1975: 165). And Paul Wiebe, while disclaiming any connection with the systematic theologies taught at seminaries, maintains that Religious Studies is a constructive science, not merely self-reflective and historical, and therefore indistinguishable from theology (1975: 18, 23). He states his position: "the creation of norms is the final good of religious studies. This is to say that the real impetus behind the investigation of religion is not a mere intellectual or aesthetic curiosity, but is a desire for existential truth" (23). This of course makes it obvious that the so-called academic discipline is at the same time a religious activity. And it is certainly reminiscent of Paul Tillich's nebulous view of the History of Religion's being merely a form of theology in the process of transformation into "the religion of the concrete spirit" (1963: 87). Charles Davis similarly maintains that once one recognizes theoretical theology for what it really is—and has been since at least the Middle Ages— the modern development of the science of religion will be seen to be in continuity with that medieval progression (1975: 207).[47] On one level he insists that to study religion is not in itself a religious exercise (207), but on another he maintains that theology cannot simply be seen as a datum on a different level from the science of religion (208). Consequently he advocates a convergence of the two disciplines, with each having as its primary concern religious data *qua* religious (219), even though this seems to contradict his earlier disclaimer about the religiosity of that study. In conclusion he states "the science of religion is [. . .] a more advanced stage of systematic theology, [and] not an essentially different enterprise (219).

A twist on the identity thesis is often found in the literature as well. It is often claimed, that is, that the so-called academic study of religion is itself a religion and therefore simply rivals religious faith of the established traditions. This was the thrust, for example, of W. C. Smith's 1984 presidential address to the American Academy of Religion (1963).[48] The most vocal exponent of this thesis, in my opinion, however, is R. N. Bellah. He readily admits that he has no anxiety about blurring the boundary line between religion and the teaching of religion—of infecting the study, so to speak, with its own subject matter (1970c: 4). Indeed, boundaries cannot be erected since "whatever fundamental stance one takes in teaching about religion is in itself a religious position" (4), though he does elsewhere refer to it as implicitly religious (1970a: 95).[49] In the latter article he refers to his position as one of "symbolic realism" which is both academically sound, according to him, and self-consciously religious. Indeed, he maintains that it "is the *only* adequate basis for the social scientific study of religion" (1970a: 93, my emphasis).[50]

Paul Ingram captures the sentiments of Bellah well in his methodological statement against the "cartesian methodology" that is "basically a technology for manipulating 'religious data' into precise intelligible patterns that can be understood by anyone who followed the same technical procedures" (1976: 392). Rather than attempting to seize the truth about religion the students must be seized by truth and insight in spite of the methodologies they may hold (1975: 394). And Walter Capps also talks about the need to fight against "the monopolizing compact between the Enlightenment and religious studies . . ." (1978: 104). Religious studies, that is, must involve itself, as does theology, in the process of the formation of the truth (1978: 105). This, then, is the dominant story one hears from an ever-expanding circle of spokespersons for Religious Studies.

Although rather lengthy, this review does not at all exhaust the bewildering variety of arguments calling for a return to Theology in Religious Studies— calls to turn to religion and the Supermundane, to Ultimate Reality and the Truth. There is, however, sufficient documentation here to support the claim that the objective, detached, and scientific study of religion, so eagerly sought in the heady days of the late nineteenth century, is no longer a major factor in the study of religion in our universities. We have now a return to religion under the apparent pressure of a breakdown of our culture,[51] but to believe that we are returning to our "origins" is sheer illusion. The "limitations" of the classroom in our attempt to understand religion[52] have not so much led to a misunderstanding of religion, I would suggest, as they have fostered the creation of what R. Michaelson calls "classroom religion."[53] Bellah's symbolic realism is an example of precisely that, but it is arguable as to whether—with respect to the religious traditions originally studied by the academic community—such an interpretation is not itself reductionistic.[54]

Before leaving this matter I should like to focus special attention on my own academic community in Canada which I think is aptly described as having "lost its nerve" in this enterprise—if it ever had it—as evinced in the work of Davis discussed above. In a more recent essay on theology and religious studies Davis categorically insists that a scientific study of religion cannot operate devoid of religious faith (1981: 13). That view, moreover, presents itself in a more general fashion in Davis's work as editor of the Canadian journal *Studies in Religion (SR)*. The conclusion drawn by P. B. Riley after close analysis of the journal's content over the first ten years of its existence is that the journal has been devoted to (quoting Davis) "collaboration between theologians and religionists" (1984: 427). Indeed, he correctly suggests that this is the distinctive contribution of the journal and, I would maintain with only slight qualification, that the groups for whom the journal serves as official organ are quite happy with the ideological direction it has taken.

The editorial policy of Davis, moreover, perpetuates a long tradition. In this regard it is interesting to note that, in some sense, *SR* is a continuation of the old *Canadian Journal of Theology.* That journal, experiencing financial difficulties and being unable to secure Canada Council funding because of its "religious character," signed away its existence to the new religious studies periodical able to secure such financial support. In return, however, the *Canadian Journal of Theology* received assurance from W. Nicholls, the first editor of *SR,* that the new journal would not abandon its theological readership. That promise has been kept (Riley, 1984: 444).[55]

This is not, of course, the only indication of the state of Religious Studies in Canada. The influence of Wilfred Cantwell Smith on the Canadian scene is almost all-pervasive, and it most certainly influences the "re-theologizing" of Religious Studies. Riley, in his look at *SR* claims that Smith's "work and influence perhaps more than that of any individual, permeates the pages of *SR*"[56] and the claim applies, I think, to his general influence on Religious Studies elsewhere as well,[57] although space does not permit substantiating that claim here. Finally, other events in the emergence and operation of departments for the study of religion in Canada could be cited to support the claim.[58]

It was with some surprise that I found myself taken to be an exponent of the very position I have argued against here and elsewhere.[59] It is true that in my discussion of the possibility of a Science of Religion I admitted that

Religious Studies might well contain theological elements (Wiebe, 1978). But the theology I had in mind was of a scientific nature, capable of accepting the demands of intellectual honesty to the point of abandoning any absolute or ultimate commitments, and leaving itself open to radical change (1978: 125).[60] In this sense, which I may not have explained clearly enough, theology (philosophical, theoretical, or scientific) as "the rationale of God or the gods" permits the possibility of reductionism, although, quite obviously, it does not necessitate it. It is for this reason that I found it justifiable to talk of the possibility of the study of religion as proceeding from the point of view of the "critical participant" (or "detached devotee") while refusing to recognize an "autonomous discipline" presupposing an independent subject matter—that is, God, the gods, the Transcendent, Ultimate Reality, and so on. For the *a priori* acceptance of the reality and existence of the Ultimate is a species of religious thinking and, if it is to be called theology at all, ought to be referred to as "confessional theology." And it is this kind of theologizing which I argue is incompatible with Religious Studies since it in fact constitutes the subject matter of that study. As I have pointed out in my discussion of Davis and others above, to accept without question (as a condition of the study) the existence of an Ultimate Reality is to espouse confessional theology, even if it is of a more "ecumenical" variety than in the past. So, to avoid any further ambiguity, I reiterate here: theology, when it commits itself to the existence of the Ultimate, constitutes a form of religious thought which cannot complement the academic study of religion but can only "infect" it.[61]

Imprecision on this matter may unfortunately have been fostered by my failure to point out clearly there that the "critical insider" and "sympathetic outsider" converge—and ought to do so—on the descriptive level only and not necessarily on the explanatory and theoretical level.[62] The confusion is due, it appears to me now, to my earlier, predominant apologetic concerns.[65] In my work on the role of explanation in the study of religion (Wiebe, 1975), however, even though showing some sympathy for the argument of the "insiders," I expressed nagging doubts about the matter but did not pursue the issue at that time.

In this paper I have taken up a matter which has challenged me over many years, and I think I have assessed it here a little more clearly. I have shown that the explicit agenda adopted by the founders of Religious Studies as an academic (university) concern committed the enterprise to a detached, scientific understanding of religion wholly uninfected by any sentiment of religiosity. I have also pointed out that the study was—and still is—dominated by a hidden theological agenda, but that the *epoché* invoked by its practitioners had nevertheless provided the ground for beginning a new tradition of thought on matters religious. Finally, I have shown that the crypto-theological agenda informing that study is becoming more overt, actually being touted as the only proper method for the study of religion. This last step, I argue here, dismisses the tentative move toward the development of a scientific study of religion that was heralded by the first generation of *Religionswissenschaftler* and, therefore, constitutes a failure of nerve in the academic study of religion.

Notes

1. This essay is a revised version of a paper prepared for the Eastern International Regional Meeting of the AAR held at McMaster University in the spring of 1984. I wish to thank the participants (especially Lorne Dawson) for helpful comments and criticisms. I am also grateful to Peter Slater, whose criticisms of an early draft of this paper were also of assistance.

2. See R. H. Drummond, "Christian Theology and the History of Religions" (1975); A. R. Gualtieri, "Confessional Theology in the Context of the History of Religions" (1972); and D. Wiebe, "Is a Science of Religion Possible?" (1978).

3. See Carl-Martin Edsman, "Theology or Religious Studies?" (1974); W. Pannenberg, *Theology and the Philosophy of Science* 1976); Eric J. Sharpe, *Comparative Religion: A History* (1975) and *Understanding Religion* (1983); and B. Hebblethwaite, "Theology and Comparative Religion" (1980).

4. See N. Smart, "Resolving the Tensions between Religion and the Science of Religion" in *The Phenomenon of Religion* (1973); R. J. Zwi Werblowsky, "The Comparative Study of Religions: A Review Essay " (1959), and "On Studying Comparative Religion" (1975).

5. For examples of such imagery see Drummond, "Christian Theology" (1975); and J. M. Kitagawa, "*Verstehen und Erlösung:* Some Remarks on Joachim Wach's Work" (1971).

6. The phrase "failure of nerve" is borrowed from G. Murray (*Five Stages of Greek Religion* [1955]). For Murray, a "failure of nerve" characterized the shift from confidence in human effort and the enlightened mind from the presocratics to the rise of asceticism and mysticism after Plato and Aristotle. See also S. Hook, *The Quest for Being* (1961). Other scholars have used the phrase in quite a different way, even to the point of reversing its original intent. See, for example, Carl A. Raschke, "The Future of Religious Studies: Moving Beyond the Mandate of the 1960s" (1983); Eric J. Sharpe, "Some Problems of Method in the Study of Religion" (1971); and, especially, J. C. McLelland, "Alice in Academia: Religious Studies in an Academic Setting." The Enlightenment, as I point out below, constitutes the source from which the academic study of religion emerged. If Peter Gay's (1966) interpretation of that period as the re-establishing of the derailed presocratic Enlightenment is anywhere near the truth, then Murray's "failure of nerve" concept applies particularly well to the subject of my essay.

7. See J. P. Mostert, "Complementary Approaches in the Study of Religion." In the hope of avoiding confusion I use the concept "theology" in a less specific sense than do theologians, so that its rejection as a part of Religious Studies ought not to be taken as an argument for the rejection of theology *per se*. As used here—and in general methodological literature pertaining to Religious Studies—"theology" denotes religious thought, whether carried out by the naïve devotee or by the systematically reflective, intellectually sophisticated devotee. The term "theoretical theology" will be used to refer to a "religiously neutral" discipline—although, as will become clear, there is question as to whether that constitutes a discipline—a distinct mode of thought—as its supposed task is indistinguishable from that of the philosophy of religion.

8. See especially Phillip B. Riley, "Theology and/or Religious Studies: A Case Study *Studies in Religion/Sciences Religieuses* 1971–1981" (originally presented at the 1983 meeting of the Canadian Society for the Study of Religion). A version of the paper that revises his 1983 judgment somewhat appears in *Studies in Religion*.

9. Charles Davis, "The Reconvergence of Theology and Religious Studies" (1975). If space permitted, I would dispute this claim. I agree with Davis that theoretical theology emerges in the Middle Ages, but I would argue that he does not adequately grasp the import of that development. Bernard of Clairvaux did see the significance of the "new theology" of Peter Abelard (and others) more clearly than Davis. A descriptive account of this state of affairs can be found in J. Leclercq, *The Love of Learning and the Desire for God* (1961), and a persuasive alternative interpretation of the Bernard-Abelard conflict can be found in B. Nelson, *On the Roads to Modernity: Conscience, Science and Civilization* (1981). The tension separating "new" and "old" theology, I would maintain, resembles that found between religious and scientific communities of recent Western history. I have addressed this problem more comprehensively in a monograph, *The Irony of Theology and the Nature of Religious Thought* (1991a).

10. On the distinction between the reality and existence of the Focus of the devotee's attention see N. Smart, *The Phenomenon of Religion* (1973).

11. The kind of theology I have in mind here is to be found, for example, in the work of L. Feuerbach or, more recently, in the Christian atheism of the 1960s.

12. Such a scientific theology is undertaken, for example, by W. Pannenberg in his *Theology and the Philosophy of Science* (1976).

13. It might be argued that a further distinction within "capital-c" confessional theology is also necessary in order to account for the differences between the main confessional churches of the Reformation and the left-wing or more extreme groups who explicitly distinguished themselves from the mainstream and did not consider themselves confessional in that sense. This is not, however, a problem to be settled here. (I wish to thank Thomas Yoder Neufeld for drawing this point to my attention.)

14. Similar arguments are to be found in F. J. Streng, "The Objective Study of Religion and the Unique Quality Of Religiousness" (1970), and K. K. Klostermaier, "From Phenomenology to Metascience: Reflections on the Study Of Religions" (1977).

15. For a philosophical discussion of this matter, see A. Flew, "The Presumption of Atheism" (1972).

16. Davis's argument here might on first sight seem to find support in the attempt by R. Morgan and Michael Pye to recall the argument of Ernst Troeltsch. Troeltsch maintained that the positivist or materialist method of study was unacceptable in this field because, in an *a priori* fashion, it precludes the possibility that religion is veridical rather than illusory. A closer reading of Troeltsch, and of the commentaries by Morgan and Pye, however, reveal Troeltsch's methodological idealism to be guilty of a similar *a priorism*. Unfortunately, space does not permit elaboration of that critique here. See the essays by Troeltsch and the Morgan and Pye commentaries in *Ernst Troeltsch: Writings on Theology and Religion* (1977).

17. The scholarly study of world religions has, for many, been a religious exercise. On this point see K. K. Klostermaier's "The Religion of Study" (1978). On the suggestion that the academic study of religion should substitute as a religious exercise, see E. R. Goodenough, "*Religionswissenschaft*" (1959).

18. Likely the best source for details on this development is E. J. Sharpe, *Comparative Religion: A History* (1975). See also M. Jastrow, Jr., *The Study of Religion* (1981), and J. de Vries, *The Study of Religion: A Historical Approach* (1967).

19. See C. Dawson, "Natural Theology and the Scientific Study of Religion" in *Religion and Culture* (1948); also S. M. Ogden, "Theology and Religious Studies: Their Difference and the Difference It Makes" (1978). Some may argue that the early practitioners of the new style of Religious Studies wished to liberate that study from direct ecclesiastical control and therefore were ready to "give up" only "capital-c" confessional theology while seeking to integrate the new study with their "small-c" confessional stances. Yet even a superficial reading of the methodological literature of the period shows that the rejection of confessional theology was much more radical in intent. For it was to allow students of religion to avoid having to settle the apparently unresolvable ontological and metaphysical questions that preclude "convergence of opinion (belief)" even on the level of "small-c" confessional theology. Nevertheless, as I point out below, it is true that much of the work of the early practitioners in this field could appropriately be described as a species of confessional theology.

20. See Sharpe, *Comparative Religion* (1975).

21. See Sharpe, *Comparative Religion* (1975), ch. 6.

22. Many influential members of the IAHR signed the document. It is important to note that Eliade and Kitagawa did sign this positivist-sounding statement despite their sympathies lying elsewhere, as I point out below.

23. My use of this phrase recalls William Warren Bartley's "retreat to commitment" in *Retreat to Commitment* (1962).
24. These sentiments are also expressed in the following essays by R. J. Zwi Werblowsky: "Revelation, Natural Theology and Comparative Religion" (1956); "The Comparative Study of Religions: A Review Essay" (1959); "Marburg And After" (1960) and "On Studying Comparative Religion" (1975).
25. See, for example, C. Davis, "Theology and Religious Studies," *Scottish Journal of Religious Studies* 2 (1981): 11–20.
26. I apply quotation marks to the word "discipline" to show that it is being used for convenience—I am reluctant to call the academic study of religion a discipline in the formal sense. See my essay "Is a Science of Religion Possible?" (1978); and *Religion and Truth: Towards an Alternative Paradigm for the Study of Religion* (1981).
27. See, for example. W. C. Oxtoby, *"Religionswissenschaft* Revisited" (1968); and U. Drobin,"Psychology, Philosophy, Theology, Epistemology—Some Reflections" (1982).
28. See D. Wiebe, "Is a Science of Religion Possible?" (1978).
29. See D. Wiebe, "Explanation and the Scientific Study of Religion" (1975), and "Theory in the Study of Religion" (1983).
30. On this see especially C. J. Bleeker, "The Relation of the History of Religions to Kindred Religious Sciences, Particularly Theology, Sociology of Religion, Psychology of Religion and Phenomenology of Religion" (1954); "Comparing the Religio-Historical and the Theological Method" (1971); and "The Phenomenological Method" (1963).
31. See also Bleeker (1974), W. B. Kristensen, *The Meaning of Religion* (1960), W. C. Smith. "Comparative Religion: Whither and Why?" or *The Meaning and End of Religion* (1963); or "The Modern West in the History of Religions" (1984).
32. The concept of "understanding" used in this fashion has an existentialist, religious connotation, for it suggests that "understanding" constitutes not simply knowledge about religion but perception of a reality that surpasses knowledge or, succinctly put, that constitutes a special kind of knowledge beyond ordinary knowledge. This state of affairs certainly demands further analysis—unfortunately not a task that can be taken up here. On this matter consult J. Waardenburg, "Introduction: A View of a Hundred Years of Religion" (1973).
33. See Oxtoby, *"Religionswissenschaft* Revisited" (1968).
34. This constitutes, I think, a kind of "theology of humanism" and, therefore, an implicit religion. It is clearly on display in, for example, D. R. Blumental, "Judaic Studies: An Exercise in the Humanities" (1977).
35. I do not wish here to assess why the agenda is becoming apparent—nor what is behind these attacks on the scientific study of religion. Some discussion of these issues can be found in C. W. Kegley, "Theology and Religious Studies: Friends or Enemies?" (1978); or G. D. Kaufman, "Nuclear Eschatology and the

Study of Religion" (1983). The image of an "attack" on the scientific study of religion is appropriate given the level of hostility evident in the work of a number of authors. Much of this approaches invective and is thus not worth analysis, but it does display the vehement reaction to what I have referred to as a "failure of nerve," as well as a fear (initially generated by the Enlightenment) that academic life might transcend, and thereby threaten the "intellectual" work of the faithful. Among others see M. Marty, "Seminary/Academy: Beyond the Tensions" (1983); M. Novak, *Ascent of the Mountain, Flight of the Dove: An Introduction to Religious Studies* (1972); and "The Identity Crisis of Us All: Response to Professor Crouter" (1972); and B. Ladner, "Religious Studies in the University: A Critical Reappraisal" (1972), and David Burrell, "Faith and Religious Convictions: Studies in Comparative Epistemology" (1983). Other offenders, such as R. Bellah and W. C. Smith, are discussed below.

36. I have in mind here the example of the development in Canadian universities of rather close, official ties to church-related colleges characterized predominantly by their "advocacy-learning" environment. See R. W. Neufeldt, *Religious Studies in Alberta: A State-of-the-Art Review* (1983). It is also important to note that some Canadian universities have funded appointments financed by religious groups in the community, since such a procedure contributes to a blurring of the distinction between religion and the study of religion. This type of funding activity has received some attention with respect to "study conferences" underwritten by the Unification Church in a recent "Symposium on Scholarship and Sponsorship" involving I. L. Horowitz, B. R. Wilson, J. A. Beckford, E. Barker, T. Robbins, and R. Wallis.

37. See also R. Holley, *Religious Education and Religious Understanding* (1978).

38. Bolle in effect is asking that "capital-c" confessional theology be replaced by "small-c" confessional theology.

39. On this subject see my "Theory in the Study of Religion" (1983).

40. See as well Wach's "General Revelation and the Religions of the World" (1954): 83–93, and "Introduction: The Meaning and Task of the History of Religion" (1967).

41. See especially J. Kitagawa, "Theology and the Science of Religion" (1975), and "*Verstehen und Erlösung*" (1971).

42. Paul Tillich, *Christianity and the Encounter of World Religions* (1963), and "The Significance of the History of Religions for the Systematic Theologian" (1966). See also Howard R. Burkle, "Tillich's 'Dynamic-Typological' Approach to the History of Religions" (1981).

43. See, for example, the essays in M. Eliade's *The Quest: History and Meaning of Religion* (1969).

44. See, for example, *Imagination and Meaning: The Scholarly and Literary Worlds of Mircea Eliade* edited by N. J. Giradot and M. L. Ricketts.

45. The concept of "meaning" is complex and ambiguous, requiring a good deal of clarification if it is to be of use to the student of religion. Minimal bibliographical orientation would take more space than is available at present, and must, therefore, be left for another essay.

46. The literature, I suggest, shows an increasing number of the latter, which, however, neither time nor space allow for analysis here. See, among others, F. Streng, "Objective Study of Religion" and his "Religious Studies: Processes of Transformation" (1974); N. Ross Reat, "Insiders and Outsiders in the Study of Religious Traditions" (1983); C. Vernoff, "Naming the Game—A Question of the Field" (1963); J. Arthur Martin, "What Do We Do When We Study Religion?" (1975); and Blumental, "Judaic Studies" (1977). There are several essays by J. Neusner which seem to support this kind of position—but they do so ambiguously. For this reason I reserve discussion of his position for another context. Further studies, moreover, seem to be in preparation for publication. The *Journal of the American Academy of Religion,* I understand, is soon to publish papers on this topic by J. Neusner, W. May, J. Cahill, W. Capps, and L. O'Connell. (See L. O'Connell, "Religious Studies, Theology, and the Undergraduate Curriculum" [1984]). O'Connell's article appeared after this paper was written and so no account of it has been taken into consideration here, although the paper is wholly in "the failure of nerve" stream as I have developed it above. O'Connell does, however, refer to the forthcoming articles that he prepared for publication (146). [These papers were published in that journal as what Strenski calls "The Report of the Saint Louis Project" (see I. Strenski, "Our Very Own 'Contras': A Response to the 'St. Louis Project' Report"). W. Nicholls's recent paper to the Canadian Society for the Study of Religion annual meeting in Guelph (1983), entitled "Spirituality and Criticism in the Hermeneutics of Religion" and J. Wiggins' paper on "Theology and Religious Studies," read to the Eastern International Regional Meeting of the American Academy of Religion at McMaster University (1983), are also likely to see publication in the near future (to my knowledge, neither paper has appeared in print).

47. See also G. Baum *et al.,* "Responses to Charles Davis" (1975).

48. It is, in fact, the bulk of Smith's methodological message to the community of academic students of religion. Since I have discussed his position on a variety of occasions I shall say no more here; see especially my essays "The Role of Belief in the Study of Religion: A Response to W. C. Smith" (1979), and "Three Responses to *Faith and Belief:* A Review Article" (1981).

49. See also the response by James Tunstead Burtchaell to this paper and Bellah's reply in the *Journal for the Scientific Study of Religion* 9 (1970: 97–115).

50. For similar statements see also his "Religion in the University: Changing Consciousness, Changing Structures" (1972), and "Religious Studies as 'New Religion,'" (1978).

51. See, for example, T. J. J. Altizer, *Oriental Mysticism and Biblical Eschatology* (1961): 161, 172–174.

52. See Neusner, "Being Jewish" (1977).

53. See R. Michaelson, "The Engaged Observer: Portrait of a Professor of Religion " (1972). A slightly different view can be found in J. C. McLelland, "The Teacher of Religion: Professor or Guru?" (1972).

54. Bellah's attempt to salvage religion from the students of religion, I am afraid, is about as effective as Durkheim's attempt to rescue the reality of religion

from its "demise" at the hands of the intellectualist (largely British) anthropologists. But this argument cannot be taken up here. See, however, R. Aron's parallel critique of Durkheim (Aron, 1967: 56).

55. In fairness, it must be noted that clarification of this whole matter is needed, as Professor Nicholls recently informed me that the "theological turn" taken by *Studies in Religion* was not an intentional policy of his nor the result of any promise freely given by him. Whether or not his disappointment and mine with that "theological turn" converge is something we need not explore further here.

56. The sentence appears on page 13 of a draft of the essay distributed by Riley at a 1983 meeting of the Canadian Society for the Study of Religion. For some reason, it was deleted from the published version.

57. In support of this claim see, for example, A. R. Gualtieri, "Faith, Tradition and Transcendence: A Study of Wilfred Cantwell Smith" (1969), and "'Faith, Belief and Transcendence' According to Wilfred Cantwell Smith" (1981). Gualtieri's work itself provides a good example of the results of that influence; see, for instance, his "Descriptive and Evaluative Formulae for Comparative Religion" (1968); "Confessional Theology in the Context of the History of Religions" (1972) and "Normative and Descriptive in the Study of Religion" (1979). There are a number of other prominent Canadian scholars whose thought shows a like influence and even others who argue a similar case quite independently of Smith. I regret to say that these scholars appear jointly to dominate the Canadian scene.

58. See note 36 above.

59. See note 8 above.

60. I expressed that understanding of theology earlier in my essay "'Comprehensively Critical Rationalism' and Commitment" (1973).

61. W. Burkert expresses this conflict between religion and the study of religion most succinctly in his *Homo Necans: The Anthropology of Ancient Greek Sacrificial Ritual and Myth* (1983), which is worth citing here: "The language that has proved the most generally understood and cross-cultural is that of secularized scholarship. Its practice today is determined by science in its broadest sense, its system of rules by the laws of logic. It may, of course, seem the most questionable endeavour of all to try to translate religious phenomena into this language: by its self-conception, a religion must deny that such explanations are possible. However, scholarship is free to study even the rejection of knowledge and repudiation of independent thought, for scholarship, in attempting to understand the world, has the broader perspective here and cannot abstain from analyzing the worldwide fact of religion. This is not a hopeless undertaking. *However, a discussion of religion must then be anything but religious*" (xxi; my emphasis).

62. This was the primary focus of my doctoral work at the University of Lancaster (1974). My early views and subsequent re-evaluation of them are to be found in the volume entitled *Beyond Legitimation: Essays in the Problem of Religious Knowledge* (1994e).

Chapter Nine

The "Academic Naturalization"
of Religious Studies:
Intent or Pretense?

Initial reaction to my argument in "The Failure of Nerve in the Academic Study of Religion" was not encouraging.[1] There was no appreciation of the essay's aim to draw attention to the possibility of fundamental contradiction in our practice of Religious Studies in the university setting—which contradiction may be responsible for the identity crisis the field suffers, threatening not only the future development of the enterprise but its very existence.[2] Nor was there any apparent recognition of the essentially historical character of my thesis—let alone refutation of the argument and evidence provided.[3] Although my account of the emergence and academic establishment of Religious Studies was left unchallenged, my essay nevertheless came under sustained attack. It drew this fire, I suspect, because of the methodological and political implications for Religious Studies stemming from that analysis. To follow my methodological tack could leave me open to charges of reductionism, of being "intent" on explaining religion away in terms of nonreligious social factors rather than understanding it on its own terms; my political argument incites apprehension that the truth and value of religion will be undermined by persons unsympathetic to its aims if they gain control of departments and centers established for its study. Reflecting on the thesis of my essay—that the academic study of religion (Religious Studies) should concern itself with objective knowledge about religions and religion—Charles Davis complains: "We are not led by this philosopher of religion so as to find ourselves at 'the still point of the turning world"(1984: 393), apparently quite oblivious that that had never been my intention. He continues in his critique: "What . . . is the point of religious discipline if any worldling of a philosopher has access to the same level of religious meaning as the tried ascetic?"(394)—as if the cognitive intentionality of the academic student of religion is coincident with the soteriological views of religions and their devotees.

If my aim in that essay had been to set the world straight, then the Davis critique has some justification. However, that was not my aim, and it is beside the point for Davis "to note" that the essay is a "failure" in that regard. Furthermore, it seems impertinent for him to suggest I ought to have been concerned with such an agenda—perhaps because it is the one he wishes to have resolved or because it is the agenda of religions and religious persons. My actual aim had been merely to show that the study of religion, as an academically legitimated enterprise, stands in danger of dissolution in a crisis created by recent clamoring for its "reconvergence" with theology. After all, Religious Studies had achieved its academic status as a legitimate scholarly undertaking—housed in its own political structure within the academic and university community—precisely on the basis of a clear demarcation between itself and theology. But the new "discipline," despite the adoption of the rhetoric of demarcation, failed to emancipate itself completely from its theological and religious roots.[4] And the residual theology characteristic of many of the publications of the earliest generation of scholars in this field shows the (unintended) result of failure in their practice. The failure of the first generation of *Religionswissenschaftler* suggests, unfortunately, either dullness of perception or a failure of nerve in living up to their scholarly commitments.

The study of religion, then, having achieved academic legitimation as a positive science, was included in the curriculum of the modern university, but did not become fully "academically naturalized"—to borrow an image used by the late Professor W. Clebsch in his 1980 AAR Presidential address.[5] It did not live up to the obligations of all "naturalized citizens" of that community, namely, the obligations of neutrality and objectivity. It did not restrict its cognitive concerns to describing the behaviors and beliefs of religious communities nor to drawing empirical generalizations about particular religious traditions and about religion per se by means of testable hypotheses. Whereas the "naturalized" study of religion aims at understanding religion (where "understanding" is mediated through intersubjectively testable sets of statements about religious phenomena), the "theologized" version aims at something "more." As the comments quoted from Davis above indicate, the latter version of Religious Studies, despite having accepted the privileges of legitimation, ignores some of its responsibilities, seeking more than merely public knowledge of public facts—it refuses to follow the rules governing the rest of our public discourse about public facts.[6] It pretends to be what it is not, and in so doing thwarts the intention of the original founders of Religious Studies. If not a "failure of nerve," this certainly constitutes a betrayal of the "discipline."

Contrary to the suggestions of Davis and Slater in their responses (1984) to my "failure of nerve" thesis, the methodological framework it assumes appropriate for the academic study of religion reflects neither a "naïve foundationism" nor a "scientism" endorsing that stance assumed by logical positivists. Although I admit that absolute objectivity is not possible, I must nevertheless insist that every scientific enterprise, in striving for objective knowledge, must be able to distinguish the subjective involvement that is an inescapable human aspect of any enterprise from an involvement that is— whether culturally or individually—blatantly idiosyncratic. The search for a set of criteria whereby we might adjudicate the acceptability or unacceptability of claims made in this field, criteria that "correct" personal, idiosyncratic judgments of individuals, is not the same activity as a search for a set of indubitable foundations upon which we can base absolutely all future statements about events, processes, and elements in the field.[7]

Although, as I have stated, initial reaction to the "failure of nerve" thesis was discouraging, subsequent discussions have, by and large, come to its defense. This is apparent not only in the critiques of what might here be referred to as "the Davis response," but also in a positive assessment of "the intellectual history of the movement to study religion scientifically,"[8] and in an espousal of the essay's central methodological claim—namely, that the academic study of religion needs to be demarcated clearly from theology-religion.[9] And yet I was disappointed to see that the majority of the criticisms had little or nothing to do with the aim and intent of my essay. Some are simply the result of misreading—although a certain lack of clarity in the explication of the thesis may be partly responsible for this. It would greatly assist in clarifying the nature of my original statement—its assumptions and implications—if I could respond to all of the criticisms that have arisen.[10] However, given the restrictions of space I shall limit myself to treating one major issue: the critique of reductionism. Implicit in the initial responses of Davis and Slater, this pointed misunderstanding is raised to explicit and insistent attention by Bruce Alton and, to some extent, by Lorne Dawson.

According to Alton, my understanding of the role of reductionism in the study of religion is indicative of a confused understanding of what it means to take up a "scientific approach" in Religious Studies. There is, he insists, a naïveté in my evocations of that approach that jeopardizes much in my otherwise reasonable understanding of the nature of this field of study as an academic exercise.[11] He maintains, for example, that I argue for a reductive explanation of religious activity (because of my search for causes), although I fail to see where he finds textual warrant for such a claim. He insists that I depict reductionism as necessarily causal in nature and suggests that I am blind to—or ignorant of—a "logic of intending" characteristic of all human behavior. As far as I can tell, Alton infers this from what he believes must attend my understanding of the nature of scientific explanations. Such unfounded surmising on his part is carried out, ignoring the fact that I have devoted an essay to that precise question(Wiebe, 1975), in which I do indeed recognize "the logic of intention" yet show that the causality-intentionality distinction does not preclude theoretical reductionism in this field.

With respect to his opposition to my reductionist approach, Alton's assessment of the "state of the science" of human actions, frankly, leaves me baffled. For he appears to be engaged in little more than a semantic quid pro quo of minimal value to the matter at hand. A few examples will suffice to illustrate my point: his substitution of "processes consequent upon . . ." for "causes," and "mechanisms" for "preceding chain of events," in accounting for the peeling of skin after sunburn, makes little sense. His move from talk of "a logic of intention" to questions about religious intentionality, as if one were dealing with two different kinds of psychological-intellectual processes in these two cases, adds to the confusion. At the end of it all, Alton seems to be advocating a form of anti-reductionism that would force the scientific student of religion determined to explain phenomena to be dependent upon an extra-natural source of information for such explanation. Although insisting that the scholar may not appeal to "a sacred source of conviction" in explaining religion, Alton nonetheless maintains "neither can the scholar *insist* on external factors or on a chain of psychological influences. They are restricted *to the proper domain of religious action—self-caused action* . . ."(1986: 164, my emphasis). He does not suggest how "religious action" differs from other kinds of action, yet in insisting on the distinction he implies that religion is a *sui generis* phenomenon and, therefore, nonreducible (that is, wholly explicable without reduction).

Given the brevity of Alton's treatment of the issue of reductionism, as well as the consequent ambiguity of many of his criticisms, I shall not attempt to refute his claims here. I shall instead state briefly what I see implied by reductionism in the scientific study of religion, for that should indicate how distorted is his conception of the role of explanation (and theory) in the study of religion.[12]

Alton assumes that the only reductionism possible in the study of religion is a nonteleological one that attempts to show that consciousness, sensation, perception—as well as the behavior that stems from them—can be accounted for simply in neuroscientific terms. I am in entire agreement with Alton that reductionist accounts of either religious or nonreligious behavior have met with very little practical success, although I would argue that failures in this quest are due largely to the prematurity of the enterprise. Indeed, in seeing how little of biology, for example, has yet been reduced to the molecular level, it is difficult to conceive how anyone could believe that philosophers at this stage of the game would talk simply of "reducing" the social sciences—lock, stock, and barrel—to the level of physical science, and I certainly do not assume anything of the kind. That such an aim is impossible, however, is also too much to assume, especially given some of the "incredible" reductions of organismic biology to the molecular level already witnessed by the scientific world.

Another kind of possible reductionism is one that explains intentional action in terms of the more general notion of purposiveness that, however, is teleological without being supernatural. Such a reductionism was effected, for example, by Charles Darwin in biology. To explain the behavior of plants that maximize their exposure to the sun in terms of their wanting to do so is simply no longer acceptable. Yet some such explanations were wholly reasonable before Darwin, for the teleology of nature was then founded on the intention or conscious design of a creator-god. Darwin, thus, de-theologized biology but without effecting a nonteleological reduction.

A reductionism comparable to that in Religious Studies is to be found in the behavioral sciences. Unlike biology, the latter treat teleological behavior not simply as purposive behavior but as action derived from conscious intention—wishes, fears, desires, hopes, beliefs, and so on. However, not all such explanations assume conscious intentional or cognitive states, as scholars concerned with nonreductionism in Religious Studies would suggest. Projectionist theories of religion, whether philosophical (Feuerbach), sociological (Durkheim), or psychological (Freud), are considered reductionistic, but they are not on that account nonteleological or even nonintentional. Those theories explain religious behavior, rather, in terms of unconscious intention and cognition, thereby showing that the religious can be understood in terms of human behavior not specifically religious. The de-theologization of Religious Studies, therefore, implies reductionism, but not necessarily of the proportion envisioned by Alton; although it might be admitted that it seems a long-range goal of biology eventually to "reduce" (that is, account for) the conscious and unconscious intentional or cognitive states invoked by the social sciences, structuring their explanations of human action in terms of the *organic* states they invoke to explain other biological behavior.

It is important here to recognize that this kind of reductionism in Religious Studies, as in the other sciences, amounts to a commitment to the methodological unity of the sciences—concepts and methods successful in one area of scientific endeavor will be so in others. Furthermore, such reductionism deepens the explanations sought by inviting expanded application of the theory to account for broader ranges of human experience.

Dawson's concern with my reductionism is expressed less directly. He seems to share my "negative" concerns regarding the de-theologizing of Religious Studies, but he thinks I fail to provide positive formulations of the presuppositions of that study. His own suggestions for grounding Religious Studies, he claims, are epistemological, but he persists in assuming the object of that study to have a peculiar, transcendent character. I find Dawson's proposal interesting but not persuasive, given its metaphysical commitments. For, otherwise put, it rests on an assumption of the autonomy of Religious Studies necessitating a subject matter that is *sui generis*—thus irreducible—and consequently beyond scientific comprehension.[13]

Despite the criticisms raised against it, I feel that the essential thrust of "The Failure of Nerve in the Academic Study of Religion" remains intact. Indeed, the call sounded there for a "de-theologization" of this field of research—and, therefore, for the "academic naturalization" of Religious Studies—has found significant support. Although the essay may not have converted many it may at least have generated interest in a major problem too often and too easily ignored. I hope this exchange of views will not bring an end to the discussion, for there is much still to be learned with respect to such issues as the epistemological foundations of Religious Studies, the theoretical object of attention for the scientific student of religion, and the nature of explanation in the study of religion.[14]

Notes

1. This includes Charles Davis's "'Wherein There Is No Ecstasy" (1984) and Peter Slater's "Comment on Wiebe" (1984). I should also mention the response by Gordon Kaufman, whose helpful critique of an earlier draft of the paper is not publicly available. (Many of the points raised by Davis and Slater were noted by Kaufman.)
2. On this see my essay "A Positive Episteme for the Study of Religion"(1985).
3. Hans H. Penner (1984) notes in passing that he does not find my descriptions of the players in this historical scenario problematic, although he himself, it seems, would have expanded the critique of the role of the historians and phenomenologists of the period. A positive assessment of the historical aspect of my argument can be found in E. Perry's "Identifying Religion Itself" (1985).
4. As noted in my essay "The Failure of Nerve," "discipline" is in quotation marks to indicate that I use the term only for convenience and not because I think Religious Studies a true discipline or autonomous science. Alton (1986) maintains that I do see Religious Studies in this way, despite my disclaimer in the original essay (1984: 408n39).
5. This is discussed in passing in my essay "A Positive Episteme for the Study of Religion" (1985).
6. In phrasing the matter as I have I do not mean to rule out the place of theory. The question of the nature of the theoretical object of attention for the scientific student of religion is obviously of central concern, as both Penner (1984) and Perry (1985) point out. I hope in the near future to take that matter up in an extensive critique of the positions of W. C. Smith, C. Davis, and G. Schmid.

7. Dawson's contribution to the discussion (1984) makes this point abundantly clear.

8. This phrase is borrowed from Perry (1985).

9. I use the hybrid term "theology-religion" to indicate that what I mean by the "de-theologization" of the study of religion is its study from within a nonreligious framework. (Theology in that locution, however, does not include what I refer to as nonconfessional theology discussed in chapter 8 of this volume.) It is important that the reader bear this in mind, since Davis (1984) attempts to make much of the distinction he sees between them. For Davis, those who call themselves objective students of religion may not carry a theological agenda into their study, but they do, he insists, carry a religious agenda with them, created by their failure to come to terms with their personal religious inheritance. How Davis presumes to know this to be the case for all students professing to take an objective approach to the study of religion is not revealed.

10. I include the charges of scientism, foundationism, and nihilism (among others in my essay). Bruce Alton's misunderstanding of my use of the concept of "discipline" (see note 4 above) and his claim that I fail to provide examples of nonconfessional theologians (which in fact I do provide in notes 12 and 13 of the original version of the essay, "The Failure of Nerve"—reprinted as chapter 8, notes 11 and 12 in this volume) need correction if further confusion is to be avoided. His suggestion that my claim that the majority of scholars entered Religious Studies with a theological agenda is a "sceptical instrument wielded with reckless abandon" is simply groundless. His critique of my use of the concept of "nonconfessional theology" is also ill-conceived, as are the charges of a "failure of nerve" on my part in the Religious Studies enterprise also lodged by Davis and Slater. I have dealt at length with some of these issues in two addresses: "Why the Academic Study of Religion?: Motive and Method in the Study of Religion" (1988), and "Postulations for Safeguarding Preconceptions: The Case of the Scientific Religionists" (1988).

11. Alton's interpretation that at this point in my argument I become "normative" is odd, since he himself notes that I do not posit the necessity of reduction but only its possibility. This more subtle view is clearly perceived by Dawson. It seems that both Dawson and Alton feel that, had my views been presented less polemically or more logically, this nuance of argument would not have been lost on Davis. Both have failed to see, however, that the refinement of argument to which they refer was not, in fact, lost on Davis (1984: 397). Moreover, what they see as a reasonable argument—even if somewhat obscured—is nonetheless rejected by Davis as "a mock battle in the name of a false certitude" (397).

12. The comments on reductionism here draw on the discussion of the topic in the biological sciences. The reader might profitably consult A. Rosenberg, *The Structure of Biological Science* (Cambridge: Cambridge University Press, 1985).

13. See Lorne Dawson, "Neither Nerve nor Ecstasy: Comment on the Wiebe-Davis Exchange" (1986). A similar position is argued by some philosophers

of biology on behalf of biology as an autonomous science. There are some teleological claims that so far seem incapable of being translated into causal—therefore reductionistic—descriptions. Some philosophers therefore accept that teleological descriptions are inevitable in biology, accounting for the difference between the physical and biological sciences as based on a radical difference between the subject matters under consideration. But knowledge of this difference could only be metaphysical and, of course, not open to independent confirmation.

14. Of the essays printed on this theme in *Studies in Religion* (1986), only that of Barry W. Henaut ("Empty Tomb or Empty Argument: A Failure of Nerve in Recent Studies of Mark 16?") has gone without mention. I wish to note here that exercises of the kind undertaken by Henaut constitute important support for the claim I have made about the failure of nerve in Religious Studies.

Part III

—◦◦◦—

Case Studies in the Failure of Nerve

Chapter Ten

*Phenomenology of Religion
as Religio-Cultural Quest:
Gerardus van der Leeuw and the
Subversion of the Scientific Study of Religion*

In this essay I will be discussing the fundamental contradiction at the heart of van der Leeuw's phenomenological enterprise; that his phenomenology of religion is directed to both scientific and extra-scientific goals that are mutually exclusive. He responds to the crisis of religion in the radical secularization of Western culture from the vantage point of the academic study of religion, but in so doing he undermines the very foundations on which the legitimacy of the study of religion was established in the Dutch universities. In his attempt to arrest what he sees as cultural deterioration in the West, he draws not only upon Christian spiritual resources but also upon analogous non-Western traditions. This in itself is not a problem. However, his appropriation of the phenomenology of religion in this crusade shows his failure to recognize that it involves a radical transformation of the academic study of religion. In deliberately refusing to draw a clear line of demarcation between religion and the academic, scientific study of religion (which includes the phenomenology of religion), he effectively makes of the latter but another religious quest.

In surveying the approaches to the Old Testament in modern research, Herbert F. Hahn in 1956 concluded that the field was in a state of crisis caused by what I have referred to elsewhere as a "failure of nerve" with respect to the scientific attitude of objectivity that had increasingly come to characterize the field. As Hahn put it:

> [T]he crisis grows out of a loss of confidence in the historical approach on the part of many who formerly favoured it. They have come to doubt whether a detailed and objective method of investigation can interpret the inner mean-

ing of religious literature. The historical method had been content to discover the origin and growth of religious ideas in the Bible and to place them in proper perspective in the religious history of mankind. But of late, the conviction has been growing that historical understanding divorced from commitment to belief is unproductive of true insight where religious conceptions are concerned. (1956: xi-xii)

The political and social turmoil of the twentieth century, claimed Hahn, had convinced many scholars that the scientific approach to research on the Old Testament would not contribute to a better social order and that, consequently, it was necessary to replace "the optimistic belief in mankind's progress toward a better social order and a firm faith in the ability of human reason to discover and apply general principles for successful living" (xii) with the eternal verities of religion. It was therefore the failure of society in coping with the social and political problems of the day—rather than objective, scientific considerations—that led to a revival of traditional dogma and the establishment of a new religious orthodoxy as the framework within which a socially and spiritually relevant understanding of the Old Testament texts was to be achieved.

According to Hahn, there was not simply a rejection of the scientific method and principles of objective research hitherto characteristic of the critical approach to the Old Testament (41); there was also a dissatisfaction with the concomitant refusal to deal with "the inner significance" of that literature (43). Such a scientifically critical approach, it was admitted, "contributed greatly to the increase of knowledge," but, the critics of the scientific approach charged, "it did not deepen understanding" (43). Scholarship, that is, came to be considered "meaningless" if it restricted itself wholly to objective claims (129). The following extended passage from Hahn illustrates the dissatisfaction of many scholars with the "objectivity" of the Wellhausen school:

> Examination of the Old Testament writings by the same methods as were used in the study of other ancient books did not seem to result in an interpretation that gave significant meaning to those writings. The critical reconstruction of Old Testament religious history, setting forth as it did the ideas of the Old Testament only in relation to the circumstances from which they arose, made the viewpoints of the biblical writers simply an expression of an ancient way of life and the embodiment of a particular historic culture. It did not interpret them in terms that gave them universal validity as the expression of general principles. To those who were aware that the importance of the Bible in human history was not due to the accuracy with which it reflected the viewpoints of an ancient culture, but to the permanent significance of its most basic ideas, the emphasis on descriptive fact rather than normative principle

seemed like "mere antiquarianism." Even when the results of critical study were accepted as scientifically correct, the feeling remained that the real value of the Old Testament, as essentially religious in content and point of view, had somehow been missed. (228–229)

A survey of the approaches to the study of religion in modern research should bring us to a similar conclusion about this field of study. Raffaele Pettazzoni, for example, in his essay on "History and Phenomenology in the Science of Religion," seems to echo the same concern with respect to the academic study of religions that is voiced by the critics of the objective study of the Old Testament. "We have told ourselves," he writes, "that it is not enough to know precisely what happened and how facts came to be; what we want above all to know is the meaning of what happened. The deeper understanding cannot be asked for from the religions; it springs from another religious science, phenomenology" (1954: 217). Phenomenology, for Pettazzoni, must therefore be an independent science whose concern is to achieve an understanding of the interior experience of religion. This understanding (*Verstehen*), however, must be combined with the objective knowledge of the history of religion and not be merely an addition to it. Though phenomenology, therefore, is independent, Pettazzoni nevertheless sees it as part of a composite "Science of Religion" that can breathe life into the other elements of the science—such as the History of Religions—that provides merely historical treatment of the exterior manifestations of religion. A "proper" recognition of the symbiotic relationship between the history of religions and phenomenology, he maintains, will assist in the recovery of the unity of what he sees as the ideal sources of the field of religious studies, namely, theology and the humanist sciences. Given his abhorrence of dualism, the emergence of phenomenology of religion is for Pettazzoni the most important innovation of the first half of the twentieth century, and he encourages further development of this trend of thought.

The phenomenologist Pettazzoni had in mind was Gerardus van der Leeuw. And it seems that Pettazzoni correctly understood both the nature of van der Leeuw's phenomenology and its implications. But what Pettazzoni sees as a most important innovation to revitalize the academic study of religion I argue is essentially its subversion. In his analysis of the reaction to the scientific study of the Old Testament, Hahn raises the question as to whether it represented a "new path forward" or rather signified a return to a "theological exegesis" ultimately obscuring the gains made by the critical historical studies undertaken (1956: xii). The same question is equally appropriately raised with respect to the phenomenology of religion, for here we see the same insistence that the scientific scholarship related to religious phenomena concern itself with questions of meaning that go beyond the scholarly scientific mandate.

Van der Leeuw, I shall argue, was concerned to transcend such a mandate; he was also concerned to show that transcending that mandate constituted not the abrogation of science but rather its ultimate fulfillment. In that respect, his reaction to the detached, objective-history-of-religions approach to understanding religion mirrors the neo-orthodox reaction to critical biblical studies for whom, as Hahn puts it, "[s]cientific detachment was tantamount to divorcing oneself from the possibility of understanding." For them, he continues, "no merely intellectual understanding was adequate; there [had to] be the kind of 'spiritual' appreciation that comes from personal commitment as well" (241–242).

There have been a number of works on the thought of van der Leeuw and particularly on his contribution to the phenomenology of religion—and I do not wish here simply to cover ground gone over before.[1] However, I think it is not unfair to say that his understanding of phenomenology and the phenomenology of religion, especially as found in his *Religion in Essence and Manifestation,* is far from clear, and that comments on his phenomenology to date have not been a great deal clearer. Further discussion, therefore, is called for. I do not mean this to be as critical a comment as it first appears, for I am not sure that anyone could provide a very coherent account of van der Leeuw's position since, as Ake Hultkrantz has pointed out, it is in some places simply incomprehensible (Hultkrantz, 1970: 72). My intention in this brief recounting of his phenomenology is not to provide a comprehensive and wholly perspicuous description of his position but rather to discover its central thrust—to bring into focus what Pettazzoni considered its critical innovation in the academic study of religion.

Van der Leeuw's brief history of phenomenology in the epilegomena of *Religion in Essence and Manifestation* (1938) displays quite clearly his view of the significance of the phenomenology of religion. He maintains that the latter results from the various investigations undertaken within the framework of the history of religions. Although van der Leeuw links phenomenology with the work produced in the Enlightenment period by historians of religion, he nevertheless sees the chief impetus to the phenomenology of religion in Romanticism. He goes further, however, to identify an even stronger impetus in "Philosophic Romanticism," which viewed religious phenomena (manifestations) as signs of a primordial "revelation" requiring a mythological apperception—that is, "a religious immersion within the data of the history of religions" (691).[2] But neither of these movements, in his opinion, contributed significantly to the development of a phenomenological understanding of religion, although each explored new territories with "incalculable results." He points out that the wealth of discoveries made in these stages of the growth of the study of religion forced scholars to consider new ways to handle the enormous amount of information needing attention. Thus was the ground prepared for the phenomenological approach, which in its seeking to understand the essence of religion would simultaneously account for its emergence. Consequently, van der Leeuw suggests, the objective and historical study of religions—which is essentially the source of the development of the phenomenology of religion—is also transformed by it; the phenomenology of religion, that is, occasions a "change of direction of the history of religions" (694). The question I wish to raise here is whether that change of direction in fact amounts to a subversion of the objective historical study of religions.

Although the phenomenological study of religion may have been a by-product of the history of religions in van der Leeuw's eyes, the two are contradictory, and in fact phenomenology could be seen as inimical to any scientific approach to the study of religions. From the preface to the epilegomena of *Religion in Essence and Manifestation,* van der Leeuw talks as if the phenomenological study of religion were involved in a power struggle with scientific studies of religious traditions. "Imperious" and "dominating" theory, for example, is entirely banished from his work, for it is detrimental to a study aimed at *understanding* Religion. Explanation differs from understanding when it applies to religious phenomena. In the opening chapter of the book van der Leeuw rejects theoretical approaches to primitive religions characteristic of British scholarship. Although his anxiety about much of the theoretical discussion is to some extent justified, he does not by any stretch of the imagination provide an adequate foundation for its outright rejection—and certainly not for the rejection of recourse to theory overall. Nevertheless, he remarks in a note that the methods characteristic of such scholarship "can in no case attain *our* goal which is the comprehension of the phenomena in accord with their spiritual content" (27n4). Although the reference to "our goal" might be an innocent remark about the peculiar aims of one of many disciplines concerned with religions, I think it is indicative of a deeper intent—that of bringing about a transformation of the generally accepted academic goal of the study of religion: the acquisition of objective, scientific knowledge of religions.

In chapter 5 van der Leeuw elaborates somewhat on his opposition to theory (and to evolutionary theory in particular) and reveals more clearly an agenda tainted with political overtones. He appears to attribute the ready acceptance of the evolutionary explanation of religion to an "unhealthy" view of the nature and power of a science that effectively subordinates religion. Science, and the desire for explanation, it appears, is destructive; it seems religion can only be restored to its proper status if such reductionistic explanation—and therefore science itself—is subverted. In fact, he attempts to persuade us that this has in part already occurred, although the argument he provides is very much open to debate. He writes: "Today . . . the need to 'explain' religion has substantially lost ground; at all events we realize that re-flection on the causes of natural phenomena cannot of itself constitute reli-gion" (52). Clearly then, an important aspect of van der Leeuw's aim is to point out the limits of scientific explanation and thus to see its secondary role when the study of religion is framed by the quest for *understanding* rather than knowledge. He is concerned not only with developing an ap-proach to the discipline that will facilitate an essential understanding of re-ligion but also to show that the new approach both supersedes the old, objective-scientific approach, and actually fulfils it. And he believes the ac-quisition of such understanding is not possible without undermining the le-gitimacy of a purely objective and scientific approach to the study of religion. Van der Leeuw does not deny the possibility of studying the his-torical forms of religion from a scientific point of view, but he claims that scientific students are in error if they ask such explanations to provide them with total knowledge of the nature of religion. Their adoption of objective, "external" approaches to the study of religion amounts to a refusal to see, as he puts it in his chapter on "The Religion of Love," that "religions are not wares that one can spread out on a table" (646)[3] for purely objective scien-tific research; religion can only be understood from the inside and not "by contemplative observation from a distance" (683).

Having shown to his own satisfaction that objective knowledge gleaned by practitioners of the science of religion must necessarily distort the very thing they set out to examine, van der Leeuw posits the existence of an ap-proach that can provide an understanding not only of the historical forms in which religion is manifested but also of its "essence." That approach is the phenomenology of religion.

Analysis of van der Leeuw's understanding of phenomenology and the phenomenology of religion—and especially as found in the epilegomena—is not an easy task, as many scholars have found. In their discussions of the phenomenology of religion, C.J. Bleeker and Ake Hultkrantz complain about van der Leeuw's use of speculative philosophical ideas and ignore his methodological discussions in the epilegomena, although this may simply be from a lack of understanding.[4] And it is little wonder that scholars such as Hans Penner ("Is Phenomenology a method for the study of Reli-gion?"[1970]) or Sanford Krolich ("Through a Glass Darkly: What Is the Phenomenology of Religion?"[1985]) display like puzzlement; or that Eric Sharpe insists that van der Leeuw's methodological principles are subtle and not easily followed (1986: 234). J. Waardenburg, on the other hand, has at-tempted a close reading and explication of van der Leeuw's notions of phe-nomenology and the phenomenology of religion, as well as to outline the steps in the process of such a study of religion.[5] Without proceeding to analyze the success of his venture, I wish to draw attention to that aspect of phenomenology of religion seen by van der Leeuw as distinguishing it from all other approaches to the study of religion, making it superior to empirical and theoretical approaches in the field. My assessment of his position, briefly, is as follows.

In the chapter on "Phenomenon and Phenomenology," van der Leeuw writes: "Phenomenology . . . is neither metaphysics, nor the comprehension of empirical reality. It observes *restraint* (the *epoché*), and its understanding of events depends on its employing 'brackets'. Phenomenology is concerned only with 'phenomena', that is with 'appearance'; for [phenomenology], there is nothing whatever 'behind' the phenomena" (1938: 675). But it is important to recognize that the "restraint" of which he speaks is not merely a methodological device but also involves a (subjective) *attitude* to reality. Such an attitude, he argues, should block out all "the accidental coefficients of the existence of objects in the world in order to get at their essence" (676). The "attitude" that does this "blocking out"—allowing the "phenomenological reduction" and intuition of the essence of the phenomenon to take place—involves a persistent application of "intense sympathy" or "empathy" allowing for what van der Leeuw calls the "interpolation" of the phenomena into one's life. By "interpolation" he means a re-experiencing of the event or phenomenon, by which it is *understood* rather than known scientifically. In this respect, he insists, phenomenology is a vital, engaging activity rather than merely an abstract and artificially constructed method of gaining information. This vital activity he identifies as an objective discernment of the essence of things. The phenomenologist, then, is not the "cold-blooded spectator" (684) of the world but rather fully involved in it, assigning to the events both form and meaning:

> Phenomenology aims not at things, still less at their mutual relations, and least of all at the 'thing-in-itself'. It desires to gain access to the facts themselves; and for this it requires a meaning, because it cannot experience the facts just as it pleases. This meaning, however, is purely objective: all violence, either empirical, logical or metaphysical, is excluded. (677)

This sphere of meaning, as van der Leeuw puts it, is a realm neither wholly subjective nor wholly objective. The "meaning" derives from a connection between events or phenomena that is neither an abstraction from the data nor directly experienced—rather, it is a structure that is "intuited." In his words, the "structure is certainly experienced, but not immediately; it is indeed constructed, but not logically, causally, or abstractly. Structure is reality significantly organized" (672). The significance or meaning intuited, therefore, belongs "in part to reality itself, and in part to the 'someone' who attempts to understand it" (672), and it is impossible to distinguish what is one's comprehension from what is "real." Yet in the act of comprehending, these two become one and constitute the gateway to the reality of primal experience.

It is clear from this brief description that for van der Leeuw, what lends phenomenology its superiority over the empirical and theoretical sciences is that it has rejected "the attitude of the cold-blooded spectator" and embraced a subjectivity that clearly recognizes the participatory nature of human existence.[6] In further elaboration of the subjectivity of the phenomenologist (in the chapter on "The Phenomenology of Religion"), van der Leeuw points out that the sympathetic "interpolation" of the chaotic data that attributes meaning is understood as a "self-surrendering love." For were that not so, he writes, "then not only all discussion of what appears in religion, but all discussion of appearance in general would be quite impossible; since to him who does not love, nothing whatever is manifested" (684). When this is understood in terms of his seeing "meaning" as tending toward the Ultimate Meaning (in the chapter on "Religion"), it is difficult to avoid concluding that any comprehension of religion is (and must ultimately be) religious comprehension. Indeed, van der Leeuw claims: " . . . all comprehension, irrespective of whatever object it refers to, is ultimately religious; all significance sooner or later leads to ultimate significance" (684).

Phenomenological understanding for van der Leeuw, then, is something *other* than the knowledge wrought by empirical facts and scientific theories. Rather, as Waardenburg (1972) points out, it discloses a reality that is not spatio-temporal—consequently it distinguishes the results of the phenomenological researcher from that of the historian of religions (and all social-scientific students of religion). But the disclosed reality must also be distinguished from the reality of the metaphysician and theologian, which transcends the spatio-temporal level of existence. Phenomenology, therefore, is as distinct from theology as it is from the empirical and theoretical sciences. Its "reality," at least at first sight, is a kind of psychological reality, or a reality that is neither empirical nor Ultimate.

From this mode of analysis of what phenomenology of religion achieves, it is obvious that there need be no tension between phenomenology and the objective, scientific study of religion. For phenomenology would serve merely to "complement" the other studies, further contributing to the non-theological academic study of religions. And this is precisely how many scholars (including Bleeker and Hultkrantz, to whom I referred above) have in fact interpreted van der Leeuw. But van der Leeuw explicitly rejects such an understanding of his position. Phenomenology of religion is broader than the psychology of religion because religion is far more than the merely psychical. As he puts it, "the whole man participates in [religion], is active within it and is affected by it. In this sphere, then, psychology would enjoy competence only if it rose to the level of the science of Spirit . . ." (687). The phenomenology of religion, exceeding the capacity of psychology, gives the student access "to the reality of primal experience [which is] itself wholly inaccessible . . ." (673).

Thus even though neither a theology nor a metaphysics, van der Leeuw's phenomenology of religion, unlike the other sciences, has implications of a theological and metaphysical kind that makes the *understanding* achieved a more scientific, and therefore, for him, a better knowledge than the knowledge obtained by the objective sciences.[7]

The depreciation of the scientific study of religion, it can now be seen, has effectively been accomplished. Van der Leeuw does not reject empirical analysis—that would hardly be possible given the spectacular achievements of the scientific study of religious traditions. He suggests, in fact, that it plays a critical role in the testing of phenomenological insight, claiming that all phenomenological comprehension must be subject to factual correction. However, this claim cannot be understood in the Popperian fashion—understanding phenomenology to provide theoretical conjecture about the nature of religion that can then be critically tested. On the contrary, van der Leeuw explicitly argues that the objective sciences must be taught the restraint (*epoché*) characteristic of phenomenology if they are to be useful in the understanding of religion. Thus his conclusion regarding the crucial role of the objective, empirical sciences in testing phenomenological comprehension is much more ambiguous than it first appears, for its ultimate result is the undermining of those sciences and the subtle inversion of our understanding of the nature of science. He writes: "[The phenomenological insight] must . . . always be prepared for confrontation with material facts, although the actual manipulation of these facts themselves cannot proceed without interpretation—that is, without phenomenology . . ." (677). Restricted to analysis of religion's *manifestations,* the objective sciences can play a role in bringing the essence of religion into view, but they can never in themselves achieve that end.

I have referred above to the "depreciation" of the objective sciences by van der Leeuw because his phenomenology of religion, even though fueled by empirical research, ultimately undermines the results of that research. This appears to involve him in a contradiction, for he seems to be both accepting and rejecting the validity and value of the scientific undertaking. Moreover, he seeks to evade such a charge of incoherence by "limiting" the role of the objective sciences to relating *wholly* to the externals of religion. For van der Leeuw, only phenomenology can deal with the essence of religion, although he admits it is in some respects dependent upon the results of scientific research. Both the objective sciences and the phenomenology of religion, then, are necessary enterprises in coming to understand religion, but neither is necessary and sufficient. They are complementary undertakings and together can provide the result for which the student of religion strives—or, according to van der Leeuw, for which the student of religion ought to strive. The "unified science" of religion, he goes on to suggest (without providing an explicit argument, however), resembles his phenomenology, for both reveal the essence of religion. As a conduit to a deeper level of understanding, then, phenomenology is seen as the more important element of the two in the "unified science." However, the result of combining empirical study with phenomenology leads to the "denaturing" of the essential character of the sciences originating from Enlightenment thought; in other words, in van der Leeuw's thought the substitution of *understanding* for knowledge as the goal of science amounts to a revolutionary transformation of science itself.

A brief look at the study of religion already extant in Holland will reveal just how radical a change of attitude van der Leeuw's phenomenology of religion represents and how much his own proposals constitute a politically significant revolution in the academic study of religion—"politically" significant in regard to the existence and role of the scholarly study of religion in the academic, university setting as well as in society at large. Not intending to present a history of the study of religions in Holland overall, I shall restrict myself here to some comments on the work of C. P. Tiele, who, as Waardenburg puts it, "created the study of religion from the sources practically out of nothing and made it to [*sic*] an autonomous and recognized discipline . . ." (1972: 136),[8] and who, as van Proosdij insists, defined the goals of that discipline for the new century (1970).[9] I illustrate my point with reference to Tiele's account of the conception, aims and methods of the science of religion as he sets them out in volume I of his Gifford Lectures, *Elements of the Science of Religion* (1897).

Tiele opens his lectures with the claim that the study of religion has already in his day "secured a permanent place among the various sciences of the human mind" (I: 2), implying thereby that the study of religion as a discipline was confined to an "exclusively scientific ground" (I: 4), whose task was to "investigat[e] religion as a historical, psychological, social and wholly human phenomenon . . ." (I: 5). This is not to say that Tiele denies his own religious conviction; but he believes that the scientific study of religion will ultimately benefit religion, and he strongly opposes those who take up the "science of religion" either apologetically or destructively—that is, in order to support or to undermine religion. To the scientist and the scientific enterprise, such extra-scholarly positions would be unconscionable, since for the scientific student of religion "all religions [ought to be] simply objects of investigation" (I: 9).

Like van der Leeuw, Tiele also speaks of the "limits" of the scientific study of religion, but in quite a different vein. He does not see these limits, for example, as a barrier to gaining an objective knowledge about religions, but rather as an indication of the difference of intent between science and theology. Consequently he writes: "The rights of the religious conscience must not be limited; but science, too, vindicates her right to extend her investigations over everything human, and therefore over so important and mighty a manifestation of man's inmost nature as religion has ever been and ever will be" (I: 10).[10] The concern of science, then, is "to explain" and "to know what religion is, and why we are religious"; by contrast, theology's concern is with the development and growth of faith (I: 12). Thus Tiele clearly distinguishes the Science of Religion from Theology, whereas van der Leeuw is less definitive.[11] For the latter, the sciences are a propaedeutic to Theology; and for Tiele, the Science of Religion—as distinct from history and other empirical studies of religion—seeks explanations for the development of religion without which theology would remain incomplete.

It may be obvious, but should nonetheless be stressed, that Tiele does not mean by "science" (in the study of religion) the application of the exact methods of the natural sciences, but he does nevertheless (unlike van der Leeuw) insist that this new science operates within the same *general objectivist framework* of the natural sciences (I: 216–217). For Tiele, then, understanding and knowing are not diametrically opposed as they are in van der Leeuw's thought. The following description given by Tiele of this "critical science" clearly sets out the significant difference between his notion of the scientific study of religion and the philosophical notion at the heart of van der Leeuw's distinction. He writes:

> I think that we need not hesitate openly to proclaim the philosophical character of our science, and to apply to it the method adapted to all philosophical branches of science—namely, the deductive. Not the one-sided empirical method, which culminates in positivism and only ascertains and clarifies facts but is powerless to explain them. Nor the one-sided historical method, which yields exclusively historical results. Nor again the so-called genetic-speculative method, a mixture of history and philosophy, which lacks all unity. Still less, I must hasten to add, the warped speculative method which has no foothold on the earth, but floats in the clouds. For when I speak of the deductive method, I mean this speculative method least of all. On the contrary, our deductive reasoning must start from the results yielded by induction, by empirical, historical and comparative methods. What religion is, and whence it arises, we can only ascertain from religious phenomena. *Our inmost being can only be known by its outward manifestations.* (I: 18; emphasis added)

The objective sciences, therefore, as Tiele puts it more explicitly a few pages later, are in a position to penetrate to the origin and inmost nature of religion (I: 27)[12]. Tiele, like van der Leeuw, may well believe that the results of scientific study will never clash with religion, but he does not believe that, logically, such a clash is impossible. But what is of overriding interest here is the avowed intent of Tiele to apply as detached an outlook as possible when studying religious phenomena. There are places at which Tiele's Christian theology is clearly evident in his analysis of religion and the nature of the study of religion. But Tiele is not attempting for all that to "theologize" that study—to bring the sciences "into line" with his theological agenda. He identifies the task of the student of religion as the quest for an explanation of phenomena that will satisfy the criteria of scientific investigation.[13]

A similarly scientific understanding of the study of religion is to be found in the work of Tiele's contemporary, Chantepie de la Saussaye, who first coined the phrase "phenomenology of religion."[14] Chantepie divided the study of religion into philosophical and historical components concerned respectively with the essence and the manifestations of religion. Although, as Waardenburg maintains, it appears that for Chantepie the understanding of outward forms of religion is predicated upon an understanding of inward processes (1972: 137–138), it is nevertheless also true as James points out, that Chantepie's work was for the most part a call for "a perspicuous description and arrangement of a specific object of study" (1985: 327). In this, Chantepie seems to parallel Tiele, assuming that the student of religion can get to the essence beyond the phenomena by means of the phenomena themselves. The study of religion dominating the Dutch academic scene until about the third decade of this century (van Proosdij, 1970: iv), therefore, assumes we can "know" religion from the outside in. And it is this assumption and understanding of the nature of the scientific study of religion that is undermined by van der Leeuw.[15] As Sanford Krolich maintains, the call to empirical research seemed to fall on deaf ears, and a resurgent idealism was fostered in the new description of phenomenology emerging with scholars such as van der Leeuw (1985: 199). Jacques Waardenburg similarly notes: "[T]he phenomenology of religion in its classical forms encouraged explicit or implicit views of religion which were not empirically developed and tested, and it brought the data, so to speak, under the spell of religion as an autonomous reality" (1978: 199).

Although van der Leeuw's revolutionary impact on the study of religion has been widely felt, it has not, I think, been ultimately successful in defining the framework of the field. For there have been repeated attempts to recover and develop the academic tradition that he questioned and ultimately undermined. As van Proosdij notes, this program of recovery began immediately with van der Leeuw's successor: "The position of phenomenology as a method, which penetrated the field of religious studies although originally a philosophical technique, has been contested by van Baaren, to name but one" (1970: x). Van Baaren makes this matter very clear in his contribution to the "papers of the Groningen working-group for the study of fundamental problems and methods of science of religion" collected together under the title *Religion, Culture and Methodology* (Van Baaren et al., 1973). His central concern, he tells us, is to show the groundlessness of a notion of religion that transcends the framework of culture. He therefore claims that the Science of Religion must be seen to be "limited to an empirical study of religions as they are." And, he claims, "because it does not acknowledge the authority of any religion to influence or determine the results of this research," the Science of Religion is wholly different from theology (42). Consequently he rejects van der Leeuw's attempt to replace the "objective knowledge" of the sciences with the "subjective understanding" of phenomenology. "The knowledge arrived at in this [phenomenological] way," he writes, "is no valid form of science, its scientific exactness or falsity has to be demonstrated and checked by scientific methods" (45–46). Van der Leeuw, says van Baaren, did not possess insight into the cognitive validity of the various methods of acquiring knowledge, although he does not think this alone can account for the path van der Leeuw chose to take. "Why [he] himself transgressed these rules [of knowledge] so frequently," suggests van Baaren conclusively, "can only be solved by a study in depth of his life and work" (49).

I do not accept that it was for theoretical or philosophical reasons that van der Leeuw rejected the scientific method and the application of the principles of objective research as the essence of a sound academic approach to Religious Studies. Rather, it appears that van der Leeuw had his intellectual sights trained elsewhere and that he deduced the limitations of science by assessing how well or poorly they functioned with respect to his own particular interests. His primary concerns were religious and cultural, and a study of religion that was a purely academic matter simply had no religious or cultural value, being without relevance to the well-being of society. Indeed, as Sharpe puts it, "to be thoroughly empirical [and, we might add, theoretically objective], was, in a manner of speaking, the foremost symptom of what van der Leeuw held to be the typical twentieth-century sickness" (1986: 235). Van der Leeuw gives a clear indication of this aspect of his thinking in the preface to the German edition of *Religion in Essence and Manifestation*. Admitting the shortcomings of the book, he nonetheless writes, "I trust that my book will contribute somewhat towards the comprehension of Religion, equally as regards its incalculable cultural wealth and the appeal to faith which it addresses to mankind" (1938: 10).

In keeping with his analysis (in chapter 1) that power forms the basis of most—if not all—religions, van der Leeuw writes in the epilegomena: "He who does not merely accept life . . . but demands something from it—that is, power—endeavours to find some meaning in life. He arranges life into a significant whole: and thus culture arises" (679). However, that search for meaning is not exhausted by cultural manifestations alone, but rather by the grasping of that "ultimate significance" or "final meaning." And religion is the bearer of final meaning, according to van der Leeuw; with such a conviction, as Waardenburg puts it, van der Leeuw thought to "connect religion and society, christianity and culture, theology and the Arts and Sciences" (1972: 183). His phenomenology of religion was inevitably tied to his theology and his concern for society; it therefore involved extra-scientific goals requiring a transformation of the original academic, scientific goals of the scholarly study of religion. Finally, Waardenburg warns that van der Leeuw "should be seen against the background of the secularization of Dutch society and the theological crisis in Dutch protestantism between the two world wars" (183).[16] It is obvious even in *Religion in Essence and Manifestation* that van der Leeuw saw religion as a cultural—and "more than cultural"— orientation to life, and that a purely objective and academic study of religion could jeopardize that orientation. It is equally obvious that, in what amounts to what I have termed a religio-cultural quest, he attempted to combine his scientific and extra-scientific goals in the new discipline, but that the scientific goals originally espoused in the academic study of religion were undermined (radically transformed) in the process.

Van der Leeuw would not, I think, be left without reply to arguments of this kind. His response is contained implicitly in his discussion of the study of "The Religion of Love" in *Religion in Essence and Manifestation* (645–649). He argues there that to exist in the world is to do so in some quite specific way. Consequently, to think that one could study religion— or the character of one's own religio-cultural quest—in a detached, unprejudiced way is simply naïve and, in fact, deceptive; for it prevents the investigator's biases from being recognized and critically (scientifically) clarified. "Unprejudiced" investigators, he maintains, themselves have an ultimate—and therefore religious—interpretation of the world from which they proceed; consequently, his study, which is controlled by a consciously—and therefore critically—espoused "Christian prejudice," is more "scientific" than what has been taken to be the only proper scientific approach. But to argue in this fashion is to proceed arbitrarily (and rather circularly)—he assumes precisely what it is he sets out to demonstrate. It is an exercise in the persuasive redefinition of terminology that ignores the critical differences between religion and the academic, scientific study of religion. In erasing the line of demarcation he had inherited, he effectively destroyed the academic study of religion because he transformed it into the very thing from which it had originally emerged—namely, Theology. With van der Leeuw, therefore, the study of religion not only does not advance beyond the stage already reached by that discipline in Holland, but rather it returns to an earlier theological approach—one that amounts to a subversion of the scientific study of religion. The desire to reclaim social, cultural, and religious values in response to crises in one's own culture is one thing; to call that activity "scientific" is quite another. Van der Leeuw's theology—and his intention to arrest the cultural deterioration he sees in modern Western culture—is not problematic, but the use to which he puts his phenomenology in support of religion demands a critical response.

Notes

1. See, for example, John B. Carman, "The Theology of a Phenomenologist: An Introduction to the Theology of Gerardus van der Leeuw" (1965); Jacques Waardenburg, "Gerardus van der Leeuw as a Theologian and Phenomenologist" (1978); and Jacques Waardenburg, "Leeuw, Gerardus van der," in Mircea Eliade et al., eds., *The Encyclopedia of Religion* (1987). Other essays bearing on his work will be cited below.

2. The work of thinkers such as Hegel, Herder, and Schleiermacher, he suggests, reduced the efficacy of Enlightenment thought. He recognizes, however, that there were reactions to Romanticism, although he (rather strangely) refers to these developments as "a period of romantic philology" and "the age of romantic positivism."

3. A little later he insists that religion "is an ultimate experience that evades our observations, a revelation which in its very essence is, and remains, concealed" (683).

4. See Ake Hultkrantz, "The Phenomenology of Religion: Aims and Methods" and C.J. Bleeker, "The Contribution of the Phenomenology of Religion to the Study of the History of Religions" (1972). Hultkrantz and Bleeker both see van der Leeuw as an empiricist. Hultkrantz, for example, sees phenomenology as a systematically descriptive study "identical with the older term 'comparative religion'" (75); and Bleeker insists it is "a systematization of historical facts in order to grasp their religious value" (41) and "meaning" (51).

5. In addition to the essays mentioned in note 1, see Waardenburg, "Religion Between Reality and Idea: A Century of Phenomenology of Religion in the Netherlands" (1972).

6. In this respect, I think Eric Sharpe (1986) is right to draw attention to van der Leeuw's evaluation of Lévy-Bruhl's notion of the primitive mind and the emergence of the "modern mentality" as being an abstraction. An empirical approach to the study of religion resulting from the acceptance of such abstraction was for van der Leeuw, Sharpe claims, merely a symptom of a sick society that failed to recognize its wholeness, which led to "the scholar's [failing at the] most vital and most sensitive point, the point of genuine understanding" (235). I have presented quite a different reading of Lévy-Bruhl's significance for the academic study of religion in my essay "The Prelogical Mentality Revisited" (1987).

7. Eric Sharpe remarks that van der Leeuw's categories (especially that of "holiness") are understood by *homo religiosus*, but not by the academic, who

finds instead that van der Leeuw is embarked "upon a hazardous voyage on a metaphysical ocean." He continues: "But to van der Leeuw phenomeno-logical scholarship was not to be sharply differentiated from metaphysics or from theology" (1986: 234).

8. Though correct on one level, from another point of view this is an exagger-ation. Histories of this field of study (such as that of Eric Sharpe cited above) for the most part fail to deal adequately with the history of the intellectual ethos that permitted the development (initiated by Max Müller in England and C. P. Tiele in Holland). An excellent account of the emergence of the ethos (with a history of the diverse institutional development of the field) is provided by S. Preus in *Explaining Religion: Criticism and Theory from Bodin to Freud* (1987). (See also my review of the work: "Explaining Religion: The Intellectual Ethos"[1989], and chapter 1 of this volume). Further study of the issue is to be found in Christina Banman, "The Study of Religion: Nine-teenth Century Sources and Twentieth Century Misconceptions" (1989).

9. Though this claim may at first appear extreme, I think it justifiable in re-spect of the work of Müller and Tiele. One might note here the somewhat exasperated response of John Baillie to the emergence of the new discipline in his *Interpretation of Religion: An Introductory Study of Theological Princi-ples* (1956): "Here we seem to have 'science' masquerading in a new guise as compelling us not to make any use in our inquiry of a truth of which we are nevertheless 'convinced,' and which is of such a kind as to bring us to the core of the very issue that is being inquired into"! We are analysing human faith, yet we must not bring the light of our own faith to bear upon the analysis! As a matter of fact, if there is one point rather than another con-cerning which we should expect the 'Elements of the Science of Religion' to enlighten us, it is just the real inward nature of the very kind of 'conviction' and 'faith' which Tiele claims to possess himself in regard to the truth of Christianity" (123–124).

10. In a later discussion Tiele is more ambiguous, claiming that all academic study leaves religious conviction untouched, and suggesting that it somehow constitutes an insoluble mystery (I: 51,52).

11. See E. J. Sharpe, 1986: 234.

12. There is some ambiguity in later discussion on this subject, in both vol. I and vol. II. For example, in vol. I Tiele talks about "religion itself," which is entirely independent of the historical forms in which it appears, and claims "that [the] forms may change and vary without sacrificing the eternal ideas and the immortal aspirations which constitute the essence of religion" (222). This, taken with the distinction between faith and knowledge in vol. II (36), might make it appear that Tiele's position is significantly similar to that of van der Leeuw. However, he writes further: "Between faith, which strives, on the basis of inward perception, to form an idea of what lies beyond percep-tion, and science, which, kept within its proper bounds, makes the percep-tible the sole object of its research, the opposition is not so absolute as is commonly supposed" (II: 37–38). See also vol. II, 191 ff.

13. Tiele believes that objective, scientific explanations will, ultimately, harmonize with a religious truth of necessarily quite different derivation. Baillie (see note 9) acknowledges Tiele's faith and asserts that Tiele does not keep his academic study of religion free of its influence. He writes: "[S]tudents of this science are nearly always far better than their word and do, in spite of all their protestations, bring their own religious intelligence and the light of their own religious experience to bear upon the otherwise chaotic mass of fact which it is their business to set in order . . ." (124). But Baillie fails to recognize that such influence could be inadvertent; he complains that " . . . it is remarkable how seldom in such writing we are able completely to escape the impression that we are here having religion described to us by one who either lacks a religious experience of his own or has left that side of his spiritual equipment behind him at home when he came to this workshop" (124).

14. See George A. James, "Phenomenology and the Study of Religion: The Archaeology of an Approach" (1985): 311–335.

15. Chantepie de la Saussaye's contribution in this matter is somewhat ambiguous, as is shown in Richard Plantinga's brief exposition of Chantepie de la Saussaye on the relationship of the History of Religions to Theology. Plantinga quite correctly points out his influence, for example, on such religious phenomenologists as Söderblom, van der Leeuw, Heiler, and Bleeker (6). Plantinga also notes, however, that whereas Chantepie did not consider Theology a subdivision of *Religionswissenschaft* (4), van der Leeuw did (7). In the latter's inaugural address and in his *Introduction to Theology,* Plantinga states, "van der Leeuw explained his version of the theological encyclopedia in which history of religion plays a key part" (7). This suggests, I would argue, that Chantepie's work shows a significant agreement in structure to that of Tiele. Van der Leeuw was, no doubt, dependent upon Chantepie's work, but, as Plantinga rightly notes, he did more than simply tidy up and expand the latter's work. The nature of van der Leeuw's development beyond Chantepie, especially in the divergence on the place of the History of Religions in the theological encyclopedia drawn to the reader's attention by Plantinga (7), is indicative of a change fundamentally subversive of the conscious framework within which Chantepie seemed to operate. It is equivalent, I think, to the revision John Baillie hoped to bring to the Science of Religion by getting its students to recognize that their personal religious convictions cannot (even on methodological grounds) be kept distinct from their work as scientists (see note 9 above). Not without sarcasm, Baillie remarks: "The candour and ingenuousness with which we are sometimes recommended in the name of this Science of Religion to stand aside from the faith that lives in our hearts when we are trying to understand the faith of mankind as a whole is indeed enough to make us rub our eyes and wonder whether we have read correctly" (1936: 122, 123). Only by seeing History of Religions as an essential element of the theological encyclopedia can we properly understand it: "It is the duty of theological science to provide the

historical study of religion with a proper point of view, proper presuppositions and a succession of proper questions" (131). Van der Leeuw's position is structurally indistinguishable from Baillie's, but Baillie, unlike van der Leeuw, openly recognizes the antagonism of this position to the notion of the new scientific approach to the study of religion that had emerged in the latter part of the nineteenth century. A similar conclusion, ambiguously defended, can be found in Lammert Leertouwer, "C. P. Tiele's Strategy of Conquest" (1989: 153–167).

16. A full assessment of the theological roots of his phenomenology is, obviously, to be found in his sermons and religious and theological writings, but their analysis is a task that neither can be nor need be undertaken here.

Chapter Eleven

―○○○○―

On the Value of the World's Parliament of Religions for the Study of Religion

In reviewing Eric Ziolkowski's *A Museum of Faiths* (1993), I became aware that two stories are being recounted, if only by implication. While on the one hand Ziolkowski is interested in the World's Parliament of Religions as a significant religious and cultural event, on the other hand he focuses particular attention on the Parliament as a major landmark in the development of university education in North America. For the student of religion, the more important question that emerges from the study of the Parliament is whether (as is often claimed) it reflected and promoted the scientific study of religion.

Ziolkowski's *Museum*, like R. H. Seagher's *The Dawn of Religious Pluralism* (1993), is concerned with restoring the Chicago World's Parliament of Religions of 1893, as he puts it, "to its rightful place in Western memory as a landmark in religious and cultural history . . ."(48).[1] Moreover, where Seagher is primarily concerned with providing a selection of texts "that represent important positions or were delivered by noteworthy people" in order to include "the many different voices that gained expression in the first global, ecumenical assembly in world history" (Seagher, 1993: 2), Ziolkowski's essays concentrate more narrowly on matters of methodological significance to the student of religion. "This book," he writes in the introduction, "has a circular aim, which is to reassess the meaning and significance and the histories and legacies of the 1893 parliament as a meeting of religious faiths and to shed light upon the role of the event as a critical moment in the development of the very perspective from which we now reassess it: that of the academic study of religion" (1993: 4). As a consequence Ziolkowski has selected the following for reissue: the six papers contributed to the Parliament by the participating scientists—the only papers, he suggests, "devoted explicitly to expounding the history, scope, aims, and methodologies" (48) of the Science of Religion (part I); two early appraisals of the Parliament published in 1894 (part II); and eight subsequent reassessments appearing between 1983 and 1993 (part III). Ziolkowski himself contributes a lengthy and helpful introduction to the collection, providing both a summary and an overview of the Parliament's organization and overall significance.

Although the papers in part I of this volume are by scholars interested in promoting the scientific study of religion, they are not all concerned simply with academic or scientific questions. Merwin-Marie Snell, for example, in the "Service of the Science of Religions to the Cause of Religious Unity"(69–73), essentially points out the indispensability of this new discipline to a demonstration of the truth and unity of religion. At the same time she notes that, unlike other persons concerned with "understanding" religion, the scientist studies religion "from a pure love of his science" (71) and need not be concerned about practical results. Eliza Read Sunderland, in "Serious Study of All Religions," similarly focuses attention on the role of the comparative study of religion in judging the "worth of any religion" (117). Like Snell, she acknowledges that the results of this new science (which she calls "hierology") form "part of the great body of scientific truth" (111)—just another element of, as she puts it, "the century par excellence in scientific research and classification, which has given us the new lessons of the telescope, the spectroscope, and stellar photography; the new earth of geology, chemistry, mineralogy, botany, and zoology; and the new humanity of ethnology, philology, psychology, and hierology" (111).

Albert Réville, in "Conditions and Outlook for a Universal Religion," and Charles Joseph de Harlez, in "The Comparative Study of the World's Religions," are both apologetically orientated, concerned respectively with "the sacred path that shall one day bring man to the truly humanitarian and universal religion" (89) and the establishment of the fact that religion is not simply "a creation of the mind of man" (101). Jean Réville's paper on "Principles of the Scientific Classification of Religions," however, is a more clearly scientific paper, urging the acceptance of a methodological view that would ground the study of religion (singular) in a scientific study of the particular historical religions (92). C. P. Tiele's "On the Study of Comparative Theology" is also essentially a scientific paper concerned with understanding the origin and nature of the new scientific approach to the study of religions (82).

According to Ziolkowski, the papers in part I of the book, even though written by scientists, "hardly amount to a showcase for scholarly objectivity" (51). Yet this ought not to be read as a criticism of their work in general, nor of the Science of Religion per se, because, as Seagher makes clear in the general introduction to his collection of essays, the mission of the Parliament was religious and theological rather than scientific, and those invited to participate in it were well aware of the fact. Indeed, Ziolkowski also acknowledges this when describing the substance of Barrows's and Müller's essays appraising the success of the Parliament (in part II), for he notes there the concern on the part of those who conceived and organized the Parliament that the conference sessions reflect an appropriately religious tone. In his conclusion, Barrows expressed confidence that the Parliament would have an important role in popularizing the study of religion, and he was entirely right, as Kitagawa and others in part III of this book note. However, contemporary scholars, I think, may seek to argue with Ziolkowski about the actual contribution of the Parliament to the further *scientific* development of the discipline, for there is reason to believe quite the contrary, as I shall suggest below.

The appraisals of the Parliament found in part III range over a broader spectrum than those of parts I and II. Martin Marty's essay, "A Cosmopolitan Habit in Theology," is a general assessment of the Parliament and of the theology of its organizers, leveled as a liberal religious protest against materialism and irreligion. Richard Hughes Seagher's focus in his essay is the pluralism, introduced by the Parliament into mainstream American religion, that helped foster a new approach to understanding the religious history of America. Referring to the proof represented by the Parliament itself, Seagher asserts: "[t]he parliament was a protean phenomenon which could mean different things to different people, a fact which itself hinted at the passing of a consensus-dominated vision of American religious history [based on a notion of unity rather than diversity]" (209). With a more critical focus, James Edward Ketalaar's essay, "The Reconvening of Babel," emphasizes how deeply suspect the notion of consensus regarding the religious history of humankind became because of the Parliament. He notes that the participants in the Parliament, whether from the East or the West, used it to further their own religious and political views. The Oriental representatives used the occasion to show the West that Buddhism rather than Christianity would make the better spiritual guide for a technologically orientated culture (298), while the West clearly saw all religions predominantly in terms of the Christian message and mission (274). Sunrit Mullick's essay, "Protap Chandra Majumdar and Swami Vivekananda at the Parliament of Religions," and Tessa Bartholomeusz's "Dharmapala at Chicago" in some respects support Ketalaar's claims of ethnocentrism in the organization of the Parliament. Mullick emphasizes the role Majumdar and Vivekananda played as messengers of Indian spirituality to America, and Bartholomeusz focuses on what she sees as Dharmapala's interest in returning to Sri Lanka with a Buddhism legitimated by the West. Ursula King's contribution, "Rediscovering Women's Voices at the World's Parliament of

Religions," although not obviously spiritually partisan, reveals an agenda not wholly focused on the legacy of the Parliament: Though women were represented there, and spoke in their own voices, as King puts it (341), she argues that they were not there in sufficient numbers, and she pleads that women today be given a more representative voice in the debate on religion and spirituality (342–343). Finally, Ziolkowski's contribution to the reassessment of the Parliament has little bearing, if any, upon its practical import; he addresses an independent theme, namely, "The Literary Prefigurations" of the Parliament in the "kernel idea of a fraternal meeting of the world's religions" (307) to be found in the Western literary tradition. So in fact, these seven essays have very little to say in a pointed manner about the actual contribution of the Parliament to the growth and development of the scientific study of religion. Some of the essays, in fact, are openly apologetic. Ketalaar may make some important points about the "politics" of the treatment of religions in this ecumenical gathering that have significant implications for methodology, but those points are not developed; nor would their elaboration have illustrated the influence of the Parliament on the growth of such a scientific study in any case. To a certain extent, the same may be said of Seagher's concern about the historical treatment of religions in America. In fact (and here I return to a reference made at the beginning of my article) it may be said that the mere suggestion of the Parliament's positive influence on the growth of the Science of Religion derives mainly from Ziolkowski's understanding of Kitagawa's essay "The 1893 World's Parliament of Religions and Its Legacy." In attempting to identify the Parliament's several layers of meaning, Kitagawa argues that it provided a stimulus to the study of religions in America. Despite the fact that this was not a gathering of scholars, and that what united the participants in the Parliament "was the religious quest, the hope, and the longing of the children of the one God, the Christians and the Jews, and adherents of other faiths" (184), Kitagawa maintains that it still "called attention to the need for scholarly approaches and resources in dealing with the fact of religious pluralism on the global scene" (176). (If so, this was surely an ironic development.)

In many respects, the introduction Ziolkowski provides for this volume of essays is the most interesting piece of all, because it provides a general overview of the Parliament's organization and contribution. This is not to say, however, that his assessment of the importance of the Parliament to the development of the Science of Religion is beyond criticism. Indeed, as I will show here, he is actually quite inconsistent in his claim that the Parliament had a definite methodological, scientific impact upon the academic study of religion. He stresses that an "adequate study of the Parliament must ultimately take into account the history of the very enterprise of studying religious faiths from 'scientific' and 'comparative' perspectives" (4), yet he acknowledges that the primary purpose of the conference was religious (seeking harmony among the different religious traditions) (28) rather than scientific (achieving an explanatory understanding of religious phenomena) (33). Given this fact, it is not clear why Ziolkowski would claim that the scientific study of religion had any bearing at all on the Parliament, or the Parliament on the scientific study of religion; it seems instead that he is simply appropriating (uncritically) Kitagawa's assessment of the Parliament's legacy. Furthermore, in the preface Ziolkowski acknowledges the blurred distinction at the Parliament between "religious" and "scientific" representations of religion, but he does not see that blurring as undermining the Parliament's scholarly, scientific value.

Bringing representatives of the world's religions "into dialogue" in this unprecedented fashion no doubt created broad public interest in understanding religions, which indirectly encouraged interest in some circles in the academic study of religions. But in itself, I would argue, the Parliament made no contribution of a scientific or methodological kind to such an academic enterprise. Indeed, it may have hindered any such contribution precisely because of the "blurring" mentioned; that is, by ignoring any demarcation between the religious and the scientific pursuits, the Parliament made it impossible to formulate a clear methodological framework for such an academic enterprise. Kitagawa may be right in saying that the lack of clarity about the nature of the scientific study of religion—a problem actually exacerbated by the imprecise thrust of the Parliament—could have contributed ironically to its popular accessibility (187); but that, surely, does not bespeak progress in its development as a discipline. Ziolkowski comments on the diminution of apologetics in the subsequent Paris Congress of 1900, but he does not associate this trend with the inconsistency of method or inconsequentiality of results—for the Science of Religion—emanating from the 1893 assembly. In fact, he maintains (despite proof to the contrary) that the Parliament has ultimately been beneficial to scholars' concerns today. Such a position, however, can only be maintained by conflating the tasks of the student of religion as scientist with those of the student of religion as a morally accountable member of society. He insists that the Parliament is relevant to scholarly concerns because "the problem it highlighted of trying to reconcile the scholar's vocation toward 'purely scientific research' with his or her 'cultural task,' to borrow words from a speech by C. J. Bleeker at the Marburg IAHR congress several decades ago, continued to hound scholars of religion throughout our century" (44). But putting the matter this way does not point to a reconsideration of the blurring of the religious and scientific tasks; it seems, rather, to encourage that the blurring remain unresolved, since to "reconsider the blurring," would be to reconsider whether religion in fact can be studied in a scientific manner at all. If this apparently condoned (if not promulgated) blurring of science and religion forms the basis of the "contribution" made by the 1893 Parliament to the scholarly study of religion, it is a dubious contribution indeed.[2]

Notes

1. Ziolkowski acknowledges here that he is following Kitagawa's lead in this respect.
2. The Marburg Congress to which Ziolkowski refers (in regard to the issue of blurring the religious and the scientific enterprises), it should be remembered, is the occasion for the reaffirmation by the International Association for the History of Religions of a clear distinction between the task of the student of religion qua scholar-scientist and the cultural task of the student of religion qua member of society. That demarcation of the academic and scientific study of religions from apologetic religio-theological approaches to the study of religions was clearly embedded in a five-point statement of the "basic minimum presuppositions" for the pursuit of the scientific study of religions drawn up by Zwi Werblowsky and printed in the journal of the Association (see A. Schimmel, "Summary of the Discussion," 1960).

   One wonders whether the official distancing of the Paris and subsequent Congresses from the Parliament can be taken as proof that the academic study of religion has headed—as indeed it had to, if intellectual respectability were to be maintained—in a direction opposite to that implied by the 1893 Parliament. Demarcating the religious from the scientific is precisely what occurred at the Paris Congress, which indicates that the scholars there considered such a demarcation an essential element of the academic, scientific study of religion.

Chapter Twelve

—◈—

The Study of Religion:
On the New Encyclopedia of Religion

The *Encyclopedia of Religion* (Eliade et al., 1987), as one might expect from any work of this kind, attempts to bring within our command the sum of current knowledge about the world's religions. It supersedes its predecessor, *The Encyclopedia of Religion and Ethics* [*ERE*] (Hastings et al., 1908–1926), in several respects, for it not only makes available the vast store of information about the history and cultural significance of religion accumulated in the decades since the publication of the *ERE*, but it also focuses on questions of method and theory in the study of religion in a way not undertaken before. And it has structured what it has to say about religions and the study of religion in a more helpful fashion, providing a network of information by cross-references interconnecting some 2,750 articles organized under four rubrics. Those rubrics are: "The Religions," which treats not only major, extant "world religions" but also ancient and primitive traditions; "The Study of Religion," which is concerned less with particular historical realities than with a method for understanding them; "Religion and Philosophy," which confronts the systematic aspects of religious thought; and "Religion and Culture," which deals with religion's links to science, the arts, and society.

My attention here will be focused primarily on the essays falling into the category "The Study of Religions." It will only be possible, however, to address a very limited selection, since nearly a quarter of the *Encyclopedia* is devoted to the subject, directly or indirectly, including, for example, articles on various religious phenomena, on technical terms used in the study of religion, on histories of the various fields of study, and on methodological approaches (general and specific) for the study of religions. Furthermore, I will restrict my comments almost exclusively to those essays concerned in a general way with the academic, scientific method for the study of religious phenomena. They are relatively few in number, but, significantly enough, they reflect a great deal about the nature of the *Encyclopedia* as a whole.

Joseph Kitagawa, in the "Foreword" to the *Encyclopedia,* maintains that it is a product not only of a different time but also of a different sort of scholarship from that responsible for the *ERE.* The *ERE,* he insists, is pervaded by theological interests and therefore presents us with a normative (Western) understanding of religion; but it is limited in its failure to treat the theological implications of the view that assumes religion to be unique and irreducible. By contrast, he insists that the new *Encyclopedia* "has made a serious effort to balance the inner, theological, soteriological meanings and the outer, historical, sociological, anthropological . . . and cultural meanings" of religion, although he also recognizes that it is the product of a "total hermeneutics" employed by Mircea Eliade (the editor-in-chief) "to decipher the meaning of human experience in this mysterious universe" (1: xv). As Eliade himself points out in the "Preface," reductionism must be excluded if modern people are to be capable of radically changing their existences—that is, if they are to be "saved." He sees knowledge of religion, then, as a "religious knowledge" that enables one to understand more clearly the real meaning of religion. He maintains, therefore, that "knowledge of the religious ideas and practices of other traditions better enables anyone to understand his or her own. The history of religions is the story of the human encounter with the sacred" (1: xi). Though his *Encyclopedia* may demonstrate a greater awareness of methodological issues and of methodological diversity in the study of religion, this deliberate exclusion of all forms of reductionism is indicative, I suggest, of a lack of critical rigor due to a hidden theological agenda. Not only does Eliade detect a longing in modern Western people for a *renovatio* that can change an individual's existence, he also assumes that the study of religion must be directed toward such an end. But that kind of understanding is indistinguishable from the religio-theological. Consequently, one might well call the new encyclopedia the *RER*—the "Religious Encyclopedia of Religion."

There are several key methodological entries that receive brief analysis here: the multi-authored articles on "Study of Religion," "Phenomenology of Religion," and "History of Religions"; as well as the entries on "Comparative Religion," "Comparative-Historical Method," and "Dialogue of Religions." Before proceeding to these, however, I turn to Winston L. King's entry on "Religion" (12: 282–293) because its specific focus on the definition of religion provides a kind of general introduction to the positions elaborated in the other entries.

It is difficult to ascertain whether in his definition of religion King is seeking to determine the essence of religion or merely establishing a point from which the academic study of religious phenomena might proceed.

The ambiguity, however, ultimately reflects the editorial line already identified. King points out that "religion" is a Western concept ingrained with specifically Western cultural presuppositions favoring nonreligious accounts of religious phenomena. The concept is problematic, therefore, because for the devotee, "what is happening in religion seems also to contain some extrasocietal, extrapsychological, depth-factor or transcendent dimension, which must be further examined" (284). King examines a range of definitions that avoid such reductionism but ultimately he admits their severe limits. Nevertheless, he insists that a nonreductionist understanding is possible—and necessary—since, as he puts it, almost every culture "displays elements that, if not wholly other from their context, do show a certain discontinuity with [that culture]" (285). Even though he attempts to make a case for the "other-than-ordinary" in religion, he nonetheless admits that the assessment "other than ordinary" is arrived at by means of "culturally constructed ultimate priorities," and this undermines the nonreductionist position he advocates. His characterization of religion as the "depth-factor" of cultural experiences is ambiguous but seems in the final analysis to indicate a (religious) reality beyond the culturally perceived. This dichotomy is clearly enunciated as follows: "Religion is the organization of life around the depth dimensions of experience—varied in form, completeness, and clarity in accordance with the environing culture" (286); all of the characteristics and structures of religious life elaborated by King in this article seem to reflect precisely that dichotomy.

The "Study of Religion" section contains three essays: "History of Study" by Seymour Cain (14: 64–83), "Methodological Issues" by Eric J. Sharpe (14: 84–88), and "Religious Studies as an Academic Discipline" by Thomas Benson (14: 88–92).

Cain opens his essay by evoking problems of method and theory, but his analysis neither clarifies his concern nor contributes to solving the problems in question. He does suggest in the introduction, however, that the proper approach to the scholarly study of religion will be other than a reductive, scientific one. Referring to the work of M. Jastrow, he intimates that at its inception the scholarly study of religion was a purely natural, scientific enterprise, yet he claims that this study took a wayward turn.

After a quick review of diverse influences on the modern, scholarly study of religion—going back as far as classical antiquity—Cain proceeds to focus attention on the beginnings of the new discipline. Though he claims that a critical and comparative study of religion can be found in the discipline's early stages, he argues that at that point it was not undertaken "in the self-consciously theoretical and methodological manner of modern disciplines" (68) that first emerged in the last part of the nineteenth century with Max Müller and others. He then reviews the development of the study of religious phenomena in terms of the anthropological, historical-phenomenological, psychological, and sociological approaches adopted by various scholars. The anthropological approach, especially as found in A. R. Radcliffe-Brown, is seen as "rooted in nineteenth-century biological notions and in an outmoded and inappropriate view of social science as the formulator of universal laws" (73). The psychological and sociological approaches are sparsely treated, with little focus on the role the great reductive theories played in the development of this field of study. Positive reference is made, however, to the hermeneutical-dialectical kind of understanding inimical to the notions already mentioned. The contributors cited in the section on the historical-phenomenological approach to the study of religion are all hermeneutically, rather than social-scientifically, orientated; these include N. Söderblom, R. Otto, F. Heiler, G. van der Leeuw, J. Wach, and Eliade. In them he detects not only a philosophical, but also a religious-theological influence on the scholarly study of religion. The essay is brought to a conclusion by a glance at the current situation, briefly reviewing the work of C. Lévi-Strauss, C. Geertz, and M. Douglas. However, the real issues raised in the various reviews, some of which I suggest below, are left untreated.

Cain's essay, then, does not really accomplish its task. It covers ground requiring attention, but it lacks focus. Moreover, it ignores much that is essential, while dwelling on remote influences hardly central to its concerns. Cain does not, for example, elaborate on the contribution of pivotal figures such as M. Müller, C. P. Chantepie de la Saussaye, or C. P. Tiele. Nor does he mention the history of the emergence of this field as related to curricular concerns of the modern university. Finally, institutional developments—such as the formation of societies and the establishment of journals for the study of religions—are overlooked entirely.

One might have hoped the companion essays by Sharpe and Benson would pick up the slack in Cain's general overview. This unfortunately is not the case. For they present less-than-adequate treatments of even their own topics. Sharpe's essay, though directed to methodological issues, reflects and reinforces present trends in the study alternating between censure and largesse, rather than critically analyzing the issues at stake. His attention is given diversely to whether the study of religion ought to be undertaken "from the inside out," or "from the outside in." According to Sharpe, some people tend to assume objectivity to be "a pipe dream, and methodological discussion a necessary meeting place of competing subjectivities." The concern for laws—explanations and theories—therefore would not be appropriate for the study of religion. He then notes that the contrary view is held with equal force in other circles, and he insists (rather amicably) that "[n]either view can be maintained as a general principle" (84). This, of course, does not constitute an assessment of matters, for Sharpe merely sets out the range of positions possible.

Sharpe admits that the academic study of religion is by its origin a Western enterprise and that "it was, in intention at least, a science" (86). He nevertheless comes down clearly on the side of metaphysics when he insists that in religion there is yet something beyond the culturally conditioned—something timeless and transcendental—lying beyond the methods of science. He does not defend this statement but rather claims we have already been brought to this realization by something he refers to as "the experiential wave," implying that religious studies is an art rather than a science; so that it is quite naturally "sustained by impressions, furthered by dialogue, and transmitted as an aspect of a wider personal desire for self-realization and self-expression, 'method' in any strict sense [is] rendered obsolete in the process" (88). Any demarcation of religion from the study of religion, therefore, is erased. And Sharpe justifies the erasure by advocating the benefits of methodological pluralism.

To insist that the study of religion in the university setting should be strictly scientific, he tells us, would amount to a methodological sectarianism. It is worth noting, however, that in other volumes of the *Encyclopedia* Sharpe appears to contradict his own position (one of the weaknesses of his contribution to the work overall). In his earlier essay "Comparative Religion" (3: 578–580), he lays out without commentary the conditions of the early study of religion in the university setting, relating that the term "comparative religions" was used as a synonym for the "science of religion." The desire of the discipline, he points out, was to discover laws in terms of which religious phenomena could be understood nonreligiously and entirely independently of the notion of revelation—that is, just as understanding is achieved in other disciplines. No suggestion of methodological pluralism— or its benefits—is made. His essay on "Dialogue of Religions" (4: 344–348), however, returns in some degree to the thorny problem of demarcation. For he notes, "at least the 'dialogue period' helped to banish some of the impatience and the inaccuracies of the past, although doubtless creating fresh problems of its own" (347); but he does not clarify the thrust of his argument; these key methodological issues are left undeveloped and the potential of dialogue as a tool for research unheeded.

Since he deals only with the years following World War II, Thomas Benson's essay does not make up for Cain's oversight on the institutional history of this subject. Nor does his essay really concern the issue of religious studies as an academic discipline. Rather, Benson provides an uncritical account of the redefinition of the seminary programs in American colleges and universities that came to be called Departments of Religious Studies. He notes that, occasionally, apprehensions were voiced concerning Church-State relations here, but he points out—perhaps missing the irony—that such fears were "easily allayed" by laying claim to a distinction between teaching religion and teaching about religion.

With Ugo Bianchi's dense (and sometimes abstruse) essay on "History of Religions" (6: 399–408), we enter a different sphere, for Bianchi sees the history of religions as a scientific discipline that emerged out of a context in which religion was taught normatively. It is a "fundamentally empirical discipline" (401), contrasted with the hermeneutical and phenomenological approaches, both of which he sees as extensions of the irreducibility of religion. Such imprecise characterization on his part assumes direct insight into the nature of religion (derived, it appears, from the experiential sensitivity of the researcher)—that is, from some kind of a priori reasoning or personal conviction. (Bianchi also contrasts this kind of historical approach with both the historicist and theoretical approaches, but I will touch on this below.)

History of Religions, he further claims (somewhat enigmatically), is tempered by "a dialectic between its object of study and its method of research" (400). Such a study does not operate with a "univocal" notion of religion but rather with an "analogical" one, which allows for the production, as he puts it, of a complex, multidimensional map of religion. He further "explains" that such history is not mere ideographic research since it aims at establishing "networks" of continuities and discontinuities (both structural and temporal) able to account for more than just a single historical religious tradition.

As I have stated above, Bianchi's essay is dense and therefore somewhat difficult to assess. The stark contrast between his suggested approach and the historicist and theoretical approaches presents a problem, for in his assertion that religion, even though a decidedly historical phenomenon, cannot be "reduced" to history he has made the two in effect irreconcilable. And though I find value in his critical comments on Hegel and others in this regard, Bianchi's pointed objection to reductionism in general seems limited if not unwarranted; he himself seems to see this, at least partly, as he concedes (somewhat inconsistently) that *theory* in the study of religion ought not to be rejected out of hand. His claim that "all forms of reductionism have in common an appeal to a univocal conception of religion located within a preconceived frame of reference" (400), therefore, surely hides a certain measure of unsubstantiated assumption, the precise nature of which escapes me.

Despite the fact that the *Encyclopedia* includes an essay by Sharpe on "Comparative Religion," and another by Bianchi on "History of Religions," it includes yet another essay on "Comparative-Historical Method," this time by Ninian Smart (3: 571–574). Smart takes up issues masked elsewhere in the volume. Like Bianchi, he emphasizes the similarity between the scientific study of religion and the other sciences—that is, the concern with objectivity (whether in regard to descriptive-historical accounts of tradition or to their explanation within a broad theoretical framework). And he does not fail to indicate that it is precisely in this approach to the data (rather than simply in the selection of data) that the study of religion is differentiated from religion and theology. Questions of transcendental truth are not of concern here; the focus, rather, is on "religion's actual influences and effects within the world of human history" (572). Smart refers to this kind of study of religion as a "dynamic phenomenology" that, in its concern for history and theory, somewhat blurs the neat lines drawn between the two.

The last essay to be considered here is Douglas Allen's "Phenomenology of Religion" (11: 272–285). Following an overview of the diversity of phenomenologies, classified as "non-philosophical" and "philosophical," he lists the central characteristics of the latter (itself divided into three types). He admits that philosophical phenomenologists have not had much interest in religion, but he maintains that it is they who have largely influenced methodological vocabulary in the religious studies field. He notes the intimate connection between phenomenology of religion and history of religion and then proceeds to review the positions of the major phenomenologists (W. B. Kristensen, R. Otto, G. van der Leeuw, F. Heiler, C. J. Bleeker, and Eliade). He enumerates those criticisms leveled at this kind of approach to the study of religions, and observes somewhat tentatively that, generally speaking, phenomenology has undermined the demarcation between religion and the study of religion—and has, therefore, become a form of religion masquerading as a methodology. He sees the challenge to this approach in its need to construct a "scientific" framework that "allows the description of essential structures and meanings with some sense of objectivity" (282). He thus proposes adoption of a phenomenological induction "in which the essential structures and meanings are based on, but not found fully in, the empirical data" (283). Though he admits this induction will involve imaginative construction and idealization, he nevertheless, contradictorily, insists that the results of those activities must—like all scientific hypotheses and theories—be subject to test and verification.

Weighed in the balance, then, the *Encyclopedia of Religion* falls short of the level of scholarship required of the discipline as a science. It has so embraced the Eliadean perspective on religion that it scarcely does justice to the range of opinion and debate in the field. The extensive discussions of the scientific study of religion from the time of its emergence as a bona fide element of the university curriculum—distinct from theology—are ignored. The history of the battle between Theology and Religious Studies seems never to have occurred, so that its perseverance into the present is played down if not suppressed. Little wonder then, that such slight attention is given in the *Encyclopedia* to such matters as the nature and role of explanation and theory in the academic study of religion—for its assumed antireductionism would preclude any thought in this direction.

This new *Encyclopedia,* then, though it brings up to date the results of research in religious studies since the publication of the *ERE,* does not contribute to the field in any significant fashion. Indeed, in important respects it actually blocks new developments, for it consciously and determinedly espouses the metaphysical assumptions lying half-hidden in the structures of its predecessor—and this despite the claim to have moved beyond them. In sum, though new, it is also old; though just published, it is already obsolete.

Chapter Thirteen

~~~~~

Alive, But Just Barely:
Graduate Studies in Religion
at the University of Toronto

Although the academic-scientific study of religion is still institutionally alive at the University of Toronto, there is a sense in which its
future at the graduate level has been seriously compromised. A primary indicator of this, I suggest, is the recent amalgamation (1992) of the
university's graduate Centre for the Study of Religion with its undergraduate department. As unlikely as this suggestion may at first appear, this essay
will show why this is the case, in light of the history of the study of religion
at the University of Toronto at both the undergraduate and graduate levels.[1]

There is sufficient reason to question whether a "genuine" religious studies program at the University of Toronto has ever existed at the undergraduate level. There is, to be sure, a Department for the Study of Religion, but
it is clear that, despite insistent endeavors on the part of some of its members, it has not really committed itself to the kind of academic study of religion and religions one might have expected of the field. For Religious
Studies at the University of Toronto has been unable (from the earliest creation of an undergraduate department in 1969) to free itself from Christian
(theological) domination—an inability stemming from its historical associations with the federated Christian colleges with their required "religious
knowledge" components in all undergraduate arts programs. As a mid-
eighties review put the matter, the department was diligent in fulfilling its
self-ascribed role by offering a curriculum reflecting "current student interests, the origins of the department in college 'religious knowledge' courses,
and wider conceptions of religious studies . . . ," but it failed to recognize
how drastically that curriculum diverged "from the recent development of
the discipline" (Drummond et al., 1984: 1). It emerges from the review,
moreover, that the department saw its role primarily "in terms of 'service' to

students who seek knowledge and truth through religious studies" (1984: 1), therefore emphasizing the pastoral "function" of the department to the detriment of scholarship and critical analysis in the classroom. The authors of the report state it clearly:

> . . . since the University of Toronto does assign priority to scholarship and to research, a department which ignores these activities is not likely to be taken very seriously within the University. The point is worrying to us, because it is not clear to us that the Department does see itself in a way that parallels these University priorities. (Drummond et al., 1984: 2)

By contrast, at the graduate level of the university's program for Religious Studies there appears to have been an attempt to demarcate the task of the student of religion from the pastorally orientated task of the "Religious Knowledge" professor and the theologian. According to a recent state-of-the-art review of the study of religion in educational institutions in the province of Ontario, however, that demarcation was not a simple undertaking:

> The road to graduate degrees in religious studies at the University of Toronto was long and rocky. What had to become clear, both within the University and to the OCGS [Ontario Council of Graduate Studies], was that the study at the graduate level was a legitimate academic enterprise and that any institutional embodiments of such a study would be distinct from the Toronto Graduate School of Theological Studies (TGSTS) founded in 1944 (succeeded in 1969 by the Toronto School of Theology [TST]), although some faculty of TGSTS might also serve as religious studies graduate faculty. (Remus et al., 1992: 60)

Moreover, the Centre for the Study of Religion was to be independent of the undergraduate Department of Religious Studies, although the specific reasons for this were not spelled out clearly. It is not difficult, however, to determine the motivations behind the relevant reports and documents. The original "Report of the Religious Studies Consultants" involving V. A. Harvey, H. E. Duckworth, and N. Smart to ACAP (Advisory Committee on Academic Planning) (Duckworth et al., 1974a), which ultimately recommended that the proposed Centre not be established, simply claims that most of the people interviewed by the consultants

> agreed that the teaching core of the proposed program could not be based on the present staff of the undergraduate program in Religious Studies because many in that faculty are not competent to guide graduate research and the entire program does not enjoy the confidence of many of the faculty in those

other departments whose cooperation would be necessary to the success of the proposed program. (in Duckworth et al., 1974a)

The consultants did not, admittedly, make specific and direct reference to the "Religious Knowledge" character of the undergraduate program, but they did nevertheless accuse the graduate proposal of being only "*allegedly* in Religious Studies" (A-22; my emphasis). They also claimed that

> . . . because of the weakness of the existing faculty in Religious Studies and because of the prestige and overwhelming number of scholars in the related theological schools, it seemed almost inevitable that the hegemony of the program would drift quite naturally to members of those faculties, which is to say, to scholars in Christian studies. (A-21)

Dean A. E. Safarian seems to have understood the term "allegedly" in the consultants' discussion above as direct reference to the failure of the proposal to make a clear distinction between Theology and Religious Studies (Safarian, 1974: C-12, C-13). Safarian maintained that the consultants failed to recognize that mechanisms were in place in the university to prevent the theological programs of TST and the Institute for Christian Thought (ICT—an undergraduate program of St. Michael's College) from swamping the program of graduate studies proposed for the new Centre. He also argued that they did not properly understand the role the undergraduate department would play in complementing the graduate program, despite the "peculiar nature" of its own genesis (Safarian, 1974: C-9). But the consultants were not convinced, and in their "Reply" to ACAP they wrote:

> The Dean's letter does not in our opinion speak to the problem constituted by the quality of the undergraduate department of Religious Studies. His statement . . . boils down to the claim that 21 [of 32] of this department have been engaged "in graduate teaching in the university *or* one of the theological programs . . ." ([emphasis] ours). Unfortunately the conjunction "or" in the above sentence masks the distinction between being engaged in graduate teaching in a University and in a theological school. Nor are we told how many are engaged in each of these. The fact that a great proportion teach in a theological program isn't in itself an impressive fact and only raises our question about the overwhelming emphasis on Christian studies in the department. Moreover, it raises the incidental question why if 21 are so competent in this respect that only 11 are being proposed for membership in the Centre. (Duckworth et al., 1974b: C-22, C-23)

The consultants, despite these comments, insisted that their concern was not the confrontation of "theological studies versus Religious studies" (Safarian,

1974: C-23), nor the proposed Centre's relation to religious inculcation, but rather the overwhelming "Christianness," so to speak, that would come to characterize the program. The disclaimer, however, stands in some tension with the consultants' views on the nature of the study of religion in general, and with their specific comments about "The Relation of Proposals to Faculty Resources and Competence" at Toronto in their original report, in which they point out that "faculty trained in theology seem especially prone to claim themselves competent in secular sounding fields . . . even though they appear to have been trained conventionally as theologians, published nothing in these areas, and are not recognized by colleagues outside of the department as established scholars in them" (Duckworth et al., 1974a: A-12). The perception of a "darker hint" in their Council of Ontario Universities report (Safarian, 1974: C-12), moreover, suggests that Dean Safarian also saw implicit in that report a further claim about "theological studies versus Religious studies."[2] It is interesting to note that, in the report's "System Recommendations," Theology is not included among the "human studies" applicable in the field of Religious Studies. Moreover, that portion of the report makes quite explicit the problems for the field with respect to the "Theological-Studies-versus-Religious-Studies" issue:

> The academic study of religion emphasizes neutrality and objectivity. To a considerable extent, this emphasis has arisen recently in universities of the Western world and is to be contrasted with "committed" accounts of religion which were the norm for a long time and, of course, still are the norm where religion is treated *from a theological point of view.*
>
> The study of religion may thus be characterized as concerned with man's relation to the transcendent, to God or the Gods and whatever else is regarded as sacred or holy. *Its present-day concern is predominantly descriptive and explanatory and embraces such various disciplines as history, sociology, anthropology, psychology, and archaeology. This is in contrast to the traditional orientation of religion toward truth claims which is properly the concern of theology.* (Yolton, 1974: 6; emphasis added)

The ACAP obviously did not follow the advice of the original consultants and recommended that the proposed graduate Centre for Religious Studies be established. Evidently, they thought the concerns with objectivity and neutrality—and with the possible domination of the program by "Christian Studies"—had been properly solved by Dean Safarian. A new team of consultants—C. Adams, R. B. Y. Scott, and J. Pelikan—created in early 1975 to undertake the task of appraising the program in detail, also maintained that the fears of the ACAP's consultants were exaggerated.[3] And if one of them (R. B. Y. Scott) looked for an eventual closer relationship between the undergraduate department and the Centre, none argued that an "amalgamation" would be of any benefit to the Centre.[4] The assessors for the aforementioned 1984 review of the department, it is true, recommended a merger of the two units "so that the Department of Religious Studies would be responsible for both [undergraduate and graduate] levels of activity" (Drummond et al., 1984: 5), but they also acknowledged that the department still reflected its historic, "college" character and that many of the members of the department were very much involved with the TST (1–2, 4). Regrettably, those assessors failed to perceive the implications of such a merger for the future development of the Centre. These were not overlooked, however, by the acting director of the Centre, Professor Ronald Sweet, who, in his report on the 1981–1986 quinquennial review of the Centre, wrote: "Since the state of the Department is still perceived today to be very similar to what it was in 1974, it would be folly, from the point of view of the Centre, to merge the Department and the Centre forthwith" (Sweet, 1985: 16). Unfortunately, Sweet also argued that the Centre should be given more time—"at least another five years of independence"—so that it could continue to build on the respect it had already earned (1985: 16), instead of insisting that no amalgamation or merger take place until the department had secured its academic place in the university. Despite the qualifications, Professor Sweet's fears for the Centre in the case of a merger are well founded; yet, as I shall show below, they were little heeded, if at all, by the Provostial Task Force (1992) that eventually effected the merger. Drummond et al., unlike Sweet, did not recognize that although the merger with the Centre might help re-create the department and give it some degree of national and international stature, it could also lead to the destruction of the ethos, program, and reputation the Centre had established by handing over control of its program to a department incapable of carrying out the mandate of the Centre.

In the third edition of his *Guide to Religious Studies in Canada,* Charles Anderson claims that the creation of university faculties or departments of Religious Studies was based on "the acceptance by the university community of a distinction between the religious study of religion and its secular study [that is] . . . between the religious and the academic study of religion" (Anderson, 1972: 8). He continues: "This important distinction was the ideological prerequisite for the founding or evolution of several new departments of religious studies around 1960. . . . By the mid-1960's . . . the concept of religious studies as a respectable academic enterprise had been widely accepted in the university, despite some pockets of resistance" (1972: 8, 9). Although Anderson's reference here to "pockets of resistance" refers to the reluctance of some universities to accept Religious Studies as a bona fide academic enterprise, the term might equally well be applied to the refusal by some theological "holdouts" to acknowledge a distinction between Religious Studies and Theology. It is my claim here that a resistance of that kind—theological in effect if not in nature—to the establishment of a program of Religious Studies has been in operation for some time at the University of Toronto. Nor am I alone in holding such a view; to support this claim I shall draw attention briefly to the published perceptions other Canadian scholars have of Toronto's place in the field.

Harold Coward's summary assessment of Toronto's program of Religious Studies—based in part on his reading of the state-of-the-art reviews of the study of religion in the provinces of Ontario and Quebec—is highly critical with respect to Toronto's failure to embody the ideological (academic) prerequisites of which Anderson spoke. He maintains, for example, that "[t]he shift, from the mentality of 'Christian establishment' and the missionary thrust that dominated the place of religion in the early history of Canadian universities to Religious Studies departments in which Christianity has no privileged position, is far from complete" (Coward, 1991: 32). Coward also claims, and for the most part rightly so, that departments established in institutions without denominational allegiance have stronger, more balanced programs of study than those with such connections (Coward, 1991: 32). It is important, however, to note that this is not unambiguous, as can be seen in the review for the provinces of Manitoba and Saskatchewan (Badertscher et al., 1993). The Religious Studies program at the University of Manitoba, as Gordon Harland's contribution to this study makes clear, has fewer such religious-ecclesiastical ties than does the University of Winnipeg, yet it seems more committed to a religiously orientated program: "a diffused sense in the culture of the need for a religious perspective, and even a quest for religious experience ... [was] an important ingredient in conceiving the aims and goals of the department" (1993: 32). This still seems to be the motivation behind that department's offerings, as is clear from Gordon Harland's contribution to a recent conference there on "Religious Studies: Directions for the Next Two Decades." He explains:

> For my part I thought the times required that we become livingly aware of the resources of a deep religious heritage. It was, of course, a risky business then, as it still is, to use terms like heritage and tradition. For many people these terms conjure up images of 'the dead hand of the past,' or a retreat from the complexities of the present to the supposedly simpler days of the past, all in the spirit of nostalgia. Nothing could have been further from my concern. My concern, then as now, was that we engage the depths of our religious traditions as a way of laying hold of those energies and values that will enrich the present, and help us shape the future. Indeed, one of the few convictions that I have is the belief that it is only those who are in touch with a vital heritage who possess the resources to shape a new age. (Harland, 1991: 3)

Despite Harland's disclaimer above regarding a nostalgic recovery of one's "heritage and tradition," it is obvious that for him the task for Religious Studies is not simply an academic or scientific one, but rather (as in the past) a moral and religious undertaking: "Our task in Religious Studies is to engage the issues of our time, in their particularity, with all the knowledge we can muster, but also in a larger framework of meaning from which may be gained the values and the visions to help humanize our world" (Harland, 1991: 12). Religious Studies, unlike other disciplines in the university, is able to do this, claims Harland, because it facilitates "the recovery of the Bible to exercise a more active presence in our culture" (Harland, 1991: 10).

Roland Miller's contribution on Saskatchewan in the same review provides an important contrast to that of Harland. Miller acknowledges that, as in the case of Manitoba, "university education [in Saskatchewan] grew out of a close association with an original perspective that viewed arts and theology as colleagues in the educational enterprise" (Badertscher et al., 1993: 101), but he points out that such religious "contribution" in the shaping of the Religious Studies curriculum took place only at the University of Saskatchewan and not at the University of Regina. Although there are several legally and financially independent religious colleges integrally related to the University of Regina, Miller argues that its Religious Studies program (department) "grew out of a genuine recognition of the importance of the subject material and out of a concern for a secular approach to its academic study" (Miller, 1993: 83).

In elaborating upon his assessment of departments with and without religious connections, Coward claims that the Department of Religious Studies at the University of Toronto is one of those institutions heavily influenced by ecclesiastical and theological concerns. "Its failure to develop strongly," he writes, "is at least partly due to the unwillingness of the University of Toronto denominational colleges to appoint specialists in non-Christian religions" (Coward, 1991: 32). To some extent this judgment is accurate, for the department at the University of Toronto was—and, indeed, still is—largely a department of Christian studies. Coward does not find this surprising, given the origin of the department; nor do I, even though I am aware that some interpretations of its development would not support the implications Coward and I would draw—and in particular that the department's background was conducive to fulfilling many of the aims and goals of the earlier "Religious Knowledge" programs of the federated denominational colleges. Whether the establishment of the department in 1969 constituted a radical departure from the "Combined Departments of Religious Studies" or was simply a continuation of the old programs in a new package (with at best minor modifications) is the issue in dispute. It can be shown that, despite the hopes of some members of the "combined departments" (and their successors) to found a genuine academic study of religion at the University of Toronto, the new university department (established in 1975) has ultimately retained its religious aims and intentions.

Until 1965, religious knowledge courses were taught at the federated denominational colleges (University of Victoria College, University of Trinity College, and University of St. Michael's College) as a required component of the undergraduate degree program. By 1965 there was growing dissatisfaction on the part of the students with this requirement and alternatives were proposed, even though there was some doubt that the federated colleges would accept radical changes. As a result of a "Memorandum Regarding Religious Knowledge and Religious Knowledge Options" at the University of Toronto, prepared by Gordon Watson of Trinity College [1965; unfortunately available only indirectly],[5] it was agreed that the current religious knowledge courses be discontinued and replaced by interdisciplinary seminars. It is through this change of program, so it appears, that the "combined department" was brought into being as an institutional administrative framework. It is true, furthermore, that, as Professor Joanne McWilliam points out in "A Short History of the Department of Religious Studies," the department, in the process of being formed, saw itself as engaging staff not only from among those involved in the religious knowledge program but also cross-appointed faculty from "Near Eastern, East Asiatic, Sociology . . . and other departments" (McWilliam, 1990: 2). She does note, however, "[a]t the beginning the teaching staff was almost exactly the same as it had been for 'religious knowledge'" (1990: 2), although she claims this changed gradually over the next six years. The claim is dubious, for it is clear from the ACAP consultants' report in 1974—five years after the establishment of the department—that it was still predominantly involved in Christian studies. This is no surprise, however, in view of the fact that St. Michael's College, the largest of the three federated university colleges, had the greatest influence on the departmental politics that shaped the development of Religious Studies at Toronto; and at St. Michael's, cross-appointments between Theology and Religious Studies were common (McWilliam, 1990: 2). Furthermore, none of the new appointments between 1969 and 1974 (at St. Michael's or elsewhere) really reflected a radical change within the department, since in each case the study of non-Western religious traditions was carried out largely as "inter-religious dialogue" rather than as a critical historical exercise. What new appointments were made, therefore, do not indicate a "paradigm shift" but rather merely a broader theological development. Moreover, the ethos of the "combined departments" and new university department had not really changed a great deal, as can be inferred from Gordon Watson's recommendation that the arrangements go beyond the apparent goal of the "religious knowledge program" to provide instruction in Christian doctrine and to deal "with the ultimate directions or foundations or concerns of human life" (quoted by McWilliam, 1990: 1).[6] After reviewing the early history of the University of Toronto's new Department of Religious Studies,[7] one is inclined to agree with the authors of the Ontario state-of-the-art review when they note—echoing Charles Anderson—that changes in the pattern of the traditional teaching of religion, such as are to be seen at the University of Toronto, "did not automatically transform the *status quo ante* into a religious studies department, any more than changing the names of departments of 'Religion' or 'Theology' to 'Religious Studies' in other Ontario universities . . . effected instant transmutations" (Remus et al., 1992: 59). N. Keith Clifford makes a similar observation in "Church History, Religious History, or the History of Religions?"; he notes, for example, that very little anxiety was experienced by departments concerned with theology and religious knowledge (such as McGill, Queen's, or the University of Toronto) in becoming departments of Religious Studies because, as he put it, the change was little more than one of name only, "without changing their teaching staff or their conceptions of what they were doing. . . . [T]here was little or no dissonance, for everyone continued doing what they had always done" (Clifford, 1991: 172–173). The same individuals who taught Religious Knowledge courses to University of Toronto students, for the most part, still staffed the new department, and to a large extent the same religio-theological approach to the study of religions that had characterized the combined departments persisted within the new university department created in 1975.[8] This is quite clear from the department's rather grandiose description of its agenda in its first handbook:

> To expand human awareness in areas which affect directly the foundations and quality of life is not easy, but in our age it is vitally important. To prepare for life, in addition to preparing for a career or for graduate study is, among other things, to learn how to formulate ultimate questions and work toward their answers. The Department of Religious Studies is committed to encouraging this process and to critical and creative extension of it into areas of individual and corporate concern. (Handbook, 1975–1976: 5–6)

Although this statement is not repeated in subsequent department handbooks, similar sentiments are expressed in a variety of forms right down to the present: the reference to theologians on the staff, for example, was deleted only in the 1981–1982 and subsequent handbooks (even though there is no indication that the composition of the teaching complement has been significantly changed), while information regarding advanced studies at both the graduate Centre and the Toronto School of Theology was not removed until the 1990–1991 handbook. It would appear that such vestiges of the old (combined) departmental concerns only disappeared as a result of internal pressures from those faculty in the new department who wished to wean the program from its original religio-theological agenda. The successes of the "secularists" were limited, however, for by 1986–1987 the handbook had recovered much of the tone of the first edition in 1975–1976. In describing the department, the later edition states:

> The study of religion offers useful preparation for participation in a religiously diverse world. As an inquiry into an important dimension of human experience it is intrinsically valuable and satisfying; it also prepares students for a wide range of careers (e.g., social work, law, politics, from the local to the international level, teaching, medicine, leadership in religious organizations). (Handbook, 1986–1987: 2)

Moreover, in the list of approaches the department employs in the study of religion, the current handbook (1994–1995) has reinserted the "normative" approach, reflecting once again the religio-theological character or ethos of the department. A review of the program and course offerings contained in the handbooks over the years further indicates that little advance has been made in diversifying the direction of "Religious Studies"; Christian studies is still overwhelmingly dominant, and the balance in course offerings spread over the major world religious traditions, despite some additions to the teaching staff, simply did not take place in 1975—and still has not taken place, as one might have expected in light of the consensus that Anderson thinks the Religious Studies community in Canada had achieved on demarcating religion from the study of religion and in broadening the study of religion to traditions outside Christianity.[9]

In his report to the School of Graduate Studies with regard to the 1981–1986 quinquennial review of the Centre, Acting Director Ronald Sweet argues that an important reason for the SGS's drawing only selectively from available TST personnel and other resources is "that the committed approach of theological method—*fides quaerens intellectum*—is not appropriate in the religious studies enterprise of a secular university" (Sweet, 1985: 12). He did not elaborate the point, however, as he thought this would be done by someone else.[10] This was an unfortunate omission as it resulted in an inadequately serious perception of the threat to the Centre's program from its relationship to the TST.[11] Sweet also took too lightly the threat to the Centre of being overwhelmed by Christian studies because of its connections to both the TST and the undergraduate department, whose program was in many respects difficult to differentiate from that of the TST. He notes that the University Appraisals Committee (Adams, Scott, and Pelikan) claimed that the fears of the ACAP's consultants (Duckworth, Harvey, and Smart) were likely exaggerated, and that ACAP had "met the university representatives [Safarian, Watson, et al.] and referred a statement of the university's revised position to the consultants" (Sweet, 1985: 12).

However, Sweet provided no support for the claim that the fears of the ACAP's consultants may have been exaggerated; and (without a copy of the University's "revised position" before him) he suggested: "it is reasonable to assume that it contained an assurance that Christian studies would not be permitted to swamp the study of other religious traditions" (Sweet, 1985: 12). Moreover, in adopting such an ill-founded position, Sweet was all the while aware of at least two major "decisions" by the university that actually confirmed the ACAP's consultants' worst fears, as I shall show below: namely, the proposal to hire the theologian Hans Küng for the Centre, and the joint University of Toronto/Toronto School of Theology proposal to establish a Graduate Department of Theology (GDT) in the School of Graduate Studies.

Members of the Centre became aware sometime in late 1983 or early 1984 that the university was about to hire Dr. Hans Küng for the department and the Centre for Religious Studies. The news came as a surprise, for no advertisement of a position had been published and no search undertaken. The processes leading to this decision had been brokered by a few senior members of the department who were also members of the Centre, and it was conducted through unofficial—if not improper—channels until a deal had been worked out, one presumes, to Küng's satisfaction. Fortunately for the Centre, news of the impending deal leaked out before the contract was sent to Küng. This provided sufficient time for concerned members of the Centre to press Dean Leyerle of the School of Graduate Studies (SGS) and President Strangway of the University for an explanation of the decision to hire for a purportedly scientific program a world-renowned Christian theologian—a move that would tip the balance in favor of Christian studies even further. In the early days of a protracted series of discussions and consultations, it became evident the Dean of SGS did not care to be informed about the concerns expressed by ACAP's consultants (Duckworth, Harvey, and Smart) regarding the likelihood of a hegemony of Christian studies in the Centre. Nor was he concerned with the danger such a major and highly visible appointment presented to the emerging nontheological ethos of the Centre. The agenda of the Dean of SGS and the President of the university seemed totally at cross-purposes to that of the Centre; it seemed almost as if they perceived the Centre as providing some kind of beneficial religious quality to a spiritually needy secular institution.[12] In light of this, Dean A. E. Safarian's letter of 13 May, 1974, assuring the Council of Ontario Universities that the University of Toronto was sensitive to ACAP's concerns in this regard and possessed "mechanisms" to deal with such problems, rings hollow; for the "mechanisms" in mind involved the attention of a "vigilant" Dean of graduate studies (Safarian, 1974: C-10) and a "vigilant" Director of the Centre (C-14); yet a former Director of the Centre had been a primary impetus behind the Küng proposal, and a Dean of the School of Graduate Studies (with the support of the then current Director of the Centre) was doing all in his power to see it through to a successful conclusion.[13]

Under some pressure, the (then) current Director of the Centre called for a special general assembly of the members (both faculty and students) of the Centre (1984) in order to canvass opinion in the graduate program of Religious Studies on the Küng appointment. Many acknowledged Küng's scholarly contribution to the Church and its theological community but nevertheless objected to his appointment to the Centre. Of these some had economic concerns, in that the large sum of money to be expended in that appointment could be used to better effect in the Centre, while others took exception to the less-than-open process employed in the attempted appointment. In addition, however, the majority involved in the discussion clearly objected on the grounds that this kind of appointment would be detrimental to the ethos and program of the Centre, whose operating principle had been the academic-scientific study of religion. Fortunately for the Centre, those opposed to Küng's appointment won the struggle, as can be inferred from Professor Sweet's statement in his 1985 Report to the School of Graduate Studies: "Professor H. Küng is teaching the graduate course REL 1029F: Models of Interreligious Dialogue in the first term of 1985–1986. He is in Toronto at the invitation of the Dean of SGS, however, and his salary, which is provided by special funds from the President's office, is not administered through the Centre" (Sweet, 1985: 14). Just how effective the opponents to the appointment were, however, in persuading others of the validity of their (academic) principle was very much in doubt; for the undergraduate department had already gone on record (in its response to the report of the department's 1984 external review) that it considered theology an appropriate element in the "religious studies mix," and that the undergraduate department, as has been indicated, eventually would gain control of the Centre's programs. In the opening paragraph of that document it is stated that the department feels compelled to formulate more explicitly than before, "a general theory of the academic study of religion and an application of that theory to the specific context of this University," given the several issues raised by the external assessors, including the question of the department's "relation to Church-related Colleges . . ." (University of Toronto, 1985: 1). The statement points out that "there is no agreement within the 'discipline' of Religious Studies about the appropriateness of theological studies within the [university] framework," and that the department would, therefore, be behaving inappropriately if it refused to hire any staff in theology (3). The department's justification for the hiring of theologians is inadequate, however, for it confuses the distinction between the critical-historical study of theological systems of thought (which everyone in the field admits is a part of the subject matter needing analysis) with the study of the Divine, which as "object(s)" of such systems of thought are considered by students in this field to be beyond their mandate of investigation. The statement therefore continues: there are "no illegitimate questions [in the field], (e.g., about the existence of object(s) of theological reflection—the god(s)" (3).

As stated above, the second major factor which threatened not only the integrity of the Centre but its very existence was the university's willingness to consider the establishment of a Graduate Department of Theology (GDT). The Centre's 1981 Review Committee recommended "that the Dean [of SGS] be urged to seek, through the President, the establishment of a joint committee between the School and TST to study the relationship between the University and TST in the hope that each could utilize the resources of both institutions. In particular the sharing of resources between the TST and the Centre of Religious Studies should be examined" (quoted by Sweet, 1985: 11). This is an astounding about-face, given the ACAP's consultants' report and Dean Safarian's assurances that the Centre's program would not be "swamped" by Christian studies or by a theological ethos. It is true that Dean Safarian insisted the Centre capitalize on its strengths in the "sub-field" of Christian studies, but this could not have included making all of TST's graduate faculty available to the students in the Centre's Religious Studies programs. Yet that is precisely what would have occurred, had the report of "The University of Toronto/Toronto School of Theology Joint Council" (established in 1984) been adopted.[14] Although rumor of the Joint Council's workings had been circulating for some time, it was not until September of 1987 that some members of the Centre became aware of its agenda and voiced their concerns.[15] It was, again, astounding—and most irregular—that such discussions could have proceeded as far as they had without input from members of the Centre. As far as I am aware, even though a former Director of the Centre was a member of the Joint Council, no information came to the Centre about the content of those discussions.[16]

On September 24, 1987, Professor Paul Gooch, the fourth Director of the Centre for Religious Studies,[17] sent a notice to all faculty members of the Centre about the possibility of the creation of a GDT, enclosing with the memorandum a draft statement on the "CRS and a Possible Graduate Department of Theology" that, to some, seemed an inappropriate (if not cavalier) response to the formation of what would amount to a Graduate Department of Christian Theology. It seemed that neither the university officials involved in the secretive deliberations regarding the GDT nor the Director of the Centre had adequately considered how greatly such a department would skew a variety of issues—from funding to supervision to the composition of the student body of the Centre. Fortunately for the Centre, again, its Director was persuaded of the threat posed by the Joint Council proposal, as indicated in his letter to me of October 8, 1987:

> I take it that you believe the chief threat to the CRS to be the danger of muddling: more courses and supervisors will be available to CRS students, and these will be in theological areas, with Christian content, taught by people who are not academically suitable for Religious Studies. I agree completely that this is a danger. (Gooch, 1987a: 1)

Professor Gooch concluded that letter with the assurance that the Centre would formulate a paper on the matter, having the support of its Executive Committee *and* its General Assembly, which would then be sent on to SGS. The result of those deliberations amounted in effect to a repudiation of the 1981 Review Committee's assessment that easy access to one another's resources by the TST and the CRS would be beneficial to both, and in the end, the Joint Council proposal for a GDT came to nothing.

Given the concerns raised by ACAP's consultants about the religio-theological and predominantly Christian character of Religious Studies in Toronto—concerns apparently acknowledged by the backers of the proposal for the CRS (and other university officials)—such threatening proposals to the Centre's programs certainly ought never to have got off the ground, let alone approach fulfillment.[18] One can only assume that they did so because opinion within the Centre—like that in the undergraduate department—was still seriously divided on both the ethos of the Centre and the balance of its offerings.[19]

The difference of opinion with respect to its ethos became obvious in a Centre symposium in the fall of 1984, organized on the topic: "The Relationship between Theological and Religious Studies: What Should the Toronto Model Be?" Many thought the Centre should be open to theological thinking and research, although not of the kind involving confessional commitments. This, for example, was the position of Professor Peter Slater, then of Wycliffe College and cross-appointed to the Centre. He argued:

> The God who is to be discussed in the University courses is not yet God if this God is not one who may be worshipped. On the other hand, no God is worthy of worship whose names do not include the name Truth. . . . Talk of God in the University is appropriate, even though non-empirical, as is talk of the mind in the mind-body dichotomy of philosophy. Anyone who's

going to teach theology in a university department has to be committed to a sense of reverence which also allows for that kind of openness of inquiry. (Wyse, 1986: 19)[20]

Professor William Fennell, a TST theologian and member of the symposium panel, provided a critical review of my article "The Failure of Nerve in the Academic Study of Religion" (1984, and chapter 8 in this volume) as a point of departure for a similar argument in support of the place of theology in the study of religion in the university. I argued that such a position failed to understand the historical development of the field of Religious Studies in general, and that it ignored local commitments (the graduate study of religion at the University of Toronto would not merge its program with a religio-theological enterprise). The ensuing discussion by the panelists led to some rather uncivil exchanges in the symposium, thus providing a clear indication of just how deeply the theological issue still affected the Centre for Religious Studies, and of how keenly felt was the pressure to integrate Religious and Theological Studies. Not only those cross-appointed from the TST to the Centre, but some of the (originally college-based) staff of the undergraduate department (of whom some were also involved in one way or another with the TST or other college-based religion programs, such as the Institute for Christian Thought at St. Michael's College) had a vested interest in establishing a religio-theological ethos in the Centre and in maintaining the dominance of Christian studies in it.[21]

It was this residually religious character of the study of religion in the undergraduate department, along with the dominance of Christian studies in the department, that the proposed Centre for Religious Studies was created to escape.[22] Various University officials and committees, as I have indicated above, gave assurances to those who were skeptical that the escape could be managed, but those officials were apparently disingenuous. The undergraduate department, despite strenuous and persistent efforts on the part of several of its members, has remained essentially where it was in the mid-seventies; and now—with the recent amalgamation of the department and the graduate Centre for the Study of Religion, against the advice of numerous external assessors in various reviews of the Centre and of its then Director and Associate Director (N. McMullin and D. Wiebe)—it has virtually total control over the graduate programs. Although the renamed Centre for the Study of Religion still exists as an element within the new (also renamed) Department for the Study of Religion, its existence is largely nominal; for the restructuring of the new department has virtually subordinated the Centre to governance and administration by the members of the undergraduate department. The forceful role played by the General Assembly of the old

CRS (involving graduate students and all those cross-appointed to the Centre) in blocking both the long-term appointment of Küng and the formation of a Graduate Department of Theology within the university's School of Graduate Studies has been undermined; the General Assembly is now merely a body to which the Chair reports on matters considered "appropriate" to that body.[23] Even discussion of the "RLG [Religion] Departmental Planning Document," a response to the university's overhaul of its structures and programs (which will therefore set the frame within which Religious Studies is to continue into the next century) was restricted "to regular members of the Department" (McWilliam, April 1994).[24] It is no surprise, therefore, that the morale among graduate students and a number of the teaching members of the Centre is at an all-time low.[25] There seems little hope at this point that the academic study of religion at the University of Toronto—even at the graduate level—will escape being a mere embellishment of Christian studies undertaken in a broad, liberal, religio-theological framework. And if one sees these developments in light of the 1982 Centre brochure, vaunting "the teaching and research resources of three Catholic and five Protestant theological colleges," one might naturally conclude that the Centre has always perceived itself as but another element of the TST mix.

The story of the merger of the Centre with the undergraduate department is a sad tale indeed. Although I cannot here recount in detail its convoluted plot (involving decisions by upper-level University of Toronto administration who simply ignored the advice of both their own external assessors of the Centre and the majority of the members of the Centre), something of that story ought to be related in order to show that my conclusion regarding the present state of affairs is not simply conjecture.

The "Report of the Task Force on Religious Studies" (Iannucci et al., 1991), in discussing the previous reviews of the Department and Centre, points to only the reports written by the Deans or their representatives when dealing with the establishment of a unitary organization for the study of religion at the University of Toronto. Although this practice might be considered "proper," it nevertheless fails to acknowledge that some of those reports were hotly contested within the Centre because they ignored major issues of concern raised by their own external assessors. This is particularly so with respect to the Perron report (1986), which many members of the Centre found unacceptable. The report suggested that moves be made toward bringing about a merger between the Centre and the department, despite Coward's rejection (1986) of the Drummond report (1984), which had advised the merger in order to strengthen the undergraduate department. Coward had stated:

> This question is rightly a key concern of many with whom I spoke, and opinion seems quite split. I see two dangers for the Centre in such a union. First,

there would be a tendency for a more standard graduate program to be established (e.g., on the mode of McMaster [University]) and this could submerge the special qualities of the current Centre program. Second, if the department took over the operation of the graduate program I doubt that the same level of over and above support would be forthcoming from other departments. . . . Thus, to maintain what is unique and attractive about the Toronto graduate program I would not advise union with the undergraduate department. (Coward, 1986: 5–6)

Professor Steven Katz, another external assessor of the Centre, wrote the following with regard to its "Faculty Relations with the Undergraduate Department" (1986):

This continues to be a "sore" point for all those involved. It is not saying too much to say that the undergraduate program is perceived as: (a) academically weak, (b) heavily theological in its bias, (c) too narrowly Christian in orientation, [and] (d) containing a faculty weak on research and uninterested in same. The efforts underway to make . . . appointments of *scholars* (research scholars) in non-Christian areas is certainly a step in improving this situation as is the recent appointment of a new distinguished Chairman. However, until the perception of change follows upon these actual changes—and hopefully other changes in the same positive direction—I would demur in recommending that the CRS and the Undergraduate Department merge or even become closer. Certainly they should continue to co-operate and seek ways to improve the overall situation, but given the present reality the CRS would, *I strongly believe,* be *ill*-served by the proposal either (a) to join the two; or (b) even to locate the two together in Robarts [Library] (or elsewhere). Though this latter proposal has the weight of the previous two Directors (Professors Oxtoby and Simpson as indicated in a memo to the Review Committee) behind it I think, at the present juncture it would be a major error. The fact is that though everyone wishes there were better relations between the CRS and the Undergraduate Centre [sic], until such time as the Undergraduate Department changes considerably any of the present proposals would, almost certainly, tend to swallow up the CRS in the Undergraduate program, a result which is not desirable. (Katz, 1986: 7–8)

The 1991 (Iannucci, et al.) task force report attempts to make a case for a radical change in the character of the undergraduate department, but this persuaded few who knew the situation even superficially. That thirteen of the sixteen full-time tenured faculty are members of the graduate Centre, as the report notes, does not provide automatic indication of a change of attitude within the department, as it seems to suggest. That theologians may have been cross-appointed to the Centre surely does not suggest that they too have a transformed attitude, diluting, so to speak, their theological aims.

Similarly, in noting that specialist programs are available in five major streams (Religions West; Religions East; Christian Origins; Religion, Ethics, and Society; and Philosophy of Religion), the report seems to suggest that the shortcomings successively noted by the assessors of the department have been overcome. The task force obviously failed to see that some of the categories of specialist programs overlap considerably: Religions West, for example, includes much of the territory of Christian Origins; and the remaining three Specialist programs, as the curriculum shows, deal predominantly with issues in Western religious traditions. Moreover, although the task force report fails to mention it, it is a fact that even at the time of the deliberations of the task force the undergraduate department was still making use of theological students from the Toronto School of Theology as teaching assistants despite a surplus of available School of Graduate Studies students in the Centre in need of training and employment. The department of which the 1991 task force writes, therefore, is still essentially the same Department to which Coward (1986) and Katz (1986) referred.

It is unfortunate that the later task force was not set up to examine simply whether or not it would be advisable to merge the two institutional structures dedicated to the study of religion. Such an endeavor would have reflected considerable integrity. Instead, the Provost required of the task force that it "bring forward recommendations whereby the resources of the University in the field of Religious Studies would be brought together under a single structure" (Foley, 5 Nov. 1990). Even though this decision to merge the two units caused considerable opposition, no genuine change of direction was ever considered. The handwriting was on the wall; for good or for ill, the Provost intended to merge the two units—revealing an apparent disregard for the academic merit of the decision. And the clarification issued by the Provost ("that the task force was 'asked not whether there should be a single structure but what one would look like were it to be implemented'" [Iannucci et al., 1991: 1]) appears to indicate an overriding financial concern to the detriment of the program's quality. Although the report claims that the task force "took note of the concern of some in the Centre that union with the Department might weaken the Centre's academic activities" (1991: 8), its authors did not outline those concerns, nor did they disclose how the university planned to deal with them. Once again, it would appear obvious that the task force was not established by the Provost to find out what were the best conditions for the study of religion at the University of Toronto, but rather to provide justification for administrative maneuvers already approved.

But if it is possible to conclude somewhat less bleakly, in spite of the unfortunate decision made by the Provost, one might argue that the "RLG [Religion] Department Planning Document" (to which I refer briefly above) may in fact chart a course for the undergraduate department to bring about the radical change in the nature of the department and a fundamental shift in the current imbalance of its teaching staff that will mitigate the dangers the department has presented to the Centre in the past. That of course does not justify the action taken by the Provost in the merger. Furthermore, it is difficult to know whether that planning document will in fact initiate a move as described, since the members of the Centre who are not also members of the undergraduate department have been excluded from discussion of the document. That fact alone might suggest that the department has not changed a great deal and that it wishes to have total control of the program, fearing how the non-Religious Studies scholars outside the department might affect the future shape of the program. It is difficult to say unequivocally that it is a backward-looking document; I can only say that some in the department are struggling to have the document cohere with a more broadly accepted understanding of the study of religion as an academic-scientific enterprise. Should the "reformers" in the department be successful in their efforts to play down the past connections of the department with religio-theological issues and concerns, and should they be effective in advocating a hiring policy to address the problem of the dominance of Christian studies, the future of the Centre will appear brighter than it has since the Provost's merger. Success in these two areas, however, would not alone guarantee the future of the Centre's program because there is no telling whether the changes proposed in the planning document would receive the support of the university's upper management—whose record on such matters, as I have pointed out in several places in this essay, is not encouraging. For this reason I have argued and must continue to insist that the merger of the Centre for the Study of Religion with the undergraduate Department of the Study of Religion has put the former at risk. Sound administrative action would have been collabrative rather than unilateral.[26]

Notes

1. This essay was written, at the invitation of Professor Gary Lease (Lease, 22 Feb. 1994), as a contribution to the special issue of *Method and Theory in the Study of Religion* (7/4; 1995) on "the place and future of the academic study of religion(s) in North America," which he edited. My analysis here of the current state of affairs in the study of religion at the University of Toronto is based on my experience as a member of the graduate Centre for Religious Studies (1981–1994), and my two years as its Associate Director (1990–1992). It is not a dispassionate analysis of the situation, even though I have attempted to ground my judgments upon historical accuracy and to prevent the distortions that often accompany the assessments of events in which one is actively involved. Some of my colleagues in Toronto will no

doubt think me excessively harsh. I wish to note here, therefore, that I have been a strong supporter of the study of religion in Toronto and think that the Graduate Centre has in many respects functioned admirably under often very difficult circumstances. My aim in writing this account, therefore, is not to undermine the achievements of the Centre, its students, or its staff, but to sound a warning about recent developments I think likely to be detrimental to its future. The documentation cited is that in my own possession or filed with university archives, as noted. Although most of the documents came by way of my participation in the Centre, I am grateful to a former student, Marion Wyse, for copies of some University of Toronto archival materials she collected for a paper in her Toronto School of Theology program, and to the Toronto School of Theology itself for making available to me materials in regard to deliberations of the University of Toronto/Toronto School of Theology Joint Council. (The documents with attributable authorship are cited in the text by name and date, while those without such clear designation are cited by abbreviated title as found in the references.) I am deeply grateful as well to several members of the Centre, especially Professors Peter Richardson and Neil McMullin, for critical comments on an early draft of this essay that were helpful in matters of interpretation and in getting the facts straight. I did not always heed their advice, so I alone am responsible for errors that remain. Thanks are also due to Professor McMullin and to Martha Cunningham for their views on matters of presentation.

2. The context for the remark is as follows: "We do not intend in any way to downgrade the enormous strength of the resources for Christian studies on the Toronto campus. On the contrary, presumably it is both a University and an ACAP objective to encourage graduate programs in fields where comparatively strong resources exist. The consultants rightly observe that our strength in this area is drawn in significant part from the Toronto School of Theology and the Institute for Christian Thought. . . . Indeed, there is their darker hint in this context that the proposal is a cover for the simple transplanting of the T. S. T. and I. C. T. programs to a more 'respectable' University of Toronto base. To refer in this connection to the program spelled out in the proposal as 'allegedly' in Religious Studies is mistaken and ignores several important facts which were drawn to their attention" (C-12).

3. It may be of value here to read the precise views of the three assessors. Pelikan wrote:

Throughout the documents that I studied in preparation for my visit and throughout many (perhaps even most) of the interviews I had during my visit there ran the undercurrent of the relation between Religious Studies and Theology. The institutional form of the problem is the question of what the creation of the proposed Centre would do to the Toronto School of Theology and to the Institute for Christian Thought and what they would do to it, but the intellectual and scholarly issues at stake transcend the rivalries of the various staffs. At most universities in the Western world, and a fortiori at Toronto, the academic study of religion has been nurtured by the enterprise of Christian theology, and it would truly be cutting off one's nose to spite one's face if the nascent Centre for Religious Studies were to be deprived of the scholarly riches represented by this tradition at Toronto. *On this issue I find myself considerably closer to the priorities expressed in Dean Safarian's letter than to that of the Consultants.* . . . I see little ground for the anxiety of the consultants that the result of the creation of the Centre would be to "incorporate the present theological studies now given by the Toronto School of Theology and the Institute for Christian Thought into a program allegedly in Religious Studies." (Pelikan, 1975: 12–13, 14; emphasis added)

Adams claimed: "I do not consider the possible threat of domination by a Christian specialization to be serious. The proposed Centre will have committees to regulate admission to its program and to supervise the courses of study that students will pursue. It should not be difficult for these committees to insure that the constituency of the Centre, both on the staff and the student side, remains diverse. All that is required to protect the multi-disciplinary, plural, and comprehensive nature of the program in the Centre is a determination by the Executive and other committees that the Centre shall remain true to its original purposes" (Adams, 1975: 7–8).

Scott approved the proposal without qualification and claimed "[t]he consultants' substantive criticisms of the *Proposal* have largely been met since their visit, through changes in the form of the *Proposal* though not in its principles. Their view that what was contemplated was simply integration of the TST/ICT resources with those of the University was erroneous; as was their contention that a good program must be based on an already strong undergraduate department" (Scott, 1975: 3).

The naïveté of these assessments, however, will become clear in the remainder of this paper. It will become obvious, I think, that these three scholars did not look deeply enough at the entrenched political problems with which the proposal was riddled.

4. Scott wrote: "The radical administrative distinction between the Centre and the University Department of Religious Studies is not a good thing academically and in other respects, though it appears necessary in present circumstances. It is to be hoped that in time this unnatural division of forces can be remedied" (Scott, 1975: 5). It would have been appropriate, I think, for Scott to have detailed the reasons why it was considered necessary at that time to keep the two units separate—it may well have awakened him to the serious concerns expressed by ACAP's consultants. As I will show below, I do not think the required remedy had surfaced by the time of the merger in 1992; nor do I think the problems of the department have yet been solved, even though several members of the department are working hard to achieve their resolution.

5. I have not seen a copy of this memorandum but have gleaned information about it from Joanne McWilliam (Chair and Acting Chair of the Department of Religious Studies, 1990–1994). Most of the historical account of the department in this and the next paragraph have drawn heavily upon the McWilliam essay (1990).

6. Watson obviously saw the Department of Religion as involving more than simply an academic enterprise; it was also a religious one, and that is why he could understand the colleges' worries over the loss of autonomy in the teaching of religion. Although I have not seen the text of his memorandum, a similar view seems to be presented in Watson's earlier essay "A Brief in Support of a University Department of Religion" (1960): "As one of the Humanities, then, the study of Religion can provide the student with an opportunity, at the very least, to deepen his understanding of man and human institutions, and, at the most, to find a basis for interpreting the many facets of human activity *within an ultimate frame of reference*" (Watson, 1960: 16; emphasis added).

7. [Since writing this essay a brief historical account of the early development of Religious Studies at the University of Toronto has appeared. "Religious Studies in the University of Toronto: A History of Its Foundation Written to Celebrate the Twentieth Anniversary of the Centre for the Study of Religion, 1976–1996," by Gordon Watson, was published by the Department for the Study of Religion (Toronto, 1997). There is nothing in this account that would require a re-evaluation of the views I present in this paper.]

8. It is true, of course, that after 1975 and the creation of the new university department, the colleges no longer had the kind of control over appointments they had once held. Thus, both Coward's and Clifford's comments about staffing need refining. To be specific, those within the new department who attempted to bring about a radical transformation of the conditions for the academic study of religion point to three significant developments: a) the old combined departments died away in order to make room for a new university department, so that one ought not to talk about an evolutionary development; b) the staff of the new department was not restricted to simply teachers of the old religious knowledge programs; and c) there was a deliberate attempt (if unsuccessful) to hire new faculty with expertise in non-Western religious traditions. Nevertheless, in large part the continuation of the ethos that characterized the earlier study of religion at Toronto still wielded much influence in the development of the new department. In response to the "significant developments" just cited, I will show below how a) the change in the new department was not revolutionary in any respect save administratively; b) even though staff for the new department was not necessarily restricted to members in the old college departments of Religious Knowledge, nevertheless the latter came to dominate in number and in influence; and c) the new faculty hired did not represent a sharp break in research interests or with the pedagogical style of their predecessors.

9. It should be noted here that it is not altogether clear, as the discussion of other institutions on the Canadian scene in this section of the article suggests, that the departments without (a history of) dominant religious or ecclesiastical connections fared better in the "Theology-Religious Studies demarcation" issue, despite the fact that they had a freer hand in hiring practices, making possible the study of a broader spectrum of religious traditions. As Keith Clifford pointed out, the scholars who founded Religious Studies departments in Canadian universities belonged to a "transitional" generation because, for the most part, they still carried a religio-theological agenda, having been trained in theological institutions, and they adapted the traditional theological disciplines of Bible, Theology, and Church history to the context of the modern university. This is obvious in the case of the University of Manitoba discussed above, and it seems to me that it is also true of Coward's former department at the University of Calgary, despite the plurality he sees as characteristic of that department—for in his view the balance Calgary achieved should be lauded not in terms of the increase in knowledge about religion it provided, but rather for the religious contribution it made to a secular university and a secular society (see Coward, 1991: 34–35).

10. Sweet stated in a rather offhand manner: "Space need not be taken here to elaborate the point, as I am sure Professor Wiebe will make a passionate statement to the Review Committee on this topic" (Sweet, 1985: 12). Although I did respond to the issue, it could not have the authority of an official response by the Director of the Centre on that occasion.

11. Although there was no formal (legal) relationship between the Centre and the Toronto School of Theology, the historical connection between the two meant that the TST exerted considerable influence on the former. Until 1986, for example, the Director of the Toronto School of Theology was an *ex officio* member of the Centre's Executive Committee; and more than one external reviewer has remarked on the number of TST members on that committee. It is useful in this regard to consider the role some at TST saw themselves having in the Centre. For example, Douglas Jay, the first Director of the Toronto School of Theology, wrote in a memo to Marion Wyse concerning her paper on the question of the relation of the TST to the Centre:

In the next section, one element that is missing in the establishment of what became the Graduate Centre for Religious Studies is significant involvement on the part of TST. So far from opposing the goals of graduate study in religion in U. of T., many of us were very much involved in the process of trying to bring it about. As Director of TST, I was secretary of the original committee of which Gordon Watson was chairman. *We saw the various theological disciplines as one way of engaging in religious studies in a university context, without in any way wishing the programme to be dominated by the Christian tradition and without minimizing the importance of other methodologies than those used in theological inquiry. I don't think that this is adequately reflected in your second paragraph on page 25, when you draw a very sharp distinction between the aim of the Centre and the aim of TST.* The aim of TST was and is much more broad ranging; it includes preparation for ministry in the various traditions, but it also includes the academic study of religion through methodologies that enable TST theologians to participate in a graduate centre of religious studies on all fours with 'secular' colleagues, as they have done from the beginning. (Jay, 1986: 2; my emphasis)

It is of interest to note that Jay presented an argument to the Governing Council of the University of Toronto insisting that the religious commitment theologians consider an essential aspect of their methodology and pedagogy would also benefit university education in general (Report 131 of Governing Council, 9 March 1978: 7).

12. It should be noted in this regard that Directors of the Centre were customarily asked to open University of Toronto convocation ceremonies with prayer. Not until 1990 did this surprising practice cease. Professor Neil McMullin, appointed Director of the Centre in that year, refused to perpetuate the custom, informing University officials that if every other academic unit were to share in the practice, the Centre would also participate. (His point, of course, was to try to educate the University's academic administrators about the nature of the Centre's program as an academic and scientific enterprise rather than a religious one.) In a memorandum of October 21, 1990, having expressed his surprise at the practice, McMullin wrote:

Whereas the role of the university Chaplains is to conduct public, formal religious rituals, the purpose of the Centre for Religious Studies is to study the phenomenon of religion and the various religious traditions. Just as it would be an error to assume that a member of the clergy is professionally trained to examine, analyze and critique his/her own religious tradition or some other religious tradition according to the methodological canons of the humanistic and social sciences, so it is incorrect to assume that the faculty and students of the Centre for Religious Studies are professionally trained to perform religious rituals. This is not to say that the members of the Centre for Religious Studies do not practice religion: many, perhaps all, of us practice some or other religion, but that is not relevant to the present consideration; most people in the Faculties of Medicine and Forestry also practice some or other religion. It is no more appropriate for the Director of the Centre for Religious Studies, or the Chair of the Department of Religious Studies, to be invited to conduct a religious service than it would be for the Dean of the Faculty of Engineering to receive such an invitation. . . . I trust that the Offices of the President and the Chancellor will understand that the Centre for Religious Studies stands with the other Centres and Departments as an academic enterprise, not with the Chaplain's Office or any other church organization, and that they will support the role and scholarly activities of the Centre for Religious Studies, as I have briefly described them, in the University.

That Professor McMullin was not asked to continue as Chair/Director of the new combined Department-Centre for the Study of Religion may not be wholly unconnected with this and other similar decisions by the Director. McMullin, that is, made it very clear that he intended to change the course of development of the Centre so as to distinguish its mandate from that of the TST and from the historically linked theological mandate of the undergraduate department. (And as can be seen in his decision to make the director of the Centre for the Study of Religion the SGS representative on the Advanced Degree Council of the Toronto School of Theology, the Dean of the School of Graduate Studies continues to disregard the distinction between theology and the academic study of religion. It is, of course, no more appropriate for someone in Religious Studies to fill that role than it would be for someone in physics, mathematics, or any other department.)

13. The Director of the Centre referred to here is Professor Willard Oxtoby, who, despite concern about cross-appointments from the TST, informed Governing Council of the University of Toronto (Report 131, 9 March 1978: 7) that he "felt that the Centre would regard the Toronto School of Theology as a large pool of resources from which to meet the needs of the Centre [and that in] his view, there was nothing but usefulness to be derived from the contractual arrangement."

14. I have "telescoped" developments here somewhat, because these matters are too complex to be discussed in detail in this essay. The fact of the matter is that the Dean of the School of Graduate Studies in the early eighties was concerned as well about the scholarly value of the TST degrees. Those degrees were being conjointly awarded by the University and the individual TST colleges, and the Dean (as documentation could show) wished to have greater control over them. Establishing a Joint Council to resolve the matter did not seem to present any peculiar problems, given the Centre's 1981 Review recommending seeking closer relations between the Centre and the TST. Consequently, no probing questions were raised about the possible effects of such a development on the long-term viability of the Centre.

15. It is difficult to see why the discussion of the Joint Council needed to be kept confidential if those involved had no anxiety with respect to what impact their deliberations might have upon members of the Centre. (On this matter see note 16 below and the report of Vice-Provost Brian Merrilees of 8 Jan. 1987: "Statement of the Joint Council U of T/TST.")

16. Requests I made at that time for information regarding the U of T-TST discussions of a GDT were simply dismissed; their deliberations were "confidential." The discussions were apparently meant to be secret, and it is not altogether clear why no information about them was shared with the Executive Committee of the Centre. Given the potential impact of changed relations of the Centre with the TST, one would have expected the Director of

the Centre (John Simpson) to have sought the advice of his Executive Committee on this matter. The university's concerns in this regard, to be sure, were broader than simply those of the relation of Theology to Religious Studies; as intimated, they involved the credibility of the degrees being conjointly granted by the U of T and the TST. What is of particular importance, however, is that it seems the university—including Centre officials—were on the point of jeopardizing the University's program in Religious Studies in order to achieve its goals with respect to the TST's programs. It is difficult not to conclude, therefore, that the secretive nature of these discussions was intended to prevent the undermining of a proposal very much desired by both institutions.

(It should be noted here that the delay by the Joint Council in presenting a proposal for a GDT was caused by somewhat tangential difficulties regarding the assurance of tenure for TST faculty at St. Augustine's College [MJC, 1985: 1]).

17. It should be noted here that, in the brief history of the Centre (1976–1992), it has had no fewer than seven Directors. Numerous changes of Directors and Associate Directors were made without considering the effect such changes may have had on students and on the program. Early assurances by Dean Safarian that the quality of the program would find at least a partial safeguard in the Office of the Director were subsequently negated by the "revolving-door" practice of the Centre's administration.

18. Thus, despite what would have appeared a solid position against the merger in September, Gooch kept up talks with the Joint Council about conditions under which the proposal could go forward. On can deduce this from his comments the following December to the Joint Council: "Professor Gooch said members of CRS have agreed that if TST is to become a graduate department, theology would have to be taught in an atmosphere of academic freedom. . . . No one at CRS has said it would be better off, although it is generally acknowledged that the 9 cross-appointed people from TST provide some supervision of CRS students. If a Graduate Department of Theology were to be created, barriers would have to be erected so that there would not be an overemphasis on the study of Christianity" (MJC, 3 Dec. 1987: 4). These are, in fact, the sentiments expressed by Gooch in a letter to me (24 Sept. 1987) that included his "Draft Statement on CRS and a Possible Graduate Department of Theology." In my opinion, having acknowledged the dangers of the creation of a GDT—dangers similar to those pointed to earlier by the ACAP's consultants—discussions with the TST ought to have been terminated.

19. It was not easy to assess opinion within the Centre because of the nature of its composition. On the one hand, most of the people cross-appointed to the Centre come from other university departments and most, though not all, have no hidden theological "agenda" they are seeking to address by means of their membership in the Centre. On the other hand, many members of the Centre cross-appointed from the Toronto School of Theology and from the

undergraduate Department do bring their religio-theological concerns with them. Even though the former group is far larger than the latter, and one might expect its influence on the ethos of the Centre to dominate, that is simply not the case. The reason for this is not all that difficult to discern: unlike those members concerned to bring about an integration of religious and theological studies, these cross-appointees do not constitute a cohesive group with a "mission." They are dispersed in various departments throughout the university and seldom function together, whereas among those cross-appointees from the Toronto School of Theology and the undergraduate department there is a good deal of academic and social interaction. The dominant ethos of the Centre, therefore, derives from the minority group of cross-appointees. It is not the case that the larger group of cross-appointees has no view about what the Centre ought to be, nor any power with respect to Centre politics—as the incidents of the Küng appointment and the formation of a Graduate Department of Theology clearly indicate. Nevertheless, given the assumption held by many of the non-TST and non-departmental cross-appointees that the Centre is like any other academic unit in the University (that is, concerned with an academic-scientific rather than a religio-theological study of religions), there is a tendency to presume that the TST and departmental cross-appointees (by virtue of their acceptance of a university appointment in the Centre) operate with the same set of assumptions. Consequently, these "outsiders" function in the Centre untroubled by the "re-theologization" issue (that would not matter if their number were not occasionally cited as a back-up to official policy).

20. I quote this passage as it is found in M. Wyse (1986). Wyse transcribed the quotation from a tape of the symposium placed in the University of Toronto Archives under accession number B84–0043.

21. This generally liberal religious attitude surfaces in other aspects of the Centre's activities such as the attempt to establish Sikh studies through recourse to Sikh funding. Though there is not space here to discuss the details of the matter, it appeared to a number of scholars that the university's response to Sikh complaints about the way in which Sikh studies were being pursued in the Centre jeopardized the objective, neutral academic study of that tradition (Cook, 1994a). As a subsequent letter from the Vice-Provost makes clear (Cook, 1994b), the university moved—under pressure, it appears—to repudiate any suggestion that it was willing to subordinate its academic programs in the study of religion to adjudication by a religious community (a point reiterated by Provost A. Sedra in a newspaper interview [see G. Bruce Rolston, 1994]). It is not at all clear, however, that this constituted an end to this religio-political interference in the academic study of religion in the Centre. A conference on "The Academic Study of Religion [with a] Focus on the Sikh Tradition" was hastily convened for the fall of 1994 *with funding from the Provost's Office* (and one might ask whether the Department had not been pressed into a kind of public-relations exercise to play down the fiasco of the Provost's earlier intervention in the Sikh dispute. Answers to

queries in this regard were not supplied) (Wiebe, 1994a and 1994c; and Cook, 1994c).

22. I say "residual" religious character because the whole of the University of Toronto was in many respects a religious institution in its foundation and development. Despite official status as a secular institution, its curriculum, like that of the federated religious colleges, also included Religion and Theology (although in a nonsectarian fashion). See here, for example, John Moir's comments (1982) regarding the teaching—even if not explicit—of Christian theology at the University of Toronto through its Orientals program in the opening decades of the twentieth century. Of one Chair of department he writes: "McCurdy had developed in 'godless' University College a four-year course on Hebrew literature and history comparable to the religious knowledge courses offered in the federated denominational colleges" (50). And he quotes McCurdy's justification: "Religious education was the primary motive and purpose in the creation of the Semitic department. . . . The intelligent study and teaching of the *essential* Bible should be a function of every university. . . . Unless Religion and science are first harmonized, they also will never be reconciled . . ." (54). This theological attitude in the departments of Orientals and of Near Eastern Studies, however, was modified, according to Moir, "after World War II when a rapprochement of the two points of view [scientific and theological] was attempted with good will but little success" (73). The approach to the Bible by the two departments mentioned, that is, was now "of a markedly different character from that of their theological colleagues" (73). Unfortunately, the approach to the study of religions by those in the undergraduate Religious Studies Department did not—nor does it now—differ substantially from that of their theological colleagues. (It is possible that Moir's assessment of a marked difference in character in the approach to the Bible in the university and its federated colleges is a little exaggerated, but this is not a question to be tackled here.)

23. See the "By-Laws of the Department for the Study of Religion, University of Toronto, 1993."

24. In regard to the university's plans for restructuring its approach to university education, it is interesting to note that the merging of the Centre for the Study of Religion with the undergraduate department runs counter to the university administration's claim that it wished to transcend departmental and disciplinary boundaries in order to make more effective use of the expertise of its scholars (See "Planning for 2000," 1994). Sadly, the administration has expressed no intention to review the merger in light of these goals (Wiebe 1994c; Prichard 1994).

25. This of course is not something I can substantiate with hard facts and figures. My judgment, however, is based on views expressed to me by students and colleagues over the past two years. [Such opinions have continued to trickle in, despite my having further distanced myself from the Centre.]

26. Peter Richardson, a member of the undergraduate department and the Centre for the Study of Religion, has written a critical rejoinder to this essay under the title "Correct, But Only Barely: Donald Wiebe on Religion at Toronto" (1997). He maintains that there was not only more determination to change the ethos of the department than I am ready to admit, but that such change was successfully implemented to the benefit of both the undergraduate department and the graduate Centre. Richardson does not, unfortunately, respond directly to my argument about the development of the department and the Centre, nor does he provide reasonable ground for ignoring the documentary evidence I have adduced in support of that argument. Furthermore, the evidence he provides in support of his view of the development of the study of religion at the University of Toronto is profoundly problematic. Placing doctoral dissertations in one of five categories—Religions of Classical Antiquity; Philosophy, Ethics, Religion and Art; Non-Western (and Comparative) Religious Traditions; Social-Scientific Studies of Religion; and History of Christianity—he claims, without argument, that it is in the last category that theological interests are most likely to occur. It appears, moreover, that Richardson is working with a very limited notion of "theology"; he clearly thinks of it as a Christian phenomenon, failing to recognize equivalent enterprises in non-Christian traditions. He is also wholly unaware of the distinction between "capital-c" and "small-c" confessionalism that assists one in seeing that a theological intention need not be tied to one or another historical religious tradition. Adjusting for that lack of nuance suggests the need for more than the anecdotal evidence he provides. Similar problems affect other elements of Richardson's argument: that students' places of employment show that the Centre's ethos is anything but theological; that the number of courses offered by teaching staff who are neither in the department nor in the TST constitutes three-quarters of all course offerings; and that the combined Religious Studies and TST staff constitutes only 30 percent of staff resources in the Centre. The employment issue is hardly determinative, given that a theological agenda can be carried out in a range of contexts other than overtly religious ones. Further, significant figures for purposes of determining the ethos of the Centre are not the absolute number of courses offered by staff outside of the department and the TST, but rather by enrollment figures in the courses concerned. (It is interesting to note that the paucity of teaching staff from the social sciences receives no comment from Richardson as to its significance for the nature of the study of religion in the Centre.)Richardson also argues that teaching staff employed since 1975 reflects a radical reshaping of the department since its "Religious Knowledge" days. A closer look at the stances taken by the majority of these appointees on such matters as "advocacy teaching" will, I think, suggest a very different conclusion.

I agree with Richardson that he and I "want exactly the same things and have conspired together over the years to the same end,"—namely, that the academic study of religion be comparative and nonconfessional. In my opinion, his desire that it be so has very much colored his assessment of that enterprise at the University of Toronto. He has not in any way refuted the argument of my paper, nor has he undermined the evidence provided in its support. Neither has he provided convincing argument or evidence for his claim that Religious Studies at the University of Toronto has transcended the confusion of Religious Studies with Theology.

Chapter Fourteen

---~ঙ৹ঌ৲~---

Against Science in the Academic Study of Religion: On the Emergence and Development of the AAR

It is a great pleasure for me to have this opportunity to pay tribute to Edmund Perry. My concerns regarding what I like to refer to as the welfare of the academic-scientific study of religions have very much overlapped his, and he has graciously provided encouragement and support over the years when it was most needed. Edmund was much more aware how dangerous it is to focus too much attention on such topics, especially in the North American scene, than were the younger scholars he took under his wing. Knowing full well his involvement in theological reflection and construction—not only in relation to his own Methodist tradition but also for the religious community in general—I have very much admired his commitment to the spirit of scientific inquiry in the study of religions.

In his address to the 15th International Congress of the International Association for the History of Religions (IAHR), Professor Perry directs his attention to how we might recover the scientific study of religion, the foundations of which, he quite correctly maintains, had already been laid by such nineteenth-century students of religion as Friedrich Max Müller and P. D. Chantepie de la Saussaye (Perry, 1986). He insists in that essay "a person might have predicted reasonably that the idea of the scientific study of religion, once announced and advocated, would be able to make its way on its own" (8)—a judgment with which I fully agree. He is quite aware, however, that no such claim can yet be made: "Regrettably," he writes, "that did not occur and even more regrettably it still has not yet occurred" (8). Not wanting simplistically to attribute this state of affairs in the field of Religious Studies to a single cause, Professor Perry offers the general assessment: " . . . all who are familiar with the history of our discipline, its research literature and its present constitution, must concede that its delayed development and unsteady course results from the perennial obstructions of theology and other normative religious outlooks" (9).

Although I agree with this assessment of the current situation in the field of Religious Studies—and especially as it applies to North America—my guess is that most will find this claim unwarranted, if not extravagant. I hope in this brief essay to justify, by means of a case study, his complaint regarding the suppression by theology of the scientific study of religion. A review of the emergence, development, and current status of the American Academy of Religion (AAR) should provide a clear indication of the dominance among its members of religio-theological concerns over those of an academic-scientific nature in the study of religions.[1] Since the AAR is by far the largest professional association for those involved in the field of Religious Studies in the United States, this analysis may be taken as indicative of the present state of the art (although it must be noted that there are other societies and associations in the United States that approach this field of research in quite different ways[2]).

Some clarification of the notion of "theological interference" in the study of religion will be useful before proceeding with this brief study of the AAR. "Theological" in this context is used not in some narrow, technical sense, but rather in a more general, "symbolic" fashion. It refers not only to the direct influence that ecclesiastical institutions have had (and in some instances still have) on the way the study of religion is executed, but also to the role that religious belief is permitted to play in the structuring of the set of enterprises that constitute the field of Religious Studies. Where a particular set of religious beliefs is taken as a framework within which the student of religion operates (or is expected to operate), one might speak of "confessionalism" in the study of religion. "Confessionalism" may be either narrow or broad, though among students of religion today one usually finds the broad variety. By this I mean simply that few students in the field approach the study of religious phenomena from their own specific denominational perspectives, although many do approach that study from the wider perspective of the Christian, Buddhist, Muslim, Hindu, and so on. In the North American context, we are of course familiar with the fact that many Christians undertake the study of religion with reference to their own beliefs and commitments as Christians. And, as Edmund Perry points out in the article to which I have referred, "we have learned that other normative systems of religion can equally viciate [sic] *Religionswissenschaft.*" He continues: "Two months ago when I spoke in person with Walpola Rahula about this matter, he commented that contemporary Buddhist scholars who study *other* religions tend to *Buddhize* their investigations and conclusions" (8). Whether narrow or broad, such "confessionalism" in the study of religions could be referred to as "capital-c" confessionalism to distinguish it from a more general set of religious commitments not tied to a particular historical religious tradition. The latter kind of confessionalism, by contrast, could be designated "small-c" confessionalism and would refer to the study of religion undertaken within a framework constructed from general religious convictions about the "reality, truth, and value of religion," to which the activity of the devotees in particular historical traditions provides equal testimony.

Edmund Perry, himself involved in developing a general, normative religious outlook as a theologian, adopts this distinction (raised in my essay on "The Failure of Nerve in the Academic Study of Religion"[1984 and chapter 8 in this volume]) because of its potential in clarifying discussion of this kind. Having acknowledged the problem of the "Christianization" and "Buddhization" of the study of religion, he writes: "Likewise the search for a normative religious outlook sourced from the religions generally . . . tends to confuse theology with the object of the study of religion" (8). Often such a "theological" attitude—that is, the assumption of the truth and value of religion—in some sense or other is only vaguely affirmed and not at all explicitly articulated and might well, therefore, be referred to as a crypto-theology, for such an implicit set of affirmations—referred to earlier as "theological interferences"—bears heavily upon the kinds of analyses of religion permitted.[3]

In arguing here that the AAR provides a clear indication of the dominance of religio-theological concerns in the scholarly study of religion, it should be clearly understood that I am not suggesting it would countenance explicit ecclesiastical interference in the enterprise it attempts to oversee. What I wish to point out, however, is that much (if not most) of the work done under its auspices is influenced in one way or another by confessionalism of both the capital-c and small-c variety. This, of course, is not to say that nothing of scholarly or scientific value is contributed by those scholars who work within such a framework; for scholars, even when subservient to a mythic framework, can in varying degrees operate according to scientific standards. The concern here, rather, is that even if called "scientific," that scholarly work is still hampered by religious convictions that prohibit the development of a fully scientific study of religious phenomena, for its antireductionism makes virtually impossible a fully theoretical approach to understanding religions.

Having expanded somewhat on Perry's perception of theology, (and its relation to Religious Studies as it supports my own methodological convictions), I shall proceed to the analysis of the emergence and development of the AAR.

The AAR, as most scholars in the field are aware, did not spring into existence *ex nihilo* but rather emerged from the remnants of an earlier society of scholars in the field of religion called the National Association of Biblical Instructors (NABI) following a self-study by that association in 1963 (R.V. Smith. et al., 1964: 200–201). A similar self-study was undertaken by the AAR in 1993 (De Concini et al., 1993a and b)[4] and it is the period between the two studies that will define the brief review provided here of the emergence and development of the AAR. In order to present a reasonably clear picture of a continued religio-theological agenda from the old NABI to the new AAR, I will rely essentially on the documents produced by the Self-Study Committees as well as the various assessments and evaluations of them found in the official publications of the respective organizations.

It is important to begin this study with the recognition that even the National Association of Biblical Instructors did not tolerate direct ecclesiastical interference in the academic study of religion, although that is not to say that there was no ecclesiastical involvement at all. Indeed, it is clear that a variety of "confessionalisms" pervaded the study of religion as carried on by the NABI membership. One of the published aims of NABI, for example, states that its intention is "[t]o increase the spirit of fellowship among themselves and to [assist in the] . . . practical development of the religious life of their students" (R.V. Smith et al., 1964: 200). The 1957 presidential address by then president A. Roy Eckardt, "The Strangeness of Religion in the University Curriculum" (1957), also paints a clear picture of the essentially confessionalist character of the study of religion fostered by NABI; in brief, neither Eckardt nor the Association takes the study of religion to be on the same level as other enterprises in the university curriculum. Some elaboration of Eckardt's position in this essay will help significantly, I think, in understanding the character of NABI, as well as that of its successor organization, the American Academy of Religion.

Eckardt acknowledges in this address that the classroom is not—and should not be—a Church, but he nevertheless posits a clear role for religion in that same context. Making explicit that role reveals its problematic character. For although the study of religion, as with other objects of investigation in the university, ought to require an objective approach to the data, Eckardt requires instead that it "be supplemented by participating knowledge or insight" (1957: 6). Eckardt is not unaware that the goals of secular education imply the possibility of an adequate scientific knowledge of religion as a phenomenon of human culture (8), but he thinks such an approach to religions fails to see its full significance in human affairs and is therefore inadequate. Having characterized religion under four headings (4)—implicit (or inevitable), explicit (or behavioral), finite, and ultimate— he maintains that such a secular (and therefore external) approach only addresses religion as explicit and finite, failing to arrive at an understanding of "the decisive issue of ultimate versus finite religion" (8). According to

Eckardt, only when the questions of faith that deal with the ultimate concerns of humankind are considered can one say that an attempt has been made to understand religion in its totality. On such grounds Eckardt claims that "the professor concerned to advance learning in religion can scarcely rest content with external, descriptive analysis" (6), and he insists that the study of religion in the university curriculum is an enterprise *sui generis* (11).

In studying religion in its "totality," one must of necessity direct attention to "ultimate concerns," and in the process be open to "the Truth that, in judging us all, redeems us" (10). And in so doing, one is not just a student of religion but perforce a religious person with religious concerns. Consequently, Eckardt concludes: "We do not get very far when we assume that problems in the teaching of religion no more than reproduce problems in teaching other subjects. The uniqueness of the problem of religion overshadows similarities" (11). Although it should be noted that Eckardt insists this "uniqueness" does not condone reducing religion to a mere spirituality unassailable by scholarly analysis, his primary intention is to show that religion is not reducible to a mere secular reality to be studied in the same scientific fashion as any other. For Eckardt this means that the study of religion must be undertaken in a religious fashion; he therefore assumes that instruction in this field will have an important connection to religious instruction found in ecclesiastical institutions such as seminaries and divinity schools.

That this is the position of the NABI as a whole is explicitly acknowledged in the official policy of the recommendations of the NABI Committee on Pre-Theological Studies in the report "Pre-Seminary Preparation and Study in Religion" (Eckardt et al., 1959). The report notes the Association's acceptance of a "theological understanding" of all learning, although it qualifies the notion by saying that what they envisage avoids "a profanization of education at one extreme and evangelization of education at the other extreme" (139). NABI, it claims, wants to subvert both the notion of a knowledge of religions detached from faith, as well as a religious zeal devoid of knowledge. Consequently, it sees the professor's task as not only to provide scientific knowledge about religions, but also to bring the student face to face with the issues of truth, value, and the meaning of human existence (139). The study of religion, therefore, is involved (as the report puts it) in pursuing "the vital question of the relation between the sacred and the secular in human affairs [and thus] . . . addresses itself to the issues of human commitment versus, on the one hand, disinterestedness and, on the other hand, aimlessness" (141). It is in consequence of this that the authors of the report suggest "that a department of religion may serve as a focus and guidance center of the education of the pre-theological student" (139). The study of religion in the university curriculum, according to the

NABI, therefore, is not only religious, but religious in a fashion that permits a close relation between the university department and other institutions of Christian learning.

By the early 1960s it appears that this understanding of the academic study of religion was being subjected to scrutiny and that (in part at least) this was due to the diversity of religious views of the Association members. There was no withdrawal from the commitment to a "small-c" confessional approach to the teaching of religion (which permitted individual members of the Association to work within their own "capital-c" confessional frameworks), but it was obvious from the theological pluralism of NABI that the Association needed to provide a forum "for all responsible advocates of diverse positions, so as to enable those who have responsibilities in the teaching of religion in its various manifestations to be increasingly sensitive to other positions" (Buck, 1962: 2). Thus a NABI self-study was suggested in late 1961, in an effort to clarify the Association's responsibilities, as Harry M. Buck pointed out in an editorial preface to the January 1962 issue of the *Journal of Bible and Religion (JBR)* (the official publication of the NABI). The self-study committee, it was suggested, ought "both to determine the kind of public image we want to project and to increase the effectiveness of the Association" (2).[5]

Roy Eckardt leaves little doubt about the problem of the NABI's public image in his brief essay entitled "In Defense of Religion-in-General" (an editorial preface to the July 1962 issue of the *JBR*). He is concerned about those in the Association with a personal commitment to one or another "expression of religion-in-particular," as he calls it, and who oppose the increasing number of "generalist" students of religion who may not have a similar religious commitment. Although Eckardt's sympathies seem to lie with the "particularists," he ultimately maintains that when the "frame of reference shifts to the survival and growth of this Association, and to its means of self-identification, much is to be said for religion-in-general" (185). He is convinced that unless the NABI can represent not only the religious particularists, or "capital-c" confessionalists, but also the "small-c" confessionalists, the NABI "will gradually fail in its essential function and may ultimately cease to exist" (185). He is persuaded that the NABI should reflect a more general trend and be known as "The American Religion Association," and that their *Journal of Bible and Religion* should accordingly be called *The American Journal of Religion* (186).

Eckardt's editorial preface in the April 1963 volume of the *JBR* provides an indication of the disagreement on the preferred public image for the NABI, for he rejects his earlier suggestion regarding the change of name. The preface is entitled "'Theology' versus 'Religion,'" and it points to the danger of the change in name; the new name could reflect a secularizing tendency in the discussion of what the university study of religion ought to be, thus jeopardizing the traditional principles of the NABI. For Eckardt, the notion of theology embodies the *total* effort in which the professor of religion ought to be involved, whereas the notion of religion simply does not imply the same commitment (96). As he puts it, "theology" better than "religion" offers a linguistic safeguard "against the confinement of the teacher's work to either spirituality or secularity" (97). He acknowledges here, as in his earlier presidential address cited above, that the university study of religion is an academic exercise—and so resembles other disciplines—but he makes the more forceful claim that the study of religion is, and must be, much more than this; although a constituent in the domain of the academy, "it can never be entirely of that domain," and "to this extent the scholar in 'religion,'" he insists, "will find himself set apart from the gentiles in the academy" (96). For the NABI to move in any other direction, therefore, would be foolish, for, according to Eckardt, the majority of those teaching religion in the United States "think of themselves as contributing in a positive way to the nourishment of that faith . . . through disciplined thought" (95).

Despite such objections, however, the NABI opted for the term "religion" rather than "theology." And the further case for what appears a rather radical restructuring of the NABI (not incommensurate with the "secularizing tendency" so feared by Eckardt) was presented by Clyde Holbrook in his 1963 presidential address to the Association. He argued for much more than merely a change in name, citing that the discipline needed to move away from "the partialities which at present afflict the field of religion" (1964: 99). It was his view that "[a]n academy of religion should stand as a society which gives high prominence in the *academic world generally* to the serious importance attached to religion *as a scholarly enterprise*" (103; emphasis added). Significantly, the description he provided of the scholarly study of religion contrasts markedly with the notion that had hitherto prevailed within the Association. The new conception, Holbrook argued, meant that the field of research a) should not be infringed upon by religious bodies (99); b) should not be judged on the basis of its immediate relevance to religious life and culture (99); c) should not be seen as the "morale officer" of the university (101); d) should be able to represent the total field and its sub-disciplines (104); and, finally, e) should be primarily concerned with scholarship and research (104).

Although the Association voted in favor of the name-change to the American Academy of Religion, it is questionable whether the members of the NABI ever fully endorsed the kind of change envisaged by Holbrook. It is not surprising, therefore, to see that the AAR continued its association with other religious and ecclesiastical bodies. In the "Report of the Secretary" of the NABI for 1963 (Priest, 1964), for example, one sees in the by-laws of the "new" AAR (Martin et al., 1964) evoked there a reference to consultations between the American Association of Theological Schools (AATS) and the AAR, indicating a continuation of the earlier relationship between the NABI and the AATS, and the commitment of the AAR "to keep open channels of communication and further co-operation" between the two Associations, especially with respect to the theological education of students preparing for the ministry (Priest, 1964: 198–199). Finally, the "new" AAR not only continued the NABI's involvement with theological education, but it even assigned to the executive director of the AATS a "representative on theological education of the AAR" (199) who, together with its two directors, would make the final decisions concerning that education. Certainly the "Report of the NABI Self-Study Committee" (R. V. Smith et al., 1964) did not advocate that kind of view of religious studies. It is true that it had opted for the term "religion," because of the possible applications of the notion to the varying concerns of the members of the NABI, but it rejected the implications of the term with respect to the non-confessionalist character of the activities in which the new association would be engaged. There is an acknowledgment that the expanded membership of the NABI had brought with it a widened interest in "*all aspects* of religion in its global multiforms" (200), and yet, the authors in summarizing the Report maintain that the new forum of the American Academy of Religion "could cope with the trilemma of commitment of faith, independence of scholarship, and public professional obligations" (201). The authors of the Report and the NABI itself, therefore, show greater affinity with Eckardt's ideas about the "proper" nature of the academic study of religion than with the ideas expressed by Holbrook in his presidential address—although it should be noted here that Holbrook himself, discussing the need for an Academy to be able to represent the *entire* field with its sub-disciplines, rather ambiguously included theology as one of them.

Eckardt's response to the establishment of the AAR in his editorial preface "An Identity Explored" also provides solid ground for doubting whether anything other than a change of name had occurred in the process. In assessing the development, he focuses essentially upon the question of professional specialization and upon the relationship of scholarship to commitment. He is aware that the move to specialization is important to the academic credibility and legitimacy of the enterprise, but he worries the move could ignore students' moral and intellectual needs (4). And it is the AAR's responsibility to attend to these needs, he insists, arguing that the AAR must "be the servant of persons and institutions that seek to maintain and advance simultaneously independence of scholarship, commitments of faith, and obligations to a profession" (4). He describes the Academy as "representative of men and women who, in a pluralist time and place, both examine religion and live by one or another of its concretions" (4). Though each individual, in Eckardt's mind, must work out the relationship between responsible scholarship and responsible faith, he sees the AAR and its *Journal* as "useful allies in the furtherance of this relationship" (4). Indeed, in another editorial preface later that same year he suggests the ethos created by the AAR indicates that higher education in the United States has been academically legitimated for its religious as well as its scholarly endeavors; for through the AAR higher education has "been granted the task of nurturing an independent intellectual tradition in religion" (1965b: 291).

Eckardt's interpretation of the name-change of the NABI to the AAR is not really at odds with Holbrook's conception of the AAR (as expressed in the latter's presidential address), as is confirmed in the debate between John F. Wilson and Holbrook over Holbrook's explication (in his *Religion: A Humanistic Field*) of the notion of the study of religion as an academic field (Wilson, 1964a). For Wilson, Holbrook starts by providing a sound basis to the academic study of religion as an empirical undertaking, but he then proceeds to undermine the enterprise by requiring that it satisfy students' moral needs (256). Such a requirement, Wilson rightly objects, makes scholarly circles wary that the study of religion will be indistinguishable from religion itself (257). In his response, Holbrook claims that Wilson's suggestions for placing religion in the faculties of liberal arts and sciences echoes his own conclusions, but he nonetheless accuses Wilson of introducing a mischievous distinction "when he attempts to limit the role of the university professor of religion, as well as the university itself, from speaking to the question of the truth value of religion or theology." This distinction, he continues,

> is neither representative of what actually goes on, nor should it be. . . . The religious professor, undergraduate or graduate, cannot so easily be called upon to give over his intellectual right to follow the question of truth in whatever his study of religious phenomena directs. In fact, with the growing strength of graduate departments of religion distinct from theological schools, the role assigned to the theological faculty by Mr. Wilson may well be taken over increasingly by faculties whose major concerns are not consonant with those found in the traditional domain described by him. (Holbrook, 1964: 265)

As author of *Religion: A Humanistic Field*, therefore, Holbrook resembles Eckardt, even though as author of "Why an Academy of Religion?" published in the same year, he does not. It is therefore Wilson who presents a consistent brief for a genuinely transformed academic study of religion (and by implication, therefore, a genuinely transformed NABI) in which the study of religion would concern itself with the analysis of religious phenomena rather than with the provision of "a supermarket of value options for the students" (Wilson, 1964b: 266).

Perhaps it is the tenor of this debate that leads Eckardt (in yet another editorial preface) to judge that "the history of the NABI-AAR can be read, in part, as a confrontation between those who construe the study of religion in primarily religious terms and those who identify it in prevailingly secular terms" (1966a: 96). The intent of his remark, however, is not to introduce an analysis of that debate, but rather to affirm the claim regarding the essential continuity between the NABI and the AAR. For while acknowledging the conflict, Eckardt asserts that the element of confrontation itself points to the "peculiar" nature of the study of religion (96)—the recognition that in religion we deal with a transcendent element and a cultural element, and the relation between the two (97). To identify the study of religion as dealing just with its cultural elements would be reductionistic (97); the assumption of the reality of religion's transcendent element, however, is not considered similarly problematic. The fact that these comments introduce the "Theological Education" issue of the *JBR* containing analyses of the Lilly Study of Pre-Seminary Education provides clear evidence of the AAR's deep involvement in confessional matters. When Eckardt insists that the academic study of religion "cannot disavow all kinship with the ministry . . ." (97) he is merely echoing the NABI document on "Pre-Seminary Preparation and Study in Religion" (Eckardt et al., 1959), which still stood as the stated policy of the AAR.[6]

It is not possible to analyze here all of the responses to the Lilly Endowment Study. It may be of benefit, however, to note Clyde Holbrook's reaction to the report, given his role with the NABI in the birth of the AAR. Even though the ambiguity of his stated position on the nature of the academic study of religion, as indicated above, is evident in his response, it nonetheless appears that a serious rift had developed between the AAR and the AATS. The report, Holbrook insists, creates problems for a number of members of the AAR, for it seems to assume that the academic (university) study of religion should be subordinated to the nurturing of prospective ministerial students (Holbrook, 1966: 158). According to Holbrook, that is, the authors of the report simply have not made allowance "for the scholarly study of religion at both the undergraduate and graduate levels without reference to ecclesiastical interests" (158). He points out that the task of the department should be to provide students with both a knowledge of and an "appreciation" for the various religious traditions of the world (159). Knowing that many members of the AAR are concerned with the educational needs of the church, he nevertheless insists that this does not warrant the AAR's becoming "an agent for the preparation of clergymen" (159). Yet, Holbrook's further comments once again echo Eckardt's concerns, for he admits that the AAR's sponsorship and financial support of the Lilly study shows its concern "for this particular aspect of the *total* problem of education in religion . . . ,"—he makes this statement despite his avowed "primary" concern to warn members of the AAR not to consider their work *solely* in the light of the Report (159).

In spite of apparently conciliatory tones, however, a rift between the AAR and the AATS did seem to emerge. It may be that these tensions account for the change of tone in Eckardt's last editorial preface in the *JBR* (which was about to be replaced by the *Journal of the American Academy of Religion* [*JAAR*]). Unlike Eckardt's earlier reference to the NABI-AAR confrontation, this preface indicates a genuine fear that perhaps something more than just a name-change occurred in the transformation; and the title of the preface— "Is There Anything Religious in Religion?"—would lend credence to such a theory. For Eckardt, the loss of the symbol "Bible" in the title of the *Journal* appears to preclude all testimony of religiousness and sacredness from the new journal; the rapid growth in this field could be but a "reflection of the prevailing secularity of the educational world" (1966b: 303). Although he knows that it is not the intention of the Academy "to promote an exclusively intellectualistic approach" to that study, "the fact is," he writes, "that religion study may conceivably come to a state where it is not dominantly or even evidently religious" (303).

If one examines the presidential address delivered to the Academy by C. Welch in 1970, it appears that Eckardt's fears about the AAR had been fulfilled (Welch, 1971). For the address—essentially a preliminary report of a study of doctoral programs in the field of religion in the United States and Canada sponsored by the American Council of Learned Societies (ACLS)— would suggest (on the surface at least) that the secularization of the study of religion had been all but accomplished. Welch asks whether the field of religious studies is suffering from an identity crisis. Like Eckardt, Welch had been aware that the growth of the field had occasioned considerable angst over what students of religion ought to be doing. And although the title of the address ("Identity Crisis in the Study of Religion?") raises the question of whether the transformation of the NABI into the AAR created a crisis of identity, Welch insists (at least in the early part of the address) that such a crisis did exist but has now passed. "The legitimacy of the organized study of religions in college and university," he writes, "has now been established, and this is so widely recognized that it need no longer be a subject for anxiety" (6). But unlike Eckardt, Welch's assurances apply not to achieving a definitive recognition of the simultaneously academic and religious character of the enterprise, but rather to the clear demarcation recognized between religion (with its apologetic interests) and the scholarly or academic study of religions. Welch writes: "The battle for recognition of religion as an appropriate and desirable area of organized study in college and university . . . has been largely won [and] in this sense, the period of emergence of a discipline of 'religious studies' (*as distinct from theology*) is coming to an end" (6; emphasis added). The trends in the field pointing in this direction include: the move away from denominational orientation by the academic study of religion; a rejection of the "confessional principle" and "insider theorizing"; the clear line of demarcation between professional education of religious leaders and the academic study of religion; and, finally, an overcoming of "the temptation to look upon the study of religion as a special and valuable means to the redemption of the university . . . (8).

Despite Welch's claim that a bona fide, nonreligious study of religion had found academic legitimation, Eckardt need not, I think, have been too concerned, for the emergence of the AAR has not really involved much more than a change in name; in spite of the hopes of many, the transformation brought about when the NABI became the AAR has been slight, and there is very little likelihood that anything more momentous will occur in the near future. Indeed, Welch himself may have sensed the lack of development in his own day, as can be inferred from his paradoxical acknowledgment that the study of religion in the North American context still suffered from a crisis of identity even though legitimated by and established in the universities. According to Welch, that is, along with those successes there existed "equally plain signs of a real struggle in which the issue [of identity] is not yet resolved" (9). A complex range of problems in the study of religion, including over-specialization, parochialism, arbitrary geographic organization of the field, methodological naïveté, and other similar shortcomings, he maintains, put Religious Studies at constant risk of "falling back into the arms of confessional interests" (12). And the fact that many (if not most) departments were built on the resources of a theologically trained professoriate was equally pernicious, for, as could be expected, "the presence of massive resources in faculty and library in the traditional areas generate momentum requiring the dominance of those areas. . . ." As Welch spells it out: "if you have six historians of Christianity it is hard to resist the pressure to admit a lot of graduate students in that area" (14).

Some twenty years after this report from Welch and the ACLS, the ambiguity with respect to the question of identity is still unresolved. This is especially revealing, I think, in the recent report of the AAR's Committee on Education and the Study of Religion billing itself as an "update" on Welch (Hart, 1991: 719). This report was written by Ray L. Hart on behalf of the Committee and is significantly entitled "Religious and Theological Studies in American Education." I say "significantly" because Hart maintains that this is the first time that the methodology of Religious Studies and Theological Studies has been critically addressed. This claim, given the account of the emergence and early development of the AAR I have been at pains to describe here, is not altogether justified, for in fact Welch himself broached the matter two decades previously. If Hart's report, therefore, is nothing more than the Welch report with an addendum on Theological Studies, as Hart insists, it would appear that the AAR has not moved very far—if at all—beyond the concerns centrally important to the NABI.

It is clear that the members of the AAR now, as of the NABI then, are still divided along "study-of-religion/practice-of-religion" lines; as Hart puts it, the division—still evident—is between those concerned with knowledge about religion and those concerned with the truth of religion (734, 778). What is of particular interest in Hart's report is that the division seems to be "glossed over"; that is, it is seen to be not so much a serious problem as an element of the study of religion the Academy endorses. Hart does admit that the question of the relationship of Religious Studies to Theological Studies reveals "[a] very deep tension in the field" (790), but he denies any need for its resolution; he excuses the "failure" to resolve it on the grounds that "we are not confident that the problem has even been named in the nomenclature of description" (790). It is quite remarkable of him to make such a claim, having lived with the problem and having witnessed repeated enunciations of it, along with possible theological resolutions, in numerous presidential addresses to the Academy.[7] And while refusing to acknowledge the problem he nonetheless advocates that we make haste to dispel it, inviting leading theoreticians in the field to develop views pertinent to a resolution of the "deep tension."

There is little indication in the years since Hart's 1991 report that his recommendation has been taken seriously or has even been forwarded vigorously by Hart himself.[8] This is not, of course, entirely surprising given the practical, political costs of such a move. For Hart warns that some constituencies in the Academy would be offended by the opting of one solution over another; and he makes it very clear that a theoretical resolution would therefore amount to "dishonoring the virtues the field is claimed to inculcate: tolerance, pluralism, respect for opposing positions, etc" (790). It is, therefore, disingenuous of him to maintain that the problem in the definition of the field has "not yet been sufficiently named to permit whatever is at stake to come to the fore" (731); for he has as much as declared what is at stake: a crippling of the AAR via loss either of a large contingent of members in the Academy or of the kind of academic legitimation the Academy so strongly desires. To obfuscate is to maintain the status quo; to define properly is to risk radical alteration in the structures of control presently dominating the field. That no such risk is to be taken is clear from the further recommendation of the report that the Academy "investigate the desirability of a world organization" (790). It appears that the tensions and divisions will be less problematic if the Academy participates in "accelerating the formation of a global field-spanning organization" (791); and as it is willing to do so in conjunction with the Association of Theological Schools (ATS) in North America, it is clear on which side of the divide—between those seeking knowledge about religion and those seeking an understanding of the truth of religion—the Academy has chosen to stand, despite refusing to acknowledge that it has done so.[9]

There are hints in the Hart report that might suggest some advance in the discussion of the nature of the field since the days of the NABI, but they do not amount to much. Although Hart notes the discomfort of many "with the nomenclature that discriminates 'religious' and 'theological' studies," he admits that Religious Studies is now generally used to refer "to the scholarly neutral and non-advocative study of multiple religious traditions" (716). He also acknowledges that younger scholars recently out of graduate school find theology a problem in the study of religion in the university context (732). All he does with these "discoveries," however, is to claim—rather lamely— that his study was unable to get to the bottom of this opposition. And Hart's definitive (if somewhat gratuitous) statement used to round off his report— "that we have done such a poor job in 'teaching' our colleagues [and the 'public'] about what it is we actually do" (792)—would warrant no comment here, were it not for its potentially ironic application; that is, one reason the public may be unsure of what we do is that the AAR has deemed it expedient to keep them in the dark.

Candor requires that the AAR admit it is as much a religious association as it was in its NABI days. The association does not wish merely to be a scientific or academic society—the concern of most of its members transcends such mundane goals. James Wiggins, immediate past Executive Director of the Academy, demonstrates only too well the befuddled ethos of the Academy in his farewell address; for he castigates "the champions of what they call a 'scientific' approach to the study of religion (Wiggins, 1992: 112)," all the while acknowledging that the Academy ought to house all approaches to religion, even if they "seem to present little compatibility with each other" (113). The "champions," according to Wiggins, fail to understand what the academic study of religion as conceived by the Academy is really all about, because they know only one approach to understanding religion and refuse to tolerate ambiguity with its intrinsic value as an avenue for achieving "insight." Thus he writes, as a description of the enterprise the Academy endorses: "Engaging the questions in the context—struggling, grappling, wrestling with passionate existential urgency—those are for me the *desiderata* and the hallmarks of humanistic study generally, and even more particularly of the study of religion" (113). Roy Eckardt, I have no doubt, would be fully satisfied with this description; whether Holbrook, Wilson, Welch, and the others would be equally happy—they who expected from the Academy a vanguard for scientific study rather than a mere religious mouthpiece—is doubtful; the recent graduates to whom Hart refers will surely be disappointed—as will, of course, those whom Wiggins labels the "champions" of the scientific approach.[10]

Three decades after the submission of the report of the NABI Self-Study Committee, the Academy has received a report from another self-study committee—this time from the AAR. Although the number of goals or aims delineated has increased in the later mission statement, the respective goals are in all essential respects identical. The seventh goal, which requires that the Academy include in its *conversation* "the various voices in the field of religion," appears wholly directed to ensuring that the academic or scientific study of religion within the Academy never exclude the "presence" of religion itself. Where this presented a problem in the early days of the AAR in its search for academic legitimation, such an intention was necessarily muted; today, however, this need not be the case, since as Barbara De Concini (current Executive Director of the Academy) puts it in an interview regarding the mission statement, it is no longer possible to assume "a clear distinction separating scholarship from advocacy," so that "all disciplined reflection on religion" must be endorsed by the American Academy of Religion, and by implication, by the academic community in general (Frisinia, 1993a: 5).[11] Indeed, she maintains that a number of the recent presidential addresses to the Academy have clearly shown "that religionists have an important contribution to make to the entire conversation in the academy—small 'a' in this regard because of their particular insights and understandings with respect to "knowledge and power, evidence and advocacy" (5). Thus it appears that the AAR has succumbed to the temptation—a temptation Welch thought the student of religion had transcended in passing from NABI to AAR—"to look upon the study of religion as a special and valuable means to the redemption of the university" (Welch, 1971: 8).

Whereas the NABI self-study triggered a change of name of the association—although not a change in substance—the AAR self-study has effectively bolstered the original substance of the NABI program, but with no change of name (and in fact the old name might have expressed better what the Academy actually supports). In his assessment of the situation, Eckardt expresses his "second thoughts" about substituting the notion of theology for that of religion in the name of the association—inspired, it might be noted, by John Hick—and in so doing displays at least a measure of integrity (1963: 95). Another change of name that would adequately capture what Eckardt had in mind here—and what the current Academy actually seems to represent—seems to me to be in order. One could follow the suggestion made by Hick that so impressed Eckardt, and change the name to the "American Academy of Theologians" (AAT); or, if the notion of religion implies a greater degree of ecumenicity, one might consider "The National Association of Religion Instructors" (NARI). On the other hand, the Academy could consider taking seriously its obligations to the academic community, which has given the study of religion whatever intellectual legitimacy it possesses, and commit itself to the support of the scientific study of religion. This, I admit, is not likely to happen.

At the very least, the Academy could take on something of the character of an umbrella organization—which in some senses it already is—in which members from both sides of the acknowledged divide within its ranks would find representation. It could check its practice of accepting the religio-theological study of religions while castigating the "scientific types" for unseemliness. This, no doubt, is unacceptable advice, for affirmation of a scientific approach to the study of religions would be taken by most members of the AAR as casting a negative light upon their own work. Perhaps, then, the exclusion of the nonreligiously, nontheologically orientated scholar from support within the Academy is indicative of its intention—through political action—to redefine scientific-academic acceptability within the university community. Such a hypothesis in any event might explain the Academy's negative, if not hostile, behavior toward other, scientifically grounded, associations committed to the study of religious phenomena. It is a hypothesis worth further examination.

Notes

1. Ralph V. Norman, like many others, has assumed quite the opposite. In assessing the contributions to the University of California (Santa Barbara) project reappraising graduate education in Religious Studies, referred to as "The Santa Barbara Colloquy" (*Soundings* 71 [1988]: 171–420), he quite correctly claimed that the panelists spent a fair amount of time "casting out demons," including the demon of theology, which, he asserted, was "long associated with the late dogmatic slumber from which scholars awoke upon the occasion of the founding of the American Academy of Religion in 1967" (Norman, 1988: 181). I will question here whether such an "awakening" ever occurred. Norman notes that after expelling the demons, panelists proceeded to call them back "for a second opinion" (180). In similar fashion, if scholars were really awakened from their dogmatic slumber on the occasion of the founding of the AAR (in 1964 rather than 1967, the Articles of Incorporation being signed in February of that year and printed in *The Journal of Bible and Religion* 32 [1964]: 296–300), evidence will show that they very promptly fell back into the slumber from which they had ever so briefly—if at all—awakened.

2. Some of the Societies and Associations include the Religious Research Association (RRA), the Society for the Scientific Study of Religion (SSSR), the

American Society for the Study of Religion (ASSR), and the North American Association for the Study of Religion (NAASR). A fuller understanding of the true character and intent of the American Academy of Religion would be provided, were time and space available for an analysis of its relations to these and other similar organizations, as well as its relations to other bodies such as the Association of Theological Schools (ATS) and their like. At several points in the essay, however, I will take time to note significant characteristics of those various relations.

3. The notion of crypto-theology is heavily charged, and I have raised it in various contexts for a considerable while. It is most simply linked to the term already employed, "small-c" confessionalism. "Crypto-theology" actually contains or points to a more complex, if not insidious, set of assumptions— a topic so rich in analytical potential that it cannot be addressed here.

4. De Concini (et al., 1993). The "Findings" (which contain the bulk of the report of the Committee) are introduced by Warren G. Frisinia under the title "AAR Board Adopts New Mission Statement, Sets Goals for the Future, (1–2), which is supplemented by an interview with the AAR Executive Director, Barbara De Concini, entitled "Barbara De Concini on the AAR's Self-Study" (Frisinia, 1993a: 5).

5. The suggestion, as Buck notes, was made by a former editor of the *Journal*, Dwight Beck, in a letter printed in vol. 29 (1961): 361.

6. See here William A. Beardslee, "The Background of the Lilly Endowment Study of Pre-Seminary Education" (1966), "The report was not ready by the next meeting, but was presented to the 1958 Annual Meeting, where it was adopted as expressing the policy of the NABI. The document was published in the April, 1959 issue of JBR under the title, 'Pre-Seminary Preparation and Study in Religion,' and is republished in the current number. *This statement, which still stands as the stated policy of the AAR*, is worth careful reading today as a predecessor to the Lilly Study" (98–99; emphasis added). Clyde A. Holbrook makes the same point in "The Lilly Study: Challenge to College and Seminary" (1966: 157).

7. An analysis of the presidential addresses to the Academy since its inception in 1964 is very revealing. Of the thirty addresses delivered (twenty-seven published to date), eleven deal directly with the problem of the relation of Theology to Religious Studies, of which nine argue strenuously for a kind of merger or integration of the two (if not a subordination of the latter to the former). The other two addresses argue the opposite—or appear to do so: C. Welch's address, as discussed above, argues the matter ambiguously, while William A. Clebsch ("Apples, Oranges, and Manna: Comparative Religion Revisited" [1981]) clearly favors a scientific, academic approach over the religio-theological in the comparative study of religion. Three addresses— the only ones not on (Western) Christian themes—address the Theology/Religious Studies issue indirectly, all favoring some form of integration. Hart's claim that the problem has not "even been named," therefore, has no basis in fact. It should also be noted here that of the addresses not

evoked, ten are directly concerned (rather traditionally) with Christian religio-theological issues and topics, and the final three deal with issues of humanism and hermeneutics, clearly Western and Christian in their inspiration. Overall, therefore, and contrary to the claims made by the Academy regarding its pluralist stance and its openness to all disciplined reflection (referred to in the discussion of the new mission statement), it is apparent that the "conversation" of the Academy at this official level undermines its stated pluralist intentions. Indeed, that "conversation" is virtually indistinguishable from the "conversation" that preceded it in the NABI.

8. The topic has been on the programs of the AAR for a few years, but it is significant that the scholars who view themselves as approaching the study of religion from a scientific, nonreligious point of view are not invited to participate. They have been considered "exclusivistic" and thus unworthy of the "conversation." See the discussion of Wiggins, among others, below.

9. It should be noted here that the NABI had similar aspirations; the AAR's concerns for world influence, therefore, is not new. Harry M. Buck, for example, wrote: "The Association and the *Journal* have much to contribute to present conversations in theology, biblical studies, philosophy of religion, and *Religionswissenschaft*, and we ought to become not simply a national organization but a truly international forum as well" (1962: 2).

The AAR, it also needs to be pointed out, has refused to co-operate in such a world-wide venture in that it has repeatedly ignored—or rebuffed—the one truly international organization presently in existence to foster such work, namely the International Association for the History of Religions (IAHR). No explicit reasons have ever been provided by the Academy for its attitude to the IAHR, but it would not be far off the mark to relate their behavior to the attempt on the part of the IAHR to demarcate clearly between religion and theology on the one hand, and the academic, scientific study of religion on the other. This appears symptomatic as well of the AAR's relationship to the Society for the Scientific Study of Religion (SSSR), as I point out in note 10 below.

10. It is interesting in this regard to note K. O. Alexander's assessment that the debate over reductionism in the academic study of religion "figured in the withdrawal of the Society for the Scientific Study of Religion [SSSR] in the mid-seventies from the alliance forged between the SBL [Society of Biblical Literature] and the AAR" (1988: 393). Unfortunately, Alexander does not provide convincing grounds for this claim. One finds some information, however, on the emergence of the SSSR as an academic rather than a religious or quasi-religious undertaking in William M. Newman's essay "The Society for the Scientific Study of Religion: The Development of an Academic Society" (1974).

11. It needs pointing out here, however, that the AAR is apparently less interested in varying forms of "disciplined reflection" on religion than it claims to be. It is not widely known—yet nevertheless true—that the Academy rejected the request of the North American Association for the Study of Reli-

gions (NAASR) to become a so-called Related Scholarly Association, for reasons inconsistent with the stated intent of the Academy on the plurality of voices in the study of religion. (NAASR had applied for affiliation with the IAHR at the time it proposed a formal relationship with the Academy, and it thought it could be of some use to the Academy in representing those members of the AAR whose interests leaned in the direction of the International Association's approach to the study of religions.) A letter from the Executive director of the AAR to the Executive Secretary of NAASR puts the case as follows: "The reasons were, as I heard them, essentially these: 1.) Nothing about such a relationship is required for the NAASR to achieve its affiliation with the IAHR. 2.) Nothing in such a relationship is required for any AAR members so inclined independently to have a relationship with the NAASR. 3.) Since the NAASR was not seeking an Affiliated Society relationship with the AAR, the AAR would gain nothing from it. 4) All three of the AAR initials appear in the NAASR letters" (Wiggens, 14 December 1987). On these grounds "the Board [of the AAR] was overwhelmingly opposed [to such an association], in terms of numbers" (Wiggens, 14 December 1987). It is obvious, in light of the attitude expressed in this letter, that the Academy's empathy for the apologetic and theological approach to the study of religion and its consequent antipathy for the attempt to come to a scientific understanding of religions has been firmly fixed, despite its claim to openness.

Chapter Fifteen

———

A Religious Agenda Continued:
A Review of the Presidential Addresses to the AAR

Introduction

In a recent essay on "American Learning and the Problem of Religious Studies" D. G. Hart (1992)[1] has argued that with the emergence of the American Academy of Religion (AAR) in 1964 there has been a marked change in the way religion is studied and taught in the United States. For it signaled not only the demise of the traditional Protestant and humanistic dominance of the field (214), but also the establishment of the field on a more objective, scientific foundation. From that point, "[t]o be religious was no longer as important for Professors of religion as methodological sophistication and academic achievement" (213). George M. Marsden[2] echoes Hart's judgment about the transformation of religious studies after the emergence of the AAR in his recent book *The Soul of the American University* (1994), in which he laments the fact that "normative religious teaching of any sort has been nearly eliminated from standard university education" (5), having been replaced by a lifeless phenomenological study of religion whose "object of study [is] . . . the abstraction 'religion,' the common traits of which could be exemplified by looking at particular religions" (1994: 414). This development, argues Marsden, is the result of the "professionalising impulse" within the field, institutionalized along with the formation of the American Academy of Religion in 1964. The Academy, he writes, "grew principally out of the National Association of Bible [*sic*] Instructors [NABI] (which had long lived with this less professional name)" (414). "While the AAR embraced both the humanistic and the social scientific impulse," he continues, "the latter signalled the dominant direction for the future" (414). More recently, Conrad Cherry[3] makes a similar claim regarding the effect of the 1964 "transformation" of the NABI into the AAR in his book *Hurrying Toward Zion* (1995), a history of the development of university-related divinity schools in the United States. "Those occupying the field now," he claims, "would measure their task neither by the religious trends in the larger American culture nor by the programs of study in the divinity schools. They would gauge their work, instead, by how well it conformed to the canons of the disciplinary specialties in the contemporary university" (116).

The picture painted for us by these authors of a religiously neutral study of religion created by the emergence of the AAR is idealistic at best—and the ideal, moreover, has not been fulfilled. A more realistic appraisal of these developments would suggest, in fact, that even though the early rhetoric of the creators of the AAR bespeaks an academically respectable discipline, their intention was not actually to create a scientific study of religion. I have sought to show this in two essays: "Against Science in the Academic Study of Religion: On the Emergence and Development of the AAR" (chapter 14 of this volume)[4] and "Theology and the Academic Study of Religion in the United States" (chapter 5 of this volume).[5] In each essay I suggest that an analysis of the presidential addresses of the AAR would demonstrate that claims cannot be sustained as concerns the AAR's reorientation of the study of religions from religious to scientific. (I have chosen to elaborate on that state of affairs here as a contribution to this special issue of the journal dedicated to the debate on the relations between religion and method in the study of religion.[6]) The argument to be constructed is a simple one: if the change in name of the National Association of Biblical Instructors to the American Academy of Religion signals as radical a transformation in the nature of the study of religion as has been so often claimed, one would expect that change to be reflected in the work of those who led, shaped, and directed the enterprise after 1964. One would expect as well to see a significant difference in the issues and concerns raised in the presidential addresses to the Academy from those raised by the presidents of the National Association of Biblical Instructors. Although all the presidential addresses since the formation of the AAR in 1964 will be examined in this regard, I shall restrict my discussion of the addresses to the NABI during its last decade (I exclude the address by Clyde A. Holbrook in 1963 from this list, giving it special attention below, because it constitutes a transition point between the conclusion of the work of the NABI and the birth of the AAR). Little will be lost in doing so, since Carl Purinton's 1953 address on "The Task of Our Association" not only provides a concise account of the Association's perception of itself, but does so in terms of the original goals of the Association stated in an earlier historical overview of the Association's growth and development.[7]

NABI: The Presidential Addresses 1953–1962

Of the addresses delivered to the NABI in the last decade of its existence, only nine appear to have been published.[8] All of the addresses to be reviewed in this section of my essay—save that of Holbrook—are directed essentially to religious or theological issues, although five only indirectly, in that they focus specific attention on questions of pedagogy and the role of the teacher of religion in the university setting but make religio-theological assumptions in the process.

I begin this review of the NABI presidential addresses with Carl Purinton's contribution of 1953. As already indicated, it is useful to begin here, as Purinton focuses his attention upon "The Task of Our Association," and he does so by way of a review of the role the NABI has played in the academic community since its inception in 1909. NABI's purposes were, and must remain, he insists, to provide for the "fellowship of friends" (1954: 104) and to make "the teaching of Bible and religion intellectually respectable" (105). If the Association cannot do this, he argues, undergraduate education will be lacking in serious religious instruction (106). The task of the NABI, therefore, is essentially a religious one—to help the student come to terms with the most fundamental questions of religion, which will require that the teacher "believe knowingly and . . . know with conviction" (106). Thus, Purinton writes: "The task of members of our Association in this day is to orient our teaching more directly to the basic religious needs of students" (106). Though for Purinton the religion that needs to be taught is Christianity, he claims to be interdenominational rather than sectarian. He writes: " . . . religion courses have frequently provided illuminating examples of the benefits of American democracy in action and have strengthened the conviction that in American religious life there is beneath our differences a common faith" (109). Even though Purinton ostensibly directs his attention to pedagogical issues, it is clear that his overriding concern is with the inculcation of religious belief—in a broadly based Christian form—and that a primary aim of the Association was to make available to undergraduates a "reasoned" Christianity "appropriate to an academic classroom" (106).

The addresses by H. Neil Richardson (1958), Lionel A. Whiston, Jr. (1960), and Robert V. Smith (1961) are clearly centered on traditional biblical and theological issues. Richardson's "A Decade of Archaeology in Palestine," for example, provides a brief survey of archaeological projects in Palestine undertaken with respect to the Dead Sea scroll studies; and Whiston's "The Unity of Scripture and the Post-Exilic Literature" argues the Bible's fundamental cohesion despite its evident diversity—it is "basically a confessional literature which finds its unity in its witness to the great actions of God" (1961: 290). It is important to stress this understanding of biblical theology, he concludes, "so that it can make its own contribution to the history of biblical interpretation" (291). Smith's address on "Analytical Philosophy and Religious/Theological Language" focuses on philosophical theology in an effort, as he puts it, to delve into deeper levels of meaning and questions of truth (1962: 107).

The remaining addresses, although concerning issues of pedagogy, are actually religio-theological. W. Gordon Ross's "Thesaurus in Crackable Pottery" (1954), for example, is essentially a *confessio fidei* pointing to the Bible instructor's responsibility to treasure the religious truth found in the Bible (1955: 3). Ross fears that the NABI as a professional organization does not give sufficient attention to its "treasure-bearing role"; indeed, he warns that much will be lost if that role—and the "traffic with ultimates" (7)—is sacrificed. Arthur C. Wickenden treats the same theme in his address the following year: "Rightly Dividing the Word of Truth." Bible study, he maintains, is the medium for the Revelation of God (1956: 3), and the scholar must not let technical, scholarly minutiae undermine that fact (4). The Bible instructor's task, therefore, is not to turn students into amateur biblical scholars but rather to make the Bible a source of living values. "We are called," he writes, "to be teachers of values rather than teachers of fact" (5). This does not mean, Wickenden insists, that the Bible instructor should become a preacher or a leader of devotional studies, but that facts and theories should not impede the teaching of values, for that would be to exchange our birthright "for a mess of intellectual pottage" (5).

In "The Strangeness of Religion in the University Curriculum," A. Roy Eckardt takes up the same theme, although his focus is not simply the Bible as the source of living values but methodological questions in the study of religion as well. The professor must not be content with external, descriptive analysis but must be sympathetically related to the "faith or faiths" under study (1957: 6). Thus, he, maintains that "professional work in religion and ultimate commitment simply cannot be kept apart" (5). Eckardt distinguishes "finite" religion, which can be studied like other subjects in the university curriculum, from "ultimate" religion, which overshadows those similarities, and he argues that it is only possible to understand religion in its totality when its finite and ultimate elements are considered together (8). Taking ultimate religion into consideration "as a live intellectual alternative" (9) shows that the study of religion involves issues of a *sui generis* kind (11). If we understand this, he claims, it follows that we must show that all university education stands under the judgment of Jesus Christ (9). Lauren E. Brubaker reiterates these views in his 1959 address ("What Are You Doing Here, Elijah?") devoted to a kind of self-examination of the NABI. Like Eckardt, Brubaker insists that the teacher of religion serves both the university and the Church, claiming "[i]f we are to maintain our integrity as Christian scholars we must consciously adopt and clearly express the axioms which are established by our particular faith" (1960: 164). The task of the teacher of religion is to help the student deal with issues of truth, value, and faith, to discern matters of ultimacy, and to begin to grasp the meaning of life (165). Teaching religion in the university, therefore, is not merely a scholarly profession but a religious calling (166). Robert M. Montgomery's 1957 address to the Association, on "The Religion Instructor as Learner," is but a variation on the theme recounted by Purinton, Ross, Wickenden, Eckardt, and Brubaker. The task of the student of religion is to combat false and shallow ideals and to be the bearer of a more profound culture (1958: 103). This task accomplished, the person of faith will wield a positive influence on the modern university campus (104).

These few presidential addresses permit a clear perception of the character of the NABI and should give us a sufficient understanding of its aims and intentions for us to pass on to a comparative analysis of that Association with its successor, the AAR.

From the NABI to an Academy of Religion: 1963

It is clear from these presidential addresses to the NABI that the study of religion in American universities was essentially a confessionalist undertaking; religio-theological concerns were dominant in the work of the Association. Its members were not simply students of religion but were—of necessity, it appears—religious persons with a religious mandate. This is not to say that the Association countenanced direct ecclesiastical control or interference in its affairs, but it is quite evident that it espoused a theological understanding, not only of the study of religion but of all learning. Moreover, it perceived its work as being of direct value to the Church, in that it allied its own educational task to that of the Church's preparation of persons for ordained leadership. And although this is only implied in some of the addresses reviewed here, it is explicit in the report of the NABI Committee on Pre-theological Studies entitled "Pre-Seminary Preparation and Study in Religion," published in the Association's journal (Eckardt et al., 1959).[9] The task of the Association as argued there is to avoid "a profanization of education at one extreme and evangelization of education at the other extreme" (1959: 139).

It appears from the record of discussions and debates in the Association that their ecclesiastical connections became problematic—not because there was concern among members regarding the propriety of its religious character, but because of the denominational pluralism of its membership. The Association, that is, appeared to be tied rather closely to specific Christian denominations, although it did not deliberately exclude others—whether Christians or non-Christians. To review concerns of this kind the Association undertook a self-study in 1963; the tasks it set for itself were to determine the most appropriate public image for the Association and to investigate how it might increase its effectiveness in the academic community.

The report acknowledged that an expanded membership of the NABI had brought with it a widened interest in the study of religion beyond the interests of its founders, and the report's authors therefore suggested the Association change its name to the American Academy of Religion. In summarizing their report they advocated that the new forum of the AAR continue to address those issues of concern to the NABI, maintaining attention to "the trilemma of commitment of faith, independence of scholarship, and public professional obligations" (R. V. Smith et al., 1964: 201). It should be remembered that the first of these elements has remained the dominant concern of the AAR just as it had been for the NABI. For the AAR, as I will show below, lost considerable (but by no means all) interest in the NABI's commitment to the issue of "public professional obligations," and, although its interest to protect the "independence of scholarship" by excluding direct ecclesiastical interference is evident, it did not back an objective, scientific approach to the study of religion but instead retained a commitment to the search for religious truth central to the work of the NABI and its members.

Before turning to the review and analysis of the addresses to the AAR, however, I shall give some attention to Clyde A. Holbrook's 1963 presidential address to the NABI which, in a sense, provided a charter for the Academy about to come into existence.

Holbrook entitled his address "Why an Academy of Religion?" and in it he seems to argue for a radical departure of the new body from the aims of the old. The change to be effected, he maintains, is much more than simply one of name; it is a move away from, as he puts it, "the partialities which at present afflict the field of religion" (1964: 99). The new concept of the academic study of religion, according to Holbrook, requires that this field a) not be infringed upon by religious bodies; b) not be judged on the basis of its immediate relevance to religious life and culture; c) not be seen as the "morale officer" of the university; d) should be able to represent the total field and its sub-disciplines; and, finally, e) that it should be primarily concerned with scholarship and research (99–104). Whether this agenda is as radical a departure from the NABI program as it appears at first glance, however, is doubtful. It is interesting to note, for example, that in discussing the need for the AAR to represent the total field of Religious Studies, for Holbrook, Theology is one of the *disciplines* to be included; Theology is not seen simply as an object of scientific investigation along with other aspects of religion but rather as one of the many sub-disciplines contributing to the field overall. Including Theology in that disciplinary matrix casts in doubt the strength of Holbrook's commitment—as well as that of the newly emerging AAR—to the above aspects (b), (c), and (e) of the so-called new enterprise. This criticism of Holbrook finds support, moreover, in an analysis of his fuller account published the same year under the title *Religion: A Humanistic Field.* In a critical review of that book, John F. Wilson acknowledges that Holbrook provided a sound basis for the academic study of religion as an empirical undertaking, but he also argues that Holbrook undermined that conception by requiring of the discipline that it cater to students' moral needs. This, Wilson correctly concludes, is to make the study of religion indistinguishable from religion itself. Holbrook's response to Wilson's review, furthermore, reinforces Wilson's point, for Holbrook claims that Wilson's argument introduces a "mischievous" distinction into the discussion of the nature of the study of religion "when he attempts to limit the role of the university professor of religion, as well as the university itself, from speaking to the question of the truth value of religion or theology" (1964: 264). This distinction, Holbrook continues, "is neither representative of what actually goes on, nor should it be. . . . The religious professor, undergraduate or graduate, cannot so easily be called upon to give over his intellectual right to follow the question of truth in whatever direction his study of religious phenomena directs" (265). This discussion, then, makes clear that Holbrook did not envisage the AAR's relinquishing the NABI's "commitment to faith." Indeed, there is evidence that he did not even expect the AAR to give up interest entirely in the NABI commitment to the "public professional obligations" it had espoused. And it will become clear below that, with very few exceptions, the presidents of the AAR have been primarily concerned with the issues of religious truth—in much the same fashion as their NABI forebears.

AAR: The Presidential Addresses 1964–1993

In this section I shall review the published presidential addresses in a roughly chronological order and with minimal editorial commentary, leaving to a summary statement what generalizations suggest themselves from an analysis of their contents.[10]

The first published presidential address following the transformation of the NABI to the AAR is James L. Price's "The Search for the Theology of the Fourth Evangelist." Essentially a work of Christian theology, it urges scholars to articulate the theology of the Gospel of John, determining what is of permanent and "ever-increasing contemporary relevance" (1965: 4). While Price concedes the value of a "history of religions" approach to this task, he also counters that such an approach cannot "fully illumine" the background of the fourth evangelist's theology (11). The second and third published addresses are also religious in intent, but they are not as directly theological. John F. Priest's "Humanism, Skepticism and Pessimism in Israel" directs attention not to "overt theological questions and answers"

(1968: 326) but to human concerns grounded in human experience. Thus he advocates a humanistic "theology from below," arguing that the model for this can be found in ancient Israel's recognition of the centrality of Jahweh to human existence. J. Wesley Robb's address, "The Hidden Philosophical Agenda: A Commentary on Humanistic Psychology," is a sermon-like disquisition on the responsibility of the student of religion to provide an understanding of the human psyche to ground a defense of human rights within the framework of a democratic structure of government (1969: 14). The task of the student of religion, he maintains, is to develop a philosophy and a theology to help society recover from the blow to its dignity delivered by David Hume more than two centuries ago; he suggests that humanistic psychology would constitute an important aid to the emergence of such a new theology.

The first of the non-Christian addresses delivered to the Academy is Jacob Neusner's "Graduate Education in Judaica: Problems and Prospects." It is also the first presidential address to rebuff the demands generally voiced by students of religion that the field respond relevantly to the concerns of religious communities (which demands he sees as attempts to evade the requirements of religious scholarship [1969: 321]). Neusner places his review of developments in this field within the Science of Religion framework, because he finds the work done in rabbinical seminaries to involve bias and distortion of scholarly research; the seminaries, he argues, prefer to employ only their own graduates because that will allow them to impose conditions of religious conviction and practice upon research and publication. Oddly enough, however, Neusner does not seem to espouse the Science of Religion framework as the only reasonable approach to the study of religion in general (or the study of Judaism in particular). It is thus regrettably unclear whether Neusner's approach differs radically from that of his NABI forbears, for he points to scholarship in the field as a function of the character and personality of "constructive masters" (322) who concern themselves not only with acquiring knowledge but also with constructing frameworks of meaning. He maintains, that is, that not everything worthwhile to be said about the data in this field "will be exhausted by scholarship under such [scientific] auspices" (325). No doubt it is for this reason that Neusner does not take exception to theology as an element in the structure of the modern university department of religion (324).

By contrast, Claude Welch's address of 1970, entitled "Identity Crisis in the Study of Religion? A First Report from the ACLS Study," is essentially a preliminary report on doctoral programs in the field of religion in the United States and Canada, sponsored by the American Council of Learned Societies (ACLS). Welch argues that the inability of the scholars in the field to demarcate clearly the task of the student of religion from that of the theologian was a cause for concern because it threatened the stability of the enterprise in which the members of the Academy were involved. He concludes, however, that the field is no longer characterized by a crisis of identity, as the secularization—and therefore the academic legitimation—of the field of Religious Studies was all but accomplished through the "transformation" of the NABI into the AAR. He states: "The legitimacy of the organized study of religions in colleges and universities has now been established, and this is so widely recognized that it need no longer be a subject of anxiety" (1971: 6). The move away from denominational orientation in the academic study of religion, the rejection of the "confessional principle" and "insider theorizing" by scholars in the field, the demarcation of professional education of religious leaders and of the scholarly study of religion, and the rejection of the study of religion as a means of redemption for the university Welch sees as testament to the fact that the study of religion in the university setting is no longer taken as an indissoluble mixture of the academic with the religious. A reading of the presidential addresses to the Academy since 1964, however, hardly provides warrant for this claim; therefore, some surprise accompanies Welch's conclusion. Moreover, Welch himself is not altogether sure of his stance, for in his address to the Academy he notes that along with the "successes" of the secularization of the field there are "equally plain signs of a real struggle in which the issue of [identity] is not yet resolved" (9). Indeed, he admits that there is a wide range of problems plaguing the study of religion, including overspecialization, parochialism, and methodological naïveté—putting the field at constant risk of "falling back into the arms of confessional interests" (12).

The contrast between Welch (in his *prima facie* case for the scientific character of the scholarly study of religion in the North American university setting) and his successor presidents of the AAR could not be more striking. In James T. Burtchaell's "The Ritual of Jesus, the Anti-Ritualist" (1971), for instance, we have essentially a sermon in defense of Christian liturgy and worship as a foundation for ethics and service to others (1971: 525). Burtchaell's concern here is certainly not that of the secular, scientific student of religion, but rather that of a Christian devotee intent upon correcting misconceptions of God implicit in some Christian views of ethics and worship (515). Robert Michaelson's address of 1972, entitled "The Engaged Observer: Portrait of a Professor of Religion," although not a Christian sermon, argues for an integration of the aims of the religious devotee with that of the academic student of religion. According to Michaelson, there is not only a trend among students of religion to consider the purely objective analysis of religion (1972: 420), but also an opposite tendency of scholars in the field to reject objective scholarship in favor of self-involvement (421); indeed, according to Michaelson, so strong is the latter that he can point to the emergence of a new phenomenon he labels classroom religion (422). Because the objective study of religion can "endanger the soul," the professor's task is to help the student achieve a kind of integral wholeness. The student (and teacher) of religion, therefore, ought not to demarcate the academic from the existential tasks: "That much," he concludes, "the age of involvement has taught us" (423).

Charles Long's address, "Cargo Cults as Cultural Historical Phenomena" (1974), is the second presidential address to the Academy not directly focused on Christian issues and concerns. Long's argument, however, is not in favor of a neutral, objective study of religion. He contends that a proper understanding of the emergence of cargo cults as a response to the dominating power of Western religion and culture may cause a revolution in our understanding of the nature of the social sciences, which in turn may directly affect how the AAR frames the discipline. The study of cargo cults, he continues, shows that the scientific approach to the study of religion is inadequate, because it not only alienates us from the "other" who is studied but also from ourselves (1974: 125). His advice for the AAR, therefore, is that it promote a study of religion that is self-involving rather than objective and scientific.

On the basis of the collective thought of the presidents of the AAR in its first decade of existence, then, it does not appear (notwithstanding Welch's address) that the concerns of the AAR differ markedly from those of the NABI. Indeed, like their predecessors, the presidents of the AAR are concerned that the study of religion stay focused on more than facts and theories; that the student of religion be open not only to *the knowledge about* religion but also to *the truths of religion.* And as I propose to show, the presidential addresses of the decade that follows do not deviate from this pattern. In fact, all but one of the ten addresses seem to spring from Christian tenets, and five focus explicitly on Christian theological concerns. The remaining five essays are centered on what might best be termed "methodological" issues, with four of them arguing for an integration of theology with the scientific or scholarly study of religion.

In 1974, Christine Downing's lecture on "Sigmund Freud and the Greek Mythological Tradition" proposed a reconstruction of the theological enterprise on the basis of a reappropriation of myth made possible, she maintains, by the nonrationalistic and nonmechanistic interpretation of Freud's work. Moreover, she insists this is absolutely necessary for our health and well-being. By means of Freud we can recall "those urgencies that pulled us into religious studies 'once upon a time,' to a renewed appreciation of the sacred" (1975: 3). William F. May, in his address to the Academy in 1975 on "Institutions as Symbols of Death," also speaks as a theologian. The burden of his lecture is to seek a theological response to theories of the institution, to help us avoid their predatory behavior—especially in those institutions devoted variously to health and welfare. Preston N. Williams's "Religion and the Making of Community in America" of the following year is also a theological project, addressed to the nation on the occasion of its bicentennial. Williams attempts to provide an understanding of the biblical covenant and to show how it can be helpful in dissolving the opposition, as he sees it, between "ethnicity and annihilation"; this is necessary, he argues, so as not to block the creation of an inclusive community in America and to help create a community "consonant with justice, equality, liberty, and toleration" (1976: 609). By "mediating fundamental human values" and "opening persons" to loyalty to God, he writes, such a covenant prevents the use "of religion and ethnicity for purposes of political and economic exploitation" (608). John C. Meagher's "Pictures at an Exhibition: Reflections on Exegesis and Theology" (delivered in 1978) and Jill Raitt's "Strictures and Structures: Relational Theology and a Woman's Contribution to Theological Conversation" (delivered in 1981) reflect more specifically Christian concerns. Meagher, for example, sets out to assess the adequacy of the historical and exegetical resources for studying theology. And Raitt focuses her attention on feminism because she thinks it could well undermine Christian theology by showing how religion has often sanctioned oppression. Instead, she argues, a new and more sensitive theology can be created to acknowledge deficiencies without requiring rupture with the Christian tradition.

The first of the "methodological" addresses of this decade of the Academy's history was delivered in 1977 by Schubert M. Ogden, entitled "Theology and Religious Studies: Their Difference and the Difference It Makes." Ogden's treatment of the subject is complex and subtle—and not altogether unambiguous. He begins his essay by differentiating "religious studies" from "studies of religion" (1978: 6), claiming that the former involves "reflective understanding of religion as an answer to . . . [the] questions of faith" (12) and focuses attention on "the meaning and truth of religion" (12). He denies that one must be religious in order to pursue Religious Studies, claiming rather that one need only "ask the question of faith to which religion exists to provide the answer . . ." (13). Theology proper, for Ogden, is simply a higher-level reflection in which the claims of a particular religion are subjected to critical scrutiny. Religious Studies, then, would include theology as a sub-discipline, and thus the two are not only contiguous but similar (that is, coterminous). Ogden may be right to claim that one need not be religious to "do" religious studies, but it is obvious that such a frame of mind turns the task into a religious quest—it is no longer a mere search for an explanation of aspects of religion. For Ogden, however, "studies of religion" occupy at best an ancillary role for the student of religion, whose concern is fundamentally with Religious Studies. It appears, therefore, that in creating

Religious Studies, the focus of the AAR was primarily religious and fundamentally theological.

L. Gilkey's 1979 address on "The AAR and the Anxiety of Nonbeing" carries the subtitle "An Analysis of Our Present Cultural Situation." The substance of his argument is clear and very bold: if the study of religion is neither intentionally religious nor concerned with "ultimate reality," departments of Religious Studies will be dissolved and the study of the data will be taken up by other departments in the university. Because of this, claims Gilkey, members of the AAR must argue that religion and Religious Studies are separate entities (1980: 7), although possessed of a vision that makes possible the integration of scientific with religious concerns (10). The argument for a special combination of the scientific with the religious should not be difficult to develop, he suggests, because science is itself an ideology, and all ideologies are religions—which in turn implies that the discussion between the two is in essence an inter-religious dialogue. Such a study of religion is not only relevant but necessary, because as human beings we need to answer questions that involve more than the scholarly interpretation of fact (17). In integrating our "religious" and "Religious Studies" concerns, Gilkey concludes, "the AAR is viable, academically useful, and culturally significant"; in segregating them, "each of its separate parts may well disappear without a trace" (18).

The other two "methodological" essays arguing an essentially NABI "line" are Gordon Kaufman's "Nuclear Eschatology and the Study of Religion" (delivered in 1982) and Wilfred Cantwell Smith's 1983 "The Modern West and the Study of Religion." Kaufman's address contains the apocalyptic flavor characteristic of Gilkey's contribution to the Academy: he argues that unless the advice he proffers is taken up—and soon—the world could well destroy itself. His advice is simple: students of religion must give their attention primarily to the religious and practical problems plaguing our world; we must therefore see to it that the AAR provides knowledge and other resources "for grappling with the problems of mystery and finitude . . ." (1983: 12). The student of religion must reject the notion of Religious Studies as an objective, scientific exercise in favor of normative questions of substance and value to the human community. Plainly put, Religious Studies must fully integrate with Theology to form a unified discipline. He writes: "Can we really continue, in the name of 'neutrality' and 'objectivity' to pursue our academic work in this kind of aloofness from the potential disaster that confronts humanity? To do so would be not only inhuman, it would be to ignore, or turn away from, a feature of our common life which presents us in the most overpowering and baffling way with the central issues with which human religiousness is concerned" (12).

Wilfred Smith's address to the AAR is less impassioned, but it delivers a similar message. We need a new approach to the study of religion, he argues, so that we can profit from the knowledge gained from other religious traditions (1984: 4), and that means not only learning *about* them but also *from* them. Such learning, Smith maintains, excludes the objective, scientific study of other religions and cultures. In rejecting such a secularism we can look forward to a new phase of human history, one in which a common recognition of the transcendent will bring about a convergence of world cultures. According to Smith, " . . . modern secularism, whatever its virtues . . . has been simply wrong in its conceptual negativity, and its failure to recognize intellectually the transcendent realm" (17).

William A. Clebsch's address to the Academy is the only one in this decade to argue in favor of a view of religious studies different from that held by the NABI. His 1980 address—"Apples, Oranges, and Manna: Comparative Religion Revisited"—provides a review of the place and development of "comparative religion" in the Academy, and he argues that it overcame both Christian exclusivism and the debasement of other religions in the process (1981: 6–7). He also argues, however, that on the American academic scene, exclusivism characterized the study of religion down to the 1950s, and he sees as ominous the turn toward an avowed superiority of Christianity, "and in particular toward infiltrating Christian theology into a curriculum whose integrity was supposed thereby to be recovered" (13).

The presidential addresses of the third decade of the AAR's existence, I am afraid, simply repeat a pattern by now very familiar; yet only four of these take up religio-theological themes directly, while six are, loosely speaking, methodological, focused on the "need" to integrate Religious Studies with Religion and Theology.

In "To Be and Not To Be: *Sit Autem Sermo (logos) Vester, Est, Est; Non, Non . . .* " (1984), Ray L. Hart presents what he calls the confessions of an onto-theologian (1985: 9). The primary aim of his confessions, he claims, is to make sense out of our lives which, he further insists in a sermon-like manner, cannot be done without experiencing and coming to terms with "the Not." He laments the abstract character of much of Religious Studies, which he considers more pernicious to this discipline than to Philosophy since, of course, Religious Studies "has communal constituencies of specific existence outside the groves of academe" (8–9). Nathan A. Scott's 1986 address, entitled "The House of Intellect in an Age of Carnival: Some Hermeneutical Reflections," is also a homily of sorts, although perhaps a "humanistic homily." In it Scott questions how we can live in a radically pluralistic world in which we would never achieve the "overarching *speculum mentis* that subdues all the entanglements of modern intellectual life and integrates the various fields of culture, assigning to each its proper place within the terms of some magnificently comprehensive map of the human universe" (1987: 7). He concludes that the only way for us to dwell happily together is to combine writing's *theoria* and *praxis,* which requires of us an "appropriative life stance" in our study of other cultures and religions. John Dillenberger's 1987 "Visual Arts and Religion: Modern and Contemporary Contours" is a straightforwardly theologically interested look at the visual arts in the United States in the last four decades. His argument is that in art we can find a "recovery of the human" because in it we confront the mystery of our selves. Elizabeth Clark's 1990 "Sex, Shame and Rhetoric: Engendering Early Christian Ethics" offers the conclusion that "shame-rhetoric" is a self-monitoring device for Christians to protect them from deeds that could call down divine punishment upon them.

The first of the methodological addresses of the decade is Wendy D. O'Flaherty's "The Use and Misuses of Other Peoples' Myths" (1985) the last of the three essays that I have suggested is neither the result of Christian influence nor focused upon Christian issues. Despite her stated concern with myth, it is obvious that a major question for O'Flaherty is the role of scientific objectivity in the study of religions. She argues that all creative scholarship is autobiographical in some respect or other, and that the study of myth and religion is particularly so. This implies a legitimacy of affect in the study of myth and religion despite possible violation of objective scientific scholarship. Somewhat paradoxically, she also argues that the student of religion must play by the rules of scholarship characteristic of other fields of research, although in our field we have moved too far in this direction; so that "in attempting to play the game of objectivity with the Big Boys on the playing fields of the harder sciences"—a rich metaphor she adopts both to stress the antagonistic stand-off between the sciences and religion and to question the validity of the "objective" approach to religion—we "lose out" with respect to an equally genuine sort of objectivity relevant to religious studies (1986: 233). Unfortunately, the nature of that other kind of objectivity is not elaborated upon by O'Flaherty.

Martin Marty's 1988 address—"Committing the Study of Religion in Public"—constitutes yet another criticism leveled at those who advocate the objective scientific approach to the study of religion (1989: 7). He argues that the student of religion can give allegiance to the academic community but in so doing must not become isolated from the Church; for if that were to happen, the student would be unable to contribute to humanistic study or be of service to society (8). Learning for its own sake, therefore, is not enough (12–13); furthermore, he adds—with perhaps less stress than this Pandora's Box of an argument might warrant—it will not help create a clientele for the field; the field's existence, then, would be threatened.

In 1989, Robert L. Wilken's "Who Will Speak for the Religious Traditions?" also argues that if the scholar does not "care for religion," failing to recognize its value, it is not likely that others will care either. Wilken seems to be claiming, therefore, that unless students of religion follow the advice of scholars like O'Flaherty and reject the demarcation between the discipline and the spiritual adventure, they will in fact undermine their own careers as scholars (1989: 714). Wilken is thus against the Enlightenment notion of critical reason, maintaining that the task of the student in this field is not only to study religions but to nurture and propagate the wisdom they contain (704); that study is and must be "engaged" and must, therefore, undertake dialogue with other religious traditions (707). He insists, moreover—and in a potentially explosive tangent—that those who are studied must have a say in the conclusions of those who study them (708).

Judith Berling also addresses matters of method—although she pays less attention to methodology than one might have expected—in her 1991 address to the AAR on the topic "Is Conversation about Religion Possible?" Like her predecessors, she questions the methodology implied by a demarcation between Theology and Religious Studies. Following G. Kaufman, she claims that "religionists" (students of religion) must assume a "cultural leadership" if tensions in the world are to be reduced and if we are not to destroy each other. "Cultural leadership" means acting as a kind of "religious referee" to help create a context in which all religions can act in harmony (1993: 8). We must take the lead, she writes, "in seeking alternatives to the polarity of universal truth against corrosive relativism, and in articulating the grounds for mutual cross-cultural and cross-religious understanding" (14). In conclusion she writes: "As religionists, we are facilitators who enable parties representing different positions, traditions, or cultures to move in the direction of becoming 'possibilities' to one another" (18).

Robert Neville's address on "Religious Studies and Theological Studies" (1992) is the most curious of the presentations on methodology—and the most theologically insistent. He maintains that the AAR is "at a crisis point in its self-definition, which in turn, is critical for the definition of the study of religion" (1993: 185). For Neville, that crisis is seen in the anxieties of the religiously orientated scholars in the AAR who see the objective sciences as constituting the dominant ideology of their association—despite the evidence that it is the ideology of the theologically orientated scholar in the AAR that has gained the ascendancy. Nevertheless, Neville openly supports an integration of Theology and Religious Studies, maintaining that religio-theological truth-claims are every bit as open to correction as scientific claims, and implying thereby that the two are equally scientific. This is an odd claim to make, and—significantly—no evidence is provided in its support; Neville, moreover, writes (cryptically) "[f]or a theological claim to be publicly vulnerable does *not* mean that it must be reduced to what is easily grasped by an external observer" (197). He concludes that Religious Studies provides the conditions for "authentic dialogue among adepts in different religions," and that we need to "embrace the human need for practical answers to religious questions" (197,198).

The final address of the third decade of the AAR's existence is Edith Wyschogrod's "Fact, Fictions, *Ficciones:* Truth in the Study of Religion" (1993). For Wyschogrod, meaning and truth are inseparable, which makes it impossible for Religious Studies to be reduced simply to the analysis of facts (1994: 5). She rejects the possibility of neutrality in the study of religion and seeks to flesh out a concept of truth transcending the Enlightenment's concern with mere factual and theoretical truth. To do this, she argues, requires that the student of religion take seriously narrative as *ficciones,* combining truth with value (10). This, she writes, is a strategy for "encountering the silences" of the sacred that "attest the sacred silence" and preserve it (13). In so doing, the student of religion goes beyond the facts about religion to a personal "encounter."

Summary and Conclusion

There is more than one way to categorize the presidential addresses to the AAR reviewed here. I propose, however, the following threefold classification, to account for both the superficial differences and the deeper resemblances between them: 1) addresses centered on traditional theological concerns; 2) addresses focusing attention on determining the nature of the enterprise in which members of the AAR are engaged—therefore, essentially methodological; and 3) addresses that move beyond the traditional boundaries that characterized the agenda of the NABI.

Thirteen of the twenty-eight addresses examined here fall into category one: nine of the thirteen are straight theological papers while the other four address theological issues indirectly. The addresses by Price (1965), Burtchaell (1971), May (1975), Williams (1976), Meagher (1978), Raitt (1981), Hart (1984), Dillenberger (1987), and Clark (1990) are explicitly theological while those by Priest (1967), Robb (1968), Downing(1974), and Scott (1986) come at religio-theological issues in a more round-about fashion. There is little, if anything at all, to distinguish these scholars' concerns from those of the presidents of the National Association of Biblical Instructors. In choice of illustration for their theological message they range rather widely and include analyses of traditional concerns, assessments of particular social or ethical issues, methodological comments, indirect proposals for transforming the theological enterprise, and inchoate personal assessments of the religio-theological tasks of the scholar of religion. That nearly half of the presidential addresses to the AAR are precisely the kind one finds in a formal theological context—that is, without relevance to the concerns of the historian of religions or the comparativist—ought to be of considerable concern to anyone who assumed that with the emergence of the AAR the academic study of religion would undergo a radical transformation. It is of considerable interest in this regard, as well, that only three of the twenty-eight addresses (Neusner [1969], Long [1973], and O'Flaherty [1985]) are not inspired by or focused upon theological issues, for it provides a clear indication that the historical and comparative study of religions remains relatively under-represented in the overall program of the AAR. This judgment is reinforced when one recognizes that all three of them deal with methodological issues yet encourage the student of religion to reject an objective, scientific approach to the study of religion. Neusner's paper is the least problematic in this respect, although he does argue for the inclusion of theology as an element of the discipline. Long's paper, on the other hand, advises the AAR to move away from science; and O'Flaherty uses her discussion of other peoples' myths to advise students to shun the so-called objective approaches to the study of religions and to combine theory with praxis as a more appropriate avenue to the understanding of myth and religion.

The remaining addresses (Welch [1970], Michaelson [1972], Ogden [1977], Gilkey [1979], Clebsch [1980], Kaufman [1982], Smith [1983], Marty [1988], Wilken [1989], Berling [1991], Neville [1992], and Wyschogrod [1993]) direct attention to the character of the study of religion. All twelve do so bearing advice—implicit or otherwise—for the direction the AAR ought to take in supporting "scholarship in religion." Six of the addresses (Ogden, Gilkey, Kaufman, Marty, Berling, and Neville) argue both explicitly and vigorously for a full integration of Religious Studies with Theology. Four others (Michaelson, Smith, Wilken, and Wyschogrod) argue a very similar position in proposing that the study of religion be an "engaged" one in which the student of religion becomes directly involved with the spiritual life of those whom they study. Indeed, they counsel the student of religion to move past the data of religion and to deal with "the transcendent itself." For these students the study of religion takes on the nature of a conversation with the religious devotee, making that study a religious exercise.

Of all the methodological addresses only two—Welch and Clebsch—seem to be concerned with the study of religion as an objective and scientific undertaking rather than as a religious and theological one. Welch, although misjudging developments in the field since 1964, applauds the demarcation of the religio-theological from the scientific agenda in the academic study of religion. Clebsch, a decade later, warns the AAR that the integrity of the comparative religion enterprise is being lost because of the infiltration of Theology into the Religious Studies curriculum.

The facts staring us in the face after analyzing the presidential addresses to the AAR are: 1) that at least twenty-five of the twenty-eight published addresses are primarily theological in character and insist that the academic student of religion be concerned not only with accounting for religion, but also with religious matters; 2) that at least ten of those twenty-five engage in vigorous apologetics to maintain the dual focus; and 3) that the AAR—as seen from its choice of presidents—is still essentially a religio-theological organization. This is not necessarily to suggest that it excludes scholars who are neither Christian nor religious, but clearly there is little support for those who take a scientific approach to the study of religions; the AAR has never promoted the scholarship of its scientifically orientated members, and in this it is indistinguishable from its predecessor, the NABI.

This review of the presidential addresses then, invalidates the conclusions of D. G. Hart, Marsden, and Cherry on the role of the AAR in the development of Religious Studies in the United States. It is true that, as Hart claims, the emergence of the AAR signaled the demise of the traditional Protestant dominance of the field, but it did not alter the domination of humanistic concerns in the field, nor did it provide the foundation for a more objective, scientific study of religion. Marsden's claim that the AAR embraced both the humanistic and social scientific approaches to Religious Studies is closer to the truth of the matter, but his judgment that the latter orientation predominates is incorrect. He is in error as well when he says that the work of the AAR has helped eliminate normative teaching of religion in the university, as I have indicated in this review of the addresses. Similarly, Conrad Cherry claims incorrectly that the AAR, in its role as overseer of Religious Studies departments, has been primarily concerned with the canons of the other disciplinary specialties found in the university. There is no doubt that uniform standards of scholarship are expected from the religion scholar within the university, both by their colleagues in other university departments and by university administrators (and the subject of administrative expectations has not yet been fully explored), but it is clear from the analysis provided here that not only has the AAR disregarded those scholarly ideals, but it has replaced them with others in support of a normative if not doctrinaire approach that has little to do with scholarship.

Appendix 1:
Presidential Addresses to the NABI

(Published in The Journal of Bible and Religion)
1953: Carl E. Purinton (1954). "The Task of Our Association." 22(2): 104–109.
1954: W. Gordon Ross (1955). "Thesaurus in Crackable Pottery." 23(1): 3–8.
1955: Arthur C. Wickenden (1956). "Rightly Dividing the Word of Truth." 24(1): 3–9.

1956: A. Roy Eckhardt (1957). "The Strangeness of Religion in the University Curriculum." 25(1): 3–12.
1957: Robert M. Montgomery (1958). "The Religion Instructor as Learner." 26(2): 99–106.
1958: H. Neil Richardson (1959). "A Decade of Archaeology in Palestine." 27(2): 91–101.
1959: Lauren E. Brubaker (1960). "What Are You Doing Here, Elijah?" 28(2): 161–166.
1960: Lionel A. Whiston, Jr. (1961). "The Unity of Scripture and the Post-Exilic Literature." 29(4): 290–298.
1961: Robert V. Smith (1962). "Analytical Philosophy and Religious/Theological Language." 30(2): 101–108.
1962: Fred D. Gealy (1963). [No title available; paper not published or available from AAR archives.]
1963: Clyde A. Holbrook (1964). "Why an Academy of Religion?" 32(2): 97–105.

Appendix 2:
AAR Presidential Addresses

(Published in the Journal of the American Academy of Religion, the successor journal to The Journal of Bible and Religion)
1964: Ira J. Martin III. [No title available; paper not published or available from AAR archives.]
1965: James L. Price (1967). "The Search for the Theology of the Fourth Evangelist." 35(1): 3–15.
1966: William Hordern. [No title available; paper not published or available from AAR archives.]
1967: John F. Priest (1968). "Humanism, Skepticism, and Pessimism in Israel." 36(4): 313–326.
1968: J. Wesley Robb (1969). "The Hidden Philosophical Agenda: A Commentary on Humanistic Psychology." 37(1): 3–14.
1969: Jacob Neusner (1969). "Graduate Education in Judaica: Problems and Prospects." 37(4): 321–330.
1970: Claude Welch (1971). "Identity Crisis in the Study of Religion? A First Report from the ACLS Study." 39(1): 3–18.
1971: James Tunstead Burtchaell (1971). "The Rituals of Jesus, the Anti-Ritualist." 39(4): 513–525.
1972: Robert Michaelson (1972). "The Engaged Observer: Portrait of a Professor of Religion." 40(4): 419–424.
1973: Charles Long (1974). "Cargo Cults as Cultural Historical Phenomena." 42(3): 403–414.
1974: Christine Downing (1975). "Sigmund Freud and the Greek Mythological Tradition." 43(1): 3–14.

1975: William F. May (1976). "Institutions as Symbols of Death." 44(2): 211–223.
1976: Preston N. Williams (1976). "Religion and the Making of Community in America." 44(4): 603–611.
1977: Schubert M. Ogden (1978). "Theology and Religious Studies: Their Difference and the Difference It Makes." 46(1): 3–17.
1978: John C. Meagher (1979). "Pictures at an Exhibition: Reflections on Exegesis and Theology." 47(1): 3–20.
1979: Langdon Gilkey (1980). "The AAR and the Anxiety of Nonbeing: An Analysis of Our Present Cultural Situation." 48(1): 5–18.
1980: William A. Clebsch (1981). "Apples, Oranges, and Manna: Comparative Religion Revisited." 49(1): 3–22.
1981: Jill Rait (1982). "Strictures and Structures: Relational Theology and a Woman's Contribution to Theological Conversation." 50(1): 3–17.
1982: Gordon D. Kaufman (1983). "Nuclear Eschatology and the Study of Religion." 51(1): 3–14.
1983: Wilfred Cantwell Smith (1984). "The Modern West in the History of Religion." 52(1): 3–18.
1984: Ray L. Hart (1985). "To Be and Not To Be: *Sit Autem Sermo (Logos) Vester, Est, Est; Non, Non. . . .*" 53(1): 5–22.
1985: Wendy Doniger O'Flaherty (1986). "The Uses and Misuses of Other Peoples' Myths." 54(2): 219–239.
1986: Nathan A. Scott, Jr. (1987). "The House of Intellect in an Age of Carnival: Some Hermeneutical Reflections." 55(1): 3–18.
1987: John Dillenberger (1988). "Visual Arts and Religion: Modern and Contemporary Contours." 56(2): 199–212.
1988: Martin E. Marty (1989). "Committing the Study of Religion in Public." 57(1): 1–22.
1989: Robert L. Wilken (1989). "Who Will Speak for the Religious Traditions?" 57(4): 699–717.
1990: Elizabeth A. Clark (1991). "Sex, Shame, and Rhetoric: En-gendering Early Christian Ethics." 59(2): 221–245.
1991: Judith A. Berling (1993). "Is Conversation about Religion Possible?" 61(1): 1–22.
1992: Robert Cummings Neville (1993). "Religious Studies and Theological Studies." 61(2): 185–200.
1993: Edith Wyschogrod (1994). "Facts, Fiction, Ficciones: Truth in the Study of Religion." 62(1): 1–16.

Notes

1. D. G. Hart, "American Learning and the Problem of Religious Studies," in *The Secularization of the Academy*, eds. G. M. Marsden and B. J. Longfield (New York: Oxford University Press, 1992): 195–233.
2. G. M. Marsden, *The Soul of the American University: From Protestant Establishment to Established Nonbelief* (New York: Oxford University Press, 1994).

3. Conrad Cherry, *Hurrying Toward Zion: Universities, Divinity Schools, and American Protestantism* (Bloomington, Indian: Indian University Press, 1995).

4. Donald Wiebe, "Against Science in the Academic Study of Religion: On the Birth and Development of the AAR," in *The Comity and Grace of Method: Religious Studies for Edmund Perry,* ed. G. Bond and T. Ryba (Evanston: Northwestern University Press; forthcoming). The essay is printed as chapter 14 in this volume.

5. Donald Wiebe, "Theology and the Academic Study of Religion in the United States," in *India and Beyond: Aspects of Literature, Meaning, Ritual and Thought. Essays in Honour of Frits Staal,* ed. Dick van der Meeij (London: Kegan Paul International, 1997): 651–675. The essay appears as chapter 5 in this volume.

6. *Method and Theory in the Study of Religion* 9/4 (1997). The original suggestion for a special issue of the journal dedicated to investigating the role of religious commitment in the academic study of religion came from Michael Levine. Submissions were received from Martin Jaffee ("Fessing Up in Theory: On *Pro*fessing and *Con*fessing in the Religious Studies Classroom [325–337]), Peter Byrne ("The Study of Religion: Neutral, Scientific, or Neither?" [339–351]), and from Donald Wiebe ("A Religious Agenda Continued" [353–375]). Levine provided critical comments on these contributions, in the same issue, with his "Religion and Method in the Study of Religion: Response" (377–387).

7. On this see Elmer W. K. Mould, "The National Association of Biblical Instructors: An Historical Account," *The Journal of Bible and Religion* 18/1 (1950): 11–28.

8. I have been unable to locate Fred D. Gealy's 1962 presentation to the NABI. It was not printed in the Association's journal; nor does the AAR archives have a copy of it.

9. This report, it is stated, "was adopted as an official statement of policy by the National Association of Biblical Instructors at its national meeting at Union Theological Seminary, New York, December 28–29, 1958" (142n1).

10. As with the presidential addresses to the NABI, several presentations to the AAR appear not to have made it into print: neither Ira J. Martin's 1964 address nor William Hordern's 1966 address were published, and the AAR archives themselves possess no copies.

Part IV

---~∾⊱⊰∾~---

Epilogue

Chapter Sixteen

Appropriating Religion:
Understanding Religion as an Object of Science

I consider it an honor to have addressed a conference devoted to the methodology of the Study of Religion.[1] Again, I would like to thank the Finnish Society for the Study of Comparative Religion and the Donner Institute for Research in Religious and Cultural History for the invitation and for making arrangements that permit further analysis and debate of the methodological problems of our field. I must admit, however, that as I prepared for participation in the discussions I had second thoughts because I am not myself actively engaged in the kinds of scientific studies of religious phenomena to which participants in this conference have been asked to give attention. I am not a historian of religions; nor am I an anthropologist, sociologist, psychologist, phenomenologist, or cognitive scientist. I am, rather, only a philosopher of religion, and it occurred to me that for reasons of intellectual integrity I ought perhaps to withdraw my initial acceptance to participate. Before airing my concerns in this regard, however, I took time to re-read the proceedings of the first Turku conference on methods in the study of religion, edited by Lauri Honko (1979), to see if I might find some justification for my involvement after all. My concern in this regard, I was happy to discover, was sufficiently mitigated by C. J. Bleeker's observation at Turku 1973 "that the average historian of religions should abstain from speculations about matters of method which can only adequately be solved by students of philosophy and of philosophy of religion" (1979: 176). But this, unfortunately, presented me with a further problem. In a subsequent review of the proceedings of that conference I expressed surprise that in fact no philosophers of religion or philosophers of science had been invited to participate and I ventured hastily, "[i]f progress is to be made in our methodological discussion [of this field] this oversight must surely be corrected" (1980: 633). Furthermore, I had been disappointed that the results of the conference did not provide the kind of framework for the study of religion which would allow it to take its place among the other sciences. It appeared to me, therefore, that arriving in Turku for the conference I might be expected—at least by those who could recall my rather presumptuous comments—to be able to suggest some resolution to our methodological problems. Indeed, for a time I expected this of myself, and fearing utter failure I was tempted to withdraw from the conference—although by that time it was too late to admit to having cold feet. Fortunately, I was reassured about the propriety of my participation when I recognized that despite approving Bleeker's general call for involvement of the philosopher I had expressed reservation about his suggestion that our problems could be resolved by the student of philosophy alone. And, incidentally, I should admit that I have already published a few methodological essays which fall short of resolving our central problems; nevertheless there might be some merit in approaching the issue from yet another angle.

It is, then, as a student of philosophy—a generalist of sorts—that I enter the convention's debate. I present for discussion and debate proposals for action which I hope make a positive contribution to the discipline. I do not focus attention on specific techniques or procedures in any one of the disciplines (or sub-disciplines) of the field of Religious Studies *qua* academic undertaking, but instead concern myself with the need for a clear understanding of the framework of assumptions and presuppositions of such academic techniques and procedures—a framework left undefined if not taken for granted in most of our discussions. In other words, I direct my attention to the study of religion as a scientific project, for it is the scientific interest in religion which has constituted the grounds for admitting the study of religion into the curriculum of the modern Western university. Despite that academic legitimation, however, the study of religion in the setting of the modern research university is not held in high esteem relative to the other sciences. This, I have suggested elsewhere (1984), is due to a "failure of nerve" on the part of those who succeeded Max Müller and C. P. Tiele, the founders of the science of religion;[2] their successors failed to follow through on that nineteenth-century scientific agenda for the study of religion by rejecting its implicit reductionism, and they have espoused instead a return to a so-called scholarly approach which substitutes understanding religion for explaining religious phenomena—the former being arguably humanistic in intent and therefore more gentle than the latter in affirming the value of religion. Such an approach, that is, appropriates religion for the benefit of self and society and to the detriment of academic advancement. I argue here, therefore, that if the scientific study of religion is to be legitimately ensconced in the modern research university, the notion of religion will have to be wholly appropriated by science; only then will we be able to establish a conceptual foundation from which to make valid knowledge claims about religion on a level commensurate with the pronouncements of the natural and social sciences. Indeed, to go one step further, given the hold on the concept of religion by those committed to the humanistic study of religion, we might need to talk here not of the appropriation but of expropriation of religion by science—that is, of wresting ownership of the concept from the humanists by using it solely as a taxonomic device to differentiate and explain a peculiar range of human behavior demonstrated in religious practices.

It may be surprising to some that I invoke the notion of appropriation from Robert Friedman's history of the development of modern meteorology in the early decades of this century. But I turn to Friedman's account in my attempt to propose a methodological framework for the study of religion because an understanding of the work of Vilhelm Bjerknes in the construction of modern meteorology by, as he puts it, "appropriating the weather," may be of assistance to us in defining our own task. According to Friedman, Bjerknes established a new foundation for atmospheric science by moving beyond the purely empirical method of "statistical-climatological understanding dominant since the late nineteenth century" to the larger theoretical" dynamic-physical comprehension of the atmosphere" (1989: xii). Friedman claims Bjerknes was successful in creating the new science because he was able to "appropriate" the weather for his own interests, incorporating it into the domain of theoretical physics and thereby making predictions of weather patterns possible. It seems to me that the study of religion requires a similar "appropriation" of scientific theory if it is to provide the unification needed by research in our field.

It is interesting that, despite this account of Bjerknes's appropriation of the weather, Friedman seems to insist on a constructivist reading of the emergence of the new meteorological science—interesting and of some relevance to our field, in which well-intentioned methodological ideals are too often undermined by personal engagement or other less-than-scientific occurrences. Friedman states: "Hard facts were not waiting in nature to be uncovered," rather, new concepts and models were created "by drawing upon analogy, metaphor, existing theory, and ad hoc construction [. . . thereby transforming] insights, speculations, and hypothetical entities into stable scientific 'reality' by integrating them into a structure of meaning and by devising analytical techniques with which the constructs could be regularly reproduced" (1989: 243). He claims, furthermore, that the concepts and models of the new Bergen school of meteorology "were not the inevitable result of observation and theory" (1989: 243) but that they were theory-laden and even practice-laden; they were the result not only of simple interaction with nature, but also of complex interactions between scientists and society.

Some examples given by Friedman show why he might have arrived at a constructivist interpretation. Enormous changes in the social relevance of weather significantly influenced the development of this science. Military operations during World War One, for example, obviously made improvements in prediction of weather conditions extremely valuable. Subsequently, as Friedman points out, "the understanding of weather as a resource for rational military operations suggested new possibilities for meteorology in peacetime" (1989: 142). And of course the impact of accurate prediction of weather conditions on market forces—with respect to the shipping and fishing industries and the emerging air travel industry—are almost too obvious to mention. Lastly, Friedman even draws on references to personal matters in the development of Bjerknes's career which directly influenced the development of this new science, including the "dead end" he reached in his research in physics, his attendant anxiety in taking up a new line of research in the field, his appreciation for the interest members of the international meteorological community took in aspects of his work in physics relevant to theirs, his anxiety at being too closely associated with them because of the lack of rigor in (most of) their work, and his strong desire for international recognition. Friedman summarizes Bjerknes's position (1989: 237):

> [He] made history, but not the history of his choosing. His career developed in a manner he had never envisioned; so did the science of the atmosphere he endeavored to shape. Both his professional evolution and the science he established were shaped by unexpected exigencies. He learned early that curiosity, vision, and innovative work were not sufficient to secure success in professional science. Success would depend as well on convincing other scientists to adopt his research problems and methods and on placing his disciples in authoritative situations where their reputations could contribute to both his prestige and his program. (237)

Despite Friedman's constructivist reading of Bjerknes's development of a scientific model, I think it would be going too far to claim that the new Bjerknes meteorology differs substantially from science as traditionally conceived. Friedman aside, Bjerknes was not merely engaged in subjective and constructivist work. His legitimate concern was to use meteorology to be able to predict the weather rationally; the theory upon which the predictions would be based was to be open to empirical test. Bjerknes did not somehow manufacture the reality and adapt it to his theory, for he was well aware that appropriating the weather required that it also be appropriable by non-scientists—that is, for commercial as well as academic interests. It is clear, I repeat, that the creators of the new science, despite their complex interactions with society, were not responsible for the reality commanding their attention; for there were indeed "hard facts" in nature and they had already been discovered by a wide range of interest groups—hard facts which could legitimately be exploited and discussed with reference to their newly devised methodological framework. Friedman notes correctly, "[. . .] Bjerknes and his school ably managed to combine the search for knowledge with the imperative to serve public interests" 1989: (240), and he is well aware that this required Bjerknes's bringing "the erratic and seemingly random phenomena of the seas, atmosphere, and solid earth into the domain of exact physical science" (1989: 34). Let me be clear: in seeing this science as constructive, Friedman is not necessarily denying that meteorology made discoveries. But he seems to be asserting that the science is nevertheless in some sense creating the reality with which it is dealing. He concludes by saying "[t]hrough Bjerknes's own quest to know and to succeed professionally, these issues [such as the expansion of the state's role in commercial activity and the growth of regular commercial and military flying] played a constituent role in shaping a new meteorology" (1989: 246). There is, however, a considerable difference between shaping the new meteorology and shaping the weather itself.

I trust it is obvious that I have not rehearsed Friedman's account of the development of modern meteorology because I am proposing an affinity between the weather and religion—although I can imagine someone being ready to remind me of a Christian text comparing the Spirit of God to the unpredictable movements of the wind. I do think, however, that in this one particular study there are important general lessons to be learned about methodology in science, and, by extension, methodology in the study of religion. It is fair to say, for example, that even though Bjerknes was concerned with the refinement of empirical techniques and methods necessary for predicting the weather, he was also concerned in a much more general and theoretical way with the research program as a whole; he held very clear ideas about the nature of the scientific enterprise that enabled him to appropriate the weather—that is, to provide an explanation of it, permitting predictions of meteorological patterns which made the weather in turn capable of appropriation by others.

Students of religion, I suggest, do not have a similarly cogent idea of what constitutes scientific knowledge of religion and have been unable to frame a research program to unify their field. We are partly to blame: having minimized the value of theory we have too readily espoused polymethodism (if I may so put it) as an essential aspect of our study, and as a consequence we have failed to establish firmly the science of religion envisioned, as I mentioned earlier, by Max Müller and C. P. Tiele. Furthermore, I am convinced that this polymethodism has gained, and maintains, its strength as a methodological position in the field—whether explicitly expressed or implicitly assumed—because of what amounts to a certain kind of "pollyanna-ism," by which I mean the insistence that as students of religion we must assume the goodness and "value" of religion and that we are consequently responsible for the welfare of the society in which religion plays a role. I direct my attention in turn, therefore, to an adequate response to the prevalence of polymethodism in the field, as well as to an understanding of the proper role of theory as a unifying framework in the academic study of religion. On the former matter, it will be useful, I think, to cite several religious studies scholars to indicate the differing forms this "approach" to the study of religion assumes and I shall point to the rather remarkable methodological—that is, quasi-methodological—tasks imputed by them to the student of religion which warrant comment.

I refer first to the position taken up by Ninian Smart in his essay "Some Thoughts on the Science of Religion" in a volume recently published in honor of Eric Sharpe. Although Smart acknowledges here that most departments and programs of Religious Studies indulge in theological reflection, he nevertheless maintains that there is solid ground for optimism about the future of the Science of Religion. For despite their involvement in matters religious, such departments he maintains at least provide room for a Science of Religion to exist (1996: 24),—all this assuming, apparently, that alternative institutional arrangements are impossible. And in fact he sees an advantage in blending the two, "steer[ing] a middle channel between the Scylla of secret theology and the Charybdis of reductionism" (1996: 20). Such a blending, he mistakenly asserts, would yield "genuinely scientific and objective" results. Despite the danger that "the outside world in academia may . . . misunderstand . . . what the field of Religious Studies is all about—and, categorizing it as some form of tertiary Sunday school, . . . resist it and despise it," (1996: 24) he nevertheless insists that we not narrow our conception of the nature of the field, since in so doing we may forfeit valuable philosophical insights. Where Smart's argument breaks down is in the implicit independent status of the two enterprises—(theologically informed) Religious Studies and the Science of Religion (*Religionswissenschaft*). He may seek to combine them by means of philosophical reflection (Science of Religion + "presentational concerns" = Religious Studies) but fails to identify that the very effort at reconciliation points to a fundamental difference in the essence of and approach to the two subjects. To be fair, what has been referred to here as the Science of Religion doubtless involves scientific study from a number of disciplinary angles—that is, in a variety of sub-disciplines relevant to the study of a range of religious phenomena: religious texts, beliefs, experiences, ritual practices, etc.—and is referred to in the literature, appropriately in this case, as polymethodic or polymethodological. In each of these disciplines, of course, the techniques and methods of analysis are at least empirically or theoretically grounded, whereas the so-called "discipline," described by Smart, created by the blending of Religious Studies and the Science of Religion involves a profusion of imprecise methods derived from incompatible philosophical and ontological frameworks. I therefore refer to the methodological stance of those who support such a study of religion as polymethodism; briefly put, it signifies an attempt to combine within one methodological framework both cognitive and non-cognitive agendas. Nor is Smart's "blending" approach innocuous; on the theoretical front, to claim that the Science of Religion is found at the core of Religious Studies is to taint the former and to cause disciplinary confusion within university departments; on another—financial—front, one must consider the potentially damaging effect upon funding efforts and resource-management when what claims to be a legitimate academic enterprise shows itself participating in realms of social engagement beyond its mandate.

In an essay entitled "South Africa's Contribution to Religious Studies" Martin Prozesky similarly urges the student of religion to stray beyond the academic framework. According to Prozesky, the academic study of religion includes considerably more than the Science of Religion; but his call is not just for a more fulfilling personal engagement—he goes so far as to advocate involvement in socio-political action in order to be true to the discipline. With reference to the political climate in South Africa he writes:

> Amidst all this [political oppression], Religious Studies in our context will damn itself [. . .] if it imagines that all it must do is document, analyze, interpret, and explain the reality of religions in South Africa, for the situation cries out for something more. It cries out for *a new ethic of religions, a new, creatively critical interrogation of religion in relation to both socio-personal liberation and oppression.* [. . .] [T]he field cannot now be credibly studied without prioritizing the problem of religions in the struggle for a more human world order in general, and in the apartheid state in particular. (1990: 10–11)

According to Prozesky, therefore, the task of the student of religion (in South Africa and elsewhere) must go beyond mere description and explanation to "a genuinely liberative praxis" (1990: 18), and it is, therefore, anything but apolitical. For Prozesky, such involvement is a natural by-product of religious commitment; grasping "Truth" and propagating it in a political context can only come to one who is beneficially related to the ultimate and deepest truth of religion; religion is a "humanizing" force so that the study of religion cannot limit itself to the acquisition of objective knowledge about the religious world.

However, Prozesky's insistence upon religious and political "correctness" as corollaries for scientific inquiry—just as Smart's concern for philosophic reflectiveness—will be the undoing of our science, because it is not possible within the framework of our knowledge about religion to muster and mobilize a concerted opinion on political and religious values. A blending of scientific, theological, and political interests, such as would result by adopting the combined ethos of Smart and Prozesky, does not produce scientific knowledge; extending our intellectual interest beyond cognitive matters alone may promote an ideology but never a science. Consequently, the task of the scientific student of religion as a scientist is not a moral or social one; it is merely to describe and explain as comprehensively as possible the phenomenon of religious behavior. If we are to avoid the deterioration of the academic study of religion into a pseudo-science we must leave broader Religious Studies—with its political and social agendas—to the humanists and religious devotees concerned with their place as public intellectuals in the life of society.

Consider in this regard the deliberations of William Dean, in his *Religious Critic in American Culture,* in which he advises "public intellectuals" who currently work in the university—including that religious critic whose primary concern is for religion as it pertains to the well-being of society—to consider the possibility of claiming the universities for themselves should "third sector" organizations outside the university (that is, voluntary as opposed to governmental and commercial institutions) prove an unsatisfactory home for their activities:

> [i]f voluntary organizations of the third sector do not offer the best venue and vehicle for the religious critic, and they may not, then what does? Should more hope be placed in the prospect of a deprofessionalized university? Should greater energy be lodged, after all, in reforming the university, in the effort to make it a viable psychological home and vehicle for the religious critic? (1994: 172)

Most ironic—if not downright frightening—is that many who wish to reclaim the university for their own religious, political, or other ideological agendas do so under the smoke screen of being even more truly scientific than those who hold to a naturalistic concept of science. Kieran Flanagan, for example, argues for an enchantment of the sociology of religion—that is, for a transformation of the sociology of religion into a form of theology—because, he says, "[. . .] a non-praying sociologist is [. . .] a contradiction in terms" (1996: 28). "The study of religion," he maintains, "demands a price of understanding which other belief systems and ideologies do not require. To understand the significance of a religious object or ritual is to contemplate an implication that can be transformative. Knowing what to see and what to read involves a grace of enlightenment, a point illustrated in the case of Phillip and the eunuch" (1996: 30–31). He castigates the strictly non-confessional study of religion as "pseudo-science," "untenable in the context of a reflexive sociology that is becoming positively confessional [and] a hairline away from religious belief and commitment which religious studies spurns" (1996: 92).

A further example: Much like Flanagan, Andre Droogers tries to fashion a methodological position for the student of religion—in this case the anthropology of religion—transcending "religionism and reductionism" and making possible a place for methodological theism. His personal interest in such a perspective is admittedly tied to his dual status as scholar of religion and religious scholar (1996: 51) (and of course it is the insistence on maintaining a dual status that is a central focus of my remarks today):

> As a Christian working in an ecumenical university, holding the chair of the cultural anthropology of religion, and standing in a secular science tradition, it is my job to make sense of religion. It may cause no surprise that I take the religionism/reductionism debate as my test-case and seek to go beyond the established options. (1996: 51)

The secular science tradition apparently sits lightly on him since he claims to have found a way of managing contradictions. Helpful to him in this regard is postmodernism, for by deconstructing science it "has eroded the contrast between science and religion as forms of knowledge" (1996: 60), and in criticizing the dominant scientific meta-narrative it has led "to experiment and openness, with carnival as a leading metaphor" (1996: 60). How this contributes to a scientific study of religion and a cumulative growth of knowledge about religion is hard to determine for according to Droogers, this methodological ludism, as he calls it, entertains various equally valid types of explanation of religion "even though contrasting and exclusive among themselves . . ." (1996: 61).[3]

Perhaps the most sustained effort to reclaim the university for a religio-political agenda is exerted by George Marsden in his *The Soul of the American University: From Protestant Establishment to Established Nonbelief* and his subsequent *The Outrageous Idea of Christian Scholarship*. In the earlier volume Marsden wonders "whether there are adequate grounds for most academics to insist on naturalistic premises that ignore the possibility of fruitful religious perspectives" (1994: 430). Marsden maintains that with the devaluation of neutral science there is no longer a reason to exclude religiously based claims—even divine revelation—from our research and teaching. As he puts it in the later volume, religious people can "reflect on the implications of such revelation within the bounds of the mainstream academy by talking about them conditionally" (1997: 52). They should at least have rights, he insists, similar to those who advocate "feminist, Marxist, liberal democratic, neoconservative, or purely naturalistic views," (1997: 53) ignoring among other things the danger of a concomitant balkanization of the university community into various interest and advocacy groups. This risk he is ready to accept for the sake of his own religious ideals. He insists protectively (and somewhat contradictorily, as it turns out) that, as scholars in the university setting, Christians must live up to "common standards" of practice, but

> [a]t the same time, there are limits to one's allegiance to such rules. Christians cannot play some of the games of society and they cannot accept some of the prevailing rules of other games. Nonetheless, there are many social conventions to which Christians can give limited allegiance. [. . .] Christians must remember that, much as they may value liberal institutions they are participating in them on an ad hoc basis, limited by higher allegiances. [. . .] Deeply religious people should be participating fully in [the] academy and they should be working to improve its rules, particularly those that tend to marginalize their own views. (1997: 56, 57, 58)

As for the study of religion in the academy, he laments what he sees as the attempt to raise the academic credibility by treating religion purely as an object of study and permitting a definition of the field in scientific terms only (1994: 414; 1997: 22). The remedy he seeks is to bring religion with its (Christian) salvific agenda back into the university. That of course would effectively make the university not only unscientific but actually another kind of church.

With the resurgence of religion in modern Western societies and the dominance of postmodernism and deconstructivism in humanities faculties undermining the prestige and role of science and scientific rationality, current conditions on many of our university campuses are most hospitable to the humanist and the religious devotee. And this situation can only hamper the progress of the Science of Religion. A central task for the methodologist in this latter field, therefore, must be to offset the deleterious effects of these developments wherever possible. In part, our response must involve refuting the arguments presented by religious apologists and postmodernists, but this will not in itself suffice; for it is unlikely that an argument drawing upon the resources of the very rationality they have rejected will be accepted as a properly grounded criticism of their stance. We will need to show, I think, that a broader but less-disciplined importation of political, cultural, or other non-cognitive criteria in the adjudication of scientific research simply opens the field to the articulation of individual interests and results in the accumulation of contradictory propositions or unsubstantiated claims about the nature of religion. There can be no cumulative growth of knowledge about religions with such lack of structure and our response to this methodological poverty must begin with identification of its insidious presence in our institutions.

Yet this may not be enough. I believe that we will need to intensify our response and to do this we might take a cue from Bjerknes's activity in the re-founding of meteorological science. To recall Friedman, Bjerknes saw his problem in political terms; he "[. . .] grasped the outlines of a political economy of institutionalized science, and adapted his strategies to the ecological relations within and among disciplines" (1989: 237), and paradoxical as it may sound given my comments above, we too will need to be politically active in our own way within our universities and professional associations if we are not to see our field of research and analysis overcome by politico-religious forces, becoming the avenue through which an ultimately religious agenda is re-established in the curriculum of the modern Western university. According to Friedman, moreover, "[p]assivity was never part of Bjerknes's strategy for achieving professional success" (1989: 179), and we will have to be as active if we are to re-establish the Science of Religion and counteract the "failure of nerve" which has characterized our enterprise for far too long.

First of all, we need to recognize that there is clearly a sense in which the sciences possess a political quality; that is, the very founding (or re-founding) of a science—in this case, the Science of Religion—constitutes a political act. The founders of a science are in some sense political actors because they create the framework—social and economic—within which a particular form of collective life is carried out; they determine acceptable presuppositions, assumptions, and criteria in an attempt to minimize idiosyncrasy and bias in the search for knowledge.[4] The activity which establishes a science is not itself scientific, to be sure, but that does not imply that the action is political in the narrow—party-political or practical—sense of the word. In fact, in establishing a science one creates a discourse about methods for the attainment of knowledge about the world rather than a substantive discourse on behalf of a particular set of cultural-political values within the world.[5]

Maurice Cowling's comments about politics and political science are helpful in sorting out the issues involved in the politics of the study of religion:

> Professors of Political Science who want to engage in political practice (by standing for Parliament, writing in newspapers, advising governments or joining the City Council) are free to do so. But they are, so far as they do this, abandoning their academic function for a practical political one. To do so may, if they are lucky, help them to illuminate the academic subject-matter.

But the only rational action to which scholars are committed, the only moral action to which they are commanded and the only "social responsibility" to which their *professional* position compels them, is to use their energies in order to explain in its full diversity as much as they can of the nature of the world in which they live. (1963: 209–210)

According to Cowling, therefore, failure or refusal to demarcate the study of political behavior from political behavior itself is to preclude all possibility of a political science. It goes without saying that to explain the character of the world constitutes a form of action and is therefore comparable in some broad sense to a form of political action; but explanation carries with it, as Cowling puts it, its "own conventions, rules, and institutions" (1963: 210) which distinguish it from everyday political action. Thus Cowling writes: " . . . it is desirable to rid university faculties of the pretension to be schools of political practice, not because of the confusions this induces in the conduct of politics, but because of the damage it does to universities themselves" (1963: 120).

This confusion of politics and political science is mirrored by the confusion of religion with the study of religion—in both cases we encounter the necessity of distinguishing between partisan action and theoretical discourse. And this confusion is damaging to the university because it involves the subordination of the academy to an agenda not its own—a development corrosive of the very foundations upon which our scientific work proceeds. And this would require of us, I suggest, a mode of political response more closely connected to that variety which culminates in institutionalized action. It is not enough that our methodological effort restrict itself to the techniques and methods involved in the various disciplines and sub-disciplines of our field. We must generate an organized political response. For in my opinion there is a sense in which the departments—and possibly the university itself—are subject to hostile takeover by interests far from scientific. If science, then, is simply another manifestation of what we generally see as formal political action, the university would be but another participant in party politics rather than an enterprise providing objective knowledge of the world (including politics and religion). In such a scenario those who espouse science as traditionally defined would be justified in defending their form of politics, in a party-political fashion, from imperialistic takeover by the politics of their various critics.

In any event, mapping out political action of this kind is, I think, a particularly important aspect of the task of the methodologist in our field. We need, for example, to establish more appropriate relations between our research and that of other established scientific fields, severing all relationship with religious and political interest groups including those which ambiguously (if not insidiously) engage in the kind of Religious Studies described by Smart and Prozesky. We must be far more active in our protection of the university as an institution dedicated to scientific research. Given the current intellectual atmosphere on our campuses this will require reminding university administrators and government officials of the very specific mandate of the modern university and of their responsibility to see that resources are used to that end.

Although discussion of an appropriate political response to the academic expectations with which students of religion should work is important to our methodological discussion, we are just as urgently compelled to address the question of a research program which will bring a measure of unity to the Science of Religion. We must not only reject the polymethodism of programs of Religious Studies of the kind described above; we must refuse to condone even a polymethodological concept of the Science of Religion—the two strategies are clearly complementary. Without theory to analyze independently available descriptions of religious experience, practice, and belief, (as opposed to constructivist views of religion—on lines similar to those of my criticism of Friedman's constructivism above—which make those descriptions the product of theoretical-scientific activity),[6] we cannot be said to vaunt scientific knowledge of religion; so it is to theory above all that we must look if our field is to achieve coherence. I am well aware of those critics of science who, like Paul Feyerabend, insist "[t]he world, including the world of science, is a complex and scattered entity that cannot be captured by theories and simple rules" (1995: 142) but this observation is hardly sufficient grounds for an all-out debunking of theory in our quest for knowledge of the world around us. Feyerabend's complaint, moreover, that theorists are dangerous because they often believe themselves to have found "shortcuts" to understanding nature or society—"[a] few words, a few formulas, and the Secret is revealed" (1995: 93)—is scarcely a fair or persuasive evaluation of the efforts of the history of any field. Theories may be dangerous when they place constraints upon thought, but without such constraint (which I prefer to call "structure") it is not at all clear that knowledge or insight would ever be gained at all; the alternative, an amorphous oracularism, is not a viable alternative to theory. If theories of religion are "dangerous" in the constraints they place upon our thinking about religion, they nonetheless bear the greater chance of understanding data than anything else.

In considering the need for a research program for the study of religion, it is interesting that it is on the strength of evolutionary theory that the Science of Religion initially made an appearance as a new field of research. The nineteenth-century study of religion, Sharpe notes in his history of the discipline, involved a variety of approaches—theological, philosophical, and scholarly—but he rightly argues that those approaches were devoid of a cardinal principle or idea that might somehow tie them together and provide a coherent explanatory account of the data. Each of these approaches, rather, was concerned with "understanding" religion and its value to society. "What was lacking," in all this, he writes, "was . . . one single guiding principle of method which was at the same time able to satisfy the demands of history and of science" (1986: 26). Sharpe correctly points out that it was "evolutionism" which provided the guiding principle which made the emergence of the Science of Religion possible. Here for the first time was an opportunity to understand religion in terms other than religious. Darwinism, that is, made it possible for "the real focus of the study of religion [. . .] to be located, not in transcendental philosophy, but in [. . .] this-worldly categories [. . .]" (1986: 24).

But this early theory of evolution, with its organismic metaphors often attached to simplistic notions of progress, fell into disrepute by the end of the First World War. Fewer scholars found themselves infused with the evolutionary optimism which had permeated the study of religion since the 1870s, and more and more researchers were drawn to "close and detailed studies in a limited area rather than in vast comparisons and synthetic pattern-making," (1986: 174), giving rise to the polymethodic structure which characterizes it to this day—a structure which, I think it could be persuasively argued, permits the field to return to the polymethodism of its "pre-paradigmatic" state. Furthermore, even though there may have been some enrichment of the field by the variety of approaches adopted since this "paradigmatic" phase, it is also clear that much by way of explanatory power has been forfeited. I suggest that we need to reconsider the value of a return to evolutionary theory to re-establish a unifying framework for the study of religion. Making a convincing case for this is not really possible here, because it would require not only a thorough analysis of the reasons for the rejection earlier this century of evolutionary theory as a framework but also a detailed account of how neo-Darwinian theory can actually help explain religious phenomena. But I would like at least to provide some indication of why I think the theory worth further consideration.

Daniel Dennett's analysis of the explanatory capacity of evolutionary theory in *Darwin's Dangerous Idea*, I think, provides a solid case for the application of the theory not only to biological but also to cultural phenomena. The materialistic perspective of modern evolutionary theory, he argues diminishes the sharp divide many think separates *Naturwissenschaften* from the *Geisteswissenschaften*. As he puts it, "[i]f there is just one Design Space [. . .] in which the offspring of both our bodies and our minds are united under one commodious set of R-and-D processes, then [the] traditional walls [between the two] may tumble" (1995: 189). Given that perspective, he then argues, "the central biological concept of function and the central philosophical concept of meaning can be explained and united" (1995: 185). And if this is so, then "all the achievements of human culture—language, art, religion, ethics, science itself—are themselves artifacts [. . .] of the same fundamental process. There is no Special Creation of language, and neither art nor religion has a literally divine inspiration" (1995: 144).

Dennett has not himself applied this explanatory approach to religious phenomena; there are a number of scholars, however, who have demonstrated the benefits to be gained from such theoretical analyses. Dan Sperber's work, for example, on the epidemiology of beliefs shows that a naturalistic and materialistic program for social science is more than merely conceivable; in fact, it is clearly superior to the holistic hermeneutical approaches which methodologically isolate social science, for it "establishes fundamental continuities between its domain and that of one or several neighbouring natural sciences" (1996: 5). His own attempt to account for cultural realities, therefore, is to treat culture as "the precipitate of cognition and communication in a human culture," (1996: 97) for then it is possible to find genuine material causes of culture rather than "attribut[ing] causal powers to entities such as institutions or ideologies" (1996: 99). The adoption of such a framework of explanation and the application of such techniques of analysis are fruitfully applied specifically to religious phenomena in a number of recent works by E. Thomas Lawson and Robert McCauley (1990), Pascal Boyer (1994), Ann Baranowski (1994), Luther H. Martin (1997), Stewart Guthrie (1993), and Walter Burkert (1996) among others, and are very suggestive of the benefits to be gained by the Science of Religion in a renewed emphasis upon theory. These scholars, like Bjerknes, have obviously "grasped the outlines of a political economy of the sciences" and have been able to exploit that economy in the aid of generating genuine explanations of religious phenomena. We can recognize, at least, a general agreement that whatever religion is, if we are ever to understand it, we will have to study it not simply empirically but also theoretically.

Notes

1. I wish to thank Tom Settle for his critical comments on earlier draft of this essay and to Luther Martin who took it upon himself to comment on several drafts. I also thank Martha Cunningham for her generous editorial assistance.
2. I have made a case for Müller and Tiele as founders of the modern Science of Religion in separate essays; see Wiebe 1995a (chapter 2 in this volume) and 1996 (chapter 3 in this volume).
3. The entire volume in which Droogers's paper appears is committed to the claim that "at the level of the disciplines there is no unquestioned belief in

the conflict-transcending objectivity of the social sciences" (1996: i) and many of the authors take this judgment as grounds on which to intrude their religious commitments into their academic work. For example, Droogers's colleague in the Free University of Amsterdam, Philip Quarles van Ufford, leaves the reader in no doubt about his position: "Knowledge at its most reliable arises when silently we open ourselves and acknowledge our contingencies, allowing for the presence of God" (1996: 42).

4. On this matter see Sheldon Wolin's treatment of Max Weber as founder of the social sciences (1981). For him, founding is political theorizing and he maintains that for Weber methodology served "not simply as a guide to investigation but as a moral practice and a mode of political action" (414), because it was primarily concerned with "the disenchanted world and its meaninglessness" (417). Wolin writes:

> The inherent limitations of science, its inability to make good the deficiencies of the world's meaning, provide the backdrop to the political role of the methodologist. His task is not to undertake scientific investigations or even to instruct his co-workers on how best to conduct research, much less to offer a special field of study. Rather it is to show them that significant action in their chosen realm is possible. It is, therefore, a form of political education in the meaning of vocation. Its politicalness comes from the seriousness, even urgency, of the relationship between vocational action and the world. (416)

I disagree with Wolin's interpretation of Weber's "Science as a Vocation" but there is no need to deal with that matter here.

5. K. S. Tranöy (1976), although accepting that "[p]rofessional knowledge seekers are a sub-culture [and therefore] one of the specialized tribes of the world" (7), insists that (what he calls) the "ideology of inquiry" must involve both internal and external norms of inquiry, that is, both methodological norms and policy norms. The former govern scientific research while the latter relate to issues of education and the application of the results of research. "Methodological norms and values," he writes, "do not suffice to legitimate all types of actions and activities involved in inquiry defined as the search for, and the acquisition and communication of knowledge" (3). He does not, however, provide a persuasive argument for adopting such a definition of inquiry but merely suggests that "no reasonable person ever [thought] that science and educational policies could and should be *wertfrei* and 'value neutral' [. . .]" (4). It seems to me, however, that this is precisely what Ernest Gellner (1973) maintains in his argument that the establishment of science entails the creation of the new value of objective knowledge, wholly unconnected with other political, cultural, and religious values. For Gellner, science only emerges because it has somehow obtained a "diplomatic immunity" from other values; science is knowledge for the sake of knowledge alone and is, therefore, discontinuous with other cultural values. (I have dealt with this matter at greater length in my book *The Irony of Theology and*

the Nature of Religious Thought [1991]). If this kind of argument is persuasive, then Tranöy should concede the argument I develop here. He writes:

> If these two sub-sets of the ideology of inquiry, methodological norms and policy norms, are completely separate, then a traditional and now so often disputed view of science is not only defensible but incontrovertible. [. . .]. If the two activities are thus normatively distinct, this means that responsibility in science can be divided between two distinct sets of people. The active scientist is and should be guided and legitimated by methodological norms. Others will worry about science policy and the application of results. (5, 6)

6. There are a number of scholars who take a constructivist view of religion, arguing that religion is the product of the scholar's attention rather than an independent or autonomous reality. Russell McCutcheon (1997), for example, argues such a case against Eliade and his followers who claim religion to be a *sui generis* reality. Although I agree with McCutcheon's critique of the notion of religion as wholly autonomous with respect to other aspects of our social and cultural existence it seems to me unwarranted to claim that religion is therefore the product of the scholar's study. Surely it is the product of human activity long before scholarly attention is focussed upon it; indeed, only if that were so, could we pay such attention to it.

References

Ackerman, Robert. 1987. *J. G. Frazer: His Life and Work.* Cambridge: Cambridge University Press.

———. 1991. *The Myth and Ritual School: J. G. Frazer and the Cambridge Ritualists.* New York: Garland Publishing Inc.

Adams, Charles. 1975. Memorandum to School of Graduate Studies (SGS) Dean A. E. Safarian. "Appraisal for the University of Toronto Proposal to Offer M.A. and Ph.D. Degrees in Religious Studies." 15pp.

Advisory Committee on Academic Planning, Ontario Council on Graduate Studies. 1974. *Perspectives and Plans for Graduate Studies. Vol. 12. Religious Studies.* Toronto: Council of Ontario Universities.

Alexander, Kathryn O. 1988. "Religious Studies in American Higher Education Since Schempp: A Bibliographic Essay." *Soundings* 71: 389–412.

Allen, Charlotte. 1996. "Is Nothing Sacred? Casting Out the Gods from Religious Studies." *Lingua Franca:* 30–40.

Allen, Douglas. 1987. "Phenomenology of Religion," in Mircea Eliade, et al., eds., *Encyclopedia of Religion.* New York: Macmillan Publishing Company, Vol. 11: 272–285.

Altizer, T. J. J. 1961. *Oriental Mysticism and Biblical Eschatology.* Philadelphia: Westminster Press.

Alton, Bruce. 1986. "Method and Reduction in the Study of Religion." *Studies in Religion.* 5: 153–164.

Anderson, Charles P. 1972. *Guide to Religious Studies in Canada.* 3rd edition. Toronto: Corporation for the Publication of Academic Studies in Canada.

Aron, Raymond. 1967. *Main Currents in Sociological Thought,* Vol. 2. trans. R. Howard and H. Weaver. London: Weidenfeld and Nicholson.

———. 1985. "Max Weber and Modern Social Science," in Franciszek Draus, ed. *History, Truth, Liberty: Selected Writings of Raymond Aron.* Chicago: University of Chicago Press, 335–373.

Badertscher, John M., Gordon Harland, and Roland E. Miller. 1993. *Religious Studies in Manitoba and Saskatchewan: A State-of-the-Art Review.* Waterloo: Wilfrid Laurier University Press.

Baillie, John. 1936. *The Interpretation of Religion: An Introductory Study of Theological Principles* [1928]. New York: Charles Scribner's Sons.

Baird, J. Arthur. 1961. "The Lilly Endowment Study of Pre-Seminary Education." *Journal of Bible and Religion.* 29: 16–19.

———. 1972. *Category Formation and the History of Religions.* Berlin: Mouton.

Banman, Christina. 1989. "The Study of Religion: Nineteenth Century Sources and Twentieth Century Misconceptions." *Method and Theory in the Study of Religion.* 1: 160–185.

Baranowski, Ann. 1994 *Ritual Alone: Cognition and Meaning of Patterns in Time.* Toronto: Unpublished doctoral dissertation.

———. 1998. "A Psychology of Ritual and Musical Meaning." *Method and Theory in the Study of Religion* 10 (1): 3–29.

Barker, Eileen. 1983. "Supping With the Devil." *Sociological Analysis.* 44: 197–205.

Barrows, John Henry. 1993. "Results of the Parliament of Religions." in Eric J. Ziolkowski, ed., *A Museum of Faiths: Histories and Legacies of the 1893 World's Parliament of Religions.* Atlanta GA: Scholars Press, 131–147.

Bartholomeusz, Tessa. 1993. "Dharmapala at Chicago: Mahayana Buddhist or Sinhala Chauvinist?" in Eric J. Ziolkowski, ed., *A Museum of Faiths: Histories and Legacies of the 1893 World's Parliament of Religion.* Atlanta GA: Scholar's Press. 235–250.

Bartley, William Warren. 1962. *Retreat to Commitment.* New York: Alfred Knopf.

Baum, G., Kenneth Hamilton, William O. Fennell, Paul Younger, and William Hordern. 1975. "Responses to Charles Davis." *Studies in Religion.* 4: 222–236.

Baum, Gregory. 1990. "Religious Studies and Theology." *Journal of Theology for Southern Africa.* 70: 2–8.

Beardslee, William A. 1966. "The Background of the Lilly Endowment Study of Pre-Seminary Education." *The Journal of Bible and Religion.* 34: 98–105.

Beck, Dwight M. 1961. "Letter to the Editor." *Journal of Bible and Religion.* 29: 361.

Beckford, James A. 1983. "Some Questions About the Relationship Between Scholars and the New Religious Movements." *Sociological Analysis.* 44: 189–195.

Bellah, R. N. 1970a. "Christianity and Symbolic Realism." *Journal for the Scientific Study of Religion.* 9: 89–96.

———. 1970b. "Response to Comments on 'Christianity and Symbolic Realism'." *Journal for the Scientific Study of Religion.* 9: 111–115.

———. 1970c. "Confessions of a Former Establishment Fundamentalist." *Bulletin of the Council of Societies for the Study of Religion.* 1: 3–6.

———. 1972. "Religion in the University: Chancing Consciousness, Changing Structures," in Claude Welch, ed., *Religion in the Undergraduate Curriculum.* Washington: Association of American Colleges, 13–18.

———. 1978. "Religious Studies as 'New Religion'," in J. Needleman and G. Baker, eds., *Understanding the New Religions.* New York: Seabury Press. 106–112.

Benson, Thomas. 1987. "Religious Studies as an Academic Discipline," in Mircea Eliade, et al., eds., *Encyclopedia of Religion.* New York: Macmillan Publishing Company, Vol. 14: 88–92.

Berling, Judith A. 1993. "Is Conversation about Religion Possible?" *Journal of the American Academy of Religion.* 61: 1–22.

Bianchi, Ugo. 1987. "History of Religions," in Mircea Eliade, et al., eds., *Encyclopedia of Religion.* New York: Macmillan Publishing Company, Vol. 6: 399–408.

Bleeker, C.J. 1954. "The Relation of the History of Religions to Kindred Religious Sciences, Particularly Theology, Sociology of Religion, Psychology of Religion and Phenomenology of Religion." *Numen.* 1: 142–152.

————. 1961. "The Future of the History of Religions," in G. Schröder, ed., *X. Internationaler Kongress fur Religionsgeschichte*. Marburg: N. G. Elwert, 229–240.

————. 1963. "The Phenomenological Method," in C. J. Bleeker, ed., *The Sacred Bridge*. Leiden: E.J. Brill 1–15.

————. 1968. "Opening Address" in *Proceedings of the XIth International Congress of the IAHR*, Vol. 1, *The Impact of Modern Culture on Traditional Religions*. Leiden: E.J. Brill: 3–12.

————. 1971. "Comparing the Religio-Historical and the Theological Method." *Numen* 18: 9–29.

————. 1972. "The Contribution of the Phenomenology of Religion to the Study of the History of Religions," in U. Bianchi, C. J. Bleeker and A. Bausani, eds., *Problems and Methods in the History of Religions*. Leiden: E. J. Brill. 35–54.

————. 1975. *The History of Religions: 1950–1975. The Organized Study of the History of Religions During a Quarter of a Century*. Lancaster: University of Lancaster Press. (Presented on the occasion of the 13th Congress of the International Association for the History of Religions.)

————. 1979. "Commentary," in: Lauri Honko, (ed.), *Science of Religion: Studies in Methodology;* 173–177. The Hague: Mouton Publishers.

Blumental, D.R. 1977. "Judaic Studies: An Exercise in the Humanities," in *Response at the Inauguration of the Jay and Leslie Cohen Chair of Judaic Studies*. Atlanta GA: Emory University Press, 23–39.

Bolle, K. W. 1967. "History of Religions with a Hermeneutic Oriented Toward Christian Theology?," in Mircea Eliade, Joseph Kitagawa and Charles Long, eds., *The History of Religions: Essays on the Problem of Understanding*. Chicago: University of Chicago Press, 89–118.

Boyer, Pascal, ed. 1993. *Cognitive Aspects of Religious Symbolism*. Cambridge: Cambridge University Press.

————. 1994. *The Naturalness of Religious Ideas: A Cognitive Theory of Religion*. Los Angeles: University of California Press.

Brauer, Jerald C. 1985. "Mircea Eliade and the Divinity School." *Criterion* 24: 23–27.

Brubaker, Lauren E. 1960. *Journal of Bible and Religion*. 28: 161–166.

Buck, Harry M. Jr. 1962. "The Association and Its Public Image." *The Journal of Bible and Religion*. 30: 2.

Burkert, Walter. 1983. *Homo Necans: the Anthropology of Ancient Greek Sacrificial Ritual and Myth*. trans Peter Bing. Los Angeles: University of California Press.

————. 1996. *Creation of the Sacred: Tracks of Biology in Early Religions*. Cambridge, Mass.: Harvard University Press.

Burkle, Howard R. 1981. "Tillich's 'Dynamic-Typological' Approach to the History of Religions." *Journal of the American Academy of Religion*. 49: 175–185.

Burrell, David. 1983. "Faith and Religious Convictions: Studies in Comparative Epistemology." *The Journal of Religion*. 63: 64–73.

Burtchaell, James Tunstead. 1970. "A Response to 'Christianity and Symbolic Realism'." *Journal of the Scientific Study of Religion*. 9: 97–111.

————. 1971. "The Rituals of Jesus, the Anti-Ritualist." *Journal of the American Academy of Religion*. 39: 513–525.

Byrne, Peter. 1989. *Natural Religion and the Nature of Religion: The Legacy of Deism.* London: Routledge.

———. 1997. "The Study of Religion: Neutral, Scientific or Neither?," *Method and Theory in the Study of Religion.* 9:335–351.

Cady, Linell E. 1993. *Religion, Theology, and American Public Life.* Albany: State University of New York Press.

Cain, Seymour. 1987. "History of Study," in Mircea Eliade, et al., eds., *Encyclopedia of Religion.* New York: Macmillan Publishing Company, Vol. 14: 64–83.

Capps, Walter. 1974. "On Religious Studies, In Lieu of an Overview." *Journal of the American Academy of Religion.* 42: 727–733. (Part of "A Forum on the Study of Religion" which included contributions from Randy Huntsberry and Benjamin Ladner.)

———. 1978a. "Religious Studies in an Age of Limits: Notes from the Wingspread Conference [held by the Council on the Study of Religion and the Institute of Religious Studies, Santa Barbara, CA, 16–18 Feb.]. Report to the Council on the Study of Religion." Typescript. 17pp.

———. 1978b. "The Interpenetration of New Religions and Religious Studies," in J. Needleman and G. Baker, eds., *Understanding New Religions.* New York: Seabury Press, 101–105.

———. 1981. "Contemporary Socio-Political Change and the Work of Religious Studies." *Bulletin of the Council on the Study of Religion* 12: 93–95.

———. 1987. "A Response to Dr. Strenski." *Journal of the American Academy of Religion.* 55: 125–126.

———. 1995. *Religious Studies: The Making of a Discipline.* Minneapolis: Fortress Press.

Carman, John B. 1965. "The Theology of a Phenomenologist: An Introduction to the Theology of Gerardus van der Leeuw." *Harvard Divinity Bulletin.* 29: 31–42.

———. 1971. "Inter-Faith Dialogue and Academic Study of Religion," in S. J. Samartha, ed., *Dialogue Between Men of Living Faiths.* Geneva: World Council of Churches, 81–86.

Chantepie de la Saussaye, P. D. 1891. *Manual of the Science of Religion.* trans. Beatrice S. Colyer-Fergusson (née Max Müller). London: Longmans, Green and Co.

Cherry, Conrad. 1989. "Boundaries and Frontiers for the Study of Religion: The Heritage of the Age of the University." *Journal of the American Academy of Religion* 57/4: 807–827.

———. 1992. "The Study of Religion and the Rise of the American University," in Joseph M. Kitagawa, ed., *Religious Studies, Theological Studies, and the University Divinity School.* Atlanta, GA: Scholars Press, 137–150.

———. 1995. *Hurrying Toward Zion: Universities, Divinity Schools, and American Protestantism.* Bloomington: Indiana University Press.

Chidester, David. 1987. "Religious Studies as Political Practice." *Journal of Theology for Southern Africa.* 58: 4–17.

Clark, Elizabeth A. 1991. "Sex, Shame, and Rhetoric: En-gendering Early Christian Ethics." *Journal of the American Academy of Religion.* 59: 221–245.

Clebsch, William A. 1981. "Apples, Oranges, and Manna: Comparative Religion Revisited." *Journal of the American Academy of Religion.* 49: 3–22.

Clifford, N. Keith. 1991. "Church History, Religious History, or the History of Religions?" in K. K. Klostermaier and Larry W. Hurtado, eds., *Religious Studies: Issues, Prospects and Proposals*. Atlanta: Scholars Press, 171–181.

Cook, David. 3 Jan. 1994a. Letter to D. Wiebe. 1p.

———. 10 Jan. 1994b. Letter to D. Wiebe. 1p.

———. 20 Jan. 1994c. Letter to D. Wiebe. 1p.

Coward, Harold. Jan. 1986. Submission to SGS Dean Leyerle. "Report on the Centre for Religious Studies." Typescript. 13pp.

———. 1991. "The Contribution of Religious Studies to Secular Universities in Canada." in K. K. Klostermaier and Larry W. Hurtado, eds., *Religious Studies: Issues, Prospects and Proposals*. Atlanta: Scholars Press, 17–37.

Cowling, Maurice. 1963. *The Nature and Limits of Political Science*. Cambridge: Cambridge University Press.

Crites, Stephen D. 1990. "The Religion Major: A Report." Syracuse, N.Y.: American Academy of Religion.

D'Arcy, M. C. 1939. "The Philosophy of Religion," in Kenneth S. Kirk, ed., *The Study of Theology*. London: Hodder and Stoughton, 121–147.

Darrow, William R. 1988. "The Harvard Way in the Study of Religion." *Harvard Theological Review*: 215–234.

Davis, Charles. 1975. "The Reconvergence of Theology and Religious Studies." *Studies in Religion*. 4: 205–221.

———. 1981. "Theology and Religious Studies." *Scottish Journal of Religious Studies*. 2: 11–20.

———. 1984. "Wherein There is No Ecstasy." *Studies in Religion*. 13: 393–400.

———. 1986. "The Immanence of Knowledge and the Ecstasy of Faith." *Studies in Religion*. 15: 191–196.

Dawson, C. 1948. "Natural Theology and the Scientific Study of Religion,"in C. Dawson, *Religion and Culture*. London: Sheed and Ward, 3–22.

Dawson, Lorne. 1986. "Neither Nerve nor Ecstasy: Comment on the Wiebe-Davis Exchange." *Studies in Religion*. 15: 145–151.

Dean, William. 1994. *The Religious Critic in American Culture*. Albany: State University of New York Press.

De Concini, Barbara (with Catherine L. Albanese, Judith Berling, Delwin Brown, Warren G. Frisinia, William Scott Green, Robert C. Monk, Robert C. Neville, Susan Brooks Thistlewaite, Raymond Williams, and Edith Wyschogrod). 1993a. "AAR Self-Study Committee Findings [Part I]," *Religious Studies News* 8(3): 2, 4.

——— (with Catherine Albanese, Judith Berling, Delwin Brown, Warren G. Frisinia, William Scott Green, Robert C. Monk, Robert C. Neville, Susan Brooks Thistlewaite, Raymond Williams, and Edith Wyschogrod). 1993b. "AAR Self-Study Committee Findings [Part II]," *Religious Studies News*. 8(4): 10 and 14.

de Harlez, Charles Joseph. 1993. "The Comparative Study of the World's Religions," in E. J. Ziolkowski, ed., *A Museum of Faiths: Histories and Legacies of the 1893 World's Parliaments of Religions*. Atlanta, GA: Scholars Press, 95–110.

Dennett, Daniel. 1995 *Darwin's Dangerous Idea: Evolution and the Meaning of Life*. New York: Simon and Schuster.

de Vries, J. 1967. *The Study of Religion: A Historical Approach.* trans. Kees Bolle. New York: Harcourt, Brace and World.

Dillenberger, John. 1988. "Visual Arts and Religion: Modern and Contemporary Contours." *Journal of the American Academy of Religion.* 56: 199–212.

Dow, James R. and Hannjost Lixfeld, eds. and trans. 1994. *The Nazification of an Academic Discipline: Folklore in the Third Reich.* Bloomington: Indiana University Press.

Downing, Christine. 1975. "Sigmund Freud and the Greek Mythological Tradition." *Journal of the American Academy of Religion.* 43: 3–14.

Drobin, U. 1982. "Psychology, Philosophy, Theology, Epistemology—Some Reflections," in Nils G. Golm, ed., *Religious Ecstasy.* Stockholm: University of Stockholm Press, 263–274.

Droogers, André. 1996 "Methodological Ludism: Beyond Religionism and Reductionism." in: Anton van Harskamp, (ed.), *Conflicts in Social Science;* London: Routledge, 44–77.

Drummond, Ian, Howard Clark Kee, and Joseph McClelland. Nov. 1984. Report submitted by U. of T. Assistant Dean of Arts and Science Ian Drummond. "Department of Religious Studies Review." Typescript. 6pp.

Drummond, R. H. 1975. "Christian Theology and the History of Religions." *Journal of Ecumenical Studies.* 12: 389–405.

Duckworth, H. E., Van Harvey, and Ninian Smart. 1974a. "Report of the Religious Studies Consultants to the Advisory Committee on Academic Planning, Ontario Council on Graduate Studies, on Graduate Programmes in Religious Studies in Ontario," in Advisory Committee on Academic Planning, Ontario Council on Graduate Studies. *Perspectives and Plans for Graduate Studies 12* (Toronto: Council of Ontario Universities) Appendix A, A1-A33.

———. 1974b. "Reply of Consultants to ACAP Letter of June 5 [1974]," in Advisory Committee on Academic Planning, Ontario Council on Graduate Studies. *Perspectives and Plans for Graduate Studies.* Toronto: (Council of Ontario Universities) Appendix C, C21-C24.

Eckardt, A. Roy (with J. Arthur Baird, John L. Cheek, Earl Cranston, J. Allen Easley, Edward C. Hobbs and Walter G. Williams, Walter G.) 1959. "Pre-Seminary Preparation and Study in Religion." *Journal of Bible and Religion.* 27: 139-142. (Republished in *Journal of Bible and Religion,* 1966, 34: 166–170.)

———. 1957. "The Strangeness of Religion in the University Curriculum." *The Journal of Bible and Religion.* 25: 3–12.

———. 1962. "In Defense of Religion-in-General." *The Journal of Bible and Religion.* 30: 185.

———. 1963. " 'Theology' versus 'Religion'." *The Journal of Bible and Religion.* 31: 95–97.

———. 1965a. "An Identity Explored." *The Journal of Bible and Religion.* 33: 3–4.

———. 1965b. "On Independence in Undergraduate Study." *The Journal of Bible and Religion.* 33: 291–292.

———. 1966a. "Is the Study of Religion Peculiar?" *The Journal of Bible and Religion.* 34: 96–97.

————. 1966b. "Is There Anything Religious in Religion?" *The Journal of Bible and Religion.* 34: 303.

Edsman, Carl-Martin. 1974. "Theology or Religious Studies?" *Religion* 4: 59–74.

Eliade, Mircea. 1969. *The Quest: History and Meaning in Religion.* Chicago: University of Chicago Press.

————. 1977. *No Souvenirs: Journal 1957–1969.* New York: Harper and Row.

————, ed. (with Charles Adams, Joseph M. Kitagawa, Martin E. Marty, Richard P. McBrien, Jacob Needleman, Annemarie Schimmel, Robert M. Seltzer, and Victor Turner). 1987a. *Encyclopedia of Religion.* 16 Vols. New York: Macmillan Publishing Company.

————. 1987b. "Preface," in Mircea Eliade, et al. eds., *Encyclopedia of Religion.* New York: Macmillan Publishing Company, Vol. 1: ix-xii.

Farnell, Lewis. 1934. *An Oxonian Looks Back.* London: Martin Hopkinson Ltd.

Fellman, David. 1984. "Religion, the State and the Public University." *Journal of Church and State* 26: 73–90.

Flew, A. 1972. "The Presumption of Atheism." *Canadian Journal of Philosophy.* 2: 29–46.

Feyerabend, Paul. 1995 *Killing Time: The Autobiography of Paul Feyerabend.* Chicago: University of Chicago Press.

Flanagan, Kieran. 1996 *The Enchantment of Sociology: A Study of Theology and Culture.* New York: St. Martin's Press.

Foley, J. E. 1990. Memorandum from U. of T. Provost. "Provostial Task Force on Religious Studies." 1p.

Friedman, Robert Marc. 1989 *Appropriating the Weather: Vilhelm Bjerknes and the Construction of a Modern Meteorology.* Ithaca: Cornell University Press.

Friedrichs, Robert W. 1974. "Social Research and Theology: End of Detente?" *Review of Religious Research.* 15: 113–27.

Frisinia, Warren. 1993a. "Barbara Deconini on the AAR's Self-Study [an Interview]." *Religious Studies News.* 8/3: 5.

————. 1993b. "AAR Board Adopts New Mission Statement, Sets Goals for the Future." *Religious Studies News.* 8: 1–2.

————. 1994. "Stability in Times of Trouble: University of Vermont Religion Department, [Interview with Professor William Paden, Chair.]." *Religious Studies News.* 9/3: 6–7.

Galloway, A. D. 1975. "Theology and Religious Studies—The Unity of Our Discipline." *Religious Studies.* 11: 157–165.

Gamwell, Franklin J. 1985. "Opening Remarks on the Occasion of the Establishment of the Mircea Eliade Chair in the History of Religions." *Criterion* 24: 18–19.

Gaultieri, A. R. 1981. " 'Faith, Belief and Transcendence' According to Wilfred Cantwell Smith." *Journal of Dharma.* 6: 239–252.

Gay, Peter. 1966. *The Enlightenment: An Interpretation. The Rise of Modern Paganism.* New York: Random House.

Geertz, Clifford. 1973. *The Interpretation of Culture, Selected Essays.* New York: Basic Books.

————. 1983. *Local Knowledge: Further Essays in Interpretive Anthropology.* New York: Basic Books.

Gellner, Ernest. 1973. "The Savage and the Modern Mind." in: Robin Horton and Ruth Finnegan, (eds.), *Modes of Thought: Essays on Thinking in Western and Non-Western Societies,* 162–181. London: Faber and Faber.

————. 1988. "The Stakes in Anthropology." *The American Scholar.* 57: 17–30.

Gilkey, Langdon. 1980. "The AAR and the Anxiety of Nonbeing: An Analysis of Our Present Cultural Situation." *Journal of the American Academy of Religion.* 48: 5–18.

Gilpin, W. Clark. 1996. *A Preface to Theology.* Chicago: University of Chicago Press.

Girardot, N.J. and M. L. Ricketts, eds., 1982. *Imagination and Meaning: The Scholarly and Literary Worlds of Mircea Eliade.* New York: Seabury Press.

Gooch, Paul W. 24 Sept. 1987a. Letter to D. Wiebe (including draft statement "The CRS and a Possible Graduate Department of Theology.") 3pp.

————. 5 Oct. 1987b. Memorandum to the SGS. "The CRS and a Proposed Graduate Department of Theology." 1p.

————. 8 Oct. 1987c. Letter to D. Wiebe. 1p.

————. 16 Oct. 1987d. Memorandum to SGS. "Re: Meeting of 30 October 1987 about Possible Graduate Department of Theology." 1p.

————. 30 Oct. 1987e. Memorandum to SGS. "Discussion of Proposed Graduate Department of Theology." 10pp.

————. 11 Dec. 1987f. Memorandum. "Response to Questions about a Graduate Department of Theology." 2pp.

Goodenough, E. R. 1959. "*Religionswissenshaft.*" *Numen.* 6: 77–95.

Green, William S. 22 May 1992. "Is Theology Academic?" *Sh'ma: A Journal of Jewish Responsibility* 22: 102–104.

————, ed. 1994a. *Settled Issues and Neglected Questions in the Study of Religion. Journal of the American Academy of Religion* 62 (Special Issue).

————. 1994b. "The Difference Religion Makes." *Journal of the American Academy of Religion* 62: 1191–1206.

————. November/December 1996. "Religion Within the Limits." *Academe: Bulletin of the American Association of University Professors:* 24–28.

Gualtieri, A.R. 1968. "Descriptive and Evaluative Formulae for Comparative Religion." *Theological Studies.* 2: 52–71.

————. 1969. "Faith, Tradition and Transcendence: A Study of Wilfred Cantwell Smith." *Canadian Journal of Theology.* 15: 102–111.

————. 1972. "Confessional Theology in the Context of the History of Religions." *Studies in Religion.* 2: 347–360.

————. 1979. "Normative and Descriptive in the Study of Religion." *Journal of Dharma.* 4: 8–21.

————. 1993. *Faces in the Clouds: A New Theory of Religion.* New York: Oxford University Press.

Hahn, Herbert F. 1956. *The Old Testament in Modern Research.* London: SCM Press.

Harrison, Peter. 1990. *'Religion' and the Religions in the English Enlightenment.* Cambridge: Cambridge University Press.

Harland, Gordon. 1991. "Religious Studies in a Time of Change and Conflict." in K. K. Klostermaier and Larry W. Hurtado, eds., *Religious Studies: Issues, Prospects and Proposals.* Atlanta: Scholars Press, 1–13.

Hart, D. G. 1992. "American Learning and the Problem of Religious Studies," in G. M. Marsden and B. J. Longfield, eds., *The Secularization of the Academy.* Oxford: Oxford University Press, 195–233.

Hart, Ray L. 1985. "To Be and Not to Be: *Sit Autem Sermo (Logos) Vester, Est, Est; Non, Non. . . ." Journal of the American Academy of Religion.* 53: 5–22.

———. 1991. "Religious and Theological Studies in American Higher Education." *Journal of the American Academy of Religion* 69: 715–827.

Harvey, Van A. 1970. "Reflections on the Teaching of Religion in America." *Journal of the American Academy of Religion* 38: 17–29.

Hastings, James, ed., (with the assistance of John A. Selbie and Louis H. Gray). 1908–1926. *Encyclopedia of Religion and Ethics,* 13 Vols. Edinburg: T. and T. Clark.

Hebblethwaite, B. 1980. "Theology and Comparative Religion," in B. Hebblethwaite, *The Problems of Theology.* Cambridge: Cambridge University Press, 23–43.

Henaut, Barry W. 1986. "Empty Tomb or Empty Argument: A Failure of Nerve in Recent Studies of Mark 16?" *Studies in Religion.* 15: 177–190.

Holbrook, C. A. 1963. *Religion: A Humanistic Field.* Englewood Cliffs: Prentice-Hall Inc.

———. 1964a. "Why an Academy of Religion?" *Journal of the American Academy of Religion* 32: 97–105. (Reprinted with a remembrance by William Harman, *Journal of the American Academy of Religion* 1991. 59:373–387.)

———. 1964b. "Mr. Schlatter's Dilemma Re-examined." *The Journal of Bible and Religion.* 32: 262–265.

———. 1966. "The Lilly Study: Challenge to College and Seminary." *The Journal of Bible and Religion.* 34: 157–165.

Holley, R. 1978. *Religious Education and Religious Understanding.* London: Routledge & Kegan Paul.

Hook, S. 1961. *The Quest for Being.* New York: St. Martin's Press.

Horowitz, Irving Louis. 1983a. "Symposium on Scholarship and Sponsorship: Universal Sandards, Not Uniform Beliefs." *Sociological Analysis.* 44: 179–182.

———. 1983b. "A Reply to Critics and Crusaders." *Sociological Analysis.* 44: 221–225.

Hultkrantz, Ake. 1970. "The Phenomenology of Religion: Aims and Methods." *Temonos.* 6: 68–88.

Hume, David. 1967. The Natural History of Religion [1757]. Stanford: Stanford Univerisity Press.

Huntsberry, Randy. 1974. "Secular Education and Its Religion." *Journal of the American Academy of Religion.* 42: 733–738. (Part of "A Forum on the Study of Religion in the University" which included contributions from Walter Capps and Benjamin Ladner.)

Iannucci, Amilcare, Roger Beck, Catherine Grisé, Rika Maniates, Joanne McWilliam, Nicola Denzy, Amir Hussain, Neil McMullin, and Peter Richardson.

March, 1991. Submission to U. of T. Provost. "Report of the Task Force on Religious Studies." Typescript. 12pp.

Inglis, Fred. 1993. *Cultural Studies.* Oxford: Blackwell.

Jaffee, Martin. 1997. "Fessing Up in Theory: On *Pro*fessing and *Con*fessing in the Religious Studies Classroom." *Method and Theory in the Study of Religion.* 9: 339–351.

James, George A. 1985. "Phenomenology and the Study of Religion: The Archaeology of an Approach." *Journal of Religion.* 65: 311–335.

Jastrow, Jr., M. 1981. *The Study of Religion.* Chico, CA: Scholars Press.

Jay, Douglas. 17 March, 1986. Memorandum to Marion Wyse. Wyse personal papers. 2pp.

Jeffner, A. 1981. "Religion and Understanding." *Religious Studies.* 17: 217–225.

Jordan, Louis. 1905. *Comparative Religion: Its Genesis and Growth.* Edinburgh: T. & T. Clark.

Katz, Steven. Feb. 1986. Submission to SGS Dean Leyrle. "Review of the Graduate Centre for Religious Studies." 11pp.

Katz, Wilber G. 1967. "Religious Studies in State Universities: The New Legal Climate," in Milton D. McLean, ed., *Religious Studies in Public Universities.* Carbondale, Illinois: Southern Illinois University Press, 15–21.

Kaufman, G.D. 1983. "Nuclear Eschatology and the Study of Religion." *Journal of the American Academy of Religion.* 51: 3–14.

Kegley, C.W. 1978. "Theology and Religious Studies: Friends or Enemies?" *Theology Today* 35: 273–284.

Ketalaar, James Edward. 1993. "The Reconvening of Babel," in Eric J. Ziolkowski, ed. *A Museum of Faiths: Histories and Legacies of the 1893 World's Parliament of Religions.* Atlanta GA: Scholars Press. 251–303.

King, Ursula. 1993. "Rediscovering Women's Voices at the World's Parliament of Religion," in Eric J. Ziolkowski, ed. *A Museum of Faiths: Histories and Legacies of the 1893 World's Parliament of Religions.* Atlanta GA: Scholars Press. 325–343.

King, Winston L. 1987. in Mircea Eliade, et al., eds., *Encyclopedia of Religion.* New York: Macmillan Publishing Company, Vol. 12: 282–293.

Kippenberg, Hans G. and Brigitte Luchesi, (eds.) 1991. *Religionswissenschaft und Kulturkritik.* Marburg: Diagonal-Verlag.

Kirk, James A. 1993. "The 1893 World's Parliament of Religions: In the Continuing Dialogue of World Religions." *Studies in Interreligious Dialogue* 3: 121–137.

Kitagawa, Joseph M. 1958. "The Life and Thought of Joachim Wach," in Joachim Wach, *The Comparative Study of Religion.* New York: Columbia University Press, xiii-xlvii.

———. 1959. "The History of Religions in America," in M. Eliade and J. M. Kitagawa, eds., *The History of Religions: Essays in Methodology.* Chicago: University of Chicago Press: 1–30.

———. 1971. "*Verstehen und Erlösung:* Some Remarks on Joachim Wach's Work." *History of Religions.* 11: 31–53.

———. 1975. "Theology and the Science of Religion." *Anglican Theological Review.* 29: 33–52.

————. 1983. "Humanistic and Theological History of Religions with Special Reference to the North American Scene," in Peter Slater and Donald Wiebe, eds., *Traditions in Contact and Change.* Waterloo: Wilfrid Laurier University Press: 553–563.

————. 1987. "Forward," in Mircea Eliade, et al. eds., *Encyclopedia of Religion.* New York: Macmillan Publishing Company, Vol. 1: xiii-xvi.

————and John S. Strong. 1989. "Friedrich Max Müller and the Comparative Study of Religion," in N. Smart, J. Clayton, P. Sherry, and S. T. Katz, eds., *Nineteenth Century Religious Thought in the West.* Vol. 3. Cambridge: Cambridge University Press, 179–213.

————. 1992. *Religious Studies, Theological Studies and the University-Divinity School.* Atlanta, GA: Scholars Press.

————. 1993. "The 1893 World's Parliament of Religions and Its Legacy." in Eric J. Ziolkowski, ed., *A Museum of Faiths: Histories and Legacies of the 1893 World's Parliament of Religions.* Atlanta GA: Scholars Press, 171–189.

Klimkeit, Hans. 1987. "Friedrich Max Müller," in Mircea Eliade et al., eds. *Encyclopedia of Religion,* vol. 10, pp. 153–154.

Klostermaier, K. K. 1977. "From Phenomenology to Metascience: Reflections on the Study of Religions." *Studies in Religion.* 6: 551–564.

————. 1978. "The Religion of Study." *Religious Traditions.* 1: 56–66.

————, and Larry W. Hurtado, eds. 1991. *Religious Studies: Issues, Prospects and Proposals.* Atlanta: Scholars Press.

Knight, David. 1986. *The Age of Science: The Scientific World-View in the Nineteenth Century.* Oxford: Basil Blackwell.

Knights, Ben. 1978. *The Idea of the Clerisy in the Nineteenth Century.* Cambridge: Cambridge University Press.

Kristensen, W. B. 1960. *The Meaning of Religion.* trans. John B. Carman. The Hague: Mouton.

Krolich, Sanford. 1985. "Through a Glass Darkly: What is the Phenomenology of Religion?" *International Journal for the Philosophy of Religion.* 17: 193–199.

Ladner, Benjamin. 1972. "Religious Studies in the University: A Critical Reappraisal." *Journal of the American Academy of Religion.* 40: 207–218.

————. 1974. "Why Do Ideas Illuminate?" *Journal of the American Academy of Religion.* 42: 739–745. (Part of "A Forum on the Study of Religion" which included contributions from Randy Huntsberry and Benjamin Ladner.)

Lassman, Peter and Irving Velody. 1989. "Max Weber on Science, Disenchantment and the Search for Meaning," in Peter Lassman and Irving Velody, eds., *Max Weber's 'Science as a Vocation'.* London: Unwin Hyman, 159–204.

Lawson, E. Thomas. 1967. "A Rationale for a Department of Religion in a Public University," in Milton D. McLean, ed., *Religious Studies in Public Universities.* Carbondale, Illinois: Southern Illinois University Press, 38–44.

————, and Robert N. McCauley. 1990. *Rethinking Religion: Connecting Cognition and Culture.* Cambridge: Cambridge University Press.

————, and Robert N. McCauley. 1993. "Crisis of Conscience, Riddle of Identity: Making Space for a Cognitive Approach to Religious Phenomena." *Journal for the American Academy of Religion.* 71: 201–223.

————. 1994. "Ph.D. Proposal in Comparative Religion," working paper, Western Michigan University, Kalamazoo, Michigan.

Lease, Gary, ed. 1995a. *Pathologies in the Academic Study of Religion: North American Institutional Case Studies. Method and Theory in the Study of Religion* 7/4.

Lease, Gary. 1995b. "The Rise and Fall of Religious Studies at Santa Cruz: A Case Study in Pathology, or the Rest of the Story." *Method and Theory in the Study of Religion.* 7: 305–324.

Leclercq, J. 1961. *The Love of Learning and the Desire for God.* New York: New American Library.

Leertouwer, Lammert. 1989. "C. P. Tiele's Strategy of Conquest," in Willem Otterspeer, ed., *Leiden Oriental Connections 1850–1940.* Leiden: E. J. Brill, 153–167.

————. 1991. "Gerardus van der Leeuw as a Critic of Culture," in Hans G. Kippenberg and Brigitte Luchesi, eds., *Religionswissenschaft und Kulturkritik.* Marburg: Diagonal-Verlag, 57–63.

Le Roy, Alexander. 1922. *The Religion of the Primitives.* trans. Newton Thompson. New York: The Macmillan Company.

Long, Charles H. 1974. "Cargo Cults as Cultural Historical Phenomena." *Journal of the American Academy of Religion.* 42: 403–414.

————. 1985. "The Study of Religion in the United States of America: Its Past and Its Future." *Religious Studies and Theology* 5: 30–43.

————. 1992. "A Common Ancestor: Theology and Religious Studies," in Joseph M. Kitagawa, ed., *Religious Studies, Theological Studies, and the University Divinity School.* Atlanta, GA: Scholars Press, 137–150.

Marsden, George M. and B.J. Longfield, eds. 1992. *The Secularization of the Academy.* New York: Oxford University Press.

————. 1994. *The Soul of the American University: From Protestant Establishments to Established Non-belief.* New York: Oxford University Press.

————. 1997. *The Outrageous Idea of Christian Scholarship.* New York: Oxford University Press.

Martin, Ira J. 3rd., (and Clyde Holbrook, B. LeRoy Burkhart, Bernard Phillips, Harry M. Buck). 1964. "Articles of Incorporation of American Academy of Religion." *Journal of Bible and Religion,* 32: 296–300.

Martin, J. Arthur. 1975. "What Do We Do When We Study Religion?" *Religious Studies.* 11: 407–411.

Martin, Luther H. 1993. "The Academic Study of Religion in the United States: Historical and Theoretical Considerations." *Religio* 1: 73–80.

————. 1997 "Biology, Sociology and the Study of Religion: Two Lectures." *Religio,* 5; 21–35.

Marty, Martin E. Feb. 2–9, 1983. "Seminary/Academy: Beyond the Tensions." *The Christian Century.* 100: 83–84.

————. 21 Feb. 1985. "What Is Modern About the Modern Study of Religion?" University Lecture at Arigon State University. Pamphlet.

————. 1989. "Committing the Study of Religion in Public." *Journal of the American Academy of Religion.* 57: 1–22.

————. 1993. "A Cosmopolitan Habit in Theology," in Eric J. Ziolkowski, ed., *A Museum of Faiths: Histories and Legacies of the 1893 World's Parliament of Religions.* Atlanta GA: Scholars Press, 165–170.

May, William F. 1976. "Institutions as Symbols of Death." *Journal of the American Academy of Religion.* 44: 211–223.

McCarthy, Gerald D. 1986. *The Ethics of Belief Debate.* Atlanta, GA: Scholars Press.

McCutcheon, Russell. 1997 *Manufacturing Religion: The Discourse on Sui Generis Religion and the Politics of Nostalgia.* New York: Oxford University Press.

McLelland, J. C. 1972. "The Teacher of Religion: Professor or Guru?" *Studies in Religion.* 2: 226–234.

————. 1983. "Alice in Academia: Religious Studies in an Academic Setting." (Paper presented at Victoria College, Toronto.) Nov. 28, 1963: personal papers of J.C. McLelland).

McMullin, Neil. 21 October 1990. Letter to Mrs. K. Takenaka, Ceremonials Assistant, Office of the President. 2pp.

McNeil, William H. 1986. *Mythistory and Other Essays.* Chicago: University of Chicago Press.

McWilliam, Joanne. 1990. A Short History of the Department of Religious Studies. Typescript. McWilliam personal papers. 5pp.

————. April 1994. Memorandum to Regular Members of the Department [of Religious Studies]. 1p.

Meagher, John C. 1979. "Pictures at an Exhibition: Reflections on Exegesis and Theology." *Journal of the American Academy of Religion.* 47: 3–20.

Meland, Bernard E. 1961. "Theology and the Historian of Religion." *The Journal of Religion.* 41: 263–276.

Michaelson, Robert S. 1967. "The Study of Religion: A Quiet Revolution in American Universities," in Milton D. McLean, ed., *Religious Studies in Public Universities.* Carbondale, Illinois: Southern Illinois University Press, 9–14.

————. 1972. "The Engaged Observer: Portrait of a Professor of Religion." *Journal of the American Academy of Religion* 40:419–424.

————. 1977. "Constitutions, Courts and the Study of Religion." *Journal of the American Academy of Religion* 45: 291–308.

Miller, Richard B., Laurie L. Patton, and Stephen H. Webb. 1994. "Rhetoric, Pedagogy, and the Study of Religions." *Journal of the American Academy of Religion* 62: 819–849.

Miller, Richard B. 1996. "On Not Keeping Religious Studies Pure," in *Casuistry and Modern Ethics: A Poetics of Practical Reasoning.* Chicago: University of Chicago Press, chapter 8.

Moir, John S. 1982. *A History of Biblical Studies in Canada: A Sense of Proportion.* Chico, CA.: Scholars Press.

Montgomery, Robert M. 1958. "The Religion Instructor as Learner." *Journal of Bible and Religion.* 26: 99–106.

Morgan, Kenneth W. Summer, 1977. "The Establishment of the Center." *Bulletin of the Center for the Study of World Religions:* 2–3.

Morgan, Robert and Michael Pye, eds. and trans. 1977. *Ernst Troeltsch, Writings on Theology and Religion.* London: Duckworth.

Mostert, J.P. 1976. "Complementary Approaches in the Study of Religion." Inaugural Lecture at University of Zululand, June, 1976).

Mould, Elmer W. K. 1950. "The National Association of Biblical Instructors, A Historical Account." *Journal of Bible and Religion.* 18:11–28.

Müller, F. Max. 1878. *Lectures on the Origin and Growth of Religion.* London: Longmans, Green, and Co.

———. 1881a. *Essays on the Science of Religion* [1867], in *Chips from a German Workshop* vol.1. New York: Charles Scribner's Sons.

———. 1881b. *Chips from a German Workshop,* vol. 5. New York: Charles Scribner's & Sons.

———. 1891. *Lectures on the Science of Language,* 9th ed., 2 vols. [1861, 1864]. London: Longmans, Green, and Co.

———. 1893. *Introduction to the Science of Religion* [1870]. London: Longmans, Green, and Co.

———. 1898a. *Natural Religion.* London: Longmans, Green, and Co.

———. 1898b. *Physical Religion.* London: Longmans, Green, and Co.

———. 1898c. *Anthropological Religion.* London: Longmans, Green, and Co.

———. 1898d. *Theosophy, or Psychological Religion.* London: Longmans, Green, and Co.

———. 1898e. "Science of Religion: A Retrospect." *Living Age* 219 (December 31): 909–913.

Mullick, Sunrit. 1993. "Protap Chandra Majumdar and Swami Vivekananda at the Parliament of Religions," in Eric J. Ziolkowski, ed., *A Museum of Faiths: Histories and Legacies of the 1893 World's Parliament of Religions.* Atlanta GA: Scholars Press, 219–233.

Munz, Peter. 1988. "The Philosophical Lure of the Sociology of Knowledge," in Gerard Radnitzky, ed., *Centripetal Forces in the Sciences,* Vol. 2 (New York: Paragon House): 321–342.

Murphy, Murray G. 1989. "On the Scientific Study of Religion in the United States, 1870–1980," in M. J. Lacey, ed., *Religion in Twentieth-Century American Intellectual Life.* Cambridge: Cambridge University Press, 136–171.

Murphy, Tim. 1994. "*Wesen und Erscheinung* in the History of the Study of Religion: A Post-Structuralist Perspective," in *Method and Theory in the Study of Religion* 6: 1–28.

Murray, G. 1955. *Five Stages of Greek Religion.* New York: Doubleday.

Myscofski, Carole (with Cheryl Townsend Gilkes, Roberto S. Goizueta, Yvonne Haddad, Miriam Levering, Robert Michaelson, Elizabeth Newman, Richard Pilgrim, Lynn Poland, and Rodney Taylor). 1993. "Religious Studies and the Redefining Scholarship Program: A Report of the AAR Committee on 'Defining Scholarly Work.'" *Religious Studies News.* 8/3: 7.

Nelson, B. 1981. *On the Roads to Modernity: Conscience, Science and Civilization.* Totowa, NJ: Rowan and Littlefield.

Neufeldt, Ronald. 1980. *F. Max Müller and the Rg-Veda: A Study of Its Role in His Work and Thought.* Calcutta: Minerva Associates.

————. 1983. *Religious Studies in Alberta: A-State-of-the-Art Review.* Waterloo, Ont: Wilfred Laurier University.

Neusner, Jacob. 1969. "Graduate Education in Judaica: Problems and Prospects." *Journal of American Academy of Religion.* 37: 321–330.

————. 1977a. "Being Jewish and Studying About Judaism." *Address at the Inauguration of the Jay and Leslie Cohen Chair of Judaic Studies.* Atlanta GA: Emory University Press, 1–22.

————. 1977b. "Religious Studies: The Next Vocation." *Bulletin of the Council of Societies for the Study of Religion.* 8: 117–120.

————. 1986. "The Civil War in Jewish Studies." *Jewish Advocate.* 12/11: 3–2, 11–12.

Neville, Robert Cummings. 1993. "Religious Studies and Theological Studies." *Journal of the American Academy of Religion.* 61: 185–200.

Newman, William M. 1974. "The Society for the Scientific Study of Religion: The Development of an Academic Society." *Review of Religious Research* 15: 137–151.

Nicholls, W. 1983. "Spirituality and Criticism in the Hermeneutics of Religion." Paper read at Study of Religion annual meeting, Guelph, Ontario, Canada.

Nielsen, Niels, Jr. 1984. "The Advancement of Religion *versus* Teaching About Religion in the Public Schools." *Journal of Church and State* 26: 105–116.

Norman, Ralph V. 1988. "A Season in Santa Barbara: Something Tender, Solemn, Nonsensical, Absolute." *Soundings.* 71: 171–184.

Novak, M. 1972a. "The Identity Crisis of Us All: Response to Professor Richard E. Crouter." *Journal of the American Academy of Religion.* 40: 65–78.

————. 1972b. *Ascent of the Mountain, Flight of the Dove: An Introduction to Religious Studies.* New York: Harper & Row.

O'Connell, L. 1984. "Religious Studies, Theology, and the Undergraduate Curriculum." *Council of Societies for the Study of Religion Bulletin.* 15/5: 143–46.

O'Donovan, Leo J. 1985. "Coming and Going: The Agenda of an Anniversary." *Journal of the American Academy of Religion* 53: 557–565.

O'Flaherty, Wendy Doniger. 1986. "The Uses and Misuses of Other Peoples' Myths." *Journal of the American Academy of Religion.* 54: 219–239.

Ogden, S.M. 1978. "Theology and Religious Studies: Their Difference and the Difference It Makes." *Journal of the American Academy of Religion.* 46: 3–17.

Osborn, Robert T. 1992. "From Theology to Religion." *Modern Theology* 8: 75–88.

Oxtoby, Williard. 1968. "*Religionswissenshaft* Revisited," in J. Neusner, ed., *Studies in the History of Religions: Religions in Antiquity.* Leiden: E. J. Brill, 590–608.

Pannenberg, W. 1971. "Toward a Theology of the History of Religions," in W. Pannenberg, *Basic Questions in Theology.* London: SCM, Vol 2, 65–118.

————. 1976. *Theology and the Philosophy of Science.* trans., Francis McDonagh. London: Darton, Longman and Todd.

Pelikan, Jaroslav. June 1975. Submission to SGS Dean Safarian. "Comments on the Proposed Centre for Religious Studies at the University of Toronto." Typescript. 19pp.

Penner, Hans H. 1970. "Is Phenomenology a Method for the Study of Religion?" *The Bucknell Review.* 18: 29–54.

————. 1986. "Criticism and the Development of a Science of Religion?" *Studies in Religion.* 15: 165–175.

Perron, Paul, M. R. Marrus, P. Nesselroth, I. Drummond, N. Conic, W. J. Callahan, R. Savory, P. Richardson, R. C. Hutchinson, N. Gottschalk. 1986. Submission to SGS Associate Dean Perron. "Report of the Five-Year Review Committee for the Graduate Centre for Religious Studies." 18pp.

————. 10 Dec. 1987. Letter to D. Wiebe. 2pp.

Perry, Edmund. 1986. "Identifying Religion Itself." *The Journal of the Institute for the Study of Religions.* 3: 7–22.

Pettazzoni, R. 1954. "History and Phenomenology in the Science of Religion," in R. Pettazoni, *Essays on the History of Religions.* trans. H. J. Rose. Leiden: E.J. Brill, 215–219.

Plantinga, Richard. 1989. "In the Beginning: P.D. Chantepie de la Saussaye on *Religionswissenschaft* and Theology." Paper delivered to Canadian Society for the Study of Religion., May, 1989.

Prebish, Charles, S. 1994. "The Academic Study of Buddhism in the United States: A Current Analysis." *Religion* 24: 271–278.

Preus, S. 1987. *Explaining Religion: Criticism and Theory from Bodin to Freud.* New Haven: Yale University Press.

Price, James L. 1967. "The Search for the Theology of the Fourth Evangelist." *Journal of the American Academy of Religion.* 35: 3–15.

Prichard, J. Robert. 1994. Letter to D. Wiebe. 1p.

Priest, John F. 1964. "Report of the Secretary [of the National Association of Biblical Instructors] (1963)." *The Journal of Bible and Religion.* 32: 198–199.

————. 1968. "Humanism, Skepticism, and Pessimism in Israel." *Journal of the American Academy of Religion.* 36: 313–326.

Prozesky, Martin. 1988. "Explanations of Religion as a Part of and Problem for Religious Studies." *Religious Studies.* 24: 305–310.

————. 1990. "South Africa's Contribution to Religious Studies." *Journal of Theology of Southern Africa,* 70; 9–20.

Purinton, Carl E. 1954. "The Task of Our Association." *Journal of Bible and Religion.* 22: 104–109.

Rait, Jill. 1982. "Strictures and Structures: Relational Theology and a Woman's Contribution to Theological Conversation." *Journal of the American Academy of Religion.* 50: 3–17.

Raschke, Carl A. 1983. "The Future of Religious Studies: Moving Beyond the Mandate of the 1960s." *Bulletin of the Council of Societies for the Study of Religion.* 14: 146–148.

Reat, N. Ross. 1983. "Insiders and Outsiders in the Study of Religious Traditions." *Journal of the American Academy of Religion.* 61: 457–476.

Remus, Harold E., F. Stanley Busby, and Linda M. Tober. 1988. "Religion as an Academic Discipline," in Charles H. Lippy and Peter W. Williams, eds., *Encyclopedia of the American Religious Experience,* Vol. 3. New York: Charles Scribner's Sons, 1653–1668.

————, William Closson James, Daniel Fraikin. 1992. *Religious Studies in Ontario: A State-of-the-Art Review.* Waterloo: Wilfrid Laurier University Press.

Reuben, Julie A. 1995. "False Expectations: The Scientific Study of Religion in the Modern American University, 1890–1920." *Mid-America: An Historical Review* 77: 122–144.

———. 1996. *The Making of the Modern University: Intellectual Transformation and the Marginalization of Morality.* Chicago: University of Chicago Press.

Réville, Albert. 1984. *Prolegomena of the History of Religions.* trans. A.S. Squire. London: Williams and Norgate.

———. 1993. "Conditions and Outlook for a Universal Religion," in Eric J. Ziolkowski, ed., *A Museum of Faiths: Histories and Legacies of the 1893 World's Parliament of Religions.* Atlanta GA: Scholars Press, 85–89.

Réville, Jean. 1993. "Principles of the Scientific Classification of Religions," in Eric J. Zolkowski ed., *A Museum of Faiths: Histories and Legacies of the 1893 World's Parliament of Religions.* Atlanta GA: Scholars Press, 91–93.

Reynolds, Frank E. 1985. "A Tribute to Mircea Eliade." *Criterion* 24: 20–21.

——— and Sheryl L. Burkhalter, eds. 1990a. *Beyond the Classics? Essays in Religious Studies and Liberal Education.* Atlanta: Scholars Press.

———. 1990b. "Reconstructing Liberal Education: A Religious Studies Perspective," in Reynolds and Burkhalter, eds., *Beyond the Classics? Essays in Religious Studies and Liberal Education.* Atlanta: Scholars Press, 3–18.

Richardson, H. Neil. 1959. "A Decade of Archaeology in Palestine." *Journal of Bible and Religion.* 27: 91–101.

Riley, Phillip B. 1983. "Theology and/or Religious Studies: A Case Study of *Studies in Religion/Sciences religieuses,* 1971–1981." Paper presented to the Canadian Society for the Study of Religion, 1983; Vancouver: typescript, 36 pp.

———. 1984. "Theology and/or Religious Studies: A Case Study of *Studies in Religion/Sciences religieuses,* 1971–1981." *Studies in Religion.* 13: 423–444.

Robb, J. Wesley. 1969. "The Hidden Philosophical Agenda: A Commentary on Humanistic Psychology." *Journal of the American Academy of Religion.* 37: 3–14.

Robbins, Thomas. 1983. "The Beach is Washing Away." *Sociological Analysis.* 44: 207–213.

Robertson, Roland. 1993. "Community, Society, Globality, and the Category of Religion," in E. Barker, J. A. Beckford, and K. Dobbelaere, eds., *Secularization, Rationalism, and Sectarianism.* Oxford: Clarendon Press, 1–17.

Rolston, G. Bruce. 4 April 1994. "Sikh Studies May Lose Funding," *The Varsity* [University of Toronto) 114/49: 1–2.

Rosenberg, A. 1985. *The Structure of Biological Science.* Cambridge: Cambridge University Press.

Ross, W. Gordon. 1955. "Thesaurus in Crackable Pottery." *Journal of Bible and Religion.* 23: 3–8.

Rudolph, Kurt. 1989. "Mircea Eliade and the 'History' of Religions." *Religion.* 19: 101–127.

Safarian, A. E. 13 May 1974. Letter to M. A. Preston, in Advisory Committee on Academic Planning, Ontario Council on Graduate Studies. *Perspectives and Plans for Graduate Studies* 12 (Toronto: Council of Ontario Universities) Appendix C, C5-C15.

Saunders, Ernest W. 1982. *Searching the Scriptures: A History of the Society of Biblical Literature—1880–1990*. Atlanta: Scholars Press.

Schimmel, Annemarie. 1960. "Summary of the Discussion." *Numen.* 7: 235–239.

Schmid, Georg. 1979. *Principles of Integral Science of Religion.* trans. John Wilson. The Hague: Mouton.

Schüssler Fiorenza, Francis. 1991. "Theological and Religious Studies: The Contest of the Faculties," in Barbara Wheeler and Edward Farely, eds., *Shifting Boundaries: Contextual Approaches to the Structure of Theological Education.* Louisville, KY: Westminister Press, 119–149.

———. 1993. "Theology in the University." *Bulletin of the Council of Societies for the Study of Religion* 22(2): 34–39.

———. 1994. "A Response to Donald Wiebe." *Bulletin of the Council of Societies for the Study of Religion* 23(1): 6–10.

Scott, Nathan A., Jr. 1987. "The House of Intellect in an Age of Carnival: Some Hermeneutical Reflections." *Journal of the American Academy of Religion.* 55: 3–18.

Scott, R. B. Y. Dec. 1975. Submission to SGS Council. "Report to the Appraisals Committee on the Proposal of the University of Toronto to Establish M. A. and Ph. D. Programs in Religious Studies. 10pp.

Seagher, Richard Hugh. 1993a. *The Dawn of Religious Pluralism.* La Salle, Illinois: Open Court.

———. 1993b. "Pluralism and the American Mainstream," in Eric J. Zolkowski ed., *A Museum of Faiths: Histories and Legacies of the 1893 World's Parliament of Religions.* Atlanta GA: Scholars Press, 192–281

Sharpe, Eric J. 1969. "Nathan Söderblom and the Study of Religion." *Religious Studies* 4: 259–274.

———. 1971. "Some Problems of Method in the Study of Religion." *Religion.* 1: 1–14.

———. 1983. *Understanding Religion.* London: Duckworth.

———. 1986. *Comparative Religion: A History* [1975]. London: Duckworth.

———. 1987a. "The Secularization of the History of Religions," in S. Shaked, D. Shulman, and G. G. Stroumsa, eds., *Gilgul: Essays on Transformation, Revolution and Permanence in the History of Religions.* Leiden: E. J. Brill.

———. 1987b. "Comparative Religion," in Mircea Eliade, et al., eds., *Encyclopedia of Religion.* New York: Macmillan Publishing Company, Vol. 3: 578–580.

———. 1987c. "Dialogue of Religions," in Mircea Eliade, et al., eds., *Encyclopedia of Religion.* New York: Macmillan Publishing Company, Vol. 4: 344–348.

———. 1987d. "Methodological Issues," in Mircea Eliade, et al., eds., *Encyclopedia of Religion.* New York: Macmillan Publishing Company, Vol. 14: 84–88.

———. 1988. "Religious Studies, the Humanities, and the History of Ideas." *Soundings* 71: 245–258.

———. 1990. *Nathan Söderblom and the Study of Religion.* Chapel Hill: University of North Carolina Press.

Shepard, Robert S. 1991. *God's People in the Ivory Tower: Religion in the Early American University.* New York: Carlson Publishing Inc.

Shils, Edward. 1973. "Introduction," in Edward Shils, ed. and trans., *Max Weber on Universities: The Powers of the State and the Dignity of the Academic College in Imperial Germany*. Chicago: University of Chicago Press, 1–3.

Slater, Peter. 1984. "Comment on Wiebe." *Studies in Religion*. 13: 489–490.

Slater, Robert Lawson. 1963. *World Religions and World Community*. New York: Columbia University Press.

Smart, Ninian. 1973a. *The Phenomenon of Religion*. London: Macmillan Press.

———. 1973b. *The Science of Religion and the Sociology of Knowledge*. Princeton, N.J.: Princeton University Press.

———. 1987. "Comparative–Historical Method," in Mircea Eliade, et al., eds., *Encyclopedia of Religion*. New York: Macmillan Publishing Company, Vol. 3: 571–574.

———. 1990a. "Concluding Reflections: Religious Studies in Global Perspective," in Ursula King, ed., *Turning Points in Religious Studies: Essays in Honour of Geoffrey Parrinder*. Edinburgh: T. and T. Clark, 299–306.

———. 1990b. "Review of *Marburg Revisited: Institutions and Strategies in the Study of Religion*." *Method and Theory in the Study of Religion*. 2: 298–304.

———. 1996. "Some Thoughts on the Science of Religion," in: Arvind Sharma, (ed.), *The Sum of Our Choices: Essays in Honor of Eric J. Sharpe*. Atlanta: Scholars Press, 15–25.

Smith, Huston. 1990. "Post-modernism's Impact on the Study of Religion." *Journal of the American Academy of Religion*. 58: 653–670.

Smith, J. Z. 1978. "Map Is Not Territory," in J. Z. Smith, *Map Is Not Territory*. Leiden: E. J. Brill, 289–309.

Smith, R. V. (with Dwight Beck, Harry M. Buck, Robert Eccles, Clyde Holbrook, Leo H. Phillips). 1964. "Report of the NABI Self-Study Committee." *The Journal of Bible and Religion*. 32: 200–201.

Smith, Robert V. 1962. "Analytical Philosophy and Religious/Theological Language." *Journal of Bible and Religion*. 30: 101–108.

Smith, Wilfred Cantwell. 1959. "Comparative Religion: Whither and Why?," in Mircea Eliade and Joseph M. Kitagawa, eds., *The History of Religions: Essays in Methodology*. Chicago: University of Chicago Press, 31–58.

———. 1962. *The Meaning and End of Religion*. New York: The MacMillan Company.

———. 1984. "The Modern West in the History of Religion." *Journal of the American Academy of Religion*. 52: 3–18.

———. 1995. "The Academic Study of Religion: The Challenge of the World's Parliament of Religions." *Religious Studies and Theology* 13 & 14: 5–11.

Snell, M.-M. 1993. "The Service of the Science of Religions to the Cause of Religious Unity," in Eric J. Ziolkowski ed., *A Museum of Faiths: Histories and Legacies of the 1893 World's Parliament of Religions*. Atlanta GA: Scholars Press, 69–73.

Sperber, Daniel. 1996 *Explaining Culture: A Naturalistic Approach*. Oxford: Blackwell.

Spohn, William C. 1992. "Between Church and Academy: The Dilemma of American Catholic Theology," in Joseph M. Kitagawa, ed., *Religious Studies, Theological Studies, and the University Divinity School*. Atlanta, GA: Scholars Press, 151–170.

Stark, Rodney and William Sims Bainbridge. 1987. *A Theory of Religion*. New York: Peter Lang Publishers.

Streng, F. 1970. "The Objective Study of Religion and the Unique Quality of Religiousness." *Religious Studies*. 6: 209–219.

———. 1974. "Religious Studies: Processes of Transformation," in Anne Carr, ed., *Academic Study of Religion: 1974*. Chico CA: Scholars Press, 118–131.

Strenski, Ivan. 1986. "Our Very Own 'Contras': A Response to the 'Saint Louis Project,'" *Journal of the American Academy of Religion*. 54: 323–335.

———. 1987. *Four Theories of Myth in Twentieth Century History*. Iowa City: University of Iowa Press.

———. Forthcoming a (with G. Bond and T. Ryba, eds.). "Original Phenomenology of Religion: A Theology of Natural Religion," in *The Comity and Grace of Method: Religious Studies for Edmund Perry*. Evanston: Northwestern University Press.

———. Forthcoming b. *The Struggle Over Sacrifice: Civil Religion, Social Science and Theology*.

Sunderland, E.R. 1993. "Serious Study of All Religions," in Eric J. Ziolkowski ed., *A Museum of Faiths: Histories and Legacies of the 1893 World's Parliament of Religions*. Atlanta GA: Scholars Press, 11–127.

Sweet, Ronald. Dec. 1985. Submission to SGS. "Acting Director's Report on the Centre for Religious Studies: 1981–1986 Quinquennial Review." 21pp.

Tiele, C. P. 1892. *Outlines of the History of Religion: To the Spread of the Universal Religions* [1877]. trans. J. E. Carpenter. London: Kegan Paul, Trench, Trübner, and Co. Ltd.

———. 1894. "The Study of Comparative Theology," in J.W. Hanson, ed., *The World's Congress of Religions: The Addresses and Papers Delivered before the Parliament, and an Abstract of Congresses*. Detroit: F. B. Dickerson Company, 280–286.

———. 1897. *Elements of the Science of Religion: Vol. I: Morphological, Vol. II: Ontological*. Edinburgh: William Blackwood and Sons.

Tilley, Terrence W. 1991. "Polemics and Politics in Explaining Religion." *Journal of the American Academy of Religion*. 71: 242–254.

Tillich, Paul. 1963. *Christianity and the Encounter of World Religions*. New York: Columbia University Press.

———. 1966. "The Significance of the History of Religions for the Systematic Theologian," in J. C. Brauer, ed., *The Future of Religions: Paul Tillich*. New York: Harper and Row, 80–94.

Tranöy, K. E. 1976 "Norms of Inquiry: Methodologies as Normative Systems." in: Gilbert Ryle, (ed.), *Contemporary Aspects of Philosophy*. London: Oriel Press, 1–13.

Trompf, G. W. 1978. *Friedrich Max Müller as a Theorist of Comparative Religion*. Bombay: Shakuntala Publishing House.

Tylor, E. B. 1958. *Primitive Culture: Vol. I: The Origins of Culture, Vol. II: Religion in Primitive Culture* [1871]. New York: Harper and Row.

University of Toronto, Academic Affairs Committee. 9 March 1978. "Report Number 131."

University of Toronto, Centre for Religious Studies. 1982. "Brochure."

University of Toronto, Department for the Study of Religion. 1993. "By-Laws of the Department."

University of Toronto, Department of Religious Studies. 1975–1995. "Undergraduate Handbook."

———. April 1985. "Religious Studies at the University of Toronto: A Statement of the Department." 9 pp.

———. April 1994. "RLG [Religion Faculty] Departmental Planning Document." Draft 2. 14 pp.

University of Toronto, Office of the Provost. 14 Feb. 1994. "Planning for 2000: A Provostial White Paper on University Objectives," *The [University of Toronto] Bulletin* 47 (Special Edition, 21 Feb. 1994): S1-S28.

University of Toronto/Toronto School of Theology, Joint Council. 15 Oct. 1985. "Minutes of Joint Council Meeting." 2 pp.

———. 29 April 1985. "Proposal of the Joint Council for an Agreement on Graduate Studies in the Toronto School of Theology." 8 pp.

———. 3 December 1987. "Minutes of the Joint Council Meeting." 7 pp.

van Baaren, Th. P. and H.J.W. Drijvers, eds. 1973. *Religion, Culture and Methodology.* The Hague: Mouton.

van der Leeuw, Gerardus. 1938. *Religion in Essence and Manifestation.* trans. J. E. Turner. London: George Allen and Unwin Ltd.

van Proosdij, B.A. 1970. "A Century of the History of Religions in the Netherlands." *Books in Religion: A Catalogue Presented to Participants in the 12th Congress of the IAHR,* (Stockholm, 16–22 August, 1970), i-xi.

van Ufford, Philip Quarles. 1996 "Reality Exists: Acknowledging the Limits of Active and Reflexive Anthropological Knowledge." in: Anton van Harskamp, (ed.), *Conflict in Social Science.* London: Routledge, pp. 22–43.

Vernoff, C. 1983. "Naming the Game—A Question of the Field." *Bulletin of the Council of Societies for the Studies for the Study of Religion.* 14: 109–11.

Veyne, Paul. 1983. *Did the Greeks Believe in Their Myths? An Essay on the Constitutive Imagination.* trans. Paula Wissing. Chicago: University of Chicago Press.

Voigt, Johannes. 1967. *F. Max Müller: The Man and His Ideas.* Calcutta: Firma K. Jukhopadhyay.

Vroom, Hendrik M. 1993. "Chicago 1993: The Parliament of the World's Religions." *Studies in Interreligious Dialogue.* 3: 114–120.

Waardenburg, Jacques. 1972. "Religion Between Reality and Idea: A Century of Phenomenology of Religion in the Netherlands." *Numen.* 19: 128–203.

———. 1973. "Introduction: A View of a Hundred Years of Religion," in Jacques Waardenburg, ed., *Classical Approaches to the Study of Religion.* The Hague: Mouton, Vol. 1, 3–78.

———. 1978a. "Gerardus van der Leeuw as a Theologian and Phenomenologist," in Jacques Waardenburg, *Reflections on the Study of Religion.* The Hague: Mouton, 187–247.

———. 1978b. "*Religionswissenschaft* New Style: Some Thoughts and Afterthoughts." *Annual Review of the Social Sciences.* 2: 189–220.

———. 1987. "Leeuw, Gerardus van der," in Mircea Eliade, ed., *The Encyclopedia of Religion*. New York: Macmillan Publishing Company, Vol. 8: 493–495.

———. 1991a. "The Problem of Representing Religions and Religion:

———. 1991b. "Scholarship and Subversion: A Response to Donald Wiebe," in Hans G. Kippenberg and Brigitte Luchesi, eds., *Religionswissenschaft und Kulturkritik*. Marburg: Diagonal-Verlag, 87–92.

Wach, J. 1944. *Sociology of Religion*. Chicago: University of Chicago Press.

———. 1951. *Types of Religious Experience, Christian and Non-Christian*. Chicago: University of Chicago Press.

———. 1954. "General Revelation and the Religions of the World." *The Journal of Bible and Religion*. 22:83–93.

———. 1958. *The Comparative Study of Religion*. New York: Columbia University Press.

———. 1967. "Introduction: The Meaning and Task of the History of Religion," in Mircea Eliade, Joseph M. Kitagawa and Charles Long, eds., *History of Religions: Essays on the Problem of Understanding*. Chicago: University of Chicago Press, 1–19.

Wallis, Roy. 1983. "Religion, Reason, and Responsibility." *Sociological Analysis*. 44: 215–220.

Watson, Gordon. March 1960. "A Brief in Support of a University [Toronto] Department of Religion." Watson private papers. Typescript. 17pp.

———. 1965. "Memorandum Regarding Religious Knowledge and Religious Options." (Toronto, 1965).

———. 1997. "Religious Studies in the University of Toronto: A History of Its Foundation Written to Celebrate the Twentieth Anniversary of the Centre for the Study of Religion 1976–1996." (Toronto: Department for the Study of Religion, University of Toronto.)

Weber, Max. 1946. "Science as a Vocation," in H. H. Gerth and G. Wright Mills, eds. and trans., *From Max Weber: Essays in Sociology*. Oxford: Oxford University Press, 129–156.

———. 1949. *The Methodology of the Social Sciences*. ed. and trans. Edward Shils and Henry Finch. New York: The Free Press.

———. 1973a. "A Catholic University in Salzburg," in Edward Shils, ed. and trans., *Max Weber on Universities: The Power of the State and the Dignity of the Academic Calling in Imperial Germany*. Chicago: University of Chicago Press, 46–47.

———. 1973b. "The Academic Freedom of the Universities," in Edward Shils, ed. and trans., *Max Weber on Universities: The Power of the State and the Dignity of the Academic Calling in Imperial Germany*. Chicago: University of Chicago Press, 18–23.

Welch, Claude. 1971a. "Identity Crisis in the Study of Religion? A First Report from the ACLS Study." *Journal of the American Academy of Religion* 39: 3–18.

———. 1971b. *Graduate Education in Religion: A Critical Appraisal*. Missoula: University of Montana Press.

———. 1985. *Protestant Thought in the Nineteenth Century, Vol. II: 1870–1914*. New Haven: Yale University Press.

Werblowsky, R. J. Zwi. 1956. "Revelation, Natural Theology and Comparative Religion." *Hibbert Journal.* 55: 278–284.

———. 1959. "The Comparative Study of Religions: A Review Essay." *Judaism.* 8: 352–360.

———. 1960. "Marburg—and After?" *Numen.* 7: 205–220.

———. 1975. "On Studying Comparative Religion." *Religious Studies.* 11: 145–156.

Whiston, Lionel A., Jr. 1961. "The Unity of Scripture and the Post-Exilic Literature." *Journal of Bible and Religion.* 29: 290–298.

Wickenden, Arthur C. 1956. "Rightly Dividing the Word of Truth." *Journal of Bible and Religion.* 24: 3–9.

Widengren, G. 1983. *"Pettazzonis Untersuchungen zum Problem des Hochgottglaubens: Erinnerungen und Betrachtungen."* *Studi Storico-Religiosi.* 7: 29–53.

Wiebe, Donald. 1973. " 'Comprehensively Critical Rationalism' and Commitment." *Philosophical Studies.* 21: 186–201.

———. 1974. "Science, Religion and Rationality: Questions of Method in Science and Religion." (Lancaster UK: unpublished doctoral dissertation).

———. 1975. "Explanation and the Scientific Study of Religion." *Religion.* 5: 33–52.

———. 1977. "Is Religious Belief Problematic?" *Christian Scholar's Review.* 7: 23–35.

———. 1978. "Is a Science of Religion Possible?" *Studies in Religion.* 7: 5–17.

———. 1979. "The Role of Belief in the Study of Religion: A Response to W. C. Smith." *Numen.* 26:234–249.

———. 1980. Review of Lauri Honko (ed.) *The Science of Religion: Studies in Methodology. Journal of the American Academy of Religion,* 48; 632–34.

———. 1981a. *Religion and Truth: Towards an Alternative Paradigm for the Study of Religion.* The Hague: Mouton.

———. (with P. Slater and T. Horvath.) 1981b. "Three Responses to *Faith and Belief*: A Review Article." *Studies in Religion.* 10: 113–126.

———. 1983a. "Theory in the Study of Religion." *Religion.* 13: 283–309.

——— and Peter Slater. 1983b. *Traditions in Contact and Change. Selected Proceedings of the XIVth Congress of the International Association for the History of Religions.* Waterloo ON.: Wilfred Laurier University Press.

———. 1984. "The Failure of Nerve in the Academic Study of Religion." *Studies in Religion* 13: 401–422.

———. 1985a. "A Positive Episteme for the Study of Religion." *The Scottish Journal of Religious Studies.* 6: 78–95.

———. 1985b. "Religion Transcending Science Transcending Religion . . ." *The Dalhousie Review.* 65: 196–202.

———. 24 Sept. 1987a. Letter to Paul Perron. 1p.

———. 29 Sept. 1987b. Letter to Paul Gooch. 3pp.

———. 1987c. "The Prelogical Mentality Revisited." *Religion.* 17: 29–61.

———. 1988a. "Postulations for Safeguarding Preconceptions: The Case of the Scientific Religionist." *Religion.* 18: 11–19.

———. 1988b. "Why the Academic Study of Religion?: Motive and Method in the Study of Religion." *Religious Studies.* 24: 403–413.

————. 4 Jan. 1988c. Letter to Paul Perron. 2pp.

————. 1989a. "History or Mythistory in the Study of Religion? The Problem of Demarcation," in Michael Pye, ed., *Marburg Revisited: Institutions and Strategies in the Study of Religion.* Marburg: Diagonal-verlag, 31–46.

————. 1989b. "Is Science Really an Implicit Religion?" *Studies in Religion.* 18: 171–183.

————. 1989c. "Explaining Religion: The Intellectual Ethos." *Religion.* 19: 305–309.

————. 1991a. *The Irony of Theology and the Nature of Religious Thought.* Montreal: McGill-Queen's University Press.

————. 1991b. "Phenomenology of Religion as Religio-Cultural Quest: Gerardus van der Leeuw and the Subversion of the Scientific Study of Religion," in H. Kippenberg and B. Luchesi, eds., *Religionswissenschaft und Kulturkritik: Beiträge zur Konferenz, The History of Religions and Critique of Culture in the Days of Gerardus van der Leeuw (1890).*

———— and Luther H. Martin. 1993a. "On declaring WAR: A Critical Comment." *Method and Theory in the Study of Religion.* 5: 47–52.

————. 1993b. "Religion, Science and the Transformation of 'Knowledge'." *Sophia.* 32: 36–49.

————. 17 Jan. 1994a. Letter to D. Cook. 1p.

————. 20 Jan. 1994b. Letter to R. Prichard. 2pp.

————. 28 Jan. 1994c. Letter to J. McWilliam. 2pp.

————. 1994d. "On Theology and Religious Studies: A Response to Francis Schüssler Fiorenza." *Bulletin of the Council of Societies for the Study of Religion* 23(1): 3–6.

————. 1994e. *Beyond Legitimation: Essays in the Problem of Religious Knowledge.* London: Macmillan Press.

————. 1995. "Religion and the Scientific Impulse in the Nineteenth Century: Friedrich Max Müller and the Birth of the Science of Religion." *International Journal of Comparative Religion.*

————. 1996. "Toward Founding a Science of Religion: The Contribution of C. P. Tiele." in: Arvind Sharma, ed., The Sum of Our Choices: Essays in Honor of Eric J. Sharpe; 26–49.

————. 1997a. "A Religious Agenda Continued: A Review of the Presidential Addresses to the AAR," in *Method and Theory in the Study of Religion* 9: 353–375.

————. 1997b. "Dissolving Rationality: The Anti-Science Phenomenon and Its Implications for the Study of Religion," in J.S. Jensen and L.H. Martin, eds. *Rationality and the Study of Religion.* Aarhus: Aarhus University Press.

————. 1997c. "Theology and the Academic Study of Religion in the United States," in Dick van der Meij, ed., *India and Beyond: Aspects of Literature, Meaning, Ritual and Thought. Essays in Honour of Frits Staal.* London: Kegan Paul International, 651–675.

————. 1997d. "On Theological Resistance to the Scientific Study of Religion: Values and the Value-Free Study of Religion," in A. Komendera, R. Padola, and M. Sliwa, eds., *Czlowiek I Wartosci.* Krakow: Wydawnictwo Naukowe WSP, 131–145.

————. Forthcoming a. "Against Science in the Academic Study of Religion: On the Emergence and Development of the AAR," in George Bond and Thomas Ryba, eds., *The Comity and Grace of Method: Religious Studies for Edmund Perry.* Evanston, Ill.: Northwestern University Press, 167–183.

————. Forthcoming b. "Promise and Disappointment: Recent Developments in the Academic Study of Religion in the U. S. A.," in J. Platvoet and G. Wiegers, eds., *Modern Society and The Study of Religion.*

Wiebe, Paul G. 1975. "The Place of Theology in Religious Studies," in Anne Carr and Nicholas Piediscolzi, eds., *The Academic Study of Religion: 1975.* 17–25.

Wiggins, James. 1983. "Theology and Religious Studies." Paper read at Eastern International Regional Meeting, American Academy of Religion, McMaster University, Hamilton, Ontario, Canada.

————. Dec. 1987. Letter to L. H. Martin, Executive Secretary of the North American Association for the Study of Religion.

————. 1992. "Openings and Closings." *The Journal of the American Academy of Religion.* 60: 105–115.

Wilken, Robert L. 1989. "Who Will Speak for Religious Traditions?" *Journal of the American Academy of Religion.* 57: 699–717.

Williams, Preston N. 1976. "Religion and the Making of Community in America." *Journal of the American Academy of Religion.* 44: 603–611.

Wilson, Bryan R. 1983. "Sympathetic Detachment and Disinterested Involvement." *Sociological Analysis.* 44: 183–187.

Wilson, John F. 1964a. "Mr. Holbrook and the Humanities, or Mr. Schlatter's Dilemma, A Review Article [of Clyde A. Holbrook *Religion: A Humanistic Field*]." *The Journal of Bible and Religion.* 32: 252–261.

————. 1964b. "A Comment." *The Journal of Bible and Religion.* 32: 265–266.

Wolin, Sheldon. 1981 "Max Weber: Legitimation, Method, and the Politics of Theory." *Political Theory,* 9; 401–424.

Wyschogrod, Edith. 1994. "Facts, Fiction, Ficciones: Truth in the Study of Religion." *Journal of the American Academy of Religion.* 62: 1–16.

Wyse, Marion. 1986. "Of Two Minds: A Theological Reflection on the Relationship between the University of Toronto and Its Denominational Colleges." Wyse personal papers. 26pp.

Yolton, J. 1974. "System Recommendations," in Advisory Committee on Academic Planning, Ontario Council on Graduate Studies. *Perspectives and Plans for Graduate Studies.* (Toronto: Council of Ontario Universities) 8–13.

Young, Lawrence A., ed. 1997. *Rational Choice Theory and Religion.* New York: Routledge.

Ziolkowski, Eric J. 1993a. *A Museum of Faiths: Histories and Legacies of the 1893 World's Parliament of Religions.* Atlanta: Scholars Press.

————. 1993b. "Waking Up from Akbar's Dream: The Literary Prefiguration of Chicago's 1893 World's parliament of Religions." in Eric J. Ziolkowski ed. *A Museum of Faiths: Histories and Legacies of the 1893 World's Parliament of Religions.* Atlanta: Scholars Press.

Name Index

Nicholls, W., 154, 162; "Spirituality and Criticism," 161

Norman, R. V., 250; "Season in Santa Barbara," 250

North American Academy of Liturgy, 103

North American Association for the Study of Religion, xvii, 31, 105, 135, 251–2

Novak, M., *Ascent of the Mountain,* 160; "Identity Crisis of Us All," 160

O'Connell, L., 161; "Religious Studies, Theology, and the Undergraduate Curriculum," 161

O'Donovan, Leo, 81–3; "Coming and Going," 82–3

O'Flaherty, W. D., 132, 268–9; "Uses and Misuses," 136, 268, 271, 274

Ogden, Schubert M., 265; "Theology and Religious Studies," 158, 265, 271, 274

Ontario Council of Graduate Studies, 206

Osborn, Robert T., 25; "From Theology to Religion," 25

Otto, Rudolf, 42, 44, 46, 151, 200, 203

Oxtoby, W. C., 125–6, 146, 216, 221, 229; *"Religionswissenschaft,"* 126, 136, 146, 159

Pannenberg, W., 152; *Theology and the Philosophy of Science,* 156–7

Pareto, Vilfredo, 139

Paris Congress, 30, 46, 74–5, 96, 195–6

Paris, University of, 48

Pelikan, J., 208, 214, 224–5; "Comments on the Proposed Centre," 208, 224–5

Penner, H., 132, 168, 178; "Criticism and the Development of a Science of Religion?," 132, 138; "Is Phenomenology a Method for the Study of Religion?," 178

Pennsylvania, University of, 71, 72

Peritz, Ismar J., 104, 121

Perron, P., 220; "Report of the Five-Year Review," 220

Perry, Edmund, 168, 235–7, 275; "Identifying Religion Itself," 168–9, 235

Pettazzoni, Raffaele, 175–6; "History and Phenomenology," 175

Phillips, Leo H., "Report of the NABI Self-Study Committee," 238, 242, 249

Plantinga, R., 189; "In the Beginning: P.D. Chantepie," 189

Plato, 156

Popper, Karl, 181

Prebish, Charles S., 90 "Academic Study of Buddhism in the United States," 90

Preiss, H., 48

Preus, J. S., 3–7; *Explaining Religion,* 3–7, 32, 132, 188

Price, J. L., 261; "Search for the Theology of the Fourth Evangelist," 261, 270, 273

Prichard, J. R., Letter to D. Wiebe (1994), 232

Priest, John F., 261–2; "Humanism, Skepticism and Pessimism," 261–2, 270, 273; "Report of the [NABI] Secretary (1963)," 241

Proosdij, B. A. van, 182, 184–5; "Century of the History," 182, 184–5

Prozesky, Martin, 129–30, 285–6, 291; "Explanations of Religion," 136; "Proposals for a Criteriology," 130; "South Africa's Contribution," 129, 136, 285–6

Purinton, Carl E., 257, 259; "Task of Our Association," 256–7, 272

Pye, M., xvii, 132, 158; *Marburg Revisited,* 132, 138; *Ernst Troeltsch,* 158

Queen's University, 213

Radcliffe-Brown, A. R., 200

Rahula, Walpola, 236

Rait, Jill, 265; "Strictures and Structures," 265, 270, 274

Raschke, Carl A., "Future of Religious Studies," 156

Reat, N. Ross, "Insiders and Outsiders," 161

Regina, University of, 211

Remus, H. E., *Religious Studies in Ontario,* 206, 213

Reuben, J. A., 93–7; "False Expectations," 94–5, 114; *Making of the Modern,* 93–5, 114

Réville, A., 37, 40–3, 45–6, 48, 113, 192; *Prolegomena,* 40–2

Réville, J., 48; "Principles of the Scientific Classification of Religions," 192

Reynolds, F. E., 100–1, 112, 114, 116; *Beyond the Classics?,* 116; "Reconstructing Liberal Education," 112, 114; "Tribute to Mircea Eliade," 100–1

Richardson, H. N., "Decade of Archaeology in Palestine," 257, 273

Richardson, P., xvii, 221–2, 224, 233–4; "Correct, But Only Barely," 233–4; "Report of the Five-Year Review," 220; "Report of the Task Force," 220–2

Ricoeur, Paul, 127–8

Riley, P. B., 154; "Theology and/or Religious Studies," 154, 157

Ritschl, A., 24

Robb, J. W., 262; "Hidden Philosophical Agenday," 262, 270, 273

Robbins, T., 160

Robertson, Roland, 89; "Community, Society, Globality, and the Category of Religion," 89

Rolston, Bruce, 231; "Sikh Studies May Lose Funding," 231

Rome, 105, 130

Rosenberg, A., *Structure of Biological Science,* 169

Ross, W. G., 258–9; "Thesaurus in Crackable Pottery," 258, 272

Royal Society, The, 12

Rudolph, Kurt, 127, 132; "Mircea Eliade and the 'History' of Religions," 132

Rushdie, S., 49

Ryba, Thomas, *Comity and Grace of Method,* 275

Sabatier, Auguste, 25, 48

Safarian, A. E., 207–8, 215, 217, 225, 230; "Letter to M. A. Preston,"207–8

Saint Louis Project, 132, 137

Saint Michael's College (Toronto), University of, *u.* Toronto, University of

Saint Paul, 58

Sankara, 63

Santa Barbara Colloquy, 31, 250

Saskatchewan, University of, 211

Saul of Tarsus, 58, 64

Saunders, E., 103, 117; *Searching the Scriptures,* 103, 117

Savory, R., "Report of the Five-Year Review Committee," 220

Schelling, 17

Subject Index